Library of Congress Control Number: 2015907901
ISBN: 978-0-9835820-1-4

Copyright 2015 Hadeland Lag of America, Inc.
www.hadelandlag.org

Copies of this book are available on Amazon.com

OUR HADELAND ANCESTORS

VOLUME TWO

Editor
Anne Sladky

Book Committee
Evonne Anderson
Sharon Arends
Barb Schmitt
Joy Sundrum

Dedicated to Peder H. Nelson
Editor of the *Brua* 1931-1951

In the 1937 issue of the *Brua*, page 33, Peder wrote,

"The pioneer history of Hadeland immigrants in *Vesterheim* (Home in the West) is so valuable that it ought to be published in the *Brua* so that it does not go into the *glemmeboken* (literally: the forgotten book or the oblivion book). In our *Brua*, your stories will be preserved so that future generations – on both sides of the ocean – will be able to read them in the future. Send in your reminiscences now, before they are forgotten."

Brua Editor Verlyn Anderson took this wise counsel to heart and introduced the "Our Hadeland Ancestors" column in 1997. Since that time, dozens of our members have shared the stories of their immigrant ancestors in our newsletter's pages. These stories have now been brought together in two special volumes. We trust that Peder Nelson would be pleased with all of our efforts to preserve the stories of "Our Hadeland Ancestors."

Peder Nelson's biography can be found on page 215 of Volume One.

Table of Contents

VOLUME ONE

Acknowledgements

Contributors

The following lag members, family members and friends of the lag wrote or submitted the immigrant ancestor stories found in Volume Two: Verlyn Anderson, Kari-Mette Avtjern, Sharon Sayles Babcock, Robert Brodin, Ronald J. Butler, Ruth Carlson, Brian Christensen, Frank Evenson, Connie Ferris, Geir Olav Fjeldheim, Ole P. Gamme, Bary Gammell, David Gunderson, Estella Johnson, Anne Lise Jorstad, Mrs. Clifford Koethe, Judith Bjone Liebelt, Helen Loing, John Monson, Peder H. Nelson, Morgan A. Olson, Carol Pendretti, Catherine Rossing, Alfa Olson Rud, Byron Schmid, Barb Helstedt Schmitt, Carol Emerson Schwartz, Larry Shoger, Pam Solwey, Torun Sørli, Hilma Haakenstad Stengel, Joy Sundrum, Allen Thoreson, Carrie Tollefson, Edwart Usset, Floie Vane, Carol Vind, Carol Harris Weber, Linda Weidenfeld, Arnold Zempel

Special Thanks

The committee wishes to express its gratitude to

➢ Kari-Mette Avtjern and the staff of the Hadeland Folkemuseum for permission to include their articles about Hadeland emigrants in this book

➢ Ole Gamme for his tireless work on the Emigrant Identification Project and for compiling the lists of veterans of the Civil War and World War I

About the Cover

In 1921, the Hadeland Lag met in Northwood, North Dakota. This panoramic picture was taken of those in attendance. The picture is now held by the Norwegian-American Historical Association at St. Olaf College, Northfield, Minnesota. A high-resolution digital copy can be viewed on-line at

http://www.naha.stolaf.edu/archivesdata/images/panorama/Hadeland1924.htm

Introduction

"Our Hadeland Ancestors" has since its inception been a favorite feature of the *Brua*. It has flourished because of the willingness of our members to share not just dates and places but also the photographs and remembrances of generations past.

For their descendants, the profiles of *Hadelanding* foreparents help explain and put into context family traditions, experiences, and relationships. On another level, the stories come together to create a great saga of the Hadeland emigrant experience. In writing down, sharing, and reading their stories, we bear witness to the dreams, determination, courage, family, and faith that allowed our Hadeland ancestors to put down the roots of our American families in this new land.

One of the primary missions of the Hadeland Lag is to preserve the history of Hadelanders in America. We all owe a debt of thanks to our members' continuing commitment to writing down oral history, carefully researching historical records and, most importantly, sharing the results. Kontaktforum Hadeland-America's Emigrant Identification Project has identified over 11,000 Hadeland emigrants, so there are many more stories left to tell!

In these two volumes, the biographical articles have been roughly ordered by date of publication, with some attempt made to group stories about members of the same family together. As a result, most – but not all - of the many stories submitted specifically for this project can be found in Volume Two. As well as being included in this collection, all of the new submissions will eventually find their way into the pages of the *Brua*.

A reference to the Kontaktforum Hadeland-America Emigrant Identification Project family record (form#) is included in the header or body of each story. These forms may provide additional biographical information. The Kontaktforum Hadeland-Amerika Emigrant Identification Project database and associated forms are available to lag members in the Limited Access Archive on the Hadeland Lag website, www.hadelandlag.org.

Anne Sladky, Editor

Destination: Burke County

published August 2009   *Verlyn Anderson*

Lena Ohe is seated in a rocking chair on the roof of her newly built soddie on her homestead claim in Fay Township, Burke County, North Dakota. The photo is not very clear, but it looks like she has a cat on her lap! After living on her land for five years, Lena "proved up" and received title to her property. She then moved back to Minnesota where on October 18, 1912, she married Helmer Hjermstad. Helmer's family had emigrated from Stange, Hedmark, Norway. In 1915 Lena and Helmer returned to her homestead in Burke County and lived there until 1939 when they moved to Bottineau, North Dakota.

In 1972 the Burke County and White Earth Valley Historical Society in northwestern North Dakota published a 1,287-page *History of Burke County, Homesteaders and the Early Settlers.* Included in this massive book are the histories of the eight larger towns of Burke County and biographies of their citizens, mini-histories of the thirteen smaller villages in the county, articles about each of the churches and the town and rural schools. Of the greatest value are the biographies of the individual families who lived in Burke County between 1896 and 1972. My maternal grandparents, Ole and Karen Ohe Hovland, homesteaded in Short Creek Township, Burke County in 1902. After my grandfather's death in 1980, I inherited this interesting history. I have spent many hours reading this fascinating and valuable book.

Burke County was the destination of Norwegian emigrants arriving in the Midwest during the first decade of the 20th Century. Children of Norwegian emigrants who had arrived in western Minnesota in the 1870s and '80s, particularly in Otter Tail and Wilkin Counties, also moved west to claim homesteads at that time. More than a hundred young individuals and couples who took homesteads in Burke County had their "roots" in western Otter Tail County, my home area. For example, in the spring of 1902, three young women from Rothsay each filed for homesteads on adjoining quarter sections in Section 7 of Fay Township, Burke County. They were Gunda Ødegård who was born in Vestre Gran on April 11, 1880; Lena Ohe, born November 30, 1881, the daughter of Torger and Helena Ouren Ohe, Rothsay, MN; and Stena Tollefson. Lena's father, Torger Ohe, had emigrated from Vestre Gran in 1869 and when he visited Hadeland in 1900, Gunda Ødegård accompanied Torger when he returned to America after his visit. I have not been able to uncover any information about Stena Tollefson, but she apparently was a friend of Gunda and Lena.

These three women fulfilled the legal obligations and eventually "proved up" and received ownership titles to their land. On March 14, 1903, Gunda married Joseph Grina, son of Iver O. and Oline Ohe Grina, older sister of Torger Ohe. They immigrated from Hadeland to Iowa in 1854 when Joseph was only 3 years old. Joseph Grina and Lena were first cousins. Other close relatives, including my grandparents, Ole and Karen Ohe Hovland, also homesteaded in 1903, just a couple of miles away. Karen was Lena's older sister. Ole had several Hovland cousins who also homesteaded on adjoining sections. Many other young people from the Rothsay area also took homesteads in Burke County. The new community was therefore a transplanting of young people who had spent their childhoods together in Minnesota. That surely would have made their homesteading less stressful.

There were also several dozen emigrants from Hadeland who settled in Burke County shortly after they arrived in the United States at the turn of the century. In this month's "Our Hadeland Ancestors" I am including information about some of those emigrants who settled in Burke County shortly after their emigration.

Engebret Kostad was born in Ullensaker, Norway and in 1902 came to Dale Township, Burke County. **Marthea Larsdtr was born in Gran, Hadeland on February 17, 1867** and came to North Dakota in 1899. When she married Mr. Kostad she had four children from a previous marriage to Torger Samuelson. These children were Inger and Morris Samuelson, both deceased by 1971, Ida (Mrs. Self) and Torena Samuelson who both lived in Minot, North Dakota in 1971. The Kostads were members of the First Lutheran Church, Lignite, ND. Engebret died 3 September 1938. Marthea died 13 February 1939. (*Form 496*)

Hanse Hagen, son of Per and Karen Hagen, was born in 1877 in Brandbu, Hadeland. In 1902 he homesteaded in Leaf Mountain Township, Burke County. Hanse returned to Norway in 1914 to visit relatives and there married his wife Oda, who returned with Hanse to his North Dakota homestead. Oda Gudbrandsdtr was born on Raasumshagen. Hanse died 23 September 1949. Oda lived 30 more years. In 1971, she was living in the Kenmare (ND) Baptist Home, and passed away on 15 Jun 1979. (*Form 760*)

In 1903, **Hanse's two brothers, Anders, born Sept. 24, 1883 and Karl, born March 30, 1884 in Brandbu, Hadeland** came to North Dakota. Karl filed for a homestead adjoining his brother, Hanse's homestead. Some years later he sold his homestead and took a homestead near Swift Current, Sask. Later he sold that and moved to Van Hock, North Dakota where he owned a hardware store and lumber yard. Karl married Emma Scanson in 1915. They had two children: Gjerdie and Carl Everett. Karl died in 1919 and his wife, Emma, died in 1921. Carl Everett was adopted by his uncle, Hanse, but died the next year at the age of two and a half. His sister Gjerdie was adopted by her other uncle, Anders. She later married a Mr. Johnson and in 1970 lived in Lignite, ND. Anders and Gina had no children of their own. Anders and Gina continued to live on their farm until they retired and moved to Columbus, ND. Anders died at the Crosby Hospital in 1965. Gina died in August, 1971 in Lignite, ND. *(Form 760)*

Ole Olson Kammerud was born on February 27, 1886 in Hadeland. He came to Burke County in 1913. Besides farming, he worked in the Anderson and Bonsness coal mines. Ole never married and in 1970 was living in Minot, North Dakota. Ole died in 1980. *(Form 788)*

Ingeborg Hallum and her sister Randi filed for a homestead in Cleary Township, Burke County in 1903. **They were born in Hadeland.** Ingeborg married Anton Olson in 1907. They had four children: Milo, Leaf Mountain Township; Martha Ness, Columbus; Evelyn Hanson, Lignite; and Alice Olson, Chicago, Illinois. Ingeborg died in 1945 and Anton died in 1958. They are buried in the Bethlehem Lutheran Church cemetery, rural Columbus, ND. **Randi Hallum married Carl Brothen.** According to an obituary of their son Larry M. Brothen in the *Fargo Forum*, May 13, 2009, they farmed near Columbus, ND. Larry's obituary lists six brothers: Alvin, Clarence, Palmer and Evald who were deceased. Brothers Magne, Minot, ND, and Ed, Brooklyn Park, MN, survived. *(Form 453)*

C.P. Olson was born in Hadeland in 1863 and emigrated with his two sisters in 1879 to Hartland, MN. After his first wife died in 1901, he moved to Lignite, ND where he homesteaded. He married Ragna Eide in 1928. She died in 1933. C.P. Olson was one of the early treasurers of Burke County. He died in 1937 at the age of 74. *(Form 484)*

Thorvald Dihle was born in 1889 in Gran, Hadeland. He emigrated in 1909 to his brother, **Gilbert (Gulbrand) Dihle who lived near Esmond, ND.** Thorvald later moved to Larson, ND in Burke County. Another Dihle brother, **Jorgen**, came to the area later. They built the South St. Olaf Church south of Larson, ND. Thorvald Dihle married Sella Haarstad. They had three sons and a daughter: Willard, who lived in Lignite, ND, their daughter, Ardelle McIntre, lived in Bowbells, ND. Thorvald and their two sons, Allen and Donald, drowned in the Stoney Creek Dam in that hot summer of 1936. The family had gone there to swim after a sweltering hot day! *(Forms 671, 1259)*

Thorvald Dihle's brother, Erick, was born in Hadeland in 1881 and immigrated to America in 1900. In 1903, he filed a homestead claim in Harmonious Township, Burke County.

He married Anne Hagen in 1907. They had two children: Alvin and Ethel. Anne Dihle died in 1914. In 1916, Erick married Emma Ronholdt, Murdock, MN. They had two sons, Arthur and Milo. Erick died in 1950. Emma died in 1953. They are buried in the South St. Olaf Lutheran Church cemetery, rural Columbus, ND. In 1970, Alvin Dihle lived in Crosby, ND; Ethel Lee in Mt. Vernon, Washington; Arthur in Columbus and Milo lived near Larson, ND. *(Form 671)*

Iver Hallum was born on December 9, 1874 in Hadeland, the oldest of eight children. In 1904 Iver was the first of his family to immigrate to America. After spending his first years there in Minnesota, he went to North Dakota in 1905 and took a homestead in Leaf Mountain Township, Burke County. In 1913 he married Karine Henriksen. They moved to Columbus, ND in 1924. In 1943 they moved to Vancouver, Washington where he worked in the shipyards during World War II. Iver died in 1957 in Portland, OR. Iver and Karine had eight children. Two died in infancy. Surviving children include Mabel (Mrs. Mel Larson), Portland, OR; Nettie (Mrs. Lawrence Welo), Crosby, ND; Amy (Mrs. Warren Tanner), Alpine, NY; Paul, Tonasket, WA; Irene (Mrs. Gene Haugen), Milwaukee, OR; and Lafe, Portland, OR. Iver was the brother of Ingeborg and Randi Hallum (above). *(Form 453)*

John O. Swenskrude was born in Gran, Hadeland. He emigrated to Watson, MN where he married in 1889. His wife had emigrated from Kvam, Norway. In 1899 they homesteaded near Lignite, ND. In 1907 they moved into Lignite where he opened a hardware store. He was active in civic affairs – he was elected city alderman seven times and served as mayor five terms. In 1933 he retired and with his wife moved to Minot, ND to be near their only child, Caroline (Mrs. Henry Iverson). Mrs. Swenskrude died in 1944 and John died in 1950. *(Form 131)*

Olaf Ruden was born on May 6, 1887 in Hadeland. He emigrated in 1906 and took a homestead in Sorkness Township, Burke County in 1909. He married Elsina Jensen in Neenah, WI on December 9, 1913. They had seven children: four of them died in infancy. Those who survived into adulthood were Iver, Stanley, ND; Ruth (Mrs. Arnold Feiring), White Earth, ND; and James, Williston, ND. Mrs. Ruden died on January 13, 1940. In 1947 Olaf married Josephine Asmervig Monson. They lived on the homestead until 1966 when they moved to Powers Lake, ND. Olaf died on November 15, 1971. After his death, his wife moved into the St. Olav Guest House in Powers Lake, ND. *(Form 1235)*

County histories that are well researched are excellent sources of biographic information. If you own a county history, check to see if it contains biographies of immigrants, especially immigrants from Hadeland.

Henry P. Hanson: Voyage from Hadeland

"Recollection of Pioneer Times" February/May 2010   Form 233   *Henry P. Hanson*

SS HERO, built in 1866

This story was provided by Ole P. Gamme from the Kontaktforum's "Hadeland Emigrant Identification Collection." It was given to that collection by Geir-Olav Fjeldheim, Rykkin, Norway.

Henry P. Hanson (birth name: Hans Paulsen) was six and a half years old in May, 1870 when he and his parents, three sisters and paternal grandmother left Norway. Many years later he wrote about his memories of that long journey. Henry P. Paulson died on December 17, 1916. His daughter Mabel Pauline Hanson, Watertown, SD reproduced her father's original copy in March, 1980.

The family left their home in Hadeland and traveled to Christiania (present-day Oslo) where they boarded a combination steam-and-sail ship for Hull, England, with a stop at Kristiansand, Norway. According to the *Norway Heritage* website, the Wilson Line of Hull, England traveled that emigrant route weekly, departing Christiania every Friday at 5:00 p.m. The family traveled on either the *S/S Hero* or the *S/S Albion*. Those were the only two ships on that route from Oslo to Hull during May 1870.

Since my wife and children have expressed a desire to have me write a sketch of my life and family connections, the following will have to serve as such a write-up.

My paternal grandfather's name was Hans Paul Lerbro, born Dec. 15, 1793 in Hadeland, Norway. They lived on a place called Lerbro for many years. Of occupation, he (also all his sons) was a shoemaker. He went from farm to farm making the necessary footwear and repairing the old shoes for the different families as they had need therefore. My paternal grandmother, Bertha Halvorsdatter, was born Oct. 20, 1803. To this wedlock on the place called Lerbro were born the following children: Hans Hanson (Skaarta), June 14, 1824, Anders Hanson (Lerbro), Dec. 9, 1828, Ingeborg Hanson (Anderson), April 25, 1831, Paul Hanson (Skaarta), February 21, 1834, Anne Hanson (Lerbro), April 30, 1837. Of the above named, Paul Hanson was my father.

In a certificate of qualifications, bearing the signature of S. Bugge, parish minister for Gran, he is described with the following characteristics: "Musketeer No. 10 Paul Hanson of Toten

Company, Valdres Musketeer Corps, place of birth Næs in Gran, date of birth Feb. 21, 1834; knowledge of Christianity: very good; vaccination: Dec. 9, 1838; commissioned Oct. 5, 1856 and Nov. 22, 1857." This certificate bears no date. On April 21, 1861 he was married to my mother, Siri Gunderson. After their marriage they lived in a place called Skaarta which originally belonged and had been part of a farm named Retrum. In the spring of 1870 they departed for the United States of America. To this wedlock were born the following children: Hans (Paulson) Hanson, Feb. 20, 1863; Lise (Paulson) Hanson, Feb. 16, 1865; Bertha Marie (Paulson) Hanson, Dec. 3, 1867; Gena, born March 3, 1870. As before mentioned, father was of occupation a shoemaker as were his brothers and at this work he earned the support of himself and family. He had heard a great deal about America and the great advantages of this country for a poor man. He could also see that in the future, as his family would grow up, that they would likely want to move here. So, although he realized the difficulties connected with such a journey, the loss of old friends and near relatives, the inconvenience of a strange language which he could neither speak nor understand, the change of climate and mode of living, he braved all these difficulties, sold his effects and departed from the home which was dear to him, for a place where he had not that to which he could lean his head. This move was made in the spring of 1870.

The party was composed of the following: father, mother, father's mother, my three sisters and myself. A neighbor by the name of Amund Retrum hauled our effects to the city of Christiania from which we were to take a steamer for Hull, England. While waiting for the steamer to depart, the time was devoted to seeing the city. Among the various places visited, I can remember the old fort (*Akershus*) on the fjord with the ancient cannon, the House of Parliament (*Storting*), the Steam Kitchen where we ate dinner one day and several other places. About 1:00 p.m. on the day of our departure we boarded a small boat which carried us to a larger one at anchor farther out, and about 4:00 p.m. this ship began to journey through the fjord toward the sea while thousands of people on the pier fluttered their handkerchiefs as our boat steamed out.

As darkness began to settle over the sea, we went below to the place assigned the steerage passengers, and on waking the next morning, we lay at anchor outside of Kristiansand. It was a cloudy and gloomy day as I remember it and a sadness took hold of all, including the younger members of the party. As soon as the ship had taken on board other passengers and cargo, it started on its voyage across the rough North Sea for the English coast. On a journey of this kind, even a small child will see many things which impress his mind and which he will remember as long as he lives. Among such can be mentioned the pleasures of travel by rail through a country (from Hull to Liverpool, England) so widely different from his usual surroundings as England and America are different from Norway – the beautiful landscape in England fenced with hedge, the great factories emitting black coal smoke through their immense chimneys, the fruit orchards in bloom and setting fruit, and many other things which were new sights. Therefore this was something that was impressed upon the memory and will never be forgotten.

On arrival at Liverpool, England our party boarded the Allan Line steamer, *North American*, bound for Quebec, Canada, and from that time until we neared the American coast, very little besides sky, water and seafowl were to be seen. On a day after the steamer was well out in the Atlantic Ocean, the shore being entirely out of sight, an accident occurred which ought to be related. A sailor attempting to do some work outside the rail of the boat, slipped and fell into the water. As soon as it was possible to stop the steamer, a boat manned by nine sailors was lowered into the water and these set out to rescue their wet companion. In this they were successful, rowed back to the steamer and were all taken on board. The wet clothes were exchanged for dry, and the ship proceeded on its journey. From this occurrence until we saw land, nothing out of the ordinary happened which the memory is now able to recall.

As the steamer neared the east coast of Canada, on the western horizon a bank of hills began to appear in the distance, which the crew said was land. The passengers who, on account of sea-sickness and other indispositions had taken little interest in anything lately, began to fill up the decks, and it began to be lively on board the boat. As our ship steamed up the St. Lawrence River and the city of Quebec came in sight, a small cannon was fired off, a pilot was taken on board our ship, and we reached the harbor safely toward evening. Just how long it took to cross the ocean, it is impossible for me to say, but we were told that on account of icebergs in the usual traveled routes, it had been necessary to make a detour of about 300 miles on our trip across the Atlantic.

In Quebec it was not necessary to remain very long, for as we were transferred from the boat during the night, we were taken by rail the next morning toward what was probably the Erie Canal in the neighborhood of the Great Lakes, which we crossed in a large ferry boat and we were speeded on toward Chicago. On arrival at Chicago, it was found necessary to haul the goods from one depot to another and a hack driver speaking the Norwegian language was engaged to do this work. In going to the other depot, it was necessary to cross the Chicago River and the hackman drove directly toward the water's edge, although there seemed to be no bridge in the neighborhood or any way to cross except to drive over the steep bank into turbulent and muddy water. This, however, did not become necessary, for stopping his team on the bank of the river, he pointed to two men on a long platform-like structure in the middle of the stream who were running around in a circle, turning a lever. This platform-like structure proved to be one of Chicago's many turning bridges which had been swung to admit the passage of boats in the river and now turned back to permit crossing by team. This was the first time we had seen a swinging bridge and to use it was a wonderful contrivance.

From Chicago to Janesville, Wisconsin by rail, no incident can now be recalled, but here we had to stay over from some time during the night until the next morning when the train carried us still nearer our destination. Monroe, Wisconsin was the end of the rail at this time and here we arrived in the early part of the same day that we left Janesville. From this point our effects had to be hauled in a lumber wagon. But in a strange country among a people whose language was as unintelligible to us as the twitter of the birds, it was not an easy matter to find anyone who was willing to take the time and trouble to haul our goods a distance of over 20 miles. After some search, a man from Wiota Township, Lafayette County, by the name of Ole Christian Hamerest was found who loaded some of the baggage and the emigrants into his lumber wagon and started for Henry Peterson Smerud's place in Fayette Township, Lafayette County, Wisconsin, reaching the latter place well toward nightfall on Thursday, May 30, 1870. Here we found friends and here we were welcomed with open arms. These people had all come from the same neighborhood in Norway as ourselves, and at this place for the time being, father's sister Anna Hanson was staying. The son and daughter of Mr. Peterson, Perry and Rebecca, who then were children were also at home. At this place we remained a few days until we were rested up after our journey, when Mr. Peterson took us out to a place rented and occupied by Uncle Anderson from a man named Woods, and there we remained for some time. Uncle Ole had secured a farm but it was all in timber and the buildings were almost uninhabitable. Trees and underbrush grew almost to the door and no neighbor was in sight in any direction. We, who had lived in a place from which could be seen for miles in length, the Randsfjord, with the islands, the steamers and rowboats and life in general, and the dozens of fine homes on both sides of the lake, had now come to the highly praised America, where not one neighbor could be seen from the dooryard of the house; not without going considerable distance.

It was necessary now that father should go out and seek work, and as mother and the four children were compelled to remain at home while he was away a week or more at a time, living in such a hovel, surrounded by a dense forest, time seemed long, and many tears of sorrow were shed because of our changed condition and the departure from our former pleasantly situated home.

In the summer of the same year, it was probably in the month of August 1870, sister Gina was taken seriously ill and died. Father was away at work at the time but was sent for. She was buried in the Yellowstone Graveyard. Sometime later in the fall both father and mother became sick and were unable to work. Their sickness developed into typhoid fever, and although they had some medical attention and care, nothing availed, and in the month of February 1871 both passed away; Mother breathed her last on the 9th day, and father on the 23rd of the month. I don't know Mother's age, but father was 37 years old. They are all buried in Yellowstone Graveyard, Lafayette, Wisconsin. Of the once happy family of five, only three children, aged respectively 8, 6 and 3 years, remained without any near relative who had the means to do anything for their support. It looked dark indeed and many times since we have wondered how it was possible to pull through as well as we did. But He, who is a Father to the fatherless, found a way out of the difficulty so that we suffered no insurmountable hardship. Each of us secured a home, though several miles apart. Henry Peterson Smerud in Fayette Township, Lafayette County, Wisconsin, furnished home and support for sister Bertha Marie, now Mrs. John Hammer, Volga, South Dakota; Ole Rossing of Wiota Township, same county, a home for Lise, now Mrs. Hans Vostad; and Andrew Johnson of Jordan Township, Green County, a home for myself. In these respected families, we received our little schooling and bringing up. We had to study to learn. We were taught the difference between good and evil. Discipline was strict and punishments were not infrequent, but we received the necessary food and raiment. That which was missed the most was the tender care, love and affection of a father and a mother.

Parochial teachers were Ole Peterson Veum and O.J. Sann. On the 5th day of August 1877 I was confirmed in my baptismal covenant in the Norwegian Lutheran Congregation, Green County, Wisconsin, by Rec. C.C. Aus, then the pastor of the church. Later, Lise and Bertha Marie were also confirmed by the same pastor.

From the spring of 1871 up to the spring of 1881, my support was paid for by the work I could do on the Andrew Johnson farm, and after this time I was declared on my own. The following season, from May to October, I continued to work at the same place, receiving as pay $10 per month, and in that way saved my first $50. This money was loaned out to Morgan Olson at interest and saved, and made my first start towards funds for attending school at Valparaiso, Indiana. Later seasons I had farm work, cordwood chopping and fencing from the neighbors and from J.H. Nelson and his sons near South Wayne, Wisconsin. In the fall of 1883, at the age of 20 years, I decided to attend school at the Northern Industrial and Normal School and Business Institute, Valparaiso, Indiana. Accordingly in the beginning of the month of September of that year, my books and clothes were packed into a trunk and I boarded a train at Monroe, Wisconsin for that place of learning, where seven and one-half months were spent in hard study. At the end of this time, the money earned and some borrowed besides was all spent and the only thing to do was to earn some more. In securing work, I had no difficulty, paid up the former debt and borrowed more to resume studies at the same school as before. At the beginning of the month of January, 1885, I was on my way back to Valparaiso and remained there until the end of May. This made twelve and one-half months spent at the school, and the studies taken were grammar, arithmetic, geography, penmanship, bookkeeping, commercial law and actual business. I had now acquired that which I considered most necessary to get down to earning something for myself and so decided to let this be all the time that could be offered for that purpose.

Randi Lee Hvattum

published May/August 2010   *Forms 126, 43*   *Brian Christensen*

Randi Hvattum's Passport Photo

My grandfather T. Henry Hvattum (1914-2004) often mentioned that he wished he had accompanied his mother, Randi Lee Hvattum on her return trip to Gran, Hadeland, Norway. She was an immigrant from Hadeland and made just one return trip to see her parents. Grandpa would occasionally tell family members that he made a mistake when he backed out of a planned trip. Late in life he couldn't recall the details; however he mentioned he was a boy when his mother made the return visit. His mother wanted him to accompany her, but at the time he wasn't that interested, due to farm work, school, and girls. He missed the chance to meet his grandparents and cousins back in Norway. A few times I asked Grandpa the date of this trip, but he couldn't remember. A recent discovery of family papers now tells the story about his mother's trip to Hadeland.

Fourteen year old Randi Lee emigrated from Gran, Hadeland, Norway on 20 March 1903 to Boston, in the United States – eventually settling in Northern Iowa.[1] It must have been very difficult for a young girl to leave her parents and siblings back in Norway on the Skjervum farm. The journey was made easier as she was accompanied by a neighbor boy named Ingvald from the Dynna farm. (Nothing is known as to what happened to him). Randi assumed the Lee surname – an Americanized version of the Lia farm where her father's family originated. This was also the last name chosen by her uncle Andrew Lee who immigrated in 1892 to Forest City, Iowa. For a few years she resided with Uncle Andrew on his farm, and worked for him doing housework to pay for her passage to America. Although Andrew Lee was her father's younger brother, he was essentially a stranger to her, having emigrated from Norway when she was just three years old. She undoubtedly missed her parents in Norway, but it helped greatly that her older brother Gulbrand (Gilbert) Lee came to Iowa two years earlier, and a younger brother

298

Karl (Carl) Lee arrived later in 1907. A fourth sibling, Mari (Mary) Lee also came to Iowa, but it is not known the date of her immigration.

Randi Lee married in 1909 at Osage, Mitchell County, Iowa, to another Hadeland immigrant, a man named Thorsten "Tom' Hvattum. They farmed southwest of Osage. Their children were; Ruth, b. 22 Aug 1908, Helga, b. 25 Nov 1910, and my grandfather, T. Henry, b. 17 Sep 1914.

Thorsten Hvattum

Henry Hvattum was survived by his wife Katherine, my grandmother. She died a couple years ago at age 90, and left an apartment full of belongings. Grandma was notorious for keeping everything. Perhaps it was her generation that experienced the Great Depression and simply could not discard or throw away anything that could be valuable...or perhaps Grandma was just a pack rat. Since I had limited time I gathered the things that appeared to be family heirlooms and stuffed boxes in the trunk of my car. Months later I sorted through dozens of old documents and was thrilled when I found some papers written in Norwegian. Inside an envelope I discovered mementos from Great Grandma Randi Lee Hvattum's trip to Norway! At first I wasn't sure what I found, but suddenly realized it was the dinner menu from a steam ship, a receipt for the voyage, and an old burgundy colored passport with Randi's photo.

The Receipt

Travel to Norway was an expensive proposition, and the slow economy of 1930 made the trip especially costly. The old faded receipt from the Norwegian America Line (NAL) showed that Randi put down a $30 deposit for a third class ticket on January 29, 1930. The total cost was $205. Was that a lot of money back then? I checked a couple of web sites and found that $205 in 1930 dollars is the equivalent of $2,642.94 today.[2] For another comparison, a 14-day, multiple stop, transatlantic Disney cruise with balcony view, to Madrid in the Summer of 2010 will set you back $1649.[3] Not only did you have to pay for the ocean voyage you had cover bus or train travel from the middle of the continent to reach New York City. A return trip to Norway for most immigrants was indeed expensive.

Randi's trip to Norway was at the beginning of the Great Depression. The timing of the Great Depression varied across nations, but in most countries it started in about 1929 and lasted until the late 1930s or early 1940s. The depression originated in the United States, starting with the stock market crash of October 29, 1930 (known as Black Tuesday), but quickly spread to almost every country in the world. The Great Depression had devastating effects in virtually every country, rich and poor. Personal income, tax revenue, profits, and prices dropped, and international trade plunged by a half to two-thirds. Unemployment in the U.S. rose to 25%. Farming and rural areas suffered as crop prices fell by approximately 60%.[4] It must have been difficult to spend this kind of money during this economic time, and Randi had not amassed a fortune cleaning houses and being a farmer's wife. For 27 years she must have saved every penny. Perhaps my grandfather had the details wrong – It was simply cost prohibitive to have him join his mother on this trip to Norway. It is more likely that the family could afford only one ticket.

Dinner Programs

The story truly came alive when I found two fancy colored dinner programs. One program was dated "*30 May 1930 – Stavangerfjord,*" while the other was the *"Farewell Dinner, S.S. Bergensfjord, 14 September 1930."* Now I knew the dates for Randi's return visit to Norway and the ships she took on her journey! I didn't know she stayed the entire summer in Hadeland – I assumed she had a shorter stay. Both dinner programs consisted

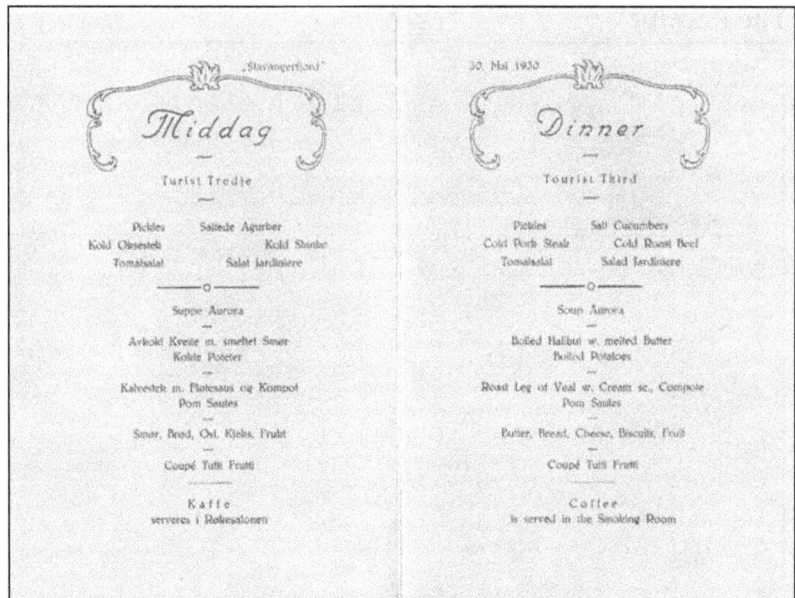

of a two-page folded paper, with the first page written in Norwegian, and the second page in English. The back of the dinner program listed the music selection for the evening. This included music by famous Norwegian composer Edvard Grieg. The "Tourist Third Class" dinner aboard the ship called Stavangerfjord on the voyage to Norway consisted of Soup Aurora, Boiled Halibut with melted Butter, Roast Leg of Veal with Cream, and Coupe Tutti Fruiti. On the return voyage to New York in September, Randi was aboard the ship called Bergensfjord, and she enjoyed Potage Reine, filet of fish Bonne-femme, boiled potatoes, Roast Young Goose with Red Cabbage, and strawberry ice cream. Third class sounded pretty tasty to me! Coffee was served in the smoking room.

The Ships of the Norwegian America Line Agency

The *S.S. Stavangerfjord* was known as the "queen of the Atlantic." Many emigrants from Norway, Sweden, Denmark, England and Ireland travelled aboard her to the US and Canada. The *Stavangerfjord* was built in 1918 at Birkenhead, England. Over her 45 years on the sea, she crossed the Atlantic 768 times and carried more than 400,000 passengers.[5] The Third Class accommodations (Randi's $205 ticket) provided for 860 passengers and the staterooms arranged for 2, 4 and 6 persons. The berths were of galvanized iron and were furnished with mattresses, pillows, sheets and blankets. The staterooms were fitted with wash-basins, mirrors etc. Commodious sitting rooms and smoking saloons were also provided for passengers traveling on the third class. The large airy dining saloons had a capacity of seating 354 passengers. Well-prepared meals were served by the ship's stewards, and every provision was made for the comfort of passengers.[6] Transatlantic service from Norway to New York continued until the ship was overtaken by Germans as a troopship in 1940. She was returned to the Norwegian America Line (NAL) in 1945. The *Stavangerfjord* was scrapped in 1964.

The *S.S. Bergensfjord* was built in 1913 by Cammell Laird & Co. of Birkenhead, England for the NAL. She carried 105 cabin class passengers, 216 tourist class, and 760 third class passengers. The ship was used on the Norway-New York service until 1940 when she was taken over by British authorities and became an Allied troopship. She was sold to Panamanian (Home Lines) in 1946 and renamed *Argentina*, for emigrant traffic from Italy to South America and Italy-New York voyages. Later she was sold to Israel in 1953 and renamed *Jerusalem*, and then *Aliya* in 1957. Two years later, in 1959 she was scrapped.[7]

The two ships of the Norwegian America Line that operated between 1913 and 1940 had many passengers with a Hadeland background, as there were 117 people from Hadeland that emigrated during these years. It is also interesting to note that 72 out of the 8,809 known emigrants returned to their native Hadeland to live out their lives.[8] It is likely that several of these individuals also had a voyage on the *Stavangerfjord* or the *Bergensfjord*. Hundreds of others like Randi Lee Hvattum came back to Norway on vacation to visit family and see friends.

Summer of 1930 – Randi visited her relatives in Gran

During this trip in 1930, Randi returned to Gran to see her father Halvor Kristoffersen Skjervum, age 72, and mother Berthe Gudbrandsdatter Skjervum, age 75. Her father Halvor was born on the Lia farm in Lunner on 17 Jun 1858, son of Kristoffer Halvorsen Lia (1833-1872), and Kari Larsdatter Ruud (1820-1867). Berthe was born 14 Jun 1858, on Skjervum farm in Gran, daughter of Gudbrand Povelsen Skjervum (1820 – aft 1900) and Kari Gundersdatter Hoff (1820 – aft 1900). Halvor and Berthe married in Gran on 1 May 1879.

Berthe was one of five daughters of Gudbrand Povelsen Skjervum. Since there were no brothers on the Skjervum farm, Halvor, having married Berthe, became the primary farmer and assumed the Skjervum farm name. Children of Halvor and Berthe included;

Halvor and Berthe Skjervum

1) Kari, b. 1879, married Nils Kamphoug of Oslo
2) Gilbert Lee, 1884-1961, lived at Osage, Iowa
3) Randi, 1888-1985, subject of this story
4) Carl Lee, 1890-1920, WWI hero, lived at Osage
5) Mari (Mary), 1892-1917, Osage, Iowa
6) Karen, 1893-1970 married Gunder Amundrud
7) Kjerstin, 1894-1974, married Johan Solbakken
8) Berte, 1898-1981 married Johan Voldengen
9) Torgeir Skjervum, b. 1917, adopted son

Because all of Halvor's sons immigrated to the USA he did not have a male heir, so late in life he sold the Skjervum farm and moved to a small cottage along the Jaren *patnet* (lake), called Skjervumbråtten. Halvor died 18 Apr 1936 and Berthe died 3 Jun 1941. During the 2005 Hadeland Lag tour I heard a fascinating story from my cousin Paul Woien of Gran. He drove me down to the edge of the Jaren lake and pointed across the water at the small white cottage called Skjervumbråtten. "That's where Halvor and Berthe lived after selling the Skjervum farm." Amazingly he then told me how he remembered his great uncle Halvor's funeral! Paul explained that they do not embalm the dead in Norway, and that it was a particularly warm day, when Uncle Halvor was laid out for burial. The strong smell made an impression on the young boy. He watched family load Halvor's remains in a horse drawn wagon for the uphill journey to the Sister Churches (*Søsterkirkene*) for burial.

It is not known how many relatives Randi was able to see during her stay in Hadeland; however I learned that her visit made a lasting impression on the children. In the late 1980s I began researching my Hadeland roots and I contacted one of Randi's elderly nieces in Norway, who was excited to tell me about her American Aunt's visit. She fondly mentioned her Aunt's delicious lemon meringue pie, gold rim spectacles, and her uncanny way of letting the children *actually* speak at the dinner table. It seems that Aunt Randi wasn't as traditional as the older generations in her native country. She must have had a lot of fun in Hadeland challenging the status quo.

Conclusion

Randi and her great-grandson, the author, Brian Christensen

A few post cards found among Randi's belongings show she maintained correspondence with her sisters back in Norway until the early 1970s, when letters stopped arriving. Randi had wondered for many years if any of her sisters were still living in Norway, and assumed she was the last remaining. She died 16 Apr 1985, at a nursing home in Osage, Iowa, at age 97.

Randi saved her money so she could see her elderly parents one last time. It is difficult to imagine leaving your parents at age 14 and then waiting 27 years to see them again. She saved her dinner programs, receipt, and passport to remind her of the summer of 1930 in Hadeland. She probably couldn't imagine that 80 years later her great-grandson would share her journey in the Hadeland Lag's *Brua*!

Sources
[1] Digital Archives, Emigrants from Oslo, 1867-1930. Research by Peter Oskar Saugstad
[2] MeasuringWorth.com: Purchasing Power of Money in the US; online calculator
[3] YahooTravel.com
[4] Wikipedia article on the Great Depression
[5] Warsailors.com
[6] Norwegian American Line booklet, 1916
[7] Darren Dypevåg's Home Page: Magne Olai Jacobsen Dypevåg Norwegian Merchant Navy, Individual Ships, photos and facts. December 4, 2009
[8] Kontaktforum Emigrant database, January 1, 2009

Annie P. Morstad

"A Pioneer Woman" published February 2011   *Form 682,130*   *Peder H Nelson*

This story was originally published in Norwegian in the 'Brua' in 1939 (#27, pp 24-27). Verlyn Anderson translated the text for the 2011 reprint.

One of the oldest pioneer women of Hadeland descent in the large Northwood, N.D. settlement is Annie P. Morstad. Last fall she celebrated her 85th birthday and we will therefore in this issue write a little about the highly respected Hadeland woman here in this *Brua*.

Mrs. Morstad was born on Guldeneiet in Gran on August 24, 1853. Her parents were Guldbrand Huser from Oppdalen in Lunner and his wife Ingeborg Guldenbakken. Her father emigrated to America in 1853 the same year as his daughter was born and when he was never heard from again, her family was left in a very dire economic situation. Annie was then placed with her grandparents, Anders and Kari Guldenbakken, and was raised in their home. In 1878 she married Peder Iversen Morstad. The young couple decided to try their luck in the much talked-about America, so in 1879 Peder Morstad emigrated to America. Mrs. Morstad emigrated the next year with their little son, Iver. The family first settled in Ridgeway, Iowa, but a short time later continued on to the large Hadeland settlement around Northwood, N.D. in Lin Township, some miles west of the village of Northwood. Some years later they moved to Minnesota where they took a homestead in Roseau County. They lived there until Peder died on January 12, 1906. Peder had been born on the Gamme farm in Gran on November 28, 1850. Mrs. Morstad moved back to North Dakota and lived 10 years in Grand Forks, but then moved to Northwood where she enjoys her retirement in her beautiful home. Her son, Miller, is at home and takes care of his mother, "and he is very good and kind to me," says Mrs. Morstad.

Annie and Peder Morstad had six children: Iver, born in Gran on July 26, 1879; Julius, born on August 31, 1881 and died in 1889; Karoline (Mrs. G.O. Brørby, Northwood, N.D.), born September 24, 1884; Miller, born February 7, 1886; and Gilman, born November 24, 1888. Gilman was a soldier in World War I and experienced many horrors and terrors of the war, until he was seriously wounded in a battle on October 3, 1918. The doctors amputated one of his legs while in the ambulance on the way to Paris, but he died a short time later. The sixth of their children, Ida Josephine (Mrs. Henry Halvorson, Northwood, N.D.) was born on February 3, 1883 and died on May 1, 1931.

In the spring of 1931, Annie Morstad received the great honor of a trip to France as a guest of the American government so that she could visit the grave of her son which was in a cemetery, located about 40 miles from Paris. On the Atlantic crossing she was a passenger on the *George Washington* passenger liner. They spent six weeks in France with two of those weeks in Paris. She visited her son's grave eight times during her stay in France. She says that she wouldn't have gone on this tour without the great arrangement and the handling of the tour in the very best way by the American military officials and the French people; they all did their very best that they could do for them. She is very happy that she could visit her son's grave, but it was also very sad to see the thousands upon thousands of white crosses that mark the graves in that large American cemetery of the young men who had given their lives for their country and their fellow citizens. The cemetery is very well taken care of and it looks like an enormous flower garden. When the visit was over, they returned to the United States on the liner *America*.

"When I had gotten comfortably settled on the train in Grand Forks at the beginning of my trip to France," says Annie Morstad, "my daughter Ida came into the train and said, 'Oh! dear Mother, what a great honor this is.' I bowed my head against my seat so far that she shouldn't see how moved I was because of her words." Ida died a short time after her mother arrived home from France.

Some days before he was injured, Gilman had written home and said that he thought the war was soon over and maybe soon he would be home again. But then he, too, was killed, just a month before the Armistice.

In spite of her high age, Annie Morstad is still quite agile and has an excellent memory. She has many interesting recollections about her childhood in Hadeland. She was baptized, confirmed and married in the *Sister Churches* in Gran, and she showed me her *New Testament* that she received from Pastor Bugge as a confirmation gift. She went to school in Nordengen and Lars Koller was her school teacher. "But many years have gone since that time," she said.

Peder and Ingeborg Stadum

published May/August 2011   *Form 751*   *Beverly Stadum*

The author thanks Verlyn Anderson and Ole Gamme for detective work finding specific information about the Stadum farm in Hadeland and the manifest list from the "Rollo" with family names.

The Peder and Ingeborg Stadum Family about 1892
Back: unknown, Annie, Peter, John
Front: Andrew, Peter, Carl, Ingeborg holding Inga, and Karin

In the spring of 1889 my great-grandparents Peder Pettersen Stadum and Ingeborg Johanessdotter Slaatland auctioned off belongings and sold their farm in Vestre Gran near Randsfjorden. Their place was called Engen, meaning "the meadow," originally part of a larger older Stadum farm that gave its name to the whole area. Thus Peder's own last name had become Stadum. He bought the farm in 1870 for about 1200 crowns and sold it for 2000; the sale was to finance emigration to America. Letters from neighbors and Peder's two sisters already living there bragged about free land for homesteading. The local clergyman - though opposed to emigration from his congregation - wrote a reference letter saying the Stadums were honest people, a respected family. Friends arranged a farewell party. Later the oldest son recalled it wasn't only neighboring farmers who came to wish them well, but people who he said were considered "the better class," a district judge and the merchant who ran the *landhandleri*, the general store.

The entire family, Peder and Ingeborg with sons Anders, Karl, Johannes and Peter (ages 2 to 15 years) and daughters Karen and Anne (5 and 10 years) sailed from Christiania on board the *Rollo* April 26 1889. The Wilson Line that owned this steamship had a near monopoly transporting Norwegian emigrants on the two-day voyage from Christiania to Hull on the east coast of England. Immigrants rode a train from there west to Liverpool to embark again by ship. For the Stadums, the destination was Quebec and then to Minnesota by train. Relatives met them at Pelican Rapids in May and took them to an area known as Norwegian Grove. Peter, the oldest son, later described their two-week trans-Atlantic voyage as "almost without incident," for his family though some passengers had been very seasick. He wrote, too, "My first impression of America was grand. I could see that here were prospects for making good for anyone who wanted to try."

In Hadeland the family farm had been small, fields were strips of open land between forest tracts. Cultivation was by hand or with one horse at the most. The local economy relied as much on industry: saw mills, wood-working and wool processing plants, as on dairy agriculture. Peder, the father, had combined farming with being a tailor; in Minnesota he continued working at that trade in the shop of a Hadelander also named Stadum. Perhaps the family's baggage had included his tailor's tools. Son Peter had taken some training in bookkeeping when he finished grade school and had begun as an office boy in a lawyer's office in Gran. But when he came to the U.S., he took the job he could find—milking cows for a farmer—something he had not done in Norway where milking was women's work; later he found a clerical job. Johannes also worked on farms in the area and for a few winters sawed trees and surveyed in Minnesota's timber industry. He took out a tree claim that gave him acreage similar to a homestead claim; the owner received land provided he planted trees and kept them alive for so many years. Johannes eventually took practical studies in engineering and blacksmithing at the new North Dakota Agricultural College in Fargo (now North Dakota State University).

Almost ten years after immigrating to Minnesota, the family moved to North Dakota to homestead. Moving away from the Hadelanders in Minnesota was not by preference but because no more land was available there for homesteading. Peter went first filing a claim in Benson County in 1898; he was 25 years old. The next year his father Peder, brother Johannes (now known as John), and sister Anne filed claims adjacent to his. All four properties met at a corner. When Anders (now Andrew) became an adult he took over his parents' farm and they lived with him; after Anne married she sold her land to Andrew and Karl (now Carl) who had earlier homesteaded a bit further west. Because available land in Benson County was soon taken, the Stadums considered themselves lucky to have come when they did. By 1900 a small town named Esmond was growing up at a railroad stop six miles from the Stadum farms, a great advantage for shipping their wheat, oats, and barley.

Peter never married, but John, Carl and Andrew Stadum married women from the Norwegian community in Rothsay, Minn. In North Dakota the families lived near one another not just geographically, but socially as well. Karen was the exception; she found her life's work in St. Paul and never married. But Anne and Inga, a third sister born in Minnesota, both married Norwegians and lived on ND farms. In old age Peder walked regularly between his sons' homesteads with the help of a carved wooden cane. A hundred years later his great-grandchildren still farm this land.

Gina Brørby Homesteads in Burke County

In 1908 when he was 32 and well underway as a North Dakota farmer, John Stadum married Gina Otilda Brørby, age 27. They are my grandparents. She was the daughter of Hadelanders Anders Jorgensen Brørby and Anna Hansdatter Kingestuen. Anders and his brother Iver had emigrated together to the Fergus Falls/Rothsay/Pelican Rapids area of Minnesota about twenty years before the Stadums came, traveling by sailboat when the Atlantic trip took six weeks instead of two.

Iver and his wife Randi Ohe had three children born in Pelican Rapids. Anders and Anna, however, had a large family with children born in both countries. The oldest, Mari, was Verlyn Anderson's great–grandmother born in Norway; my grandmother Gina was born in Minnesota, the seventh Brørby child with a twin who died at birth. Gina grew up to become a seamstress. The picture on the next page shows her in the elaborate heavy-looking wedding dress she sewed for herself. But five years before marriage, she left Minnesota to take out her own homestead claim in northwestern North Dakota, somewhat more adventuresome than Anne Stadum who had homesteaded alongside her father and brothers. Such economic ventures by females was not uncommon according to H. Elaine Lindgren in her book, *Land in Her Own Name, Women as Homesteaders in North Dakota*, which includes information about Gina.

In the September 2009 *Brua*, Verlyn Anderson described how frequently Hadelanders in the Fergus Falls area homesteaded in Burke County in northwestern North Dakota. Gina traveled by train with a female friend to Minot, ND, where they hired a wagon to take them on to Columbus, the county seat of Burke County. She satisfied legal requirements to prove up her claim by trading cooking and sewing with nearby male homesteaders (likely Minnesota Hadelanders) who did her plowing, the heaviest farm work. They also had helped build her eight-by-ten foot shack and cover it with tarpaper.

Gina dug a well for water and dug up young trees along a stream to replant around the cabin. It wasn't good land; the best had already been claimed, but she found lignite coal near the surface of the ground making it easy to keep her shack warm in winter. During a 48-hour blizzard, she stayed awake the whole time to keep watch so the fire in her stove didn't go out. The danger in summer was prairie fires; once she saw smoke on the horizon days before fire reached her but neighbors had plowed up land around her cabin which saved it from burning. She eventually achieved ownership and sold this homestead to her friend and neighbor for $1,900. The land was still in that family in the 1970s; they called it "the Gina land." She used the money later to purchase a quarter to expand the farm she shared with John in Benson County.

Life on John's and Gina's Farm

When they first married, John and Gina lived in a cook-car on his land. Building a simple barn

John and Gina married on 17 Feb 1908

and a machine shed, later a granary and blacksmith shop, had been more important to John than a house. But Gina demanded a house and their four children, Palmer, Ida, Arthur and Julian, were born in its northwest bedroom. They planted a garden every year and raised crab apple and plum trees to have fruit for canning. They had chickens, turkeys, pigs, sheep for a while, cats in the barn, and of course horses and milk cows.

Palmer, the oldest child (1909-1999), was my father, a man with vivid and happy memories of growing up in a house full of people (and too many mice). When Gina's father Anders died, his widow Anna Brørby moved in with Gina and John; she kept busy knitting stockings, hats, and gloves for everyone in the household. Gina's Brørby siblings and other Hadeland newcomers often lived there temporarily. It seemed to Palmer that women were always busy around the cook stove in the kitchen. Coffee was purchased in bulk and ground fresh every day. Breakfast was oatmeal; lunch and supper were often rømmegrøt. Occasionally on Sunday the family ate canned salmon; but if the minister (a distant Brørby relative from Minnesota), had been invited for dinner – Palmer was sent out to wring the neck of a chicken.

Fourth of July was celebrated in the churchyard or at a farm. Neighbors worked together to cut grass and set up a stand where Andrew Stadum annually volunteered to sell ice cream and cigars. The main event was the auction of a quilt sewn by Gina's Lutheran Ladies Aid that

John and Gina Stadum family about 1925
Back: Ida, Arthur, Julian and Palmer
Seated: John and Gina Stadum

met monthly (money to go to a good cause). An American flag was hung from a tree, men played horseshoes, boys played baseball and set off firecrackers. The women provided two meals and everyone drank lemonade.

Palmer Stadum (1909-1999)

Palmer was the oldest of the four children of John and Gina Stadum. He was the father of the author of this article. Palmer had a life-long fascination with all things electrical and mechanical that began when he was very young. Included in this text are quotes from the autobiography he dictated in 1994.

Modern Inventions on the Prairie

Palmer's earliest memory was going with his father to watch railroad workers lay a spur line south from the Soo Railroad and bring a train engine on it. With the railroad, the town of Baker sprang into being with a two-story schoolhouse where Palmer first learned English. Only

Norwegian was spoken on the farm. John Stadum was a forward thinking man who used his blacksmith training to upgrade equipment on his farm. In 1913 he traveled to Grand Forks, ND to an agricultural exposition to hear about progressive farming methods. He drove back home in a new Studebaker, the first car in the township. Palmer remembered how his father came into the farmyard blowing the horn in the middle of the night. Gina took Palmer and his younger sister Ida out in their nightgowns for their first automobile ride.

Palmer Stadum

The car was a disappointment, usable only in the summer and prone to flat tires that slowed down the trips to visit Brørbys in Minnesota. But on Sunday afternoons Palmer and Ida entertained themselves by going out to the shed to sit in it and pretend they were traveling. When Palmer learned to start the engine, he was allowed to drive the car up to the house for John to use in taking the family to church. In 1921 John purchased a Model T in Baker. He started the car, put 12-year-old Palmer behind the steering wheel and let him drive it home – lurching along in first gear. During World War I with high prices for grain, John bought a steam engine for threshing, the first in the township. In autumn he hired himself and the machine out to thresh at a dozen farms of other Norwegians in the area.

The steam engine was a big iron boiler on wheels pulled by horses. Straw fed into it created a fire to boil water and maintain steam channeled to run belts stretched to gears on the threshing machine that separated grain from the straw and chaff. Palmer recalled that his father used a crew of about 20 men, plus horses and wagons, to gather grain bundles in from the field, put them into the separator and eventually drive the threshed grain to the elevator in Baker. Women worked in the cook car to feed the hungry men. In the first years John's brothers worked as the steam rig's engineer and fireman. The extra harvest hands were Norwegians hired from Minnesota and Wisconsin.

As soon as Palmer was tall enough to climb onto the steam engine, his father gave him a putty knife to clean away grease. When he was big enough to handle a pitch fork, John hired him as "straw monkey" to pitch straw into the boiler to keep the fire going, then he became the fireman controlling the fire, and at about age 15, John assigned him as engineer. At dawn Palmer rode his motorcycle out to wherever threshing was to be done to clean and grease the engine parts while others were still eating breakfast. Reminiscing at age 85, he said, "When I was firing the machine, I would get up at about 4:30 a.m. and jump on my trusty motorcycle to fly out to the field." His enthusiasm for mechanics was not only encouraged by his parents who had given him tinker toys and an erector set when he was very young, but also by his Uncle Peter, the oldest of the Stadum brothers who lived down the road.

Peter Stadum was a bachelor farmer who lived out his life in his original homesteader's cabin. But he was involved in community affairs, served in various township and county offices, was an avid reader and one of the initial supporters of a newspaper for Benson County. His house was filled with books on science and classic literature, old tools, wires, metal, and inventions, one of which was a seismograph he constructed to register movements in the earth. He had subscriptions to publications including *Scientific American* and *Popular Science*. After church on Sundays it was Palmer's habit to walk over to his uncle's to read.

Palmer's Imagination and Inventions

He read Mark Twain and used old fence poles to build a raft to float in the swimming hole in their pasture – pretending he was Huckleberry Finn on the Mississippi River; he read about Roald Amundsen crossing the Antarctic and turned off the radiator in his bedroom to sleep under an open window to build up endurance to the cold. Palmer was thrilled by all modern inventions. In the eighth grade he saw a picture of an indoor bathroom in a book and bargained with his father. If John would order the piping, a porcelain toilet and bathtub from the Montgomery Ward catalog, Palmer would do all the work outside. This meant digging a hole for waste, digging a 100-foot long, 6-foot deep trench for piping and laying sand in it hauled from a lake. On Sundays John and Gina excused him from church so he could continue digging. Eventually the Stadums had a bathroom on the second story, one of the few in Benson County and according to the opinions of some neighbors — totally unnecessary.

The most exciting inventions Palmer read about came from Thomas Edison's workshop in Menlo Park, New Jersey. He said, "I was always very interested in electricity. One time I fixed up a spark box out of some old coils from a Model T car. My Dad was telling me that the sparks wouldn't be strong enough to affect him. So I laid a couple of them on one of his arms as he was sitting in the parlor. That woke him up! but he sure didn't let me do it again." Palmer also strung a telegraph wire between his bedroom and Ida's. He had taught himself the Morse Code and tried to read her messages and simultaneously type them on a used typewriter. The result? "Not so successful," he said; he was too slow.

In the 1920s wireless communication and advertisements for new radios filled the magazines. Peter was the first one to buy a radio. "He would sit and listen to operas; this is where I first heard a radio. One day when we came back from school my Dad was putting up an antennae. He had bought an RCA four tube radio; I still have that radio hanging in the garage. That must have been about 1924 because I received the *American Boy* magazine at that time and it started having articles about how to make a simple one-tube radio."

"My Dad gave me $5 to buy a tube, a socket, and a pair of headphones. I built a radio according to the instructions ....this radio worked quite satisfactorily. Neighbors would come upstairs to look at it, about three feet long with one tube in it...I made a couple of dozen kinds of radios.... I had an antenna in the bedroom with the wire going through the window and running a hundred feet southeast down toward the garden." By the time he graduated from high school in 1928, he was repairing radios for others.

Palmer continued to work on the farm in the 1930s, but hay fever plagued him and because he wanted to be an inventor, not a farmer, he rented a building in Baker for his radio workshop. In 1933 when the Century of Progress Exposition (World's Fair) opened in Chicago celebrating industrial and scientific discoveries, Palmer and a friend traveled there by train and stayed with relatives near the Fair Grounds. A World War 1 submarine, Admiral Byrd's ship to the South Pole, and the Chicago Museum of Science and Industry all impressed Palmer. However, he spent most of his carefully saved money in one place. "A little Piper Cub was being shown off at the Fair and the pilot told me that if I'd come out to a private flying field, he'd give me a flying lesson. I think it was about $7 an hour. I made several trips and he said I was catching on," reported Palmer.

Pioneer in Rural Electrification

Palmer gathered six like-minded friends from high school into the Baker Technical Club that met regularly at his workshop. They talked about future possibilities — such as space flight, but Palmer often led discussion back to the question of how they could get electricity to their area. Towns of some size had electricity, but for-profit companies were not interested in servicing rural areas. Some North Dakota farmers had their own generators - John did, but most farmers milked cows with light from kerosene lanterns. When President Roosevelt's New Deal began funding programs, Club members applied for public works money to build a new town hall for Baker and to drain the nearby slough. Then in 1935 Palmer read about the new Rural Electrification Administration (R.E.A.). The Club wrote a letter to Washington and quickly got a reply, "We are ready and willing to loan up to 100 per cent of the cost of construction of new line extension to a responsible local body which will undertake to construct these lines."

The slough was never drained but the Town Hall got built in Baker and stood until the 1980s. And approximately $65,000 came for rural electrification, but it didn't happen overnight. Palmer used John's truck to drive around the area trying to convince farmers to join the co-operative (membership cost $5 per R.E.A. guidelines, money which some couldn't afford during the Depression). And he needed right–of-ways for setting up poles and lines on farmers' land. A Board of Directors was organized; North Dakota's governor cut the red tape for them; in 1937 the Baker Electric Cooperative was incorporated and bids for construction were let. Six months later the first farm in North Dakota was electrified with lights in the house and barn. Palmer

Palmer's wife, Signe Solberg Stadum. The couple married on June 14, 1941, in York ND

directed the crew that set up the poles and climbed them himself to string the wires. (And he married the rural schoolteacher who was boarding with the family!) In 1975 when the REA celebrated its 50th anniversary nationally, Palmer was described in state newspapers as the "Father of Rural Electricity" in North Dakota. In 1996 Baker Electric Cooperative merged with the Tri-County Electrical Cooperative to become the current North Plains Electrical Cooperative.

World War II halted extension of electric lines beyond the initial townships as all wire was reallocated to national defense. Palmer joined the Seabees—the Navy's construction corps - and worked in Pearl Harbor (1943-1945) supervising electricians reconstructing the submarine base. In the early 1950s he left the REA, temporarily repaired the newest electrical miracle - television sets! He then joined and became a partner in an electric firm in Minot, ND. He wired new complexes in the area: hospitals, banks, the pumping system connected to Garrison Dam, and taught apprentice classes for the International Brotherhood of Electrical Workers.

When he retired, he was still busy eight hours a day, six days a week—building models in his Minot workshop. The first one was a miniature steam engine with movable parts, scaled one inch to the foot. He had drawn up detailed blueprints decades earlier. "As I stood behind the engine firing during threshing I would try to imagine how a model of a steam engine would look." The work took him two years. When asked how he managed to make and assemble hundreds of metal parts, he always answered, "It's just one piece at a time." More models followed, more steam engines, early tractors, train engines. His friends also built models and traveled together to steam engine threshing rallies in Rollag MN, in Iowa, and Canada. He was often asked to display models at events, including Minot's Scandinavian Høstfest in 1983.

Palmer meets Princess Astrid at Minot's Hostfest

Norway's Princess Astrid, daughter of King Olav V, sister of the present King Harald, was a guest that year. Amidst the activities she visited a Model Railroad Show where Palmer was displaying. My mother wrote to relatives, "Can you imagine his amazement when Princess Astrid & Co. walked in the main door and came to him, shook his hand and began asking questions about his models!! Needless to say, he just hates to wash the hand that shook the hand of royalty!" Someone took a picture of Princess Astrid, Palmer, and a model; it is hanging on my wall in Øyer, Norway, and pictured on the right.

Might he and the Princess have spoken to one another in Norwegian? Perhaps. Palmer never stopped using Norwegian with his parents and old friends. In 1978 he traveled with relatives to Gran for a reunion with Hadeland family. The local paper reported that he stood up at the dinner and gave a speech in the 19th century Hadeland dialect of his grandparents, Peder and Ingeborg Stadum, and Anders and Anna Brørby.

After Palmer died, we found a journal in his workshop with a hundred-plus ideas for

Palmer in his workshop

inventions, most of them written when he was in Hawaii. Some came with detailed drawings, refined repeatedly. He was thinking about power steering for automobiles before Detroit made it available. Other things were simpler: electric toys for children, farm implements, a new kind of blinking Christmas tree light, a new kind of ink pen, and my favorite: a device that made clothes-pins pop into your hands as you stood at the clothes-line. Palmer Stadum had a curious and creative mind that ran at full speed during his entire life (22 April 1909-19 January 1999).

315

Peder and Ottine Jorstad

"Recollections of Pioneer Times" published May 2011   Form 948   Anne Lise Jorstad

Ottine and Peder Jorstad

Painting of the Jorstad farm in Gran, Norway

During a recent trip to the USA in the Fall of 2010 — almost 40 years after my study year at the University of Minnesota, I used the opportunity to visit South Dakota, where I had never been before.

During a Jorstad family event in Sioux Falls, somebody brought out several large portraits, pictures of people I did not know, but found out were related to Peder Jorstad's wife Ottine Jorstad (the Høver-bakken or -Braaten side of the family).

As an afterthought Jim Pederson brought out a large portrait from a cupboard in a gilt frame, a colored photograph of a lady in the traditional Hadeland head-gear (*skru og lue*). How did that come to be there in the basement? The story is a long one, but if you read on, you will find the answer.

Emigration

The youngest brother of my great-grandfather Peder Jorstad had emigrated in 1878 and he claimed land around 1880 and settled on the fertile farmland near Freeman, in Turner County, South Dakota. My own grandfather Thorvald (1867-1949) had always talked about *Pær fa`bro* (his pet-name), meaning Uncle Peder, who was born in 1851. As the younger son he worked for a while at a sawmill and at a store in Gran, then decided to emigrate in 1878, when the parish register shows his name listed on April 17, 1878 when he notified the minister of his emigration.

He left by steamship from Christiania, arrived eventually in Gayville, South Dakota, where he worked in a shop for some time and met Ottine, his wife-to-be. They married when she was

316

only 16 and they moved into a sod house on the farm near Freeman, a small town in South Dakota, which today is an hour's drive from Sioux Falls.

The Jorstad farm in South Dakota

The Jorstad farm is on a low hillside with a wide panorama of the surrounding landscape and undulating farmland around One can imagine that the view reminded the settlers of beautiful Hadeland with rolling fields, the good soil, and a brook running alongside the farm, just like in Peder's home in Norway.

Today corn and soybeans constitute the main crop of Jorstad farmland, but in those days it would have been a dairy farm with pigs, poultry and horses, subsistence farming, with corn and grain growing. The plot was 650 *decars* or 160 acres. Part of the deal for the settlers when the claim was accepted, was to plant trees on the site: cottonwood, maple, chestnut, oak. In the painting on the previous page we can see the layout of the farm with a red barn, a grain storehouse, the main house with a porch, the servants' quarters, the hen-house, the summer kitchen and another store house for corn. The rectangular yard was divided into a work area and an area for recreation with a flower garden as well as a vegetable garden. The horses would have been the main power source, while today we saw the agro-industrial farming with one man farming 3,000 *decars* with a combined harvester (corn or soybeans being the cash crop). Farmers today reckon 750-1,000 acres (4,000 *decars*) to make a living.   Today at the Jorstad

317

farm the barn is still standing and the summer kitchen also remains. Around them are the trees that Peder planted.

The family

Ottine (born 1864) was the girl from Gayville who had emigrated as a toddler with her mother from Høverbakken, near Hurdal/Toten. Her name, Ottine, means number 8, so that there were 7 siblings who had come along on the sailing ship with her mother Marie to Gayville. Her father Ole arrived in the USA earlier and built them a house in Gayville, which incidentally is still standing and in good repair.

Peder and Ottine had a daughter in the first year they lived in the sod house, Margaret, born 1881, and named in honor of Peder's mother, Margrete Jorstad, born Skiaker.

Near the Jorstad farm is the Salem Lutheran Church built in 1877. In the cemetery there are several Jorstad graves. Peder and Ottine are buried and laid at rest alongside their infant daughter Morna. Lewis Jorstad and his wife Esther are also buried nearby and their gravestone is said to have come from Norway. Next to them are the graves of those of their daughters and sons who stayed close to the farm.

There are the graves of the three unmarried Jorstad children: Ole, Thorvald, bearing the name of his cousin (my grandfather Thorvald) and Mabel, the youngest daughter, who lived from 1905 until 2000. Also the Jensens (Tilda), the Georgesons (Margaret), the Gullicksons (Helen), the Weks (Pauline) graves are there. Annie Jorstad married John Pederson. Lewis Jorstad married Esther Brodland.

The daughters buried there, beside Morna, were Margaret, Tilda, Helen, Pauline and Mabel. Inga Jorstad married Jarle Foss and moved out of the parish. One of Inga's children, Wilbur Foss, went to teachers college and later ran a hardware store in Scotland, South Dakota. I had the pleasure of talking to him on the phone, while visiting my third cousin Nancy in Minneapolis the day before my trip to Sioux Falls. I met his parents in Norway when I was 8, in 1952, when they came to visit. And I had a very interesting talk with 89-year-old Wilbur Foss, Nancy's father and Peder's grandson, who told me about the family in general, and especially about uncle Thorvald (in the U.S.). Another sister Annie Pederson is buried alongside her husband John in a nearby cemetery as well as Laura and her husband Peder Wek.

The contact between the generations in Norway and the United States has therefore been continuous. Inga and Jarle Foss visited Norway in December 1952 when I was 8 years old. Nancy, Peder's great-granddaughter who has her family genealogy at heart visited my home in Norway in 2003. Duane Luther Jorstad, son of the youngest of Peder's sons, Lewis, visited me in 2009, 100 years after his great-grandfather's visit in 1909.

Peder was a very religious man, who never would work on a Sunday if he could avoid it. His descendants knew the table prayer by heart and they still used it, singing the same tune as we do in Norway but with different words: *I Jesu navn går vi til bords*. Thorvald Jorstad had taught his nephew Duane a little nursery rhyme that may be a Jorstad reminiscence: *Tommeltott, slikkepott, Langemand, Leiesvend og Lille Petter Spillemann (Leiesvend* equals "good for

318

nothing" – while in Norway we are more polite and say *Gullebrand* (meaning gold ring finger). Little Norwegian treasures to discover were transferred from father to son to grandson and then back to the Norwegian shirt-tail cousin.

Peder also gave land for a primary school building near the farm. The site is still visible, the building has disappeared, but it was in use until the 1950s.

Next door to Peder Jorstad, his son Thorvald (1891-1984) had his own farm, with a tiny house and a barn for dairy farming, grain and corn growing as well. His nephew Duane helped out with the farm work. The youngest son of Peder was Lewis born in 1908, the year before Peder travelled back to Norway to visit family in Gran bringing his wife and infant son with him. Lewis must be the American equivalent to Lars, maybe named after Peder's brother in Norway [Lars Jorstad, at Gjefsen farm].

Lewis took over the farm after his father in 1939, when Peder died. It is said that Peder had never gone to see the doctor until two weeks before he died.
Lewis married the minister's daughter Esther Brodland. They had 3 children, Donna, Maurine and Duane Luther.

In their later years the three unmarried siblings Ole, Thorvald and Mabel moved to Freeman. They visited many times the house their grandfather had built back in the 1860s in Gayville. Ole, the oldest boy, died in 1964, Thorvald 1984, and Mabel in 2000. Her family came to visit her and got the information about the family, and she took good care of the family and the family tradition. She had looked after her parents all their lives, and was a living source of family history.

In an 1884 letter to his brother in America, Lars Gjefsen (born Jorstad) tells that in Norway they are occupied with everyday chores, and he sends family news. Peder's wife has just had another baby. In Skiaker, Peder's brother Johannes has lost a baby named Thorvald. They are longing to see a portrait of little Margaret in the U.S., because there are some cousins in Norway of the same age at Kjørven (Janna) and Skiaker [Ragna]. Peder's mother in Norway has sent him a woolen cloth for Ottine, for dressmaking, and would like to know whether it has arrived. He tells about neighbors, friends of Peder back home, and inquires about those who have emigrated (Christian Helgaker is not far away from Peder, probably near Gayville). He was married to Ottine's sister. A neighbor in Gran has started a hydro-power workshop (smithy) in Tingelstad, This is mentioned along with the great events, births and deaths. The letter also reflects a deep belief in God and in his infinite wisdom. Just like Peder, his brother is a truly religious man, quoting Job: "the Lord giveth, the Lord taketh...praised be the Lord."

Great Grandmother in the basement – where does she belong in this account?

When Peder left Norway, his mother was 65 years old. When he returned to Norway to visit her, she was 96, an old lady in her white shawl and dark everyday dress, like we could see her in the snapshot on the veranda of the old people's house on the Jorstad farm.

The picture in the basement is a large-sized portrait, picturing a lady in her prime in her best dress (above). Its style is so typical of a Hadeland wife in the 1830-40 period. We have a few of those on my wall back home. Seeing it I got so excited I ran upstairs to get a digital camera and got the picture out of the frame, taking a good look at it. It came to me that it had to be Margrete Jorstad (1813-1912). Of course I did not know her or recognize her. No one in my father's generation had ever seen the picture or talked about it. But after some thought, the story must be as follows:

Peder probably brought back his mother's picture (a young wife in the 1830s) when he returned home in 1909 for the only time in his life and saw his mother for the last time. The picture is probably a photographic copy of a daguerreotype, a technique from before the real photographic age started around 1850. It has been enlarged and colored, maybe even touched up a little! Compared to other pictures of Margrete from her older age it shows a Hadeland woman in her best outfit, in a silken dress with the magnificent headwear: a black cap with little corners, a silken bow and a white fluffy lining. I am guessing it may date back to the time when her oldest son Iver (1833) was born, because the particular head-gear (*skru og lue*) was worn only by married women. She may be between 25-30 years of age. After more than 70 years in Norway her portrait made the long trip to Jorstad farm, Turner County, S.D. Over 100 years later she was rediscovered in the basement, identified and placed where she belonged as the matriarch of the family!

The Grandchildren of Peder Jorstad

Margrete Georgeson had 4 children
  Floyd Erwin born on 5-14-1907
  Ethel Mildred born on 8-24-1909
  Esther Florence born 6-8-1911
  Verna Evelyn born 3-26-1914
Ole Jorstad was unmarried
Tilda Marie Jensen had 3 children
  Juliet Victoria born 11-8-1910
  Rueben Jens Peder born 12-12-1916
  Delores Marcella born 3-12-1925
Annie Pederson had 5 children
  Olga Josephine born 1-29-1910

      Helen Harriet born 1-19-1915
      Oliver Peder born 9-8-1917
      Selmar Robert born 6-6-1920
      Peder Alvin born 7-6-1923
Thorvald Jorstad was unmarried
Pauline Wek had 6 children
      Lawrence Richard born 10-12-1916
      Evelyn Bernice born 10-17-1918
      Judith Ottine born 12-27-1921
      Eleanor Lillian born 2-26-1926
      Gladys Marjory born 11-17-1928
      Audrey Iona born 5-23-1931
Laura Wek had 2 children
      Andrew Peder born 6-28-1924
      Morris Leroy born 3-8-1927
Ingeborg Foss had 2 children
      Wilbur Peder born 6-15-1921
      Palmer Ordell born 1-27-1923
Helen Gullickson had 2 children
      Ardell Ruth born 6-6-1925
      Kenneth Vernon born 6-27-1930
Mabel Jorstad was unmarried
Lewis Jorstad had 3 children
      Donna Regene born 10-11-1940
      Duane Luther born 9-25-1945
      Maurine Ruth born 5-4-1946

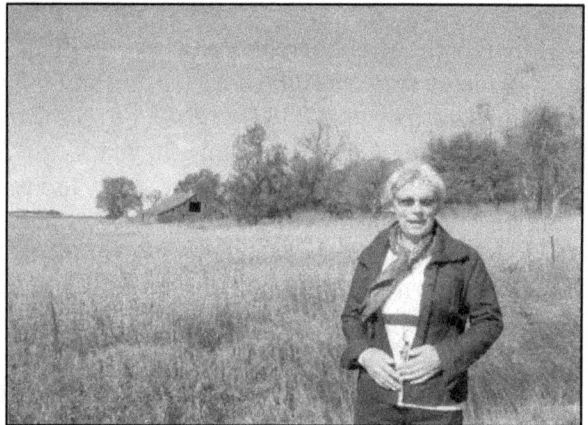

The author, with the barn at the Jorstad farm in South Dakota in the background

Halvor Velta

"A Hadeland Viking" published August 2011　　　*Form 686*　　　*Peder H Nelson*

This story was originally published in Norwegian in the 'Brua' in 1937 (#25). Verlyn Anderson translated the text for the 2011 reprint.

There are some people who because of their adventurous spirit and courage are noticed more than us ordinary people. As time goes on, they become legendary characters about whom generations tell about their adventurous experiences. It is about such a man, who is also a Hadelander, that I will write, because his life story is of historic interest.

As editor for Hadelanders in America, I am always on the look-out for anything that would be of historic interest for our Hadeland people here in the West. A year ago I wrote about Andrew C. Bakke (Anders Framstadbakken in Hadeland), a hefty Hadelander here in Northwood. One day some of his sons began to tell some stories about a Halvor Velta. Because I thought his name sounded like he may have come from Hadeland, I asked Andrew whether this Halvor was a Hadelander. Yes, he was, and Andrew had much to tell about this "frontiersman" who often traveled across the wide expanses of these prairies long before any white people had settled here on the Dakota prairie. Later Bakke and his sons took me to Aneta, N.D., to meet a man, Johnnie Evanson, who was very interested in pioneer history and who personally had spoken with Halvor Velta about those old days. He was also familiar with many of Velta's descendants. Mr. Evanson was also interested in gathering as much information as possible of Velta's adventurous life story. He promised to go to Pembina at his own expense, where Velta had lived for many years, to find out more about his history and talk to some of his living children. As readers will see from the above description, many "wheels" were set in motion to gather this pioneer history. It is these men we can thank that we are able to bring Halvor Velta's adventurous, but truthful, biography into print.

* * * * *

Halvor Velta was born on Velta, a little place in the woods near Vågavannet, far up into the east ridge of *Øståsen Allmening* (Gran Public Land). His father's name was Peder and Halvor was born in the year 1838 (*according to Ole Gamme's research in the church baptismal records, he was born in 1836*), more than 100 years ago. Already in his youth Halvor was a strong fellow who distinguished himself in many ways and many stories are told about his experiences. One time he was skiing swiftly down the steep hills toward Gran. On his back he had a sack of about 3 to 4 bushels of barley which he was taking to *Hvalskvern* (Hvals mill) to grind. When he was half-way down the hill, he came upon a woman from the Sorum farm who was walking to Ensrud, carrying a milk pail in her hand. Halvor thought he would help the woman go a little faster down the hill, so in his full speed he picked up the woman under her arms and held her thus in front of him. When they came down to the valley, he set the frightened woman down and skied on. It is said that she didn't even spill any of the milk.

Halvor grew up in the woods and the woods became his life. He was a woodsman and was constantly hunting and fishing. His great strength did him well, he had to carry all the food products and everything else needed on his back from the business center and east to his home located far up on the ridge. There was no road up to that area at that time.

In 1850 a large English-Canadian firm, the Hudson Bay Company, came to Norway and began to recruit Norwegians as trappers for the enormously large trapping area in, at that time, the wilds of Canada. The Englishmen understood that the Norwegians had good experience for this hard and severe life. They were not wrong in thinking that. When Halvor Velta found out about this offer, he immediately went to Kristiania (now Oslo) and signed up. This was something exciting for an adventure-seeking and fearless young man who, of course, he was at that time. The next we hear about Halvor is that he is an "overseer" for a large ox-cart caravan which transported pelts from Fort Garry (north of Winnipeg) and to Fort Snelling, Minn. Velta was often the only white man on these journeys and usually had up to 30 half-wild Indians to keep under control during these trips. But, as mentioned previously, there was no lack of courage in this man. The Indians had deep respect for his great strength. The caravan drivers had to be hardy and large men in order to do this work and endure all the hardships. A weak man would soon buckle under in this fight for existence. The law of

This stamp, honoring Minnesota's Territorial Centennial, shows a typical ox cart and driver

the wilderness at that time was: "An eye for an eye and a tooth for a tooth" and the revolver was the law. For many of those who live today, it would seem that Halvor Velta was a heartless type, but at that time and with the conditions in which he lived, he had to be as he was or he could never have been the overseer for the caravans of the Hudson Bay Company. He was the same type as Buffalo Bill, Kit Carson, Daniel Boone and other well-known "frontiersmen."

Halvor Velta, the man from the wooded area up on *Grans Østås* (Gran's east ridge), often traveled over the huge deserted Dakota prairie, long before any Europeans had settled in what was then the large open country in the Dakota territory. He was a well-known character among trappers and Indians.

These ox-cart caravans carrying pelts were called "The Red River Caravans." They consisted for the most of from 25 to 60 sturdy carts with wooden axles and tall wooden wheels which squeaked and squealed because of no greasing. Each cart was drawn by an ox, and the drivers were for the most part a collection of rough adventurers and often Metis (men with Indian mothers and French-Canadian fathers). The caravans made regular trips from Canada to Fort Snelling (near St. Paul) in Minnesota many times a year, a stretch of about 80 Norwegian miles (approximately 500 American miles). Going south they had heavy loads of pelts and hides, but the freight on the way north again consisted of clothing, trinkets for the Indians, staples, trade goods and manufactured goods not available at Fort Garry, and bad whiskey for everyone. The men especially earned good money hauling food products back to the Canadian wilderness, the price for a sack of flour was $32, and a barrel of pork could be purchased for $65. Coffee cost $2.50 a pound.

It was on such caravans that Halvor Velta was overseer at that time. One time he came with 30 loads of pelts from Fort Garry and was in charge of 29 Meti (half French and half Indian) drivers. On the way they arrived at a new pioneer settlement down in Minnesota, and Velta needed hay for the oxen. He saw that one of the settlers had many haystacks outside of his horse barn so he sent one of the drivers over to the settler's house to ask if he could buy hay. He came back empty-handed. He had not gotten any hay. Velta, who looked almost like an Indian, suntanned as he was from the weather and wind, went over to see the settler. When the farmer began to speak in broken English with a few Norwegian words thrown in, Velta spoke to him in Norwegian. The man was astonished to hear a "leader of Indians" standing in front of him and speaking Norwegian. The misunderstanding was cleared up, and the meeting between the two Norwegians became so cordial that Halvor got all the hay he needed.

One time Halvor Velta was hunting far north in an unsettled area when suddenly he saw a large moose swimming across a lake. Right away Halvor put his canoe in the water and rowed after the moose. He caught up with the moose, killed it with his long Bowie-knife and took the moose to shore.

Another time Halvor and some others were on a trip also far north in the wilderness. The Hudson Bay Company was very harsh with its workers and this time they had a tough English Major as commander. They encountered many difficulties and received very little food or drink so they almost perished. The men began to complain. Halvor became their spokesman. They wanted to break their contract and go back to civilization. The Major became very angry about this and refused to let them go or give them anything to eat. Velta brought out one of his large revolvers which he carried, one on each hip, and shot through the Major's hat so close to the top of his head that it scorched his hair. Then he asked if they could leave, "or else I will shoot a little lower next time." Yes, they got permission to leave. Later Halvor was imprisoned and sent to London, England to be tried for what he had done to the Major. But he was acquitted when it became known that the Major had been inhumane against his men. When he came back to Canada, Halvor Velta was a body guard and guide for an English Lord who traveled around the northern wilderness as a tourist.

The Hudson Bay Company did not like it that Halvor had shot through the Major's hat and discharged him for that and other reasons. He then went to Fort Pembina in Cavalier County, N.D., where he was well-known from his visits to the fort. Here he took land for himself and changed his name to Albert Pederson. He married a Meti woman. They had many children.

Some of them later held important positions in Cavalier County. One of their sons was an engineer for the Northern Pacific Railroad. Halvor Velta, or Albert Pederson, as he called himself, became the owner of the first threshing rig in Cavalier County. This was fired with wood.

The thirst for adventure was still in his blood and he also had many unusual experiences here. Fort Pembina was later closed, but today it is maintained by the Masonic Lodge as a memorial to the old days. In 1863 there was a large garrison of soldiers there to protect against the Indians when they were unruly. That is the last time the fort was used for that purpose. Most of the soldiers were Free Masons and the Masons later took care of the old fort which in the old days was established by the Hudson Bay Company. (*Brua* Editor's note: The first Masonic Lodge in North Dakota was organized in Pembina in 1863 by soldiers stationed there.) The officials of the Hudson Bay Company thought that their location was in Canada, but after the official boundary line between Canada and the U.S. was determined, they discovered that the fort was in the United States, and the Hudson Bay Company withdrew back over the boundary line into Canada. Because of the old fort, that area was settled earlier than the more fertile parts of North Dakota.

But back to Halvor Velta, as we will continue to call him. A band of horse thieves ran out of grass because of flooding in the Red River Valley and northward. Three U.S. marshals with a posse were hunting these horse thieves. Hadelander Iver Larsen from Mayville was one of the marshals. When they had come north to Cavalier County they came to Halvor Velta's home and asked him if he had seen any of the horse thieves. "No, and you are a surprise," said Halvor, "but come in and stay here tonight." The marshals saw the two large revolvers that hung on each of Halvor's hips but accepted the offer for a night's lodging and went in. When they got in, they saw that the room was full of suspicious-looking men, but it was too late to back out again. Both parties were fully armed, and from the descriptions of the horse thieves, the lawmen understood that they had the thieves in front of them, but Halvor Velta was in control and naturally enjoyed this dangerous situation. He thought it was exciting. But because the marshal's party was in the minority, they understood that they couldn't do anything about the situation at that time. Both groups conversed and enjoyed each other's company. They sat and watched each other's actions throughout the long night. In the morning the marshals thanked for the hospitality and headed south and the horse thieves also thanked for their hospitality and continued north. Nothing more was said about the horse thieves, and it was probably for the best, because the thieves were in the majority that night, and strength was the law in those days.

* * * *

One cold winter day in the year 1871 or 1872 Hadelander Hans Molden, who lived at Mayville, N.D., was going to walk the 130 kilometers (about 95 miles) to Fargo. The weather was bad at that time and he first walked to Caledonia in order to get to a kind of main road from there to Fargo. After a while he was overtaken by a pony team and the large fur-clad driver asked Molden if he would like to ride with him. When the strange driver understood that Hans was Norwegian, he asked where he was from in Norway. "From Hadeland," said Molden.

"That is where I am from also," said Halvor Velta, because, of course, he was. In that manner these two who had come from the same place got in contact with each other, and Hans Molden's daughter, who told me this story, could also tell about the adventures which waited for these two in Fargo.

Fargo was at that time a "frontier town" where all kinds of questionable individuals were quartered. Not least was the fact that Fargo was the headquarters of railroad building which was going ahead "full steam" at that time. There were gambling houses, saloons and many brothels, which usually sprang up in newly-built railroad towns. Halvor Velta and Hans Molden stayed together in Fargo, but Hans was not really comfortable with his wild companion, even if he were from Hadeland.

One night four saloonkeepers grabbed Halvor Velta because they wanted to get him to gamble away his money, but they did not know what kind of a man they had gotten ahold of! Not until they had sat down at the gaming table did Velta lay both of his revolvers on the table and announced that here they would play for "drinks" and not for money. The four players had to sit at that table the entire night and play with him for drinks until 6:00 in the morning. Then Halvor shot out the light with one of his revolvers, and said, "Now you little boys have my permission to go to bed." The gamblers had gotten their fill for that night!

As said before, Velta was endowed with great strength. In one of the saloons in Fargo there was a man who recognized Velta and shouted that he should come over to him. "No, you come here," said Velta. The other became angry and shouted: "Oh, you don't need to think you are such a great man, Velta, you are just married to an Indian woman." That was enough to ignite Halvor's anger. He grabbed the other man by the nape of the neck and the seat of his pants and threw him through the closed door right out into the street. At most times Halvor was a good-natured man who didn't interfere with other people, except sometimes his pranks were quite crude. But when he knew that he was in the right, he could be very severe with those who did him wrong.

Andrew Bakke, here at Northwood, remembers Halvor Velta well from the time he visited the Hadeland community here at Northwood in the early 1890s. Andrew told that he was a strong man, six and a half feet tall, not so very broad, but his body seemed as if it were built only of muscles. His neck was as wide as his head. Among other friends Velta visited Andrew's home a few days during his visit here. He told then that in the 1860s it was so dry in the Dakota Territory that he walked dry-shod over the Red River north of Grand Forks.

It did not go so well for Halvor Velta at the end. As mentioned above he was married to an Indian woman. Even though Halvor knew the Indians better than almost any white man, there were differences in their life styles and ways of thinking. Together they had many children, but his wife became more interested in the traditions and life style of her family and wanted to leave Halvor and go to live with them. Halvor was very much against this. He went so far as to threaten to kill her if she left him and the family, and sadly enough they were not only threats. He shot and killed her when she tried to leave their home. That was the end of freedom for

Halvor Velta. He received a sentence of life in prison for this murder and he ended his life in the state penitentiary in Bismarck, N.D.

Halvor died in 1912 (*according to Ole Gamme's research, he died Jan. 8, 1916*). His death marked the end of one of our most adventurous "frontiersmen." He was one of those sturdy tough fellows who went ahead and opened the country for settlers. With Halvor Velta's death, we lost one of the last daring figures from the American "frontier."

Halvor's brother, Ole Pederson, also came to America and settled as a farmer in the vicinity of Bang in Cavalier County, N.D. Ole also was a strong fellow and it is told about him that one day he came driving home with a large load of hay. Something broke on the wagon. Ole held up the hayrack on his back while his hired man repaired the damage. Ole was a man with many talents. Besides being a farmer, he was a capable blacksmith. He built his own sawmill and also made the sawmill equipment himself.

They also had a sister, Kristine, who later settled in the state of Missouri. Now they are all dead, but we write their stories here in the *Brua*, so their memories will not be forgotten.

Ingebret Svingen

WPA Interview published August 2012   *Form 1263*

The Federal Writers' Project (F.W.P.) was a United States federal government project to fund written work and support writers during the Great Depression of the 1930s. It was part of the Works Progress Administration (W.P.A.), a program of the New Deal. Established on July 27, 1935 by President Franklin D. Roosevelt, the Federal Writers' Project funded and encouraged the compiling of local histories and oral histories based on personal interviews with local citizens, plus many other types of research and writing. In each state a Writer's Project staff of editors was formed, along with a much larger group of field workers drawn from local unemployment rolls. Many of these had never graduated from high school, but most had formerly held white collar jobs of some sort.

The work of one department of the Federal Writers' Project that is of particular interest to genealogists and local historians is the interviews that were made with the surviving immigrants or with children of immigrants who were born shortly after their parents had arrived in America. These interviews were typed up and copies were deposited in the local county courthouses or museums. Copies were also sent to the National Archives in Washington, D.C. I have investigated the files of those interviews in the Otter Tail County Museum in Fergus Falls, MN. There I found an interview that was made with my grandmother, Randa Anderson in 1939. It contained a lot of very interesting primary information.

John Bye, former Archivist at the Institute for Regional Studies in Fargo, North Dakota, sent me copies of the F.W.P. interviews that were made with Norwegian immigrants who had emigrated from Hadeland and settled in Benson County, North Dakota. One of the immigrants interviewed in June, 1939 was Ingebret Svingen, Esmond, North Dakota, who emigrated from Hadeland in 1893. His interview is reprinted below.
–Verlyn D. Anderson, Editor of the 'Brua'

I was born on the Stadum farm in Elvestuen, Vestre Gran, Hadeland, Norway, January 9, 1873. Our small old house was located on a *husmannsplass* (cotter's place). It consisted of only one acre of land and a small living house. The building was a one-story structure with three rooms. The largest room had two windows, one on each side of the outside door, facing west toward the Randsfjord, a large lake. We could not see the lake from the house because of the heavy growth of timber but by going about a mile east we could from a small mountaintop located there see far out over the lake and observe the immense traffic constantly going on out there. It was always a very interesting sight that was very much enjoyed by both young and old. Girls and boys could always find that a suitable rendezvous. The nearest village was Jevnaker. It was a small town but had a large glass factory and a railroad station, post office and a general store.

The educational facilities for the common people of our class consisted of a public and parochial school combination lasting from the time we were 6 to 14 or 15 years old. We were then confirmed if we passed our catechism. It was considered a great shame not to pass.

The children of the poorer people had to begin working out while they were quite young. Their jobs were generally to herd cattle or livestock during the summer months and help in the cow barn in the winter when they were not at school. The school term lasted from three to six months per year, but the children had to take lessons at home. Their parents assigned them daily lessons which they had to learn. One of the parents heard their lessons each evening and assigned them a new lesson or if they had failed to learn the lesson prescribed then they had to study that over again and also an additional lesson. Failure to get the lessons often meant a good spanking with a bunch of long young twigs.

Labor conditions were satisfactory but the wages were very low — in fact, so low that a common laborer could seldom earn any more than what it would take to support himself and a very small family. If the family became large then it became necessary to pinch and squeeze and even go without enough clothing and not enough to eat even of the cheapest foods.

I could not say anything about farm equipment because I was so young when I left Norway that I had very little experience; however, I know that there were no harvesters or binders in our neighborhood. The grain was seeded by hand and cut by a scythe, raked up and bound by hand and placed on sharp sticks to dry out after which they brought the straw with the grain in it into the loft where it was later thrashed with a flail.

Each farm had livestock that they sent up into the mountains during the summer. These were taken care of by herders and one or two *budeier*, girls 15 to 20 years old who milked the cows and made the butter and cheese. The *budeier* would stay up in the mountains with the cattle all summer. Edvard Grieg wrote *Seterjenten's Søndag* to describe their longing for human companionship. It is a song with a very beautiful but at the same time doleful and melancholy melody.

The church attendance was very regular. Everybody went to the regular church services. Most Norwegians are serious about religion and the word of God. Going to church, however, was also a means of meeting friends and a method of maintaining a common respectability. People who did not go to church were looked down on by the community.

Confirmation Day was a day of importance, not only to those being confirmed but by members of the community. The confirmands were arranged in rows up at the altar so as to face the congregation. The preacher would walk back and forth in front of the usually long line and at the same time present difficult questions for the confirmands to answer. Much depended on how quickly and correctly the answers were made. The confirmand that answered correctly and quickly was considered by the listening congregation to be smart, and was looked up to by everybody during the future years.

In our community such recreation as dancing and many other things were considered sins and were forbidden to the children or young people by the parents. Therefore very little recreation as such was indulged in by our comrades.

A typical wedding in our community would differ somewhat from the jovial affairs of this kind in other communities because our people believed that dancing, card playing and drinking were instruments of the devil and were therefore never included in our weddings. After having complied with the law and the proper announcements had been made in the church at three previous church services, the couple would appear at the church accompanied by their friends and the church wedding would take place. This was a very serious ceremony. Many prayers and songs preceded the actual wedding and there was always a lengthy talk by the preacher. The preacher had apparently thousands of admonitions mostly pertaining to the duty of parents to see to it that their children were brought up in the Christian religion and see that the children stayed away from such sinful things as dancing and card playing. After the church ceremony was over, many of the friends of the wedded couple would accompany them home where much singing and praying was done and food was served to them both at a table and carried to them as they sat about the room. Of course the more wealthy people had great banquets.

Emigration to America

The main reason why I decided to emigrate to America was the greater opportunities that I expected to find there, and which I did find. From the standpoint of our own knowledge, conditions in Norway were good, but we heard of the free homestead land and also of the freedom of the country, and the ease with which even a poor man might work himself up and become a farm owner. This was next to impossible for a poor man to do in Norway.

No special preparation for the trip was either made or necessary, and no farewell parties were held for us. Part of the cost of my transportation was furnished by my brother Iver who had emigrated to America three years previously and was now firmly established on a farm near Pelican Rapids, Minn. My brother Gudmond emigrated with me.

I started from home in Norway on my trip to America on April 27, 1893. From home we went to Christiania (Oslo) where we boarded the boat for Hull, England, where we took a train to Liverpool and boarded the second and larger ship for New York, America, where we boarded a train and after many changes we reached Pelican Rapids, Minn., where my brother Iver met us with his team of horses and a lumber wagon and took us to his farm about eight miles out in the country. I worked on farms in that neighborhood until the spring of 1898 when I left for Benson County, N.D.

On our trip over the Atlantic we had considerable bad weather and, as we traveled third class, the accommodations were almost unbearable with all those sick people and the filth and dirt and stink, but as the weather cleared and the storms ceased, the quarters were quickly cleaned up and we soon forgot the awful days during the storm.

Arrival in America

My first impression of America was very good. I could see from the enormous great buildings in New York City that this was not a wild Indian country. However, as we traveled through the land this greatness was continually becoming smaller. The country around Pelican Rapids was a very beautiful district and I liked it very much.

As stated before I came to Pelican Rapids because my brother lived there and many others from Hadeland had settled there many years previous and owned farms there. My first work was on some of those farms at $1.50 per day which seemed big money to me then. In Norway the common people very seldom had $1.50 in their possession at any one time. Many people never had that much money. Wages were usually not paid in cash, but in wearing apparel, food and other necessities. Only a very few cents were handled by the poor people throughout a lifetime.

Homesteading in North Dakota

I filed on my homestead in Benson County in June 1898 and moved on to the land the same year. My first home was a shack, 10x14 feet, with a slant-sided roof. This shack was added on the following spring by a lean-to, 8x10 feet, which became the kitchen. The other part served as a dining room, living room and bedroom during the following 10 years. Then I built the house we are now living in.

The reason for moving here from Pelican Rapids, Minn., was that I could get a free homestead here while all the homestead land was long ago taken up back there. We have had good neighbors here. They are all Norwegians and many of them are related to me. We also have the same church affiliation and because of that, very little recreation has been carried on here by heinous dancing parties and the like. In fact, about the only recreation that we have had here is the frequent prayer meetings and some feasts which by the way are still being carried on here.

I started farming here by hiring a man to break up (plow) 10 acres which was put into flax the same year. It produced about 20 bushels per acre which was sold at a price of about one dollar per bushel. My brother Iver who had been farming near Pelican Rapids, Minn., also came and homesteaded near us. He had two teams of horses and a full outfit of farming implements. We all helped each other the first few years but kept buying extra horses and farm implements until we (my brothers Gudmond and Iver) had a complete set for each of us. There have been but few changes in farming methods except for the farm tractor, windrow stacker and combine.

As the years came and went I purchased additional land so I have a little over 400 acres on my farm. I have no complaint to make about farming, although I have not made the large amount of money that it, at times, appeared might be possible to make; still I have my farm, cattle and full outfit here almost clear of indebtedness. My poorest year was 1919 which was a complete failure and my best year was 1912, both with the crop and the price for products.

I have had no particular difficulties in farming. My best source of income has been cattle, together with raising grain. The cattle and their products have kept up with the expenses. In between them I have made a little money almost every year. I did not have to sell cattle to the government during the Depression. My standard of living has been about the same all the time. I have never demanded very much. I have a nice car but I do not go anywhere except to the nearby towns so the expense and wear is small. I had a Model T Ford from 1918 to 1934 and the speedometer showed only 30,000 miles when I traded it in on the car I now have. This car has run only 11,000 miles during the five years I have had it. But 11,000 miles is a long distance if one should walk that far.

Marriage and Family Life

On July 26, 1919, I married Mathilda "Tina" Tollefson. She was born on Jan. 1, 1886 near Wendell, Minn., of Norwegian parents. Our children are as follows: Axel, born July 6, 1920; Helen, born Oct. 14, 1921; Ingvald, born Sept. 23, 1923; Loren Oliver, born June 12, 1925; Teddy, born Nov. 8, 1926; and Edward, born Feb. 11, 1929. All were born on our homestead.

All of our children are getting high school education in our consolidated school district. The school district was organized before any of my children were of school age. The Depression has not affected my family's school opportunities since they have no desire to continue higher than high school, but it has affected their chances of getting a foothold for themselves; most of them are staying on the home farm and we are working together. The children all speak English while at home, but my wife and I generally use the Norwegian language about the house. I have always been a subscriber to our county paper and one or more Norwegian newspapers, and one or more church papers like the *Lutheraneren* published in Minneapolis.

The only form of recreation that we participate in is the church socials and parties, school programs, and visiting back and forth with neighbors and friends.

I am not in favor of entering any war unless it is to maintain law and order or to save some smaller nation from being overrun by some powerful brutal nation. I still believe that it was necessary for us to go into the World War in 1917 to stop the enemy of democracy which is today again showing its ugly head in such formidable ways as to cause us to rearm and spend millions. However, I am also of the opinion that we left Europe too early after the fighting was over. We should have stayed there then and put the European house in order and maintained our membership in the League of Nations. If we had, then thousands of innocent people who are now being slaughtered on the battlefields would have been saved because the League would then have had power. The poor Ethiopian people would then have been saved and the Spanish Insurrection impossible. All of this might be blamed to our politicians who did not have the future safety of nations in mind.

I lost no money in post-war bank failures but, of course, I lost because of others losing their money, but this loss was not great. In looking back over my past life I cannot see where I could or should have done differently than I have done. There were many instances where I could have bettered my conditions if I had known beforehand what was going to happen, but I do not suppose that I would be any wiser now if I was to be confronted with the same problems. Therefore I believe that I would do just as I have been doing.

Norway and the United States

I do not understand how the Old Country could be compared with this country because it is so different in every way. In the Old Country people live to uphold traditions and customs that have been left for them to copy and enjoy from time immemorial. They have different situations to meet and to solve. America can be self-sustaining. Norway has to depend on many different countries for supplies of various necessities such as cotton, wheat, sugar, etc.

I believe that Norway is superior to America in the scenic beauty of its mountains and valleys and the health-giving properties of its mountain air, also in the abundant number of waterfalls suitable for power plants, and of course its fisheries are superior. Since the Norwegians were among the first to initiate a government by the people and for the people and of the people, there can be no great difference in the governments, although Norway has a king instead of a president here.

America is, of course, superior to all other countries in the world, and that is not only true in its abundance of wealth and its potential wealth but in its laws and regulations under which its various classes of people live, as well as the customs and modes prevailing, which permit the lowest among men to attain the highest attributes possible. No one here need step aside and bow his head when a person of wealthier birth wants to pass. In Norway good breeding dictates and custom requires that this be done. Here no social ban prevents the hired man from making love to the farmer's daughter. In Norway a boy or girl had to confine his or her courtship to the class to which he or she belonged. When we have a party or social gathering here, we do not segregate the guests in accordance with their social standing (that is, governed by their wealth and inheritance; for example profession, education, office).

Follow-up printed in the November 2012 issue of the *Brua:*
Norma Schmitt off Fergus Falls grew up on a farm neighboring the Svigens. She wrote to say that Ingebret's son Edward was living in Rugby, North Dakota. We sent him a copy of the Brua and he passed it along to his niece, Bonnie Kuehnemund. She sent us the following:

Thank you so much for sending a copy of the *Brua* to Edward Swingen in Rugby, North Dakota. He is my uncle and he gave it to me to share with other relatives. I emailed a copy to other descendants of Ingebret. Ingebret was my Grandpa. I never knew him as he died in the 1950s just before I was born or shortly after. This interview gave me a better understanding of him and his life. Grandma Tina passed away in 1972 during my senior year in high school, so I did get to know her, for which I am thankful. She lived out her life in the homestead house with her sons Edward and Ingvald. At the very end of her life she came and lived with her daughter Helen (my Mom).

Of the five children, only Edward and Lorin are still living. Edward, as you know, lives in Rugby, North Dakota. He never married, farmed on the home farm in Benson County along with brother Ingvald (who never married) until they retired. After retiring they had a farm auction and later sold the farm land and home place. Lorin lives in Ralston, Nebraska. He is married and they have two children, Lynne and Larry. The other two brothers, Axel and Teddy, never married. Axel lived much of his life in Minot, North Dakota, after graduating from Drake University. I don't know much about Teddy, as he died in the 30s. As mentioned, I am a daughter of Helen. She was married to Richard Hagen from Pierce County, North Dakota, and they lived on a farm by Pleasant Lake where I grew up along with my two brothers and one sister. That's a little bit of descendant information on Ingebret's family. Now I understand better also why Mother didn't like cards in the house or why she was hesitant about dances. We finally convinced her that neither one is necessarily bad or sacrilegious – it's all in how it's done and they can be lots of good "clean" fun and exercise.

Thank you again so much for sending the newsletter to Edward. He's a pretty quiet, gentle man who doesn't say much, but I could tell he really appreciated getting it and reading the interview. I didn't even realize the Hadeland Lag of America existed.

Bonnie (Hagen) Huehnemund, Rugby, North Dakota

The Johnson Brothers

"About an Old Hadeland Family" published August 2011   Form 943   Peder H. Nelson

This story was originally published in Norwegian in the 'Brua' in 1937 (#25). Verlyn Anderson translated the text for the 2011 reprint.

In one of Chicago's large business buildings on one of the city's most crowded streets a person finds a large law firm which is called Johnson Brothers, and the Johnson brothers they can be rightfully called, because the firm consists of not less than four brothers, all educated as lawyers, and therefore this firm is exceptional in this city of several million inhabitants.

The reason that I am writing a little about this firm here in the *Brua* is that the four lawyers are descended from an old Hadeland family. The father of the brothers, however, was born in America in 1862, namely in Argyle, Wis., where many *Hadelendingers* can be found. His name was John C. Johnson, but his father came from Hadeland, and his name was Smedsrud. This grandfather of our four lawyer brothers also participated in the American Civil War, and took part in the war on the side of the North to free Negroes from slavery.

The Johnson lawyers' grandmother was born and grew up on the Raassum farm in Brandbu, Hadeland, where she lived until she emigrated to America. Her father came to Hadeland from Aurdal in Valdres, from the farm called Blankebraaten. All of this and more can one of the lawyer brothers, Voyle Clark Johnson, tell about his ancestors, and he has mastered the Norwegian language just as good as anyone here in the Northwest, even though both he and his father were born in Wisconsin. The names of the other brothers are Elliot, Charles Peder and Glenn Johnson.

The four brothers have an interest in anything that is Norwegian. Voyle Johnson was a pilot in the American Air Force during World War I. There he contacted an illness during the influenza epidemic, which reoccurred many years later, and then he had to be hospitalized for two years to be cured, and this hospital stay he called "his vacation." Because of his good knowledge of the Norwegian language he could pass the time with the great wealth which is found in Norwegian literature and a large part of his two-year hospital stay was spent in reading the works of Ibsen, Bjørnson, Hamsun and Jonas Lie. These authors continue to be his favorites in the order in which they are mentioned. Voyle Johnson received a solid Norwegian-American foundation in his formal education. At first he was a student at Augustana College in Sioux Falls, S.D., and later at St. Olaf College in Northfield, Minn., from which he graduated before his 18th birthday and is the youngest student up to now who has graduated from St. Olaf College. Later he studied at the University of Minnesota, Northwestern University and at Chicago University's Law School.

During recent years Voyle Johnson has won great respect as a lawyer in Chicago. For four years he was appointed assistant state's attorney. When the Chicago Bar Association was first organized, he was elected on a non-partisan basis to be on the five-man Board of Directors for this well-known law firm.

Many of our members are familiar with the famous - or rather infamous - Insull case which was written so much about in the newspapers a few years ago, when Samuel Insull swindled for himself millions of dollars, after which he fled to Europe but later, after an adventurous hunt, he was apprehended and brought back to America to stand trial for his sins. Most of the readers probably don't know that it was Voyle Johnson who succeeded in getting State's Attorney Swanson to open the legal proceedings against Insull. Insull was acquitted in that matter, even though he had much proof against him, and Voyle Johnson said, "I have never heard that the laws in this land were written for millionaires. No, they are primarily constructed for the common people."

Now these four Johnson brothers have formed their own law firm and that four brothers have entered into the same profession and opened their own firm, must be a record in a city like Chicago with more than a million people. What is certainly of great interest for us Hadelendingers is that these men are of Hadeland ancestry, both of their father's and mother's side. And it can be said with certainly about these Hadelanders that they have contributed greatly to American cultural life.

Johnson Brothers Family From Hadeland
Ole Gamme has sent the following information about the parents of the Johnson Brothers.

The Johnson brothers' great-grandfather, Jens Nilsen, born in 1798 on the Smedsrud farm in Vestre Gran, emigrated as a widower in 1854 to Lafayette County, Wisconsin. Jens was first married in 1822 to Kirsti Olsdatter, born 1799 on the Haugtvedt farm in Gran. She died in 1829 at Smedsrud. Their son, Nils, born in 1823, also emigrated in 1854 with his wife, Ingeborg Torstensdatter, born in 1824 on the Myhre farm in Land and their daughter Kirsti, born in 1850 at Smedsrud. Four years earlier Jens and Kirsti's second son, Ole born in 1827, had emigrated. Jens Nilsen then married Kari Bertelsdatter in 1829. She was born in 1804 on the Holm farm in Gran. She died in 1847. Jens and Kari had four children, all of whom went to America: Bertel, born 1830 and emigrated in 1850; Kirsti, born 1838; and Ghorer, born 1844, who emigrated with his father in 1854.

The last of Jens Nilsen's six children, Christian, born 1833, emigrated in 1861 with his fiancee, Kari Torstensdatter, born 1834 on Raassum in Brandbu. She was the daughter of Torsten Bredesen Gjefsen (Egge) and Kari Madsdatter Blegen, married 1831 in Gran. Christian and Kari were married in Argyle, Minn. the same year, and they got a farm near Argyle. Christian was also a carpenter. From 1864 to 1865 he participated in the Civil War. They had a total of 10 children and many descendants who live all over the U.S. Their oldest son, John, born October 17, 1862, married Siri "Sarah" Johnsdatter, born September 13, 1868 in Nord Aurdal in Valdres.

She was the daughter of John Knudsen and Guri Svendsdatter. They became farmers in Monona County in Iowa. John was a member of Monona County's "Board of Supervisors," president of the Board of Directors of Soldier Valley Savings Bank and for many years was a member of the town board. He died in the fall of 1940.

John and Siri were parents of the Johnson brothers, Voyle Clark, 1892-1978; Glenn, 1896-1966; Charles Peder, 1903-1957 and Elliott Amos, 1907-1993. Their daughter, Helen, born in 1898, died in 1920 of diabetes.

Helene Maria Bredesdatter

"The last baptism at Old Tingelstad Church before it fell into disuse in 1866"
published August 2012   Form 64   *Torun Sørli*

Tingelstad Old Church, also known as St. Petri Church, is a stone church built around 1220 and known for its intact interior mostly from the 16th and 17th century. Tingelstad Old Church was in regular use for the last time on November 11, 1866. Pastor Søren Bugge held the sermon and had a brief speech as a farewell to the more than 600-year-old church which fell into disuse. On this day Brede Nilsen (Nov. 26, 1826-Oct. 9, 1904) and Marte Hansdatter (Dec. 19, 1821-April 1, 1906) went to church to baptize their daughter. They were married April 13, 1852. Helene Maria was born July 13, 1866 at Marka, a tenant farm on the larger Undeli farm in Gran parish. We do not know why Helene Maria's parents waited four months to baptize their daughter, but Marka was situated in the forest more than 10 kilometers from church, in steep terrain, and so far as I know, with no roads. One can also imagine that it was a strenuous walk, carrying a four-month-child in the terrain at the beginning of winter.

A year prior to Helene Maria's baptism, in the 1865 census, the family lived on the same tenant farm with three children. In 1875 they had left the forest and settled further down the hillside. They now lived at Linvollen, a tenant farm of Horgen in Gran parish. At this point they lived there with three of their children. Birte, their oldest child, had already left the family.

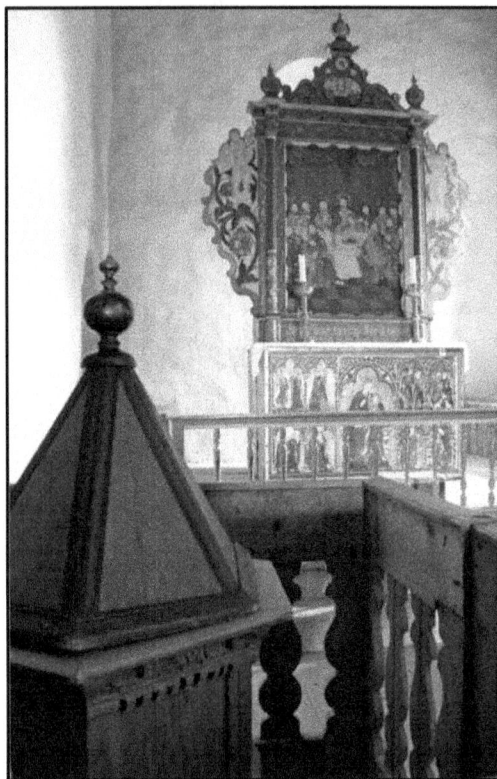

Interior of Tingelstad Old Church, showing baptismal font used for Helene Maria's baptism

On June 10, 1886 Helene Maria's father, Brede Nilsen, left Norway on the *Thingvalla*. He landed in New York on June 25th. Brede was heading for Clear Lake, Wisconsin where his uncle Ole Nielsen Framstad and his family lived. I have located Brede in the 1895 census in Black Brook Township, Polk County, near Clear Lake, Wis. By the 1900 and 1905 census he was living with his daughter Helene Maria and her family in Black Brook Township. Brede died in Clear Lake Oct 9, 1905. I do not know if Brede's wife Marte Hansdatter ever immigrated, but according to *Hadeland Lag's 1921 Yearbook* she died

April 1, 1906; unfortunately it doesn't say where. Marte is not found together with Brede in any American census, nor in the 1900 census in Gran or Brandbu, or in the church books for 1906 for Gran/Brandbu.

Brede and Marte's children:

- Birthe Bredesdatter. b. June 8, 1852 at Undelieie. She married Johan Larsen on July 6, 1879. The family lived at Kvernerud, Brandbu in the 1900 and 1910 census. Birthe died in 1936.
- Helena Bredesdatter, b. June 25, 1854 at Hvindeneie, died Dec. 11, 1862.
- Maria Bredesdatter, b. January 16, 1857 at Undelieie, died Nov. 5, 1857.
- Nils Bredesen, b. August 9, 1858 at Undelieie, married Isabella Mathilda Nelson in Clear Lake on March 12, 1888. Isabella Mathilda died on May 5, 1934, and Nils died Feb. 9, 1940, both in Cleveland, Ohio.
- Martea Bredesdatter, b. October 1, 1861. By census 1900 she lived in Rælingen, Skedsmo/Akershus with husband Karl August Andersen and three children.
- Helene Maria Bredesdatter, b. July 13, 1866.

Helene Maria leaves Norway

Helene Maria left Gran parish and arrived in New York May 18, 1891 on the *Thingvalla*, the same ship as her father left on five years earlier. Helene Maria was 25 years old and travelled by herself to America. Her destination was Barronett WI. In the 1900 census she lived with her husband Steve Harrison. They married November 18, 1892 in West Superior, Douglas County, WI. Steve was born in Norway and his given name was Steiner Høljesen. He was born on October 23, 1864 in Flatdal, Seljord, Telemark, son of Hølje (Holje) Stenersen and Anne Gregersdatter. Steiner immigrated to America about 1883, and became Steve Harrison. The last time I found them in Black Brook Township was in the 1910 census. In the 1920 and 1930 census they lived in Menomonie, Wis. Helene Maria died in Minneapolis November 5, 1948. According to the *Hadeland Lag's 1921 Yearbook* she lived in Colfax, Dunn County, Wis. in 1921, after about two years in Barronett and 17 years in Clear Lake, Wis.

Helene Maria and Steve's children:

- Hoie Harrison, b. December 12, 1893 in South Superior, Douglas County, Wis. He died Oct. 1980 in Knapp, Wis.
- Martha Bolette Harrison, b. 1896, Clear Lake, Wis., died 1988
- Anna Maria Harrison, b. April 1900, Clear Lake, Wis., married Frederick Begert, died 1991
- Blanche Sylvia Harrison, b. 1902, Clear Lake, died after 1920
- George Nikolai Harrison, b. 1904, Clear Lake, died 1978
- Esther Amalia Harrison, b. 1907, Clear Lake, died 1979

- Sophia Caroline Harrison, b. 1908, Clear Lake, died 1999
- Henry Melvin Harrison, b. 1911, Clear Lake, died after 1920

Sources for this article:
Church books, Gran parish; original documents, *Digitalarkivet.no*
1865 census, Gran, *Digitalarkivet.no*
US census 1895, 1900, 1910, 1920 and 1930;original documents, *Ancestry.com*
Hadeland Lag 1921 Yearbook
Hadeland Immigrant Identification Database, Form 64

Gulbrand Gjefsen and Martha Vien

published November 2011   *Form 1004*   *Byron Schmid*

The author grew up in Green County in southern Wisconsin. He is a retired Lutheran pastor (ELCA) and holds a Ph.D. in political science. He and his wife live in Blaine, Minnesota.

On floor from left: Byron Schmid, Sara Aeikens, Marguerite Paulson; seated from left: Lucille Paulson Gisher, Shirley Ask Harper, Laurel Ask Lange, Nancy Strommen Williams, Carolyn Larson Thompson, Joan Steen Anderson; 1st standing row from left: Shirley Paulson, Elaine Paulson Woytuck, Mary Greenwood, Charles Harper, Kristine Alm O'Connor, Margaret Alm Meyer, Gordon Grimson, Jeanne Cardinal Reiter, Kenneth Williams; back standing row from left: Leo Aeikens, Blake Paulson, David Williams, John Gishler, John Reiter, Robert Lange, James Meyer, Mark Anderson, Keith Paulson.

Reunion Tour

The Oslo bombing and the Utøya Island massacre shocked us 28 American and Canadian cousins who were going to Norway a week later. Like our Hadeland relatives, we grieved the loss of innocent lives and the attack in a country so committed to peacekeeping efforts. Our emotions were deeply stirred when our bus passed Utøya and when we visited the bombed area in Oslo at the end of the tour. But the tragedy did not dampen our enthusiasm for the homecoming return to Hadeland on the weekend of 5-7 August.

After visiting a number of places on the way from Bergen to Hadeland, we descendants of the children of Gudbrand Olsen and Martha Olsdatter, *husmenn* from Brynsås, celebrated for three days with our Norwegian cousins in the area of origin. Hans Næss guided us to Brynsås and other farms, Granavollen, the *Hadeland Folkemuseum* and the *Grinakervev*. We also visited the *Hadeland Glassverks* and were welcomed into the homes of cousins for coffees, hosted by Berit Iversrud, Olga Skovly, Liv Sørumshagen, Ruth Kari Sørumshagen, Anders Taaje/Lisbeth Follestad, and Grete Taaje. Astrid and Erik Taaje treated us to a *rømmegrøt* dinner at their home after which we were entertained by the Hadeland folk dancers. During the three days, Hans Næss and Ole Gamme also spoke to our group.

On Sunday Pastor Kari-Lette Pollestad Høghaug led the Canadian and American group, along with their Norwegian cousins, in a bi-lingual Communion service at the St. Nikolai Church. As the group leader and a Lutheran pastor, I brought the message which reflected on the legacy of our Hadeland emigrants for their descendants. Ruth Kari Sørumshagen, a cousin, was also involved in the service. At the service, I presented a 1926 oil painting of my home church (Adams Lutheran Church in Green County, WI) to Einar Raastad, board chair of the *Randsfjordmuseum*, as a gift to the *Hadeland Folkemuseum*. Then more than 70 descendants of Gudbrand Olsen gathered at the Sanner Hotel for a six-hour grand reunion meal and celebration.

Hans (Henry) Gilbertson and
wife Torina 1871

John Gilbertson and
wife Bertha

Children of Kari Horgen
Standing: Christen, Hans Quanrud, Jens Olsen
Seated: Siri (wife of Christen), Marthe Horgen
Quanrud, Ingeborg Horgen Olsen, Johanne
Horgen

The reunion tour group included persons from Wisconsin, Minnesota, Illinois, New York and Georgia, and from the Canadian provinces of Alberta and Saskatchewan.

Ancestral Roots in Hadeland

Our family history begins with Gulbrand Olsen Gjefsen who was born on Gjefseneiet, Gran, Hadeland, and baptized on 16 October 1786. He married Marthe Olsdatter Vien, daughter of Ole Larsen Soug and Berthe Larsdatter, on 2 January 1808. Both were living on *Almseiet øvre* at the time, and Gulbrand was a guard on the farm. He was a *husmann* on *Almseiet øvre* all his life. Gulbrand and Marthe bore eight children, four of whom lived to adulthood: Birthe, Kari, Paul (my great-great-grandfather) and Lars. After Marthe died, Gulbrand married Thora Joensdatter, daughter of Joen Gudmundsen Alm and Berthe Jacobsdatter, on 27 June 1848. Gulbrand and Thora had three children, all living to adulthood: Hans (Henry), Johannes (John) and Margrethe. Gulbrand died on 19 March 1850 at age 64.

All of Gulbrand's children likely assumed that they would live all of their days in Hadeland. At that time persons seldom traveled far from home and emigration across the ocean was not even imagined. So the four children of Gulbrand and Marthe married and lived the common life of a *husmann*. But they all eventually immigrated to America, except for Birthe, the oldest daughter, whose family remained in Hadeland and whose descendants are our Norwegian cousins today. However, three of her children also eventually crossed the ocean. The children of Gulbrand and Thora also made the westward journey after Gulbrand's death.

There were many factors that led to emigration to the New World. The survival rate of children had greatly increased over the years. Vaccinations had ended the outbreak of smallpox, and potatoes were a breakthrough new crop. From the late 1700s to 1865 there also was a dramatic increase in the number of *husmenn* in Hadeland, and the increasing population made it more difficult for a *husmann* to support his family. Beginning in 1836 four consecutive years of crop failure led to much famine. These factors, combined with the stories about life and opportunities in America from those who had emigrated earlier, led a large number of Hadelanders to emigrate.

Journey to the New World

Most of the Gilbertsons immigrated to the United States in the great migration wave that followed the Civil War, especially from 1866-1875. It is likely that most of our ancestors made their way on sailing ships that required an average of 53 days for the crossing. Weather conditions, of course, could vary the time considerably. Most, if not all of the Gilbertsons, made the crossing from Christiania (Oslo today) to Quebec, usually with a change of ships in England. [*A helpful source of information on the emigrant sailing ships and the conditions experienced by our ancestors when they crossed the Atlantic can be found on the website, Norway-Heritage: Hands Across the Sea, at www.norwayheritage.com.*]

The Horgens booked passage on the *Anna Delius*, departing Christiania on 28 April 1869 and arriving in Quebec on 12 June. The ship carried 389 passengers and a crew of 17. John Gilbertson traveled on the *Manila*, leaving Christiania on 23 April 1868 and arriving in Quebec

Martin Larsen & his father Lars,
c. 1876

Ole Gilbertson, another son
of Lars Gilbertson

Children of Paul Gilbertson c.1906
Kari, John, Ragnhild, Martha and Peter
Not pictured: Gilbert was in South Dakota
Thorsten died in 1890

Gilbert Gilbertson

Thorsten
Gilbertson

on 19 June. In 1876 Thorsten Paulson, son of Paul Gilbertson, and his wife and son took the *Angela* from Christiania to Liverpool where they changed ships for Quebec. Paul Gilbertson and his family came via the *Hero* in 1877 to Liverpool where they boarded another ship for Quebec.

The early Norwegian settlements in America were located in northern Illinois, Wisconsin,

Iowa, Minnesota and eventually the Dakotas. These were the open places of settlement when they arrived.

Lars Gilbertson and his family were the first of the Gilbertsons to follow their star to the New Land. They immigrated to Jefferson County in southeastern Wisconsin in 1853. Four years later, Thora, the widow of Gulbrand, along with two of her children, Hans (Henry) and Margrethe, made their way to Green County in southern Wisconsin in 1857. They settled in what became the largest settlement in the U.S. of immigrants from Hadeland and Valdres, Norway. John Gilbertson, the second son of Gulbrand and Thora, journeyed to Green County in 1868 and then made his way to St. Croix County in northwestern Wisconsin.

In 1869 the widow Kari Gulbrandsdatter Horgen, made the journey to Winneshiek County in northeastern Iowa with her married son and two of her daughters. One of her married daughters had left the previous year. Three sons of Paul followed shortly thereafter (Gilbert and his fiancé in 1870, John in 1872, and Thorsten and his wife and son in 1876) and settled in Green and Iowa counties. Gilbert and his family later moved to South Dakota and eventually relocated to the province of Alberta, Canada. Paul and the rest of his family followed to Wisconsin in 1877.

Three children of Birthe made their way to Faribault County in southern Minnesota (Johanna in 1873, Kjersti in 1877 and Martin Larson in 1878). Johanna and her family eventually settled in the Dakota Territory.

All of the sons of Gulbrand became farmers in the New World, an impossibility in Hadeland at that time. Today, of course, their descendants represent a wide diversity of occupations in the U.S. and Canada, as well as in Norway. One notable mention should be made of the more than two dozen Lutheran pastors, including a bishop, who have come out of the family, the largest number from the descendants of Kari Paulson, daughter of Paul Gilbertson. Today the descendants of Gulbrand Olson and his two wives, including spouses/partners, total almost 8,500 persons.

Compiling the Family History

The initial efforts in compiling the Gilbertson family history began in 1986 when I used an accumulated period of vacation time to begin gathering information on five of my ancestral families. In partnership with Paul Alm, we completed and printed *The Paulsons and Alms in America: The Family of Paul and Birthe Gilbertson* in 1991.

In the summer of 1991 Hans Næss, a noted genealogist in Hadeland, sent me a considerable amount of information on the family of Birthe Nygard, the sister of Paul who had remained in Norway. The following summer I spent a few days in Hadeland to gain additional information on Birthe's family. My hosts in Hadeland were Eric and Astrid Taaje who have extended hospitality and friendship on my several trips to Hadeland. They introduced me to our

Hadeland cousins. Hans Næss acquainted me with the history and places of Hadeland, and was our Hadeland guide for the two family groups that I later brought to Norway.

In early 1993 contact was finally established with the Horgen line that had settled near Decorah, Iowa. That contact made it possible to begin gathering information on the Horgen descendants in the United States. At a Horgen family reunion that summer I was able to meet several cousins who opened the door to further contacts.

In late July 1993, a group of American Strommen and Paulson/Alm cousins made a reunion trip to Norway. In addition to touring the country, the group visited Strømmen relatives in Valdres, stopped at the ancestral farm and celebrated a memorable reunion gathering with more than 120 Norwegian cousins after a joint English-Norwegian service in the *Hadeland stavkirke* that was packed with family members. The group then journeyed to Hadeland for two days. The Taajes hosted us at their home for a great meal, and the Hadeland folk dancers performed on their lawn. The group also joined a number of Hadeland cousins for a reunion dinner.

My relocation from the Twin Cities to Sioux Falls, South Dakota at the beginning of 1994 temporarily suspended the search for family information. But eventually I was able to resume correspondence with Horgen family members. While at Sioux Falls, I was also able to establish personal contact with descendants of Jens Olson and Ingeborg Horgen who had settled a short distance from Sioux Falls. And to my and their great surprise, some were even members of the church in which I served.

My move back to the Twin Cities in early 1999 again temporarily suspended work on the Gilbertson family history. But the project was resumed after my retirement in 2003 when I took another family group of Strommen and Paulson cousins to Norway. Again, the group was graciously received in Hadeland where we met with many cousins in the Birthe Nygard line.

In special trips to Hadeland in 2006 and 2008 I was able to obtain most of the remaining needed information on the Nygard line (and also participate in the *Syttende Mai* celebration!). Hans Næss and the staff at the Hadeland Folk Museum archives provided very important assistance in obtaining the older family information. In fact, it was at the archives where I learned that after Gulbrand's first wife had died, he had remarried and had three more children, all of them immigrating to southern Wisconsin. That was a real surprise, and it opened contact with a large number of cousins in southern Wisconsin whom I had known for many years. Because the line of Paul had used the surname Paulson – and some of them Alm, it had never occurred to any of us that those with the Gilbertson surname were related to our family.

Shortly thereafter I was also finally able to discover the emigration destination of Lars Gulbrandsen – to Jefferson County in southern Wisconsin. The Norwegian records did not record the information, and only an accidental stumble in U.S. federal census records located his settlement. His early death meant that he was listed in only one census record.

Now the Gilbertson family history has been compiled with information on all of the adult children of Gulbrand Olsen and his descendants, resulting in the two-volume 983 page *The Gilbertson Family History: The Ancestors and Descendants of Gulbrand Olsen Gjefsen.*

For me, the compilation of these family histories has been a search for my own past. I grew up among Strommens, Paulson-Alms and Thompsons, but left the Adams community for college at the age of 18. The family histories have allowed me to "fill in" the intervening years and gain insight into the generations back to the time of the immigration – and before. For this reason our 2011 reunion trip to Norway was another time of "homecoming," an almost sacramental re-experiencing of family "connectedness" that spans the generations and gives "root" to our emotional nature.

Carrie Aschim Tollefson

"Experiences and Memories" published February 2012   Form 672   Carrie Tollefson

This story was originally published in Norwegian in the 'Brua' in 1937 (#25). Ole P. Gamme and Verlyn Anderson translated the text for the 2011 reprint.

I am a member of the Hadeland Lag even though I have never attended any of the annual *stevner*, nevertheless I have a great interest in the lag. Unfortunately, I have had very little opportunity to be with immigrants from Hadeland since I have most of the time lived among Americans and Germans since I came to this country.

I have subscribed to the *Decorah Posten* nearly all the time since I came to this country, almost fifty years ago so I have read some about the Hadeland immigrants in that paper and often see many farm names from Hadeland I had nearly completely forgotten about. When I read about those farms and the immigrants, I got a renewed interest in the district where I was born so I got my sister to send me a subscription to the *Hadeland* newspaper. And then, I received a copy of a *Brua*, filled with names that I recognized so I was very happy to have found the Hadeland Lag.

I am the daughter of Simon Aschim and was baptized and confirmed in the Gran Church. I received confirmation instruction from Pastors Monrad and Søren Brunn Bugge during the last year that they were pastors in Hadeland. At my confirmation service, which was conducted by Pastor Bugge, there were 105 of us who were confirmed that day. It was a festive day that I will never forget.

During that time there was a big religious revival that spread through Hadeland. I had a girl friend who was sick and I had to go over the Braata creek whenever I went to visit her. There were always boys there who drank and played cards and used foul language so I was almost afraid to go, but they never harmed me. But, it was strange, when the revival came, then three of those young men were converted and fell down on their knees and prayed to God. It was remarkable to see the great changes that came over them.

A wonderful memory that I have from that time is that when I lived at the Aschim farm and my cousins, Anders Aschim and Anders Hole, went across the Randsfjorden to the west side of the lake to conduct a prayer meeting. There they sang so beautifully as we could hear them from our side of the lake. Other pleasant memories are from those beautiful Sunday evenings when the boys from the Hadeland Glassworks would take boat trips on the lake with their musical instruments and we could hear their music across the waters. Many of those boys were German and were good musicians. At that time, I thought that music was so beautiful, but since then I have seen and heard much.

I have never gotten to any of our lag's summer meetings because I had to raise my four children alone and I had to work hard to provide for them. For 17 years I lived among the German immigrants and because they did not know how to speak English, I had to learn to speak German.

I have also travelled quite a bit. One of my sons finished high school when he was only 16 years old and enrolled at the University of North Dakota in Grand Forks before his 17th birthday. But then he got influenza and also double pneumonia. When he started to get better, then the doctor said that he should go to Arizona to get completely well again, but I could not afford to do that for him. But, I had a daughter whose husband was a cook at the Hotel Jordan in Glendive, Montana so I took my son there and bought him a pony so that he could get healthy by being out in the fresh Montana air. When he regained his health, he got a job as a clerk at the hotel. There I got a job taking care of a child for a young couple who traveled around the state so therefore I got to visit much of the state of Montana. But during that time I got to see how those rough cowboys mistreated their horses and that affected me a great deal.

After my son, Alvin, had worked at the hotel for four years, the rich man who had formerly owned the Hotel Jordan at one time started to build a million dollar hotel in Orlando, Florida, and Alvin got a job there as the "Head Clerk" of the hotel. Later he got married down there. The young couple, my son and daughter-in-law wanted me to move there so I sold my house in Grand Forks and moved to Florida and lived there for fifteen months. That gave me the opportunity to visit most of that state, too. The hotel sent tourist busses to various parts of Florida and it did not cost me anything to go along on those trips because the hotel paid for those tours; however the hotel charged the tourists for these tours. This was during the "Blooming Time" and Orlando was very beautiful and became known as "The City Beautiful." After living there for fifteen months, I moved back up North again. I stopped for a time in Chicago to visit my other son and I also stayed in Minneapolis for a time before I continued on to Fergus Falls where I visited for two weeks. One day we were going to the church services and when we came to the church, I discovered that the minister was Pastor Gaulik Mona who formerly had been a minister in Grand Forks and who preached in Norwegian. It had been more than 16 months since I had heard a single word of Norwegian and the experience affected me so deeply that tears were soon running down my cheeks. That was the first time that I understood how important my childhood language was for me. When I got back to Grand Forks, I no longer had a home, but I got a room at the local rest home for the elderly.

I am 74 years old and have had many good days, but also many difficult days. I have four children, three sons and a daughter. All of my boys are dead. Two of them died at about the same time. About a year ago my son Alvin was killed in an automobile accident in Illinois. He was 34 years old. A short time after that, my son Thomas who was a head cook on the railroad, died of pneumonia in Chicago. Only a week separated the dates of their deaths. Thomas was for a time the chief cook at the Dakota Hotel in Grand Forks, but got a job with the Northern Pacific Railroad as a cook there. My daughter, Anna, Mrs. John Leppert, lives in Bismarck, North Dakota.

The Anders Langbraaten or *Wergelandsgutten* that you wrote about in last year's *Brua*, number 24 (1936), I knew in Norway, but during my childhood I was afraid of him because I once saw him butt down and tip over gravestones in the Lunner Church cemetery.

In the next year's *Brua*, number 26 (1938), on page 26, Peder H. Nelson, the editor of the *Brua* included the following short update about Carrie Tollefson and her family:

Our readers will certainly remember Mrs. Carrie Tollefson's article "Experiences and Memories" that was published in last year's *Brua* in which, among other things, she told that a year earlier she had lost two sons within a week's time, - one in an automobile accident and the other by pneumonia. Recently Mrs. Tollefson received the surprise of her life when she found out that her son, Alvin, who she thought was killed in an automobile accident, was in good health and living in Madison, Wisconsin! For the past two years, she had lived, believing that her son was dead, but recently she received a telephone call from him, telling her that the he was in good health and during the past two years he had been working for a firm and in that job he had spent most of the time abroad. When he was out of the United States, he had neglected to inform his mother about his whereabouts. A couple of years ago her son, Thomas, had written to his mother and told her that Alvin had been seriously injured in an automobile accident and she had understood that he had been fatally injured. A few days after writing to his mother, Thomas had died of pneumonia in Chicago. We rejoice with Mrs. Tollefson that she has discovered that her son, Alvin, is not dead, but in the best of health. She is a member of the Hadeland Lag and was born on the Ascheim farm in Gran, Hadeland. She is currently living in Grand Forks, North Dakota.

Peter Sterud and Jessie Birds Bill

"Hadeland Folkemuseum" published February 2012   *Torun Sørli*

Peter Sterud, or Peder Simensen Sterud, was born June 18, 1886 in Granumseie in Hov, Søndre Land in Oppland County. He grew up in a large Norwegian family. Peder left his family in 1907 and went to America. Over the years, parts of his Norwegian family more or less lost contact with him and his ancestors, so it was exciting for me to start searching for him in the United States.

Peder was the son of tanner Simen Pedersen Sterud (1859-1941) and wife Mathilde Mathiasdatter (1865-1942). Peder's parents moved many times. They lived in Hamar in Hedmark County, Hov in Søndre Land and in Brandbu. The family became large and counted 15 people altogether. Simen was a tanner journeyman from about 1886. He became a tanner in 1897. The change of residence was most likely due to Simen's occupation.

Peder's parents Simen and Mathilde were married on March 6, 1886 in Hov. Their 13 children were born "as beads on a string":

- Peder, b. June 18, 1886, d. Apr. 12, 1970 in Milwaukee. Wisconsin
- Marie (Westby), b. Feb. 6, 1888
- Sverre, b. Dec, 10, 1889, d. May 31, 1982
- Markus, b. Dec. 27, 1891, d. Oct. 13, 1972
- Asta Margrete, b. April 20, 1894
- Thora (Dahl), b. April 28, 1897, d. Oct. 1, 1982 in Minneapolis
- Gudrun, b. Nov. 9, 1898
- Peter Wilhelm, b. Dec 4, 1900
- Asbjørn, b. Nov. 11, 1902
- Signe (Lie), b. Sept. 8, 1905
- Martha, b. Jan. 13, 1908
- Aagot (Sundling), b. Feb. 1, 1912
- Else, b. April 4, 1914.

Sterud Siblings in 1967
Seated: Sverre, Peder, Marcus, Marie
Standing: Signe, Asbjørn, Aagot, Thora

As a tanner journeyman Simen lived at the farm Augedalsbro in Brandbu from about 1888 to 1894. Three of their children were born in Brandbu, among them Markus Sterud (1891-1971) who married Astrid Haagensen (1900-1992). Markus and Astrid owned the farm Søndre

351

Grinaker in Brandbu, known for hosting the ruins of Grinaker Stave Church. Sterud descendants still live on the Søndre Grinaker farm.

Peder Sterud was 21 years old when he left the port of Oslo on April 20, 1907 on the *Montebello* bound for Wisconsin. According to information from the Oslo port, Peder was a tanner just as his father. Peder changed his name to Peter Sterud after arriving in America. He is not found in the U.S. census in 1910 or 1920. The first time I found Peter was in the 1925 census. He lived in Mountrail County with his family: wife Jessie, children William, Peter Jr. and Ruth. One year later, on June 30, 1926, Jessie and the children were registered in the Indian census for the Fort

Sterud home in Elbowoods
Credit: Bureau of Indian Affairs, Fort Berthold Agency, New Town ND

Berthold Indian Reservation, an Indian reservation in Western North Dakota, home for the federally recognized Mandan, Hidatsa, and Arikara Nation. Jessie as well as her children grew up at Fort Berthold.

The Norwegian community was, and still is, very close to the reservation, and there have been quite a few intermarriages between Indians and Norwegians. Peter was employed by the Bureau of Indian Affairs as farm laborer; therefore he was provided with government housing. Jessie and Peter lived in a house in Elbowoods on the Fort Berthold Reservation.

I am told that Peter made leather belts and purses, so he carried on his tanning skills in the States. He drove a small green pickup and worked on the Indian reservation. People in the area remember that Peter spoke English with a heavy Norwegian accent.

Birds Bill with his daughters
(Jesse is second from the left)
Credit: Scott Satermo

Jessie was Hidasta and a member of the Gros Ventre tribe. She was born Oct 5, 1898 in Fort Berthold. Jessie was the daughter of Birds Bill (b. about 1873, d. Dec 27, 1945) and Plain House (b. about 1878, d. 1922). Birds Bill and Plain House were also registered with their Indian names, Tsa-ka-apash and At-i-a-tash. Birds Bill was a scout at Fort Buford. Jessie was one of 11 siblings in Birds Bill's marriage with Plain House. It is also interesting to notice that Jessie and her siblings all had English names, while their parents were registered with their English and Indian names. Jessie was registered in the Indian census for Fort Berthold from 1900 to 1939. Peter died in 1970 in Milwaukee, Wisconsin, Jessie died about 1950.

Jessie and Peter's children:
1. Marie who died as a baby
2. Carl William, 1920-1981
3. Ruth, b. 1922
4. Peter Jr., b. 1924-2010.

Peter Jr. received a high school education before he and his brother, Carl William, volunteered to the U.S. Navy during World War II. Peter served aboard the *USS Oklahoma*, and Carl William served on the *USS Maryland* when it was attacked on December 7, 1941. The brothers were on their ships when the assault on Pearl Harbor took place. In Peter's obituary in the *Daily Democrat*, Woodland, CA, I found a short personal description about the attack in 1941: Peter left the *USS Oklahoma* and went to visit his brother Carl William. It was while they were on shore in Pearl Harbor that the bombs began to fall. Peter's ship sank and the two brothers helped survivors of some of the ships. Luckily both brothers survived the attack. Peter was reassigned to the *USS Maryland* and was later honored by the Navy for his service during the attack on Pearl Harbor. Peter Jr. lived in the Mandaree area in Independence; later he settled in California. After leaving the Navy, he worked in construction and as a horse trainer for about 30 years.

According to an interview with Gail Baker on MHA Nation's website, Carl William worked as a baker while he was serving the Navy. He was also known as a good cook. In the same interview Baker also says that Carl William and Peter Jr. had learned to speak Hidatsa from their grandpa "Tony" Birds Bill. In this context it would be interesting to know if the children also were influenced by their father's culture.

In these last lines of the article, I would like to add a few words: It is a privilege for me to be able to do research about individuals in our quite close past. I have again learned that the "journey" often is linked to events in American history, which makes my work even more interesting. During the research of Peter Sterud's family I was also happy to see that some of the Sterud descendants on both sides of the Atlantic are reunited. They have embarked on a journey in Peder's footsteps via e-mail and facebook. For me it is just to wish them good luck!

Sources for this article: Church books for: Brandbu/Gran (Oppland), Hov/Søndre Land (Oppland), Vang/Hamar (Hedmark). Indian census, Ft. Berthold ND (*Ancestry.com*). Mandan, Hidatsa and Arikara Nation website: *www.mhanation.com*. Obituary, *Daily Democrat*, Woodland, California: March 11, 2010. Scott Satermo. Marilyn Hudson. Travis Woyen.

The Olson Boys from Minnesota

published May 2012   *Forms 629,648*   *Harald Hvattum*

Delos and Don Olson in front of Solobservatoriet (Sun Observatory) at Bjørgeseter in 2005

I am telling about these two fellows because they represent a dying the boys learned to speak the Hadeland dialect in their Norwegian as they grew up and can still use it today. Both of them can speak proper Norwegian but, as so many other Norwegian-speaking Americans in Minnesota, intersperse their language with some American words mixed in with it. *"Du veit je har også laga et lite hus I den sizen"* ("You know I have also built a small house of that size"), tells Donald, as he looked at a little *stabbur* (storage building) at Bislingen in Lunner, *"men det huset changed forresten bruk"* ("but that house has changed its purpose"), he continued. He could also tell that my dress shirt which had been woven by the *Hadeland Husflidslag* was not

354

the same *"kollorn"* ("color") as *busserulls* the fellows had seen in other places in Hadeland.

A generation ago there still lived many, especially in the Midwest, who were in the same situation. Now it is a long time ago since children in America learned Norwegian at home, and our Norwegian language is therefore naturally on its way out. When members of the Hadeland Lag visited Hadeland in 1977 most of the participants could understand quite a bit of Norwegian, as Verlyn Anderson, one of those participants, told me. Some of them could also speak proper Norwegian. Among the 52 who came in the summer of 2005 there were only three or four who could speak proper Norwegian.

DeLos and Donald Olson who were born respectively in 1935 and 1939 grew up on a farm near Montevideo, Minnesota. It was the custom then that the farm was named for the owner and the farm changed its name when there was a new owner. Their parents lived for a time on the Steffensen farm before they bought their own farm which then got the name, the Olson farm. They later bought a new farm in the neighborhood. The farm then changed its name. When they were growing up there were many "Hadeland farms" in the area. The Ruud farm was one. They were the Ruuds with roots in Jevnaker. Another Hadeland name in the area was the Jevnaker name Nøkleby, the Gran name of Myhre and the Brandbu name Bilden. In addition there was the Nelson farm nearby. It was that of Olaf Nelson, an early board member of the Hadeland Lag, who owned that farm. He also had roots in Jevnaker. With so many people with roots from Jevnaker it was not strange that when they built their own church in rural Montevideo in 1896, the name they chose was from the home community in Hadeland, the Jevnaker Lutheran Church.

When the boys grew up, Norwegian was the only language they spoke at home. That was not so strange, there were only people with Norwegian ancestry living in the area and they all spoke Norwegian. That is not totally true, however. There was also a German who had a farm in the area, but he spoke German. The German, besides, was a hard worker. He was part of the threshing crew and he pitched the grain bundles into the machine so quickly that it was not good to work alongside of him. The threshing machine and its crew went from farm to farm twice. The first time they threshed on each farm for only one day so that they would have grain quickly, first threshing only the wheat that would be ground into flour. After that they came back and threshed the grain from the other fields.

The boys learned to speak English when they started school. Their parents had been confirmed in Norwegian. This had been changed to English when the boys were growing up, but church services still alternated between Norwegian and English in the Jevnaker Church. This continued until around 1960. *"Men du veit at kjørka i Amerika er itte lik sånn dæ ær i Norge"* ("But you know that the church in America is not the same as it is in Norway"), DeLos explained. In America it is the congregation that appoints and pays the salary for the pastor. If one is not satisfied you only have to tell him. C.T. Jenson was pastor at the Jevnaker Church when the boys grew up. He must have done well. He came thin and inexperienced to the congregation and left the position 33 years later as a well-matured man. In the meantime there was not much income for a pastor in a rural congregation. When the Olson boys were growing up, Jenson served four churches at the same time. There were services in the churches every other Sunday. In the early days the pastor had to travel by horse and buggy so he could conduct services in two churches each Sunday.

The parents of the Olson boys were Alvin and Ingeborg Teolina Olson. Alvin's mother Karen Karlson came from Lunner to Minnesota about 1909. She was the daughter of Karl Johan Andersen of Jevnaker. The boys have many relatives in Hadeland, among others the Grinas in Lunner.

Both parents are buried in the cemetery of the Jevnaker Church in rural Montevideo. Donald and DeLos in the meantime had both left the farm for other jobs. They found another place in Minnesota, namely Rochester, where DeLos started as a carpenter. Later he got a technical job with the city. Donald started as a bricklayer and worked at that for 12 years before he got a job with an oil company. In 2005, both brothers were retired.

DeLos served on the Board of Directors of the Hadeland Lag from 2005 until his death in 2011.

Goro Andersdatter Gunderson Marion

published August/November 2013   *Form 785*   *Bary Gammell*

Goro (*pronounced Goo-roo*) was born on September 15, 1850, while her parents Anders and Kari were living in a rented cottage on the Roisum farm in Hadeland, Oppland, Norway.

After the 1865 Census for Gran and prior to her marriage in 1876, Goro moved to the Oslo area to work. She married Gunerius Gundersen June 5, 1876, who was a resident of Ostre Aker, a suburb of Oslo. Her maid of honor, or possibly who represented the bride, was Kristian Jakobsen (relationship unknown) and the best man was Gunerius' brother, Bernt Gundersen. Gunerius arranged for the wedding to take place in the Paulus Parish church of Oslo County.

Gunerius was born in May 1857 (or 1858) on the Hagamoen Farm, Eidsvoll, Akerhus, Norway.' His father Gunder Olsen, born 1814 in Oudalen, was a laborer who lodged on the farm with Gunerius' mother, Kristine Kristiansdatter, born in 1819 in Oudalen. Gunerius had an older brother Bernt (b. 1853) and a younger brother Ole (b.1860), all born in Eidsvoll. Also, living in the home was Marie Olsdatter (b. 1843 in Oudalen). Marie may be the daughter of Kristine from a previous marriage. By 1875 the Olsen's daughter Olivia (b. 1849 in Oudalen), and her son Julius Ulriksen (b. 1873 in Eidsvoll), was living and working with Gunder and Ole and the other peasants on the farm in Eidsvoll. Marte Kristiansdatter (b. 1867 in Eidsvoll) was also being nurtured *(pleiebarn)* in the home.

Just prior to and possibly up to the time of the marriage, Gunerius was working at Schou *bryggeri* (brewery) in Kristiania (present-day Oslo). The address where he lodged was Trondhjemsveien 50, Kristiania.

Their first child, and only child born in Norway, was Arthur Kristian Gundersen. He was born November 12, 1878. Goro and Gunerius were living at Thorshaug in Aker when he was born. Arthur was christened February 9, 1879, in the Vestre Aker Parish in Oslo County.'

357

Goro and her son Arthur immigrated to Minnesota in 1885. They arrived in New York harbor on June 27, 1885, aboard the ship *Hekla* which sailed from Copenhagen.' This passage is interesting. Goro is listed as Gurin, age 34. Arthur, however, was shown as age four years/ 6 months. Actually Arthur had turned six the previous November. The first page of the passenger list provides a plausible explanation for Arthur's age discrepancy. All passengers six and older were charged a higher ticket price. This was a problem for working class emigrants who needed to have as much money as possible in their new home.

Gunerius (George) Gunderson

Immigrating to a new country must have been both exciting and challenging for the family. Two of Goro's brothers, Peder and Anders, had preceded her almost 10 years earlier, but they were both living in Utah and she was headed to Minnesota. There was also some excitement and challenge with a growing family. According to family lore, Goro was pregnant before she left Norway.

Family lore also believes that she had more children than the three that are of record in this history. There is a twelve-year period from the birth of Arthur in 1878 to son Harry's birth in 1890 in Minnesota. It is not inconceivable that Goro lost more than one child in both Norway and Minnesota during that twelve-year period, including the baby which was to be born in America.

While the family lived in Minnesota, two more children were added; Harry was born June 1, 1890, and Clara in May 1892.

The location(s) of the family after first arrival in Minnesota is not precisely known. One glimpse is given by Harry's World War I draft registration card. He listed his birth location as Eagle Bend, Todd County, Minnesota." Eagle Bend was a small community that had only recently been established about 1880. It is located 142 miles west-northwest of Minneapolis.

A great number of emigrants were recruited to become farmers in the Midwest. Whatever the attraction was to settle there, it soon evaporated. It was not uncommon for immigrants to find that the ground where they settled was not well suited for farming.

Within five years after Harry was born the family relocated to Minneapolis. In June 1895, the Minnesota State Census records that the family had been living at 2118 Riverside Avenue in Minneapolis for one month.

Gunerius, now Gunirus, was a laborer and claimed to have been living in the state since 1875. This is unlikely since he and Goro, now Gurin, were not married until 1876 and Arthur was born in 1878 while both parents were living in Norway. There must have been another reason why this residency period was claimed, or incorrectly recorded by the census worker, L. Peterson.

The family did not stay long in Minneapolis. Before June 1900 the family moved again, this time to a farm in Maple Ridge Township, an unincorporated area of Delta County, Michigan. The 1900 U.S. Census records that the farm was owned with no mortgage. The census also states that "Georgia" had nine children but only three were living. This gives confirmation to the family lore about Goro having had a large number of children. We can only try to imagine the heartache and sorrow of these two parents.

The Americanization of the parents' names continued; they were listed in the 1900 census as George and Georgia. George shows a birth date of May 1856 and an immigration date of 1883. Georgia's birth date is listed as Sept 1850, Harry's as May 1890, and Clara's as May 1892.

Arthur was not with the family in Michigan and most likely never officially left Minneapolis. In June 1900 he was a private in the Army, stationed in Cuba at the Cardenas Barracks in the Provence of Matanzas. His home address was listed at 1612 7th Avenue South in Minneapolis. A brief search in records of the soldiers involved in 1898 in the U.S. War with Spain did not reveal Harry's name. This may indicate he was sent to Cuba as a part of the occupation forces. In any event Harry did volunteer and served his country.

Death was no stranger to Goro (hereinafter referred to only as Georgianna, her last known name by her family). First she had to endure the loss of six children. Next she was to lose George to an accidental death. In September of 1902 George was felling trees when a tree mortally injured him. He died September 3, 1902, from a fracture of the spinal cord. George was never able to enjoy, in this life, being a grandfather. His first of eight grandchildren, Myrtle, was born two years later.

Back in Minneapolis, Arthur, having returned from Cuba, was dating a Swedish immigrant girl by the name of Kirshta (Christine) Helgren (b. 1877) who had arrived in 1899. She was living with her sister Beda who was a servant in the home of Dr. Hugh Nelson at 25 W 15th Ave. Christine was a dressmaker in 1900.

*Arthur & Christine Gunderson
with daughter Myrtle Arlandson
and her son Norman*

On November 24, 1903, Arthur secured a marriage license and two days later, November 26, he and Christine were married. They were blessed with three children: Myrtle (1904-1987); Earl (1907-1968); and Roy (1910-1991). Both families had a history of marrying in the Church. Arthur and Christine may have been married civilly because of the still raw feelings between the

Norwegians and the Swedes, originating from the Napoleonic War. It had been 90 years since the Treaty of Kiel which ceded Norway to Sweden, but the family story indicates that a Swede and Norwegian were not allowed to marry in the church. Nonetheless, this started the history of Norwegian-Swedish marriages in the family that continued with their daughter Myrtle.

Career-wise, Arthur was a collector for a furniture company in 1910. By 1919, when he registered for the WWI Draft, Arthur moved on to his life's primary career and was a clerk at Union State Bank in Minneapolis. He was described in the draft registration as being of medium height and build with gray eyes and black hair.

Arthur remained in banking until his retirement. He rose through the ranks of Scandia Bank in Minneapolis, which was later acquired by Midland Bank, which was later acquired by Wells Fargo Bank. He went from a cashier to the custodian of the bank vault to manager of the safety deposit boxes. Arthur was promoted to Vice President at Midland Bank prior to his retirement. Christine suffered from arteriosclerosis (hardening of the arteries) and high blood pressure for over 10 years before her death May 5, 1950; she was then living at the Christian Home for the Aged. Arthur lived another 8 years until his death April 8, 1958.

After George's death, Georgianna remained in Michigan. She was not one to remain single. She met another farmer by the name of Nazaire Marion (b. 1855). They were married May 20, 1905 Court in Escanaba, the Delta County Seat. The marriage application indicated they were both residents of Perkins, an unincorporated part of Baldwin about 9 miles south of Maple Ridge. However, the 1910 U.S. Census shows them in Maple Ridge Township. Both townships were incorporated in 1873. This marriage was recorded as the second for both.

Nazaire was the son of Antoine Marion and Sophie Yvon of Lower Canada, a region of Quebec along the St. Lawrence River. He was part of a large French Catholic family. Antoine was a *journalier* (day laborer) as were many of his siblings. Antoine died prior to the 1881 Census of Canada and Sophie before the 1891 Census. Nazaire emigrated between the deaths of his parents and perhaps as early as 1880. What happened to his first wife and any children is unknown.

A search of the Lower Canada (Quebec) census and parish records revealed a great deal of information about Antoine and Sophie and their families.

Antoine was born in the area of Champlain and baptized 21 November 1822 in the Ste-Anne-de-la-Perade parish, the son of Augustine Marion and (Marie) Amable L'Heureaux. Sophie was born in 1829 in the same parish. She was baptized October 27, 1929, the daughter of Francois Yvon and Henriette LeDuc.

Both families remained in the Champlain area; Antoine and Sophie were married in Ste-Anne-de-la-Perade parish on January 10, 1853, but the marriage record shows Antoine's parents were living in St. Prosperer D'Une parish.

Nazaire Marion was the second of six children born into this family. The 1861 Census of Canada shows that the mothers of Antoine and Sophie were living next or near to them. Henriette (63), a widow, was living with relatives Nazaire Yvon (35) and Marie Sacaster (41) and Amable (64), also a widow, was living with relatives Angele Marion (24) and Esau Marion (25).

Georgianna remained in Michigan with Nazaire for several years. Her children Harry and Clara returned to Minneapolis.

Harry went to live with Arthur (then a collector for a furniture company) and Christine at the family home at 2801 Pillsbury Ave. He was unemployed in 1910 and was attending the University of Minnesota, where he played football, according to his nephew Norman Gunderson.

Clara likely also lived with Arthur and Christine. In Minneapolis, like her mother, she met and married into a large French Canadian family, the Bourdeauxs. Chester Bourdeaux's father Oliver Phillip was from Quebec. His mother Sophie was born in Minnesota, but her parents were from Quebec and Switzerland. Chester was the sixth of ten children born in Minnesota.

Chester and Clara married November 24, 1909, and shortly thereafter had five children: Clinton 0 (1910-2007); Carlton Kenneth (1911-1964); Nell "Nellie" (Mr. Nelson) (1912-Deceased); Jeanette Margaretta (Carl Robert Bowser) (1914-1988); Ruth Geraldine (John Thompson Fryhling, 2nd -Mr. Sorenson) (1915-Deceased). Sadly, Clara died of pulmonary tuberculosis June 2, 1921, while living in New Brighton Village, located in Ramsey County between Saint Paul and Minneapolis. Chester married again in 1931, to Agnes (?). Together they had 2 more children, Lillian (Chester Gardas) (b. 1932) and Patricia (Mr. Hillyard) (b. 1934). Chester was a rural mail carrier throughout his working life. He died January 20, 1943, after a six year battle with diabetes mellitus.

Clara and Chester provided Georgianna and George with a large posterity, with many great and great-great grandchildren still living in 2013.

1917 was an important year for Georgianna's son Harry. He had been working as a carpenter until April 3, 1917, when he became a Firefighter Candidate. Thus began a distinguished 39-year career with the Minneapolis Fire Department.

World War I had been raging since 1914. The United States initially "pursued a policy of non-intervention..." Pres. Wilson maintained this policy, even after 128 Americans were killed on the British liner *RMS Lusitania* in May 1915, when sunk by a German U Boat, insisting that "America is too proud to fight." Germany was intent in drawing America into this war. "The German Foreign Ministry, in the Zimmermann Telegram, invited Mexico to join the war as Germany's ally against the United States. In return, the Germans would finance Mexico's war and help it recover the territories of Texas, New Mexico, and Arizona that were lost in the Mexican War of 1848. After the sinking of seven U.S. merchant ships by submarines and the publication of the Zimmerman telegram, Wilson called for war on Germany, which the U.S. Congress declared on 6 April 1917.

The timing of this declaration, three days following the beginning of Harry's career as a firefighter, was soon to have an effect. Being single, he registered for the draft June 5, 1917, ironically the same day he took the City Oath to become a Minneapolis fireman, following his successful probation trial period. He was described in his WWI Draft Registration as being of medium height and weight, gray eyes, and light colored hair.

Harry resigned from the fire department November 1, 1917, to enter military duty. Upon his discharge from the service, he was reinstated with the Minneapolis Fire Department on July 14, 1919, and returned to live with Arthur's family on Pillsbury Ave.

Harry was well suited for being a fireman and with experience he rose through the ranks: fire truck driver (February 1922), Fire Inspector (June 1933), Lieutenant (September 1934, all Lieuten-

Harry Gunderson

ants were reclassified as Captains in January 1937), Acting Assistant Chief (January 1945), and finally District Chief/Assistant Chief (April 1947). Harry held the rank of Assistant Fire Chief until he retired January 16, 1956.

1918 was a year of more loss for Georgianna and her daughter Clara. On April 16, 1918, Georgianna's second husband, Nazaire Marion, died in Maple Ridge for the want of proper medication. Georgianna remained in Maple Ridge until after 1920 but eventually sold the farm and moved to 3525 Holmes Avenue in Minneapolis, where she first rented" and before 1940 bought the home.

Clara's father-in-law Oliver Phillip Bourdeaux died March 17, 1918. Oliver's headstone at Hillside Cemetery in Minneapolis is unusual in that it also bears the name of his great-granddaughter Jacqueline Fryhling, born in 1938. What is unusual is that the cemetery has no record of Jacqueline ever being buried there.

The WWI Draft Registration also affected Arthur Gunderson (September 1918, medium height and build, gray eyes, and black hair). Arthur was just short of turning 40 which may explain why he did not have to declare an exemption.

Clara's husband, Chester A.A. Bourdeaux, on the other hand, was only 28 or 29. He claimed an exemption from the draft to support his wife and family and was shown to have a short height, a medium build, blue eyes, and light colored hair. There are two items on his draft registration card that need further comment. First, his birth date is shown as January 30, 1889. His death certificate and the 1900 U.S. Census record 1888 as his birth year. Second, his trade was recorded as a clerk with the Cook Constructing Company rather than as a rural mail carrier. By the 1920 U.S. Census he was again a rural mail carrier.

The Bordeaux Family about 1898
Back row: Lillian, Eugene, Isabelle, Garett; 2nd row: Alfred, Oliver, Florence, Sophie, Mark; 3rd row: Marguerite, Paul (on Sophie's lap); Front: Chester, Ellen, Phillip

Harry was the last of Georgianna and George's children to marry. In 1924, at the age of 34, he married Amelia Peterson, the daughter of Erick Peterson and Lena Anderson. Amelia, age 35, was a nurse. It is easy to imagine that the handsome Norse fireman met the attractive Swedish nurse at the hospital.

Erick Peterson was born in Sweden on April 13, 1859, parents unknown. He emigrated about 1880-81. Lena, the daughter of August and Margarette Anderson, was born July 23, 1857, in Sweden. She emigrated in 1879-80. Erick and Lena married in about 1888 and settled in the Village of Morris, Stevens County, Minnesota. They had three children: Amelia (b. 1889); Mabel (b. 1891); and Henrietta (b. 1893). Lena had one known brother, Karl, who emigrated from Sweden in 1884.

Erick was a successful insurance agent in Morris, if having a servant in the home in 1900 is any evidence. In 1910 he was also the city marshall and Amelia was a public school teacher. Erick died April 23, 1918, in Morris, from liver cancer. Soon after Erick's death Lena sold the family home and moved with her three daughters to 4622 Abbott Avenue South in Minneapolis. Lena died at the home of Amelia and Harry on January 25, 1938, attributed to hardening of the arteries and inflammation of the kidneys.

After Harry and Amelia married they owned a home at 3710 Nicollet Avenue in Minneapolis where they lived for several years. When Harry was promoted to Assistant Fire Chief in 1947, his Civil Service Commission paperwork reflected that he was then living with Georgianna in her home at 3525 Holmes Avenue South, Minneapolis. Amelia died December 14, 1964, three days short of her birthday. Harry lived another seven years and died in December of 1948.

3525 Holmes Avenue is a few miles west of the historic Seven Corners. Seven Corners is located on the eastern edge of downtown Minneapolis on the west bank of the Mississippi River. Family lore tells us this was also the local headquarters of the Salvation Army and that Georgianna was a base drummer for the first Salvation Army band.

The first of Georgianna and George's grandchildren, Myrtle, the daughter of Arthur and Christine, married Harold "Hal" Arlandson in 1930. Hal (28) was an ice truck driver and Myrtle was a telephone operator for "N.W. Telephone.'" They had one child, Norman, born in 1939.

Harold and Myrtle later bought the home where Myrtle was raised at 2801 Pillsbury, Minneapolis.

Hal Arlandson was born to Swedish parents in Michigan in 1901. He was the eighth of nine children born to Charles and Maria Arlandson.

Charles (b. 1846) and Maria (b. 1861) were from the traditional province of Halland, Sweden, located on the southwest coast; they married in 1885. Their first son, Nels Edwin, was born in Halland April 25, 1886. Charles, a farmer, and Maria looked to have a better life for their family so Charles left Sweden the same year that Nels was born. Maria and Nels followed in 1887 and appear to have gone first to Wisconsin where daughter Hedwig E. "Hattie" was born October 1888. Before 1900 the family relocated to Holmes Township, Menominee County, Michigan. It is interesting to note that this county borders Delta County in the Upper Peninsula of Michigan. Holmes Township is 69 highway miles south and west of Maple Ridge, where Georgianna and George had their farm in 1900.

Having bought their own farm Charles and Maria had seven more children: George Wilford (1890-1963); Emil (1893); Ernst Fridalph "Fred" (1895-1976); Carl B (1897-1966); Oscar Lenard (1899-1955); Harold W (1901-1961); and Ellen M (1903).

Nels left the farm about 1910 and moved to Minneapolis where he married Inga Agnette Bye on December 9, 1911. They had two sons Clarence (1912-1969) and Lloyd (1914-1988). Nels was a teamster hauling coal in Minneapolis. Inga was born in Wisconsin in 1888, daughter of Isaac N. Bye (1863- Norway) and Anna Sophia (1862-Sweden).

In the decade of 1910-20 Nels was joined by his brother George who also was a teamster hauling coal.

The WWI draft registrations, 1917-1918, showed Nels and George in Minneapolis and Carl, Emil, Fred, and Oscar Lenard on the family farm in Michigan. Hal was too young to register. Charles Arlandson died during the decade of the 1920s which may be the reason why Carl, Oscar, and Hal left to join their older brothers in Minneapolis in the ice and coal delivery business. The 1921 Minneapolis City Directory records that Carl, George, Hal, and Oscar were living at 2936 Harriet St; Nels and Inga were living nearby at 2908 Harriet St. The brothers were all employed at the Lake Street Ice Company.

Hedwig "Hattie" Arlandson also lived in Minneapolis in 1921. Hattie worked as a finisher for Globe Laundry for several years. She moved (back) to Stephenson, Menominee County, Michigan sometime after 1940 where she lived until she died July 12, 1973. Hattie never married.

A review of additional *Minneapolis City Directories* (CD) up into the 1950s gives us a view of the changing family dynamics as well as the effect of modernization upon ice and coal companies. By 1925 Nels and George had formed the "Arlandson Bros Ice & Coal Co," located at 2900 Bryant Avenue South. Carl was foreman; Harold was a driver; and Oscar was route foreman.

By 1929 Carl and Oscar were added as partners/owners as recorded in the CD. Emil and his mother "Mrs. Mary" Arlandson had joined the family in Minneapolis, leaving Fred in Michigan to care for the farm. Emil was a driver for the family business. Mary moved back to the farm at Daggett, Michigan, in 1929. Emil also returned to the farm in 1929-30.

Family businesses can often prove to be a challenge for coexistence. This may have been the case for the "Arlandson Bros Ice & Coal Co." By 1932 George was no longer shown as a partner and his occupation was recorded in the CD as "fuel and fill sta." By 1940 he was a bartender at a café. As Nels' two sons grew older they both were put to work in the business. Clarence was the bookkeeper and Lloyd was a helper.

At the same time the Arlandson brothers were building their business, the ultimate extinction of coal and ice businesses as then known was being foreshadowed by the evolution of the refrigerator and non-coal furnaces.

Goro at age 100

"In 1913, refrigerators for home and domestic use were invented by Fred W. Wolf of Fort Wayne, Indiana with models consisting of a unit that was mounted on top of an ice box...The first refrigerator to see widespread use was the General Electric "Monitor-Top" refrigerator introduced in 1927, so-called because of its resemblance to the gun turret on the ironclad warship USS Monitor of the 1860s...Separate freezers became common during the 1940s, the popular term at the time for the unit was a deep freeze. These devices, or appliances, did not go into mass production for use in the home until after World War II.'"

Coal furnaces were also becoming extinct for home use.

By 1948 only Nels was left in the business. The ice business was gone and only coal remained. Carl became a custodian for several Lutheran churches in the area. Hal became a foreman for Crown Iron Works (an outgrowth of WWII) and George became a sheet metal worker for Char-Gale. Others retired.

365

George married Lillian Hostager (1894). They had four children: Adeline Margery (1919); Selmer Wilbert (1922-23); Harriet (1925); and Ellen Rose (1927). George died January 8, 1971 in Burnsville, Minnesota. Lillian died June 3, 1963 in Minneapolis. Carl married Signe S. She emigrated from Sweden in 1924 and they married in 1927. They had no known children. Carl died May 3, 1966; Signe lived 23 more years and died 24 May 1989. Oscar Lenard married Clara Schmelz. They had one son Charles John (1927-1989). Oscar died December 5, 1955; Clara died January 2, 1981. The whereabouts of Clara and her son after 1930 is unknown. In 1940 Oscar was listed in the CD as living alone in Rural Minneapolis.

Georgianna passed away at home on June 15, 1950, just three months short of her 100th birthday."

Sources: The original article contained copious footnotes which extended the article by over 6 pages and were eliminated due to space considerations. Information was credited to the following sources: Digitalarkivet (arkivverket.no/Digitalarkivet); Norwegian Historical Data (rhd.uit.no); Ancestry.com; Familysearch.org; Norman Arlandson, great-grandson of Goro; Star-Tribune newspaper, Mpls MN; findagrave.com; Wikipedia.org. The original article, including footnotes, can be found in the Hadeland Lag's Limited Access Archive (http://www.hadelandlag.org/gen/genreq/marion.htm)

Alfred Torgerson

"A Veteran's Day Story" published November 2013   Form 1178   Ronald J. Butler

Anders Torgerson emigrated on March 15, 1889 on the *SS Rollo,* pictured below. His wife Eli and children emigrated in October 1889 with Ole, Torger, Martin and Anna, also on the *Rollo.*

The *SS Rollo* was one of the steamers used expressively for the passenger trade between Hull

SS Rollo

(England) and Christiania (Oslo). Its dimensions were: length, 260 ft.; breadth, 32 ft.; and depth, 19 ft; tonnage, by register, 1500 tons. It had five water-tight bulkheads and a long deck-house, covering the engines and boilers.

The record for March 12, 1889, shows that the *SS Rollo* sailed from Christiania (Oslo, Norway) to Hull with 290 emigrants. Its cargo was wood, 11,852 kilograms margarine, 44,000 kilograms of matches, 376,300 kilograms of wood pulp and 36,200 kilograms of paper, and more.

Back row: Anna Torgerson(1887-1958), Martin Torgerson(1884-1910), the author's grandfather, Ole Torgerson(1881-1969); Front Row: Andrew Torgerson (1857-1940) holding Emma Torgerson(1893-1980), Alfred Torgerson(1890-1918), Eli Navrude Torgerson(1854-1941)holding Einar Torgerson(1894-1970).

The family settled on a farm outside Soldier, Iowa, where Alfred Navrude Torgerson was born on the November 29, 1890. Alfred became an American farm boy with his six brothers and sisters. He attended school and was confirmed in his Lutheran congregation. Alfred is shown in the photo above as a young lad of eight.

After reaching manhood on the farm, Alfred enlisted in the army on the

367

14th of July in 1918 to serve in the war in Europe. After training for two months in Mooseheart, Illinois, he was transferred to Fort Andrews in Hull, Massachusetts where he would depart for France to fight at the war front.

On October 26, 1918, Alfred wrote in Norwegian to his parents and sent them these photos.

A rifle captured on the German ship Emden

He wrote,

"We did not drill today for it rained. I thought it best to send these photos home for I have no use for them here. I am well. I guess the flu won't get me.

Love,
Alfred"

However, Alfred was wrong. A few days later he became ill from the flu and was sent to the army hospital. Here the flu developed into pneumonia. Just 11 days later on November 5, 1918, Alfred died at the age of 27 years, 11 months and 12 days. Alfred's body was brought back to Soldier, Iowa, by railroad and was buried by his family on November 12, 1918. This was a day after the war had ended, November 11, 1918, now known as Veterans Day.

Ole Andreas, born July 3, 1881, and Karen "Sadie" Johannesdatter, born May 2, 1875, grandparents of the author, are pictured here on their wedding day in May 1903 in Soldier, Iowa. Sadie was born in Kragero, Telemark, Norway. Her parents, Johannes Johnsen and Karen Christensdatter, emigrated to America on the ship *SS Hero* with their children Sadie, Gertie and Anna in 1878 and settled in Harlan, Iowa, and later in Soldier.

Alfred's Grave
in Soldier Lutheran Church Cemetery

Ole and Sadie had the following children: Ella C. (Mrs. John Hartson), Elmer C., Allen Silas, Mabel L., Gladys Opal (Mrs. Charles Butler) and Kenneth. Their daughter Gladys is the mother of Ronald Butler.

Ole died in 1969 and Sadie died November 14, 1945. Both are buried in Soldier, Iowa.

Peder Jenson (Jackson) & Inger Gaardsrud

published February 2014   *Form 95*   *Helen Loing*

This photo of Renhart's family was taken in front of their farmhouse outside Argyle, Lafayette County, Wisconsin in 1893.
Left to right: Perry, Anne (mother), Clara, Mabel, Ever, Alvida, Maria, Renhart (father), Rose and Alvin.

The earliest of my relatives who came to this country were the Jacksons who came from Jevnaker, Hadeland, Norway to Wisconsin. In explaining why these Norwegian landowners left Norway, according to Elfie Jackson Carroll, "My great-grandfather was in the government of Norway, elected and representing the Hadeland District. He became disenchanted with the trends toward socialism in the government, and as time went on, he decided he could not live with this political trend so he packed up his wife and his three-year-old son, Lewis Joseph, and soon departed for Wisconsin where other relatives had settled, in particular, a very bright and prosperous relative and cousin, Rhenhart Jackson. At that time he was the owner of a large dairy herd and financially well off."

My great-great-grandparents, Peter Jenson Gaardsrud and Inger Marie, sailed from Norway

370

to New York on April 17, 1849, along with their two children: Jens, born February 14, 1842; and Reinhard, born May 25, 1846 on the sailing ship *Vesta* captained by Plade Stranger. The ship which carried 93 passengers arrived in New York on June 28, 1849; it took 56 days from Christiania (Oslo). Peter. born on Gaarsrud in Jevnaker, on Dec. 29, 1812, and his wife Inger Maria Nilsdatter, born on Gjermunde in Ringerike, had been married March 30, 1841 in the Jevnaker church.

Peter's wife Inger was his double cousin and the twin sister to Ole Hanson. This is according to Ole's daughter-in-law, Mrs. Alvin Hanson. The Jackson and Hanson families were interrelated in Norway and this common practice continued among their descendants in America. According to Mrs. Alvin Hanson, "Marrying relatives was very common since the Norwegians were surrounded by Irish and Cornish neighbors and a lot of Swiss people, and if they were different in their make-up or characteristics, it didn't matter about being related." Young people were strongly encouraged to marry within their own congregation. It would be no wonder if the common deafness in the Jackson/Hanson family were genetic in origin. Mabel Jackson of Blanchardville said. "It was said by many that all of their descendants were bright and good-looking."

The Jacksons were among the first immigrants to come to the Wiota settlement in southern Wisconsin. Peter and his family appear in the 1850 census in Argyle Township, Lafayette County. Since the railroad was completed to Chicago by 1848, it is assumed that they went by train that far and then took a wagon the rest of the way.

The following entry occurs in *Nordmaendene I Amerika* by Martin Ulvestad, 1907:

> Peder Jackson Gaardsrud from Hadeland 1846 — settler near Argyle, Lafayette County. Brother Anders 1845. Son Renhart Jackson farms the homestead. Grandson E.R. Jackson, `rasferer` of Blanchardville State Bank, Blanchardville Wisc. since 1900.

We find also in that book that in Lafayette County in the 1840s people received $.50 to $.75 per day for work, wheat was $.50 a bushel, settlers came through Chicago and there was "malaria fever" in the settlement.

When Per and Inger Marie Gaarsrud came to southern Wisconsin to settle, they established a big farm, part of which they sold and on which the Yellowstone Church was built. Mabel Jackson said, "The old Jackson house was a stone house and was torn down. Part of the rocks or stone was used to rebuild the steeple of the Adams Church." The last name was changed from Gaarsrud to Jackson during the Buchanan administration due to a clerical error in conveying land from the government.

In addition to their children Jens and Reinhard who came with them from Norway, Peder and Inger Marie had Hans (Henry) who was born in Lafayette County, Wisconsin on March 27, 1851.

The story goes, according to Mrs. Alvin Hanson, that Inger was quite a nag but that didn't bother her easy-going husband Per. She said, "When one of Inger 's sons was to get married (Reinhart, Henry or Jens) she threw his clothes out the window and said, `He has always been like an angel. Now he seems like a devil.' This is a trait they have had. The girl who marries into this family isn't good enough."

In 1868, Jens married Ingeborg (Emily) Torstensdatter from Brandbu and they had 10 children, only four of whom lived to adulthood. In 1870, Reinhard married Anne Iversdatter from Granseiet, and they, too, had 10 children, eight of whom became adults. Hans (Henry) married Inger Marie Olsdatter (Hanson) from Jevnaker, in 1873. They had 8 children, but only three lived to become adults, and of those three, only one, their son Peter Jackson, had any children.

The Jacksons were charter members of the Yellowstone congregation located near Argyle.

Henry and Inger 's son Peter was married to Mary Larson (Pentbakken) in 1898. Mary's father encouraged the marriage even though she was only 16 since she had been going with another fellow who had a drinking problem. Peter was a few years older and a friend of the family. He was a good farmer, hardworking and didn't drink or gamble. Mabel and Orville were born to them, but Mary left Peter, took the children and resettled near the Watruds in northern Wisconsin near Rice Lake. According to Peter Hanson, the uncle of Peter Jackson, "The reason that Mary later left Peter was that hypnotism was such a fad and he tried that and she became afraid of him." Peter Jackson became "stone-deaf' and for that reason he was asked to leave his job in a machine shop in Beloit, Wisconsin. He died

Peter Jackson and his father, Henry.

from a heart attack during a flash flood.

The following information was gleaned from a centennial booklet published by the Yellowstone Church, Argyle, Wisconsin, which celebrated its centennial in 1968:

In the 1840s the whole area around the church was called "Yellowstone." Dues for the church at that time were $.01 per bushel of grain harvested. Three acres were bought from Peder and Inger Marie Jenson on December 26, 1863 for $15. That is where the church now stands. The church was built first and the congregation was not formally organized until November 11, 1889 (recorded November 16, 1889). The first burial took place in April of 1865. The church was to be built of rock at a cost of $5,500. It is the same size today with the exception of an added tower and narthex and in later years, an educational unit and sacristy. Rocks were hauled in "stone boats" pulled by horses from several nearby quarries.

Another three acres of land was bought from Peter and Mary Jenson for $15 on June 4, 1870. In 1878 a bell weighing 500 pounds was bought for $50. Alvin Hanson said that his father, Ole Hanson, was the bell-ringer and that's how he became deaf. Officially he was the sexton and it was his duty to "ring the bell before services and all funerals, ring the bell three times after the last prayer, keep the church and lamps clean and clean the church yard twice a year."

In 1873 a subscription was taken up and several members pledged and paid $100 each. Among them were Peder Gjackson (note curious spelling), Andrew Jenson, Paul Larson, and Jens Gaardsrud, Peder's father.

The first *kvindeforening* (Ladies Aid) of the Yellowstone Church was organized in 1884, but because the territory around Yellowstone was so large, another Ladies Aid was organized in 1886. Among the charter members of this second group were Mrs. Martin Larson and Mrs. Carrie Watrud who was a sister to Inger Hanson Jackson, Henry's wife. In 1889 a central *kvindeforening* was organized and among the charter members of that group were Mrs. Jens Jackson Garsrue and Mrs. Ole Hanson Elvstoyen (Ershtua), Ole Hanson's second wife.

The church was incorporated on November 10, 1889. The signers were Renhart Jackson, Hans Jenson (Henry Jackson), Ole Hanson, Peter Larson and Lars Larson (Pentbakken). Mabel Jackson King always said that both sets of her grandparents, Martin and Caroline Larson and Henry and Inger Jackson, were charter members of the Yellowstone Church.

In 1891 a Pelonbet or Pelbon organ was bought and Miss Maria Jackson, Renhart's daughter, was the first organist. The second treasurer of the congregation was Reinhardt Gaardrud (Jackson) and Jens Jackson was secretary at one time. In 1896, Ever Jackson, Alvida Jackson and Rose Jackson were in the first choir.

In 1903 it was decided to divide the Wiota Parish into two parishes: the Wiota Jordan and Apple Grove, and the Yellowstone and Hollandale. Services were held at Apple Grove 14 Sundays a year, at Yellowstone 20 Sundays a year, and at Hollandale 16 Sundays a year.

Fifteen acres were bought from Mrs. Emily Jackson for $1,000 for the first Yellowstone parsonage. $56 was paid to William Jackson for stone for the cellar.

The congregation suffered from inner turmoil in 1931, partly because the minister wanted to live in Blanchardville. In November of that year, a church meeting was held and the parsonage was offered for sale. It had 15 acres of land and William Jackson bought it for $4,000. It was thought by some that he was just going to hold it until "the battle was over," but he actually wanted it because "it was a bargain." Henry Jackson left $1,000 to the church in his will for the upkeep of the church cemetery and grounds.

Ole Christian Hanson

previously unpublished   Form 741   *Helen Loing*

Ole Christian Hanson, was born on Greftegrevseiet in Jevnaker on January 6, 1820 to Hans Christiansen (born 1779 and died 5 Jan 1859 at Elgstøen) and Kari Pedersdtr. (born 1786 and died 23 May 1868 at Elgstøen).

Ole Christian was married twice. On October 14, 1848, in Jevnaker, he married his first wife, Mari Pedersdatter, who was born at Narverudeiet in Lunner on May 4, 1826. After having two children with her, Kari b. 1849, and Inger Marie b. 1853, she was chased and killed by a bull and died on June 30, 1859 in Jevnaker.

In Norway, Ole was a bondsman and a sheriff. He was a friend of Ole Bull, the great violinist, and he was a hunting guide for Baron Ludel. Alvin said that his father was allowed to carry a gun because he was a sheriff, but that he never needed to use it because he was called "the man with the steel hands" and could grab a man by the hip and toss him.

On June 9, 1864, Ole married his second wife, Petra Hansdatter, who was born March 8, 1847 at Vesterneiet in Lunner. She was only two years older than the oldest daughter from his first marriage. Their youngest son Alvin returned to Norway in 1928, and he told about meeting the man who rang the bell for the second wedding of Ole Hanson Elgstøen. He said, "I remember Ole married a girl the age of his own daughter." Ole and Petra had two children born on Elgstøen at Nordmarka in Jevnaker, before they emigrated to America: Peder, b. 1865 and Hans Martin, b. 1868.

A man named Jacob Lynne had been to America, learned to "talk American", then returned to Norway, and rounded up emigrants for the shipload that took Ole and his family to the "new country." Behind his back, the Hadelanders called him Jacob Lynne "Troll" or "devil."

It was on May 10, 1870 that Ole and his wife and four children sailed to America from Drammen aboard the "*Colonist.*" It took six weeks to cross the ocean. Each family had to do their own cooking. They came to a farm in Argyle Township, Lafayette County, Wisconsin in July, and they planted potatoes on the fifteenth of that month. Ole and Petra's daughter, Ingeborg "Emma", was born on the 28th. Ole and Petra had 6 more children after Emma was born: Lena, Ever, Herman, Christine, John and Alvin. Alvin, their youngest, was born in 1890 when his father was 70.

The land was covered with trees, and Ole who was nearly 50 years old had to clear it in order to plant crops. His son, Herman Hanson, often said, "It was a terrible mistake when my folks left Norway. This farm was a piece of land all covered with timber, and my dad was about 50 and had a white-collar job in Norway. My brother Peter was hired out at the age of 14, and the money was used to help pay for the land."

After Ole was established here, he got the job as the sexton of Yellowstone Church. For Christmas, he rang the bell continuously from 3:00 PM to 6:00 PM. For funerals, he rang or "tolled" for the grave-side service. Sometimes the congregants would go home without telling him, and he would continue to stand up in the belfry and ring. Mrs. Alvin Hanson said, "There was a tornado that struck the area in 1900. It rolled the house over with Ole and the stove in it. He lived for two years after that." Alvin said, "My father wasn't afraid of storms."

Ole Elgstøen Hanson died in 1902 in Lafayette County, Wisconsin, and his second wife, Petra Hansdatter Hanson, died there also in 1920. They are both buried in the Yellowstone Church Cemetery.

On April 28, 1873, Ole's oldest daughter, Kari, was married to Andreas Jensen Vaterud. The young couple had only one child, Joseph Olaus b. 1874, before Kari's husband, Andreas, was killed in a tornado. Kari supported herself by becoming an itinerant seam-stress, traveling from farm to farm, doing sewing for the settlers and having her little son in tow. Kari died in Barron County, Wisconsin, in 1925, and her son, Joseph Olaus ("Joe" Watrud) died in 1958, in Rice Lake, Wisconsin.

Inger was married in 1873, in Argyle, Wisconsin, to Henry (Hans) Jackson. They were charter members of the Yellowstone Church. The couple had eight children, only three of whom lived into adulthood:

- Peter Henry (1875 – 1937)
- Inger Maria (1883 – 1925)
- Mary (1885 - 1910)

The author's grandfather Peter married Mary Larson (Pentbakken), daughter of Martin and Caroline Larson. They had two children, Mabel and Orville. (Inger) Maria married Herman Monte, and they had two adopted children. Mary married Charles Gutzmer, and they adopted one child.

When she was old, Henry Jackson's wife, Inger, the daughter of Ole Hanson, stayed with her half-sister

The author's great-grandmother, Inger Maria with daughter Mary Jackson Gutzmer

Lena in Argyle for a while. Mrs. Alvin Hanson said, "We had them, Lena and Inger, for dinner in May, 1922. In July she went to the Wittenburg Nursing Home. In January of 1923 I was sitting and writing a letter to her when word came that she had passed away. I believe she had slipped and broken a hip.

Mrs. Alvin Hanson said, "In 1923 Petra Hanson, her daughter, Lena, and husband Osmund Pedersen and their son Ralph and another daughter, Emma Hanson Buss, the first American-born of Ole and Petra, went to Rice Lake to visit Kari Watrud, Petra's step-daughter and the half-sister of Lena and Emma. Kari lived in a house by herself and had to water the cows. She seemed thankful to God, but her visitors seemed to think that she had a difficult life. Kari's son Joseph, who was a cattle buyer, admitted he wasn't treating her right. I guess he got what little she had." She goes on to say, "The Hansons didn't obtain very much education. They scorned it. That's when I heard that Charlotte Watrud, daughter of Joe, was married to a professor, Fred Yoss. I heard there was a pair of twins, Carolyn and 'Buster,' — Adeline Watrud's children. Corn was served and one of the twins said 'I beat you this one' about eating corn on the cob. Christine Hanson Davis had read 'a child shouldn't eat corn until age 9.' Lena didn't dare let Ralph eat the berries in blackberry sauce even at age 11." Mrs. Alvin Hanson goes on to say, 'Emma's son Elmer, six months younger than I, was attending the University of Illinois when I came in 1921, and Peter Hanson would call him an 'educated fool'."

Ole and Petra's last child, Alvin, was still living when Ole, Helen, their little children Kari and Inger and their great-grandpa Robert Hall stopped to see him at Blue River, Wisconsin in 1974. It is amazing to think that Ole Hanson who was born on Jan. 6, 1820 had a son who was still living in 1974.

Lars Larsen & Elina Larsdatter

previously unpublished   Form 116   *Helen Loing*

My great-grandfather, Lars Larsen Hellandshagen, born on Velo in Jevnaker, on Jan. 17, 1815, and his wife Elina Larsdatter, born on Raknerud in Gran, in 1808, left Hadeland, Norway, in 1853 for Argyle, Wisconsin.

There were four children born in Norway who accompanied them:

- Lars, born January 4, 1838 on Gagnumseiet in Gran
- Gubjor (Jane), born September 16, 1844 on Helgelandseiet in Lunner
- Karen (Caroline), born January 25, 1849 on Helgelandseiet in Lunner
- Christian, born December 20, 1851 on Helgelandseiet in Lunner

After disembarking from the sailing ship, Lars and Elina probably took the train to Chicago. From there they may have gone by wagon to southern Wisconsin as many settlers did, or they may have taken the train further, for the train had reached the Mississippi River by 1854.

It's possible that they had another child born in America in 1853 who married someone by the name of McCall. If so, that would have been before Elina died that year in Wisconsin from cholera. The story goes that Elina contracted that disease while caring for neighbors during an epidemic. Mary Larson, daughter of Lars and Elina's son Martin Larson, corresponded with a first cousin named Lillie McCall.

Gubjor (Jane) and Karen (Caroline) were reportedly adopted by an English family in Iowa after their mother died. Another version states that Caroline and Jane were adopted by a family in Mineral Point, Wisconsin by the name of McCullough. Jane took to the people, but Caroline couldn't understand their English language, cried a lot, and was sent back to her father who shifted her around among friends and relatives. It is said that Caroline worked out as a nursemaid when she was only a young child at the age of nine. She told a granddaughter that she took care of little children until she was able to work and get married.

The story was passed down that their brother Lars left to become a sailor and was never heard from again, and another story goes that there was a brother who went out West and was never heard from again. That might have been Christian.

Gubjor (Jane) who was born in 1844, in Norway, married William McCauliff (McAuliff) in 1862. William was born in New York, and the couple became farmers in Plymouth County, Iowa. Their children were Laura b. 1864, William b. 1868, George b. 1871 and Leslie b. 1881. Jane died in 1912, in Tulare County, California, and William died in 1902, in Plymouth County, Iowa.

After Elina died, Lars married again, and when he and his second wife became old and "feeble-minded" they lived with Martin and Caroline on their farm. Lars died in Iowa County, Wisconsin on September 26, 1891. It is not known when Lars's second wife died.

Karen (Caroline) who was born in 1850, in Norway, married Martin Larson (Peintbakken) in May, 1867 after he returned from the Civil War. Their families had come to America on the same ship but the families had become separated in the new country. Martin and Caroline didn't meet again until they were adults. After they were married, they homesteaded on government land near Hollandale, Wisconsin, in Iowa County. Their first home was a log cabin. The cabin was located a little southwest from the large house that they later built on the homestead: a big, five-bedroom, white farmhouse. Their daughter Mary, born in 1882, was the first child born in it. The Larsons had their own smokehouse, and they butchered and smoked all of their own meat. Sausage and meatballs were made, placed in crocks, covered with lard and stored in a cool place. Bugs got into the flour, and it had to be sifted. The early settlers in that area also had to keep an eye out for poisonous snakes. Coffee was often made by roasting barley. Children and babies were taken along to community dances. Sometimes the beds were filled with little babies while the older folks danced. Mary Larson talked of dancing all night and coming home just as it was getting light, in time to do the chores. Even when she lived in Minneapolis in the 1950s, Mary said she was going trading when she was going to go grocery shopping. It was a carry-over from the days when the early settlers actually did trade milk, butter, cream and eggs for sugar, flour and other staples.

Mabel Jackson King, a granddaughter of Martin and Caroline, remembered hearing that one of her great-uncles was buried up on the hill, southeast of the big farm house, under a big shade tree. The grave was no longer marked in 1971 when she visited there. Even though he died before Mabel was born, she remembered that the grave was marked when she was a child. That great-uncle died in the wintertime, and they couldn't get to the town cemetery.

There is a story about when a tornado struck. Martin and Caroline had just come home from town. The tornado picked up the wagon and horses from one hill where the driveway is now and dropped them on the other hill to the south. Strangely enough, the horses were not killed and the Larsons just got to the cellar in time. Other pioneers were not so fortunate.

When their daughter Mary married Peter Jackson, a smaller house was built behind the big Larson home, and that's where Mary and Peter lived and their children Mabel and Orville were born. Once when they were living there Mary needed a gall bladder operation. At that time they didn't remove the gall bladder but just removed the gallstones that had formed. It had to have been in the first decade of the 20th century when Mary and Peter had not yet been divorced. The local doctor, Dr. MacDonald, was an alcoholic and didn't feel that he could do the operation by himself because his hands were unsteady, so he asked a doctor from Madison to come to assist him. The other doctor didn't arrive until after dark, so the operation was done on the dining room table by kerosene lamp. It's hard to believe that it was successful, but Mary lived until 1962.

Son John bought the farm when his father, Martin, retired, Around 1904 Martin and Caroline Larson built a retirement home on a hill on the edge of Hollandale. A "board-walk" was made all the way down the hill to town. An orchard was planted behind the house, and they had a cow, chickens, and a horse and buggy.

Caroline with her youngest daughter Clara

Unfortunately Martin didn't enjoy many years of retirement for he died in 1908. Caroline lived as a widow in Hollandale for many years, and her many grandchildren went often to visit her and to stay with her. Her youngest daughter Clara lived with her there until she was married.

When Caroline could no longer take care of herself, she went to live with her daughter, Emma Larson Sorum. The Glen Valley Cheese Factory was located at the bottom of the hill below Sorum's farm. When it was operating in the olden days, the milk had to be hauled twice a day for Swiss cheese. In the evening the farmers would gather there and take time out to visit. In the winter, the factory closed down when most of the cows "went dry." It would open again in the spring when the cows "freshened." The Glen Valley factory was a cooperative. All of the farmers owned stock, and they hired a Swiss cheese-maker. The creek that ran behind the factory had fresh spring water which was used in the process.

Caroline died in 1936, and she was buried in the Yellowstone Cemetery, Argyle, Lafayette County, Wisconsin.

Martin and Caroline were both charter members of the Yellowstone Church. Mary told of having to walk several miles to the Yellowstone Church to "read for the minister" in order to become confirmed. She was confirmed in Norwegian, as were her children Mabel and Orville. As a matter of fact, Mabel couldn't even speak English until the age of seven when she started "English" school. Mary Larson told her daughter, Mabel, about having to plow. She said that there was nothing but woods and rocks and that the ground "had to be broken" before it could be farmed. The soil was rich, farming was diversified, and there was never a total crop failure.

The Larsons prospered in America so that, when each of the Larson children who grew to adulthood were married, Martin gave them $1,000 plus livestock and other items.

They had nine children:

379

1) Samuel Christian, born March 12, 1868, died September 9, 1869
2) Emma Louise, born June, 1869, died April 8, 1935
3) Samuel Christian, born April 30, 1872, died 1956
4) Belle Maria, born August 1874, died August 28, 1941
5) Laura O., born 1876, died May 26, 1913
6) Carl Melvin, born October 1879, died July 1903
7) Maria (Mary Ann), born March 8, 1882, died June 6, 1962
8) John O., born June 1884, died 1943
9) Clara A., born August 1890, died November, 1966

Emma Larson with husband Chris Sorum and children Adeline and Oscar

Sam Larson with wife, Emma Hanson

Gubjor Larsdatter (Jane Lewis)

previously unpublished   *Form 116*   *Catherine Rossing*

1919 Wedding of William (III) McAuliff to Alma Nordenshuld

1)Bill McAuliff   2)George McAuliff   3)Leslie McAuliff   4)Katie Flynn McAuliff
5)Mary Ann McAuliff   6) Francis McAuliff   7) William Emmett McAuliff   8) Margaret Jane McAuliff
9) Nonie McAuliff   10) Edith McAuliff   11) Harry McAuliff

Gubjor Larsdatter or Jane Lewis (and on marriage license she gave name as Lewissen) was the oldest daughter of Lars Larsen and Elina Larsdatter. She was born in 1844 in Hadeland, Norway. Jane was 9 years old when the family immigrated to Wisconsin in 1853. The family had secured permission from their church to make this move. We haven't found the ship on which the family sailed to the New world. but from anecdotal sources know they landed in port of New York and most likely took a train to Chicago.

Lafayette County, Wisconsin is where the family first settled and where Elina died soon after making a new start in this far-away place. She had contracted cholera after she had taken care of a neighbor who had the disease. Since he was not able to take care of his family, Lars placed the girls (9 and 4) with an English family according to one story but no verification has been uncovered. There were two boys who evidently stayed with Lars. Not much is known about what happened to these two siblings.

When Jane grew older she worked in home situations to support herself just as sister Karen had done according to family reports and one census report which showed Jane living as a roomer and independent young woman.. Sometime in the 1860s we believe she moved to Green County, Wisconsin. Shortly after the end of the American Civil War, Jane Lewis married William McCauliff on July 3, 1866 according to Green County records. (William had returned from serving in Union Army). They settled near or with his family in Adams township, Green County. William's father and mother, Thomas and Mary McCauliff, had been able to purchase land in early 1850s with monies Thomas earned as a wheelwright on both the enhancement of the Erie Canal and in building the Michigan, Illinois Canal near Chicago. The couple had emigrated from County Cork, Ireland.

Jane and William had four children, 3 of whom were born in Green County, Wisconsin.
- Laura born 1867 (married Philip Hayden who died and then John Tolesma)
- William or Bill 1868 (Willie when he was young but known as Bill in later years)
- George Washington 1871 (common practice of naming for US presidents)
- Leslie was born in Plymouth County, Iowa in 1881.

Jane and William made a brave decision to go west and homestead in northwest Iowa in Plymouth County. The nearest town was Le Mars, the county seat. The US Homestead Act of 1862 made it possible for US Citizen or person eligible to become one to claim 160 acres of land in areas where land had been officially surveyed. One had to live on the land for 5 years, improving the land as it was farmed and then was able to secure a deed

The couple worked hard and prospered there and were well thought of by their neighbors.as per William's obituary. All the children were healthy and the 2 older boys helped on the farm. These 2 young men were married when William died in December of 1903. Leslie was attending Iowa State University Laura was still living at home but married later as did Leslie. The three oldest all had children but Leslie did not.

After William's 1903 death, his 160 acres were divided evenly among the 4 children each receiving a quarter section of land. And by that time, the second "C" had been dropped from McCauliff making the name McAuliff.

In several years, George moved his family, favorite animals, farming & household belongings (extraordinary railroad rates at this time encouraging farmers to relocate made this move economical) to California in 1908 and Bill went there also. Both settled in Tulare County in the San Joaquin Valley near Porterville and Visalia. In-law families of both sons also wound up living in this area.

Laura remained in Iowa for her lifetime. Leslie became a newspaper editor and publisher settling for a time in Porterville. Sometime later, he and George both died in San Francisco. Since Jane or Gubjor was a widow with a minimal income, she first lived with Bill in Iowa and then with Leslie in Porterville until financial reasons forced his move. She then became a member of her son George's family until she died in 1912. She is buried in Preston Cemetery in Plymouth County, IA.

Jane lived quite an adventurous life when you review the scope of what happened. She remained a loving, caring person through it all according to one of her granddaughters, Mary. And she gave that granddaughter the Norwegian butter cookies recipe that Mary made each Christmas for her own family.

Lars Kristoffersen and Berthe Olsdatter

previously unpublished   Form 116   *Helen Loing*

With thanks to Ole Gamme, George and Nila Krenos, and Linda Lee Larson for their help in putting together this family's story

Lars Kristoffersen, born on Haureiet in Jevnaker, December 15, 1815, and his wife Berthe Olsdatter, born on Broshaug in Hurdal, March 23, 1818, were married in Aker (Christiana) before 1842. It was there that their first three children were born. They moved back to Jevnaker in 1848 where they had two more children and then returned to Aker in 1851. It was there, in 1853, that they boarded a ship, sailed to America, and then went directly to Argyle, Lafayette County, Wisconsin. Soon after, they moved north to Iowa County where they homesteaded 280 acres that remained in the Larson family for over a century.

Children of Lars and Berthe: Martin, Carrie, Laura and Mary

There were five children born in Norway who accompanied them"

- Ole Christian, born November 19, 1842 in Aker
- Martin, born April 19, 1844 in Aker
- Gina, born June 12,1846 in Aker
- Larine (Laura), born May 26, 1849 on Gulleneiet in Jevnaker
- Karen Mathea (Carrie), born April 26, 1851 on Gulleneiet in Jevnaker

When they arrived in America, Ole Christian was 11, Martin 9, Gina 7, Larine 4 and Karen Mathea 2. Lars and Berthe also had three children born in America after they came from Norway. They were Julia, born in 1856, who married Embrick Julson, Carlen, born 1858 and

Bertha, born 1859. According to one family group record, Lars and Berthe had 12 children, six of whom died at childbirth. The others attained maturity.

It is thought that Lars Kristoffersen (Lewis Christopherson in the 1860 census) homesteaded in Waldwick (Hollandale), Iowa County, Wisconsin, and that, after the Civil War in which his oldest son died, he moved to Dell Rapids, Minnehaha County, Dakota Territory with his wife and all of their other children except for Martin. It is believed that, when Martin returned from the Civil War, he stayed behind, married Karen Larson and registered the deed for the farm in his name.

At the time of the Civil War, when Ole Christian their oldest was 19, he enlisted for three years in the army on August 14, 1862, at Argyle, Wisconsin, and served in the 33rd Wisconsin Volunteer Infantry Regiment, in Company H. He died of dysentery on November 9, 1863 in the regimental hospital at Natchez,

Martin enlisted for one year on February 18, 1865. He served in Company C, 50th Wisconsin Volunteer Infantry Regiment. After 15 months of continuous service, on May 21, 1866, the 50th Regiment left for home, and Martin was mustered out in Madison, Wisconsin June 12, 1866 with an honorable discharge

Years later, Clara Ingwell wrote, "This Martin Larson Pentbakken was a war veteran. I can still see him and Martin Larson Bilden sitting inside the altar rail at Yellowstone Church on Decoration Day as it was called then – Memorial Day now. They would march and command to each grave the wildflowers that we had picked the night before."

Martin and Caroline Larson family

In May of 1867, Martin married Karen (Caroline) Larsdatter from Helgelandseiet in Lunner who had come, with her family, on the same boat from Norway in 1853.

Soon after, they homesteaded on land near Hollandale. Martin spoke of walking 50 miles, on cow paths and trails, to Madison, the capital, in order to register the deed. He carried a hundred pound bag of flour on his back on the return trip. Their first lodging was in a log house on their homestead, and in 1881-82, a large frame house with 5 bedrooms was built, and their daughter, Mary, was the first of their children to be born in it.

The following children were born to Martin and Caroline:

- Samuel Christian (1868)
- Emma Louise (1869)
- Samuel Christian (1872)
- Belle Maria (1874)
- Laura O. (1876)
- Carl Melvin (1879)
- Maria (Mary Ann) (1882)
- John O. (1884)
- Clara (1890)

The Hanson-Cleary School was established in the neighborhood in 1891. A tax of $60 was levied that year to establish the school for four months in the winter and three months in the summer. Martin Larson was elected school clerk, and his son Sam furnished wood for the winter term for $8.00. It was called an English school because English was the language spoken, and for many of the new students, it was the first time they had spoken that language.

Lars Larson Christophersen and Berthe Osdatter did not stay in Wisconsin with their son Martin, but, along with their younger children, Gina, Larine, Karen Mathea, Julia, Carlen and Bertha, they moved on to settle in Dakota Territory, near Garretson and Dell Rapids, in Minnehaha County, South Dakota.

Nothing is known of what happened to their child, Gina ("Mathilda"), after the family moved to S. Dakota.

In 1876, Larine ("Laura") was married to Edward Rood who had been born in 1845 in Norway. Five of their seven children were born in Alden, Polk Co., Wisconsin: Gusta, Minnie, Charles, Emma, and Mary. The last two, John and Addie, were born in South Dakota. Larine died in June 1923, and Edward died Jan 1911, both in Sioux City, IA.

Karen Mathea died before 1860 in Iowa County, Wisconsin.

Julia married Embrick Julson who was born in 1851, in Wisconsin. He was living in Palisades, near Garretson, S. Dakota at the time. They had two children, and she died there while quite young, but there is no sign of Julia in the cemetery records in that area. Also, their two children, Evalina (Evelyn) Julson b. 1892, and John (Johnnie) Julson b.1893 do not appear in the 1900 South Dakota census. It is known that they were brought by their father, Embrick, to Wisconsin to be raised by Martin and Caroline Larson, their uncle and aunt. Evelyn married Albert Freng in 1909, and she died in 1966. John died in 1962 at Osseo, Wisconsin.

In 1903, in Lafayette County, Wisconsin, Embrick married a second time to Ella Walrack. They had David b. 1907, Earl b. 1911, Otis b. 1913, and Pearl b. 1915.

Nothing is known about Carlen and Bertha, children of Lars and Berthe, who were born in America.

Lars Christopherson died on September 9, 1884, and Berthe died in April 1893, both near Dell Rapids, Minnehaha County, SD.

Sam and Emma Larson, daughters Marie, Eva and Pearl

Mary Larson and second husband, Robert Hall

Belinda Larson Watrud, daughter of Martin and Caroline

Clara Larson Ast, daughter of Martin and Caroline, with her niece Evelyn Julson Freng, daughter of Martin's sister Julia Larson and her husband Albert Freng.

Ole and Randi (Pedersdtr) Gilbertson

published May 2014   *Form 386*   *Ruth Carlson*

Ole Gilbertson's Third Family c. 1899
Standing: Gust, Albert, Tilla, Clarence, Cornelius, Clara, Oscar and Andy.
Seated are Magnus, father Ole, Marie, mother Kjersti and Olaf.
Ruth Carlson's mother Marie is the youngest at age 7 and is seated between her parents.

    Ole Gilbertson was born 4 September 1827 on the Sorum farm, Gran parish, in Hadeland. His parents were Gulbrand and Mari (Ericsdatter) Oleson. He was 34 years old in 1861 when he emigrated with his wife Randi (Pedersdotter) and their three children, his father, sisters Elena (Saetra-Johnson) and Siri (Braaden) and their families. Their ocean voyage was particularly long, 11 weeks and 4 days. They landed in Quebec. Their baby had died but land had been sighted so Ole prevailed on the Captain, "Please let me bury my son on land." Permission was granted, "only if you will hold the child until we disembark." Per Gilbertson is buried somewhere in Quebec.

By the time of their arrival in Wisconsin, America was in the throes of the Civil War. They settled near Richland Center. Ole's first wife, Randi, died shortly after their arrival. After a few years, he married Pernille Harper, a Civil War widow. She died when their daughter, Janna, was only a year old. In April of 1865, Ole had gone to town and he'd asked why the store fronts were draped in black. It was then he found out that President Lincoln had been assassinated.

In 1872, Ole married a third time. Kjersti (Hoghaug) Monsdatter, born September 29, 1850, was also from Hadeland (Bjoneroa). She had immigrated two years before and was assisting in the homes of other immigrant families before coming to the Gilbertsons. She had worked a year for an Irish family where she was encouraged to speak English. Another year she worked for a German family, where she was introduced to a variety of vegetables, how to grow and enjoy eating them.

They loved their home and neighbors in Wisconsin where they had lived for 30 years; but, in 1891, the decision was made to move to the Red River Valley, to a farm northeast of Halstad, Minnesota. They came by train; the older boys rode in the cattle car to care for the livestock. They had to change trains in St. Paul. When they were ready to board again, the conductor asked Mrs. Gilbertson, "Did you count, do you have them all?"

Ole died in 1906 and Kjersti in 1915.

They were members of West Marsh River Lutheran Church, north of Halstad. The inscription (in Norwegian) on the family tombstone is 2 Corinthians 5:1, "We know that when these bodies of ours are taken down like tents and folded away, they will be replaced by resurrected bodies in heaven – God made, not handmade, and we'll never have to relocate our tents again."

Kari Aschim Enger

"The Story...Wedding Dress" published August 2014   Form 480   Kari-Mette Avtjern

Each time I write an article for the *Brua,* we look through our collections to see if there is something with a connection to America. This time my colleague Grethe Johnsrud mentioned a wedding dress. The dress is 100 years old next year. It was produced in New York and used by the bride Kari Aschim Enger in North Dakota. Kari immigrated from Hadeland in 1905.

Sadly the dress is in quite bad shape and needs to be preserved. But as you can see from the picture, there is no problem to imagine how beautiful it once was. It is made of ivory silk satin decorated with machine embroidered tulle lace and shiny sequins. In front there are attached silk ribbons and a draped belt. The dress was produced by B. Schneiber & Son in New York.

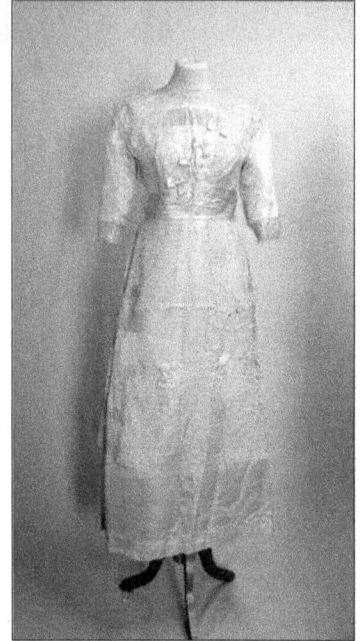

We had almost no records about the bride Kari, so I started to research. First I looked at *Kontaktforum Hadeland Amerika 's Immigration Forms.* And luckily I found information about both Kari and her family. Even more fantastic was the result of a search on ancestry.com. There I found the wedding picture from 1915. It was wonderful to actually see both Kari and the dress. Matthew D. Woods from Ypsilanti in Michigan sent me the picture.

So now we know that Kari Larsdatter Aschim immigrated from Hadeland to North Dakota in 1905. The summer of 1911 she returned to Norway to visit her family. She is registered as an unmarried housekeeper. Back in North Dakota she fell in love with Oliver F. Enger, a nine-years younger American with Norwegian parents. He proposed to her and when they married in 1915 she wore a beautiful ivory silk satin dress from New York. This dress was sent to Norway at some time and in 1989 it was given to the *Hadeland Folkemuseum* by a relative of Kari's sister Margrethe.

390

Oliver F. Enger and Kari Aschim Enger were farmers on the Lindaas farm in Traill County, North Dakota. In 1917 their only child Oliver Jr. was born. In 1921 Kari applied for a passport for Oliver Jr. She planned to bring him with her on a visit to Norway. They probably visited Hadeland the summer of 1921. Kari Aschim Enger died in 1943. She and her husband are buried in Mayville, Traill County, North Dakota.

Peder A. Andersen and His Siblings

published August 2014   *Form 3*   *George and Nila Krenos*

We have repeatedly used some simple Norwegian words where the information has been copied directly from Norwegian "kirke rekords" because we think it is very important for others to see how the original information is recorded in Norway. We are not trying to confuse anyone but feel strongly about sharing the wording of the original documents written more than two centuries ago. Since most persons do not know how to access these documents or don't want to, they still might have a great interest in seeing the original wording. Dates are listed in the Norwegian way: day-month-year.

The Anderson Siblings, taken about 1921
Front row: Thomas and Abraham. Back row: Peder A. and Kjersti (Andersdatter Grina)

Nila's grandfather Peter A. Andersen, *f. paa* (born on) the Nordbeye farm in Jevnaker *den* (the) 19-5-1844, died 13-1-1923 in Hudson, South Dakota. The location of this cotter's home is on the west side of the Randsfjorden. He was the fourth born of five siblings:

Kirsti Andersdatter, *f. paa* the Enger farm *i* (in) Jevnaker *den* 23-8-1836, died 1848 in Jevnaker; Thorer Andersen, *f. paa* Enger *i* Jevnaker *den* 16-3-1839, died 25-12-1928 in Hudson, South Dakota; Abraham Andersen, *f.* 27-9-1841 at a place which was a part of the large Buskerud *Gods* (estate) in Modum, Buskerud, died 10-8-1934 in Hudson, SD; Peder A. Andersen is noted above; and Kjersti Andersdatter *f. paa* Nordbeye *i* Jevnaker 4-1-1848, died 23-3-1925 in Lignite, North Dakota. The spelling of the name Andersen changed from "sen" to "son" in America.

Their parents were Anders Abrahamson Enger *f. paa* Enger *i* Jevnaker 8-5-1804, and Rønnaug Thoresdatter Sørumeie *f. paa* Sørum in *syvestre* (southwestern) Gran 13-8-1811, d. 22-3-1866 *paa* Sørumseiet *i syvestre* Gran.

Peder who was born on Nordbeye is profiled above. At *aar 13 udflyttede til* (the age of 13 he moved to) Gran *paa* 29-8-1857. He was confirmed in Gran on 24-5-1858. He must have been living on Enger when he left as his brother, Abraham Enger, also left Enger in 1853 to go to Gran. We know they went to Sørumeie (Daake Braatan farm) as we now find Abraham using the name Sørum when he was confirmed in 1856.

This must have been the last time the family was on Enger for we find eight years later in the 1865 census of the *gård* (farm) Daake Braaten, part of the Sørum farm, which was a part of the Sørum and Hagen parishes in Gran, "Anders Abramsen, *husmand med jord, aar 62, født i* (cotter with land, age 62, born in) Jevnaker; Rønnaug, *kone, aar 56, født i* (wife, age 56, born in) Gran; Peder Andersen, son, *aar 23, født i* Jevnaker; and Kjersti, *aar 19, født i* Jevnaker. None of these people are on the Sørum *gård* in the 1875 census but we know the whereabouts of each person.

Of special interest is a piece of information from Norway. It is Norwegian custom that *jord* (land) of the father was always passed to the eldest son. We find in Jevnaker *rekords* (records), "In 1843, owner Peder Abrahamsen Enger." Nila's great-grandfather, Anders Abrahamsen Enger, was the eldest, his brother Richard Abrahamsen Enger was the second born and Peder Abrahamsen Enger was the third-born son. We have never found where Anders was an owner so it appears his younger brother, Peder Abrahamsen Enger, must have purchased a part of the *gård* Enger. He would only hold this *jord* a short time as he left for America in 1850.

The year before Peder Andersen and his sister Kjersti left for America in 1867, their mother Rønnaug Thoresdatter, age 55, had passed away on 22-3-1866 and buried 8-4-1866. Notice the long time span from the date of death until the date of burial. Even in Norway today the burial of a person is not a "hurried" affair.

The ship *Dagne* embarked Christiania for Quebec, Canada and landed 7 June 1867. On board this vessel were 373 passengers and all but four were from Hadeland. It shows Anders Abrahamsen, farmer, Hadeland, age 64 (the age is correct but he does not use Enger); Peter Andersen, 36 (wrong by 6-8 years) and Kjersti, age 18 (correct age). We know that their mother Rønnaug had died just one year earlier, so Anders Abrahamsen Enger must have left with his children. This is supported by the ship's manifest, yet family information does not mention anything about him. Also wrong ages on a ship's manifest were not uncommon. Anders had a younger brother, Peder Abrahamsen Enger, who was living in Lafayette County, Wisconsin. Peder Abrahamsen Enger, age 41, his wife, Anna Marie Hansdatter *Glæsverket* (Glassworks), age 29, and two children ages 7 and 3 are listed in Jevnaker *udflyttede rekord "til Amerika i 1850"* (Emigration Record to America in 1850). They settled in the Argyle area of

Lafayette County, Wisconsin. In the book *Nordmændene i Amerika, deres historie og rekord* (*Norwegians in America, Their History and Record*), Martin Ulvestad, Minneapolis, MN 1907, page 600, states, *"Enger, Peder A. udb. fra Gran, Hadeland, 1845; var blandt de først norske settler i Lafayette Co. Wis."* ("Enger, Peder A. emigrated from Gran, Hadeland, 1845; was among the first Norwegian settlers in Lafayette County, Wisconsin.") While the year 1845 is incorrect (should be 1850), nonetheless it is interesting to note he was among the first Norwegians to settle in southwestern Wisconsin. They had left for America in June 1850 on the sailing vessel *Lyna* which landed in Quebec 4 September 1850. Peder Abrahamsen Enger's wife Anna Marie Hansdatter died 29-9-1862, age 41, and is buried in the Yellowstone Lutheran Church Cemetery, Lafayette County, Wisconsin. The Yellowstone Church, high on a hill, was not built until 1868 so many people of Norwegian heritage would walk the 10 or 12 miles across the rugged hills and through timber land to worship at East Wiota Lutheran Church. This limestone building, also on a hillside, is the oldest Norwegian Lutheran Church in the United States in continuous use.

When Peder, Kjersti and their father Anders Abrahamsen Enger arrived in America in 1867 they first went to the Argyle area of Lafayette County, Wisconsin. Anders' brother, Peder Abrahamsen Enger, and family were already living there, having immigrated in 1850. On 18 April 1874 Peder A. Andersen married Christine Eriksdatter (Olson Dalen) at Argyle, Wisconsin. The marriage license shows the spelling of their names as Peder Andersen and Christine Eriksdatter.

Thorer Anderson, the eldest of the Anderson children, had gone to Lafayette County, Wisconsin in 1873. In 1857 at the age of 18, he left Enger in Jevnaker and moved to Christiania where he made his home. On January 11, 1860 he entered the Norwegian army in the service *"Af hans Majestaet Konge Norges og Sveriges."* "Of His Majesty King of Norway and Sweden." He served five years, being discharged at Christiania on 11 April 1865. He then re-enlisted as a non-commissioned officer and remained in the army another six years. On 22-10-1866 in Christiania he married Inga Maria Gulbrandsdatter Opsahlager, born 1840, Eidsvold *prestegjeld* (parish), Akershus, Norway. In July 1873, the *SS St. Olaf* that had departed Bergen, Norway arrived at New York City and the manifest reads, "Thorer Anderson, age 34, farmer; Inger, age 33; Hjalmer Thoreson, age 3; and Ragna Thoresdatter, age 9 months." They had been taken on board at Bergen. They went to Lafayette County, Wisconsin, where his father, Anders Abrahamsen, brother Peter and uncle Peder Abrahamsen Enger lived.

In the spring of 1876 Peder Abrahamsen Enger and his six children, Anders Abrahamsen Enger; Peder Anderson, wife and year-old daughter; and Thorer Anderson, wife and three children left Wisconsin for the area of the Adrian Post Office, Nobles County, Minnesota. Peder's sister Kjersti had left the Argyle area earlier with other Norwegians and had gone to

Clayton County, Iowa where several groups of Norwegians had settled, many from Hadeland. She then left Iowa for Otter Tail County, Minnesota.

We have a copy of a promissory note dated 29 June 1876 executed in Nobles County, Minnesota, signed by Thorer, Peder and Abraham Anderson. We believe Abraham Anderson is their father, not their brother Abraham, who was in Monroe, Green County, Wisconsin, at this period in time. Where they were going to farm is unknown. It was either near the extreme southern border of Nobles County, Minnesota, adjacent to Lyons County, Iowa or just across the Iowa, Minnesota state line in Lyons County, Iowa. In either case the people would have gotten their mail at the Adrian, Minnesota Post Office.

In 1877 Thorer Anderson and his family settled in Sioux County, Iowa on school land in Section 16 called Settlers which later would become Garfield Township, the last of "96" townships in Sioux County to be occupied. The first school in the township was taught in a sod house owned by the Andersons on their land in Section 16. There were nine scholars. The nearest railroad and grain market was at LeMars, Iowa, which was 45 miles away. Thorer's land was close to the Sioux River which was the border between Iowa and the Dakota Territory. He had a great pair of oxen that were said to have tipped the scales at 4,000 pounds. They were so big that a man had to reach up to put his hand on them. These oxen were used to break the virgin prairie soil. When he sold this team he was paid $130 for them, which was considered a great sum in those days. An early Sioux County, Iowa history book states, "The first person to begin farming in Garfield Township was believed to be Thorer Anderson who settled in the year 1877 across the Big Sioux River from the village of Eden (now Hudson) in Dakota Territory. Anderson might be called Sioux County's first big cattle feeder, for he is reported to have had 1,500 cattle grazing between the Rock and Sioux Rivers in the wide-open spaces." Thorer and Marie were the parents of seven children.

Thomas Anderson died 25-12-1928 at his home in Hudson, SD. He was 89 years, 9 months old at the time of his death. His wife Marie died 3-5-1931, also at Hudson. Both are buried in Eden Cemetery, Hudson, South Dakota.

When Abraham Anderson came to this country as a young man in 1865 he worked awhile at Monroe, Wisconsin. Monroe in Green County is less than 15 miles from the Argyle area in Lafayette County. We know that he was attracted to the area as he had an uncle living there. He then went west and worked at Sioux City, Iowa for the government rip-rapping the shoreline of the Missouri River to keep it navigable for the steamboats that ran up the river from St. Louis to Sioux City and up river into Dakota Territory. About 1870 he homesteaded a farm about 2½ miles northeast of Beloit, Iowa where he and his wife lived until 1873 when he sold this place and bought a farm in Norway Township, Lincoln County, Dakota Territory which was seven miles southwest of Eden (now Hudson). They lived there until 1904 at which time he and his wife moved into Hudson. He had married Mari Nilsdatter, b. 5-4-1848 in Hadeland, Norway. They were the parents of eight children.

Abraham Anderson died 10-8-1934 in Hudson, SD. Marie died 4 July 1919 in Hudson, SD. Both are buried in Eden Cemetery, South Dakota.

Peter and Christine Anderson were farmers who lived in Garfield Township, Sioux County, Iowa. Their farm was just across the Big Sioux River from Eden (now Hudson, South Dakota), Dakota Territory. They farmed 160 acres in Section 17 and another 80 acres in Section 16 with their farm being between the Rock and Big Sioux Rivers. They were the parents of eight children, all being born in Sioux County, Iowa with the exception of the eldest who was born in the town of Moscow, Iowa County, Wisconsin. Christine Anderson died 26-4-1904 and Peter died 13-1-1923. Both of their deaths were in Hudson, SD, and both are buried in Eden Cemetery, Hudson, SD.

Kjersti Andersdatter (Anderson) married Hans Olson Grina, *f. paa Bjellagrinda i vest* (born on the Bjellagrinda farm in western) Gran 13-1-1847, was in Iowa about 1870-71. Hans Grina's father, Ole Hansen Grina, had immigrated in 1854 and settled in Clayton County, Iowa. He lived there 20 years and in 1871 moved to Otter Tail County, Minnesota. He was the father of 22 children from two marriages. Kjersti and Hans were living in Norwegian Grove Township, Otter Tail County, Minnesota in 1872. They were the parents of eight children.

In 1902 several of Kjersti's children went to Burke County, North Dakota to homestead land and Kjersti followed a few years later with the rest of the children. North Dakota land records in 1909 show that five of Kjersti's children each homesteaded 160 acres and she homesteaded 80 acres. She and five of her children thus owned 880 acres in Yale Township, Burke County, North Dakota between the years 1905 and 1909. Each of their quarter sections of land abutted one another. This location is three to four miles south of the village of Lignite, North Dakota and only about 10 miles south of the Saskatchewan, Canada border with North Dakota.

Hans Olsen Grina died 4-5-1898 in Norwegian Grove Township, Otter Tail County, MN and is buried at that location. Kjersti died 23-3-1925 in Lignite, ND and is buried in the old "Christ Norwegian Cemetery" which today is called First Lutheran Cemetery, Lignite, ND.

The very brief sketches on the above persons are a small portion of the vast amount of information on them from our files. Much of the information was taken from our unpublished book entitled *A Short History of our Norwegian Ancestors and their Land, the Research of the Bygdebøker, Kirkebøker and the Anderson Genealogy*. This book consists of more than 26 years of genealogy research with more than a thousand pages of recorded history on 7,500 ancestors, descendants and other relatives. This unpublished book is only in the hands of our children; however, a copy was given to the Hadeland Folk Museum in Gran, Norway several years ago as an aid to those persons in Norway seeking information about their relatives in America.

Olsen/Lia Family

published November 2014　　　*Form 384*　　　*submitted by Eunice Sankey*

The following story was written about Eunice Sankey's great-great-grandfather's family (Hans Lia/Lee) and specifically Hans 's sister, Olea. It was written by Olea's daughter Karen, years after the family came from Hadeland, Norway in 1868. It is transcribed exactly as written, with notes of explanation inserted where necessary.

Hans Lee, shortly after he was widowed for the second time about 1900. The children are Martha (born 1890), Herman (born 1892), and Ole (born 1887).

Olea Lia was born in Hadeland Norway in the year 1855. Her parents Ole and Martha Lia had a comfortable home. They owned some cattle, goats and sheep. During the summer she and a neighbor boy Per herded the livestock near mountains and lakes. They carried their lunch in a knapsack made of birch bark which was tied on their back. They often filled it with berries to take home. There were bears in the woods —they are very fond of blueberries. When they saw a blueberry bush that had been trampled they knew a bear had been near. They'd take the stock to a lake where they drove them in on a small island so were safe while they ate their lunch and rested. Other girls and boys were herding at some distance and they would all yodel to each other. Sometimes they found trees with gum on them. It was sort of sweet and very good. They also found honey combs. There was a fenced pasture where many horses were kept by a rich farmer. Per often followed the fence and picked horse hair that had been caught when the horses switched their tails. He would braid the hair into fish lines which he sold at a market. He'd pick gum and bring it to market too. He saved every cent and bought rolls of chewing tobacco. When the woodsmen were short of it he would sell them small cuts at a big profit. When he no longer herded he waited for a chance to go to the city. There he bought some merchandise which he peddled thru the

397

country. After a few years he had saved enough to buy a small store in a town. Many years later he was a rich merchant in Kristiania, the capital of Norway (now Oslo).

His sister Mari took his place herding with Olea. She was older than Olea and very mischievous. One time when they were near a big river they saw a large raft of logs which were locked together and stored until later when the woodsmen would open the locks and float them down the river to a saw mill. Mari managed to open a lock which sent logs roaring down the river. Olea never forgot how frightened she was.

Among the goats was a ram they feared. Mari fixed a dummy at the edge of a lake and hid in some bushes. When the billy goat saw it he backed up took a run at it and fell into the lake. He never bothered them after that. The girls had names for every one of the animals.

In 1867 Ole Lia's brother John emigrated to the U.S. as many of their neighbors had. John then wrote to his brother and told him about the free land in America. Ole sold his home and property, took his family to Kristiania (now Oslo) where he was to meet the sail ship *Refondo*. It had been delayed so they had to stay in the city for over a week. They had two boys: Hans, 10 years old, and Harald, 7. While there, Hans got lost one day. The police helped them find him.

When the ship finally came it took some time to get all their luggage aboard. They had to travel steerage class and bring enough food for the trip. They had chests of flat bread, dried meat, cheese, butter and some dried fruit. There was no way for them to cook and nothing to drink except water.

Martha had brought coffee and got the idea of sending Olea to the kitchen up on first class and ask the cook if he would let her put her little coffee pot on the stove. When she saw him she was scared. He was a Negro and she had never seen black people. She couldn't speak English but she pointed to the coffee pot, then to the stove. He was very kind. He made the coffee and then gave her a lot of cookies and sweets. She had her apron full of goodies.

They brought Ole's 90-year-old mother along. She was quite feeble and was bed-ridden through the journey and died 6 weeks after they landed.

It took 10 weeks to cross the ocean. (*NOTE: actual ship records indicate the journey was 7 weeks and 4 days*) With sails they had only the wind to depend on. One time they went back 19 miles and had to wait for the wind to change.

Some babies died and she said they saw little white coffins drift away. Olea did not get seasick like most of the passengers. Some days were stormy and the ship tossed a lot. They had to steer clear of huge icebergs. Once a big white bird alighted on a mast and stayed there for days.

It was a wonderful day when they saw land. The *Refondo* docked at the port near Quebec. From there they went by train to New York, then on to Wisconsin and to John's farm near Castle Rock. John and his wife Berte had a large log house and they let them stay with them until Ole acquired some land and built a log house. This land was almost covered with timber and brush. It meant a lot of hard work to clear enough in order to raise anything.

They had other relatives in that locality. Mrs. Brunstad was a cousin of Ole's. Their daughter, Bertha, was a nurse and took care of Mrs. Blaine, a woman who was ill. Sometime after Mrs. Blaine passed away Bertha married Mr. Blaine. They had a son who became governor of Wisconsin. John Blaine was governor in about 1930.

A cousin of Olea's owned a hotel in Hudson, Wis. Anders Haraldson was his name but he changed it to Andrew Harris so it would sound more American. His son was a lawyer.

Ole and Martha had two more children, Deata and Gulbran. They changed their names to Annie and Gilbert (they didn't like old Norwegian names).

Olea attended school for a couple of summers and learned English. At the age of fourteen she went out working in homes as a hired girl. She'd get up at about four o'clock and have a washing out by nine because there were no washing machines then. Clothes were scrubbed on a wash board. Top wages were $1.50 a week.

Olea sewed her dresses by hand and for her mother and sister too — no sewing machines. When she first came to Wisconsin her uncle John bought her a hoop skirt. She worked for families in La Crosse, Hudson, Boscobel and other places until she was 25 years old when she married Hans Roterud. His father lived on a large estate in Ringerike, Norway. His mother's folks had one of the best hotels in Norway and a summer resort. When royalty toured Norway they often stopped there. It was called Klekken. When Hans was of age to be taken for his military training, which was compulsory then, he did not want to be forced to go. At that time army life was very rough and hard on the soldiers. He and another young man left their homes and went to the U.S. on a small sailing ship. He had an aunt in Wisconsin, Karoline Fosholm. She lived alone except for servants, had a large farm and a horse ranch. She did a lot of riding — was a good horse woman and capable but a hard "boss." She treated him like a servant and made him work like them. He had a good education and wanted a job where he could make use of it and learn the English language.

He had an uncle, Thomas Sme, who lived on a small farm and was a neighbor of Ole Lia. He and his wife Joran had no children. They were happy to have Hans come and live with them. They were quite old and wanted him to take care of them. He could have had all their property. There was no more free land in Wisconsin but many went to Minnesota and Dakota where much was still to be had. That was before Dakota was divided into two states.

After he and Olea were married he went west to look for land. He filed a homestead on 160 acres, a quarter section of land. She stayed at home with her parents. Hans worked at different jobs. His folks did not approve of him avoiding military training and he had no help from them. The land was out on the barren prairie, far from water and woods. He, like other settlers, built a sod house and barn. It was almost 2 years before he could send for her. I (Karen) was 8 weeks old when she left Wisconsin and came to Dakota. This was 1882.

It was hard for Olea, my mother, to leave Wisconsin with its forests and a comfortable 2-story log house, and live in a sod house. Dad bought 3 oxen, Tom, Duke and Bill. With them and a walking plow he broke up 20 acres on which he sowed wheat. There was a threshing machine in the neighborhood. He hauled the grain to Garfield, a small town about 10 miles from there. This town was started because the railroad was to come through there but it came 10 miles farther east, so Garfield was moved there and named Park River. It was a 20-mile trip to town with oxen. Dad would start for town about 5 o'clock in the morning and not get home until late at night. He did not have a cow the first winter. Dad walked to neighbors and got milk and butter. The nearest was over a mile. He bought a cow and pig, also some chickens, the second year.

When I was 2¹/₂ yrs old my sister Olava was born. Jack Wooldridge, an English man, came

Olava Roterud is sitting in front of her shanty on her land claim in McWilliams County, ND. The other woman is probably her sister Karen. The family is not sure which one is Olava. She married Willie McElwain in 1912, so presumably this is before her marriage.

from Canada and rented some land a mile from our place. They had 10 children. The owner of the place had built a large house of lumber. As my sister and I grew older these English children became dear friends. The family was a happy one. They used to sing together. The older boys did a lot of hunting. One time they shot some wild geese and gave us one. They had horses, cattle and a lot of turkeys.

There was a river two miles from our place with heavy woods along the banks. Dad hauled wood from there in the fall to last for the winter. We had only a cook stove for heat. But the sod house was warm in winter and cool in summer. The walls were plastered with clay, then white washed with lime. It had a wooden roof. The window sills were deep and Mother had them full of plants.

When I was 5 years old we moved to a log house by the river, just for the winter. A bachelor named Jacob Froiland asked us to live in his house because he wanted to go back to Norway and bring the girl over whom he later married. She, Jacobina, was a beautiful girl. He was handsome too. He had been a sea captain. When they were married we had to move back onto the prairie. We had enjoyed living where there was woods. It was lovely in the spring with much in bloom. Dad took me along fishing. It was fun when I caught some. Mother worked hard to clean the house and make it livable.

I started school when I was 8 years old and had to walk 2 miles. The school house was near the river. We had school only during the summer. Some of the Wooldridge girls and boys walked with me. When the weather was hot we carried our shoes and went barefoot.

Our folks talked only Norwegian at home and we could talk nothing else until we learned some English from the Wooldridge family. The teacher laughed when I talked with a Norwegian accent. My dad started teaching me reading (Norwegian) when I was only 5 years old. When I had been in school one term I was way ahead of pupils my age and older. The teacher put me in the second reader the first summer. I already did long division and most of the multiplication tables. It took a long time to learn English though. Two years later my sister started school.

Our brother Oscar was born when I was 8 years old. At that time a baby boy was born to Mrs. Wooldridge, named Herby. When he was old enough to play, those two were pals. When Herby was 6 years old, he died with diphtheria. The doctor came too late. There was no telephone then and when anyone needed a doctor we had to drive to Park River and get one.

At times prairie fires raged over the country. When we'd see smoke in the distance dad got the oxen and plow ready. He'd make a fire break around the buildings. I remember when he and mother fought the fire with wet sacks to keep it from crossing the furrows. Many times some settlers were burned out and even lost their lives.

We had a well but the water was not fit for drinking It was hard alkali water. Dad hauled water from a neighbor. He used a large barrel on a stone boat.

The prairie was littered with buffalo bones. Farmers picked them by the wagon load and sold to a company for fertilizer. Rocks were plentiful and some built barns from them. Deer often came near. We heard coyotes howling at night. The winters were severe. Sometimes our home was entirely covered with snow. The door opened outward and Dad had to dig his way out. He opened a place on the roof of the barn and into the hay shed. The stock had to do without water so he put snow in the mangers. He had a rope from the house to the barn in case of a blizzard.

One young man, our neighbor's son, Hans Paulson, froze to death near his home. Later a family with three children also lost their lives coming home from town.

Men went hunting on skis. We had kerosene lamps for light. Someone gave my sister and me a doll head each. They were of white porcelain with hair painted black. Mother made bodies and clothes for them. That was all the toys we had. We had no books or paper. Later Dad subscribed to *Normanden,* a Norwegian paper, but there was no country post office and no mail carrier. The paper was weeks old when he'd get it in town.

Later our teacher gave us a bunch of old Sunday school papers. We read them over and over and kept them several years. A minister came and held services in another school house four miles from us. A girl taught Sunday school. We and the Wooldridge girls went there a few times. Mother walked there, too.

We went to a 4th of July celebration where there were woods. It was several miles from our place. A place had been cleared and a platform was built. They had boards laid on boxes for seats around the sides. Three men played fiddles and the young folks started dancing in the afternoon. We rode in the wagon box on a quilt spread over some hay. Ma and Pa sat on a spring seat across the top. That was a great day for us. Mother had sewed new dresses for us. There was a stand where they sold lemonade, oranges, peanuts and stick candy. I had never seen oranges. Fred Wooldridge bought an orange for me. We had never seen lemons either.

The merry-go-round was a pole in the middle with some seats. It was pulled by a horse. Some men had a beer keg in the brush and got quite drunk. We left early because it took hours to get home with the old oxen.

A year later Mother's brother, Henry, came from Wisconsin. He drove a team of horses with an old buggy all the way. He brought the horses for us. Grandpa Lia had raised them. Their names were Tom and Jack. I rode Jack often to get the cattle out on the prairie. One day in the fall I was lost in a snowstorm. He took me home. Those horses lived for many years.

Uncle Henry stayed with us through one winter, then went to Wadena MN where he filed on land. He never married and passed away in 1910. Uncle Hans married and lived on a farm near Erskine, Minnesota. Uncle Gilbert had finished high school and came to North Dakota and stayed with us several years while he taught school in 3 different districts. We left the old place and moved 15 miles farther west where Dad built a new home of lumber. It was wild country with cattle ranches, cowboys and even cattle rustlers. Three brothers, Bill, Nat and Frank Wills, were caught and put in prison. Another one, John Kaufenberg, stole two hogs from our neighbor. An expensive fur coat and a cow and sheep were stolen from another neighbor. He had a family and was not arrested — just fined.

Dad saw a man shot to death — a gambler named Thompson. That was when he first settled on the old place.

The country became quite peaceful when more settlers moved in.

Gudmund Haga and Eli Rÿa

previously unpublished   Form 452   *Barb (Helstedt) Schmitt*

My family was under the assumption that there were no relatives back in Hadeland, Norway. Even when my Dad's cousin from Minot, North Dakota (ND), traveled to Lunner in Hadeland in the 1970s to see the house that her great-grandfather, Gudmund Johnsen Haga, had built in about 1867, she was told that no one who lived there was a relative. They neglected to mention that the house next door was the *original* Haga farm, going back to the 1700s and where relatives still lived!

I became interested in my Norwegian side of the family in about 2002, and bought a map to see where family farms were located in Hadeland. I responded to an inquiry on "Rootsweb" about where to buy maps of Hadeland and mentioned my ancestor's names were Haga, Sherva, and Reah. Nothing happened for almost a year, but on Dec 26, 2003, I received an e-mail from an Ester Haga who had seen my map posting, and wrote "I am living on the family farm in Norway. I am your people." Holy cow!

Ester and I e-mailed back and forth and Ester shared that our shared ancestors were Joen Gulbrandsen Dæli (who was born Oct 25, 1802, in Norderhov parish, Buskerud, died Jan 22, 1848, in Lunner) and Anne Gudmundsdatter Haga (born Aug 31, 1816, on Haga in Lunner, died Apr 23, 1889, in Lunner). They married on Aug 27, 1839, and had four children:

1) Gulbrand Johnsen Haga, born Jan 13, 1841, on Haga, married Anne Maria Steffensdatter Olimb on Nov 9, 1865, in Jevnaker, died Dec 16, 1919, in Lunner. He was Ester's great-grandfather and he inherited the farm which was still in the family.

2) Gudmund Johnsen Haga, born Jan 22, 1843, on Haga, married Eli Halvorsdatter Rÿa on Sept 11, 1866, in Lunner. He was my great-great-grandfather. Even though Gudmund was the second son and thus would not normally inherit the family farm, his stepfather deeded almost half of the farm to him in 1867. Gudmund built a beautiful, large house which still stands today, right beside the original Haga homestead. Ester said he sold it to his older brother Gulbrand when Gudmund and his wife Eli emigrated to America in 1871 with three children. Gulbrand owned it for 7 years but it was too much for him to have both properties, so he sold it in 1878 to the Lindstad family. They are not relatives, but took the Haga name, and their descendants still live there today. Gudmund died June 4, 1914, and Eli died April 15, 1916, both in Northwood, ND.

3) Lars Johnsen Haga, born April 19, 1845, on Haga. He was the first in the family to emigrate to America, and did so as a bachelor in 1868. He probably started "America fever" which likely influenced Gudmund & Eli to emigrate in 1871. He married

Ingeborg Eriksdatter Grua in about 1873 and, after she died, married Anne Halvorsdatter in 1890. Lars died August 13, 1926, in Bergen, ND.

4) Johanne Mathea Johnsdatter Haga, born June 4, 1848, on Haga. She stayed in Norway and married Ole Halvorsen Rÿa (a brother of Gudmund's wife Eli). She died Jan 28, 1926, at Ryen in Lunner.

My husband Pete and I immediately decided we should go to Norway the next summer to meet my new relative, Ester. But behold, the Hadeland Lag's Brua came out and mentioned a planned trip to Hadeland and Norway in the summer of 2005. We thought we'd probably have access to more places and learn more with a Hadeland Lag tour group than by going on our own – that was the understatement of the year!

Pete and I landed in Oslo in June 2005 and Ester Haga was there to greet us! On the way from the airport to Haga, we stopped at Sherva, also in Lunner kommune, the area that my great-grandmother, Inga Amanda Sherva's (1883-1964) parents came from. It was a beautiful area

Gudmund and Eli Haga

with a gorgeous clear lake, and was now a recreation area in Hadeland. We drove on to the Haga farm and walked into the house where my great-great-grandfather Gudmund Johnsen Haga had been born. As we took a walk up the "old church road" to the Lunner church, Ester noted this was the path that our ancestors walked (before there were paved roads) from Haga to the church. We both got chills realizing we were walking in the footsteps of our ancestors! Ester had graciously invited us to stay 3 nights at Haga and, that first night, my heart absolutely raced as I laid in bed realizing I was sleeping in the very house that my great-great-grandfather and his ancestors had lived in!

Ester was very interested in family history and pulled out a box of old photos. She handed me a photo I'd never seen of my great-grandfather Carl Andreas Gudmundsen Haga (1871-1923) – definitely him with piercing blue Haga eyes. She had a photo I had never seen of Gudmund and Eli, as well as a photo of Gudmund's funeral in 1914 with the entire family gathered around him. Shockingly, on the back of the photo she listed a half-brother, Anders Bolgen, and a half- sister, Lise Marie Larsdatter Haga Hovland. I had not heard that there were half siblings, but I'd seen Anders Bolgen's tombstone every year on Memorial

404

Day in a rural Bergen, ND, cemetery and never realized he was a relative. (Nothing like having to go to Norway to learn about your relatives that lived in your home state)!

Ester had access to the Kontaktforum database and gave me lots of information about the Norwegian Haga family and relatives on my Rÿa and Sherva side of the family. Ester had been to Northwood, ND, where Gudmund and Eli Haga had homesteaded, and visited with Glenn Haga, Gudmund's grandson, who had lived on the Gudmund & Eli Haga farm. She also brought out a photo of Helen Haga Zablotney from Plaza, ND, who had visited Hadeland a couple of years before. I made notes to seek out these people when I got back to North Dakota to see if I could learn more about the Gudmund Haga family.

If I doubted that Ester and I were relatives, a lightning bolt struck when she brought out a book titled "Vor Martyr-Præsident William McKinley" that was sent to her great-grandfather Gulbrand from his brother, my great-great-grandfather, Gudmund. Inside it was inscribed "Reminder from Gudmund J. Haga to brother Gulbrand Haga." It was dated October 7, 1901. To think in 1901, 30 years after he immigrated to America, the two brothers were still in touch. And now 104 years later, the Norwegian and American descendants were having coffee together at Haga!

After our wonderful stay with Ester, we joined the Hadeland Lag tour. The week we spent in Hadeland was phenomenal! It was incredible to go inside the Lunner church where my ancestors were baptized, confirmed, married and buried, and see the actual baptismal font and the communion cup (that is still in use since 1739). Things are so new in the U.S.; the Lunner church dates back to the 1100's. The Randsfjord was beautiful. The Hadeland Glass Factory was a mecca of souvenirs from the homeland. We fell in love with Hadeland and particularly loved the pastoral scene outside our hotel window in Gran and taking walks in the countryside. On Saturday of the Hadeland Tour, the Kontaktforum had arranged transportation to our ancestral farms. Ester informed me the Rÿa's wanted us to visit. Ester's mother was from the Rÿa farm, so I wasn't quite sure whose house we were going to visit – her relative or mine (my great-great-grandmother Eli Halvorsdatter Rÿa, born July 10, 1844, on Rÿa, Lunner). We met Anne Marie Frøislie, her daughter Inger and her son, Per. We discovered what having coffee in Norway was like – the coffee table was laden with china and crystal and three desserts! What an occasion! Ester interpreted for us and told Anne Marie that Eli was my relative. Anne Marie shared that the cabinet behind me was brought to the house by Eli's mother, Kari Gulbrandsdatter Grua (born May 7, 1812), when she married Halvor Hansen Rÿa in 1831. Very cool!! Per studied the family history paperwork I had brought, and then he went upstairs and came down with a framed photograph of Eli's funeral in Northwood in 1916. I had brought the same picture and turned to it. At that moment, everyone realized we indeed were relatives! I was having coffee in the house that Eli was born in! We were also invited to the Else Marie

Gudmund and Eli Haga Family c. 1896
Front: Halvor, Oscar, Gudmund, Albert, Eli, Hans
Back: John, Anna, Gustav, Carl, and Kari

Paulsen Ryen farm and met Else's son, Gulbrand, and his family. This turned out to be the farm of Ole Halvorsen Rÿa (a brother of Eli) and Johanne Mathea Johnsdatter Haga (sister of Gudmund). We also saw their original house, now used as a stabbur.

Our time in Hadeland came to an end too quickly, but we couldn't have asked for a better visit. Plus, I had lots of family tree information to research when we got back to America.

Back in the U.S., with help from Geraldeen Haga Rude, Glenn Haga and Helen Haga Zablotney, I learned more about Gudmund & Eli. They prepared to emigrate to America in July 1871 with their three children, John, Halvor & Carl (my great-grandfather who was 3 months old). They first would have gone from Christiania (now Oslo) to Hull, England, a journey of about 2-4 days depending on the weather. They probably would have had to wait a few days, and then would have boarded a train from Hull to Liverpool, which was a half a day's journey. From there, they boarded the brand new steamship, *S. S. Sarmation*, on August 31st for its maiden voyage from Liverpool to Quebec – all this with a baby, 2 year old and 3 1/4 year old per the ship manifest. They arrived in Quebec on September 11, 1871. Then it was by boat and train from Quebec to Lansing, Iowa. They arrived in the United States on Sept 30, 1871, per Gudmund's Declaration of Intent to become a US citizen. They first resided at Lansing, Allamakee County, Iowa, in 1871 (a hotbed of fellow Hadelanders), then moved to Jackson County, Minnesota, in 1872. There they had three more children: Anna in 1873, Carrie in 1875 and Albert in 1877. They moved to Dakota Territory in 1879 and settled in Northwood. A note on page 166 from "Norwegians in North Dakota," which describes the settlement of Northwood Township, Grand Forks County, says that three families moved to

Northwood Township in 1877. A footnote then states "The next to arrive were Gudmund Haga, Lars Haga, Fredrick Olson, Ole and Jacob Brorby, Ole Carls, Hans and Halvor Hovland, and Fredrick and Christian Sherva."

Per Gudmund's grandson, Glenn Haga, the family had to live in a cave along the Goose River for four months before a house (which later became the granary) could be built for the family. Gudmund homesteaded 154.64 acres along the Goose River, 3 ½ miles west of Northwood, and built a large house to shelter his growing family with the additions of Gustav in 1879, Hans in 1881, Oscar in 1883 and Albert Tillius in 1886. He also had a timber claim of 148.14 acres. He later bought an additional 160 acres of land that was originally school land. Life on the prairie came with many hardships, and tragedy struck when Albert (born in 1877) drowned in the Goose River in 1883, along with his cousin, James, the son of Gudmund's brother Lars Haga. But the family was surrounded by relatives, friends and neighbors to support them in hard times. Eli's brother, Halvor Halvorsen Reah, also settled in Northwood and he had a son, Harry Reah. Gudmund's half-brother, Anders Bolgen, and half-sister, Lise Larsdatter Haga Hovland, also emigrated from Norway to Northwood.

Gudmund and Eli raised nine children to adulthood and watched their family expand and grow with marriages and grandchildren:

1) John Gudmundsen Haga, born Sept 23, 1866, on Haga, Lunner. Married January 24, 1900, in Grand Forks County, ND, to Julia Ellingson. They had 2 daughters. He died Aug 8, 1915, in Northwood, ND.

2) Halvor Gudmundsen Haga, born Dec 6, 1868, on Haga, Lunner. He never married. He died April 5, 1951, in Northwood, ND.

3) Carl Andreas Gudmundsen Haga, born May 14, 1871, on Haga, Lunner. Married Dec 4, 1901, in Grand Forks County, ND, to Amanda Inga Sherva. They had 8 children. He died Dec 1, 1923, in Bergen, McHenry Co, ND.

4) Anna Louise Haga, born Mar 10, 1873, in Heron Lake, Jackson Co, MN. She never married. She died May 29, 1957, in Grand Forks County, ND.

5) Carrie Gudmundsdatter Haga, born Mar 1, 1875, in Jackson Co, MN. Married Andrew S. Ellingson in October 1896 at Northwood, ND. They had 5 children. She died Nov 23, 1947, in Glendale, CA.

6) Albert Gudmundsen Haga, born Sept 17, 1877, in Jackson Co, MN. He drowned July 11, 1883, at Northwood, ND.

7) Gustav Gudmundsen Haga, born Sept 20, 1879, in Northwood, ND. Married Selma Kristina Mandt on Jan 18, 1911, in Grand Forks Co, ND. He died July 10, 1954, in Northwood, ND.

8) Hans Gudmundsen Haga, born June 5, 1881, in Northwood, ND. Married Gustina Iverson on Dec 9, 1908, in Grand Forks, ND. They had 5 children. He died Sept 9, 1956, in Plaza, Mountrail Co, ND.

9) Oscar Gudmundsen Haga, born May 6, 1883, in Northwood, ND. Married Thora Olava Mandt on Jan 28, 1914, in Northwood, ND. They had 2 children. He died Oct 24, 1937, in Northwood, ND.

10) Albert Tillius Haga, born Apr 26, 1886, in Northwood, ND. Married Tilda Bently on Jan 17, 1914, in Grand Forks County, ND. They had one daughter. He died July 27, 1957, in Northwood, ND.

Gudmund Johnsen Haga became a citizen of the United States on March 9, 1886. Gudmund, his wife Eli and Gudmund's brother Lars went back to Norway in May 1898 for a three month visit. It must have been an incredible reunion of relatives and friends with a chance to see their homeland of Norway again, so different from the flat prairie of North Dakota.

Gudmund and Eli "retired" to the town of Northwood in 1904 where they lived until Gudmund's death in 1914 and Eli's death in 1916. Both Gudmund and Eli's obituaries stressed their hard work, faith in God and the high esteem of which they were held in the community. Their farm, which had become large and prosperous, was taken over by their son Oscar, and later Oscar's son, Glenn Haga. Glenn and his wife Ardith Thue farmed the Haga homestead until 1960, when they moved to Northwood city. Glenn died in 2007.

In the photo of Gudmund's funeral in 1914, first shown to me by Ester Haga in Norway, a half-brother, Anders Bolgen, and a half- sister, Lise Marie Larsdatter Haga Hovland were pictured. I had to do some research to figure out how they fit into the family. It turned out half-sister Lise Larsdatter Haga Hovland shared the same mother as Gudmund. When Anne Gudmundsdatter Haga's first husband, Joen Gulbrandsen Dæli, died on January 22, 1848, she was left with 3 young sons and a child on the way – daughter Johanne Mathea who was born June 4, 1848. Anne married Lars Larsen Olimb on November 26, 1851, in Lunner. Lars was born Jan 8, 1822, in Lunner. Lars and Anne had 4 children: two died in childhood and two survived to adulthood and emigrated to America:

1) Hans Larson, born Apr 19, 1852, on Haga, Lunner. He emigrated with his dad Lars, in 1869. He settled in Waseca, Minnesota (MN), married Martha Christine Jameson. They had 9 children. Hans died August 17, 1927, in Iosco Township, Waseca County, MN.

2) Lise Maria Larsdatter Haga, born May 29, 1959, on Haga, Lunner. She emigrated around 1881 and married Halvor Steffensen Hovland who was born May 3, 1858, in Lunner. They had 10 children. She died Nov 4, 1938, in Grand Forks County, ND.

I finally figured out that half-brother Anders Bolgen shared the same father as Gudmund. Anders Johnsen Bolgen was the only child of Joen Gulbrandsen Dæli and his first wife, Anne Andersdatter Loe, and was born Feb 6, 1836, on Kjorven in Lunner. Anders' mother died when he was two, and he evidently went back to Norderhov parish, Buskerud, to live with his mother's relatives. Once grown, Anders married Oline Trulsdatter in Norderhov in 1855 and had 10 children. After his wife Oline died, Anders emigrated to Northwood, ND in 1894 and his youngest son, Peter Bolgen, came in 1899.

About June 1899, several of the Haga men living in Northwood, ND, headed west to Bergen, McHenry County, ND and filed for land under the Homestead Act – a group of 11 with 2 uncles/fathers and 9 nephews/sons. Lars Johnsen Haga (1845-1926, son of Joen Dæli and Anne Gudmundsdatter Haga) and his half-brother, Anders Johnsen Bolgen (1836-1920, son of Joen Dæli and Anne Loe), headed the group. The nephews were:

1) John Gulbrandsen Haga (1866-1935, who married Helga Strand) and
2) Stephen Gulbrandsen Haga (1873-1912, who married Gunda Ryen), both sons of Gulbrand Haga and Anne Maria Steffensdatter Olimb; and
3) Halvor Gudmundsen Haga (1868-1951),
4) Carl Gudmundsen Haga (1871-1923, who married Amanda Sherva), and
5) Hans Gudmundsen Haga (1881-1956 who married Gustina Iverson and later moved to Plaza, ND), all sons of Gudmund Haga and Eli Rÿa.

The sons were:

6) Edward Haga (1875-1965 who married Helga Hammer) and
7) Albert Haga (1877-1938, who married Rose Brørby and later moved to Vulcan, Alberta, Canada), both sons of Lars Haga and Ingeborg Eriksdatter Grua;
8) Joseph Haga (1891-1974 who later moved to Vulcan, Alberta, Canada); son of Lars Haga and Anne Halvorsdatter; and
9) Peter Bolgen (1877-1961 who married Clara Hovland), son of Anders Bolgen and Oline Trulsdatter.

My great-grandfather Carl (born May 14, 1871, in Lunner and immigrated in 1871) was in the uncle/nephews group that settled in Bergen, ND. On Dec 4, 1901, in Grand Forks, ND, Carl married Inga Amanda Sherva, born Mar 4, 1883, in Northwood, ND. She was the daughter of Anders Andersen (born May 24, 1836, on Gulden, Gran) and Ingeborg Christiansdatter Skjerva (born Aug 6, 1840, on Sherva, Lunner). They settled in Lake Hester Township, rural Bergen, ND. Their first home was a tar paper shanty. A larger two room house was built later, and when twins arrived in 1911, a large six bedroom house was built. Carl and Amanda had 8 children, all born in rural Bergen, ND:

1) Inez Haga, born July 18, 1902, married June 9, 1923 to Walter Helstedt. They had 4 children. She died May 3, 1978, in Minot, ND.

2) Gordon Haga (known as "Gook"), born Mar 12, 1904, died Oct 6, 1980, in Minot, ND. He never married.

3) Luella Haga, my grandmother, born Sept 22, 1905; married Nov 30, 1929, to Rudolph Helstedt. They had 3 children. She died Jan 14, 1982, in Minot, ND.

4) Arthur Haga, Sr., born Dec 7, 1907, married Gladys Johnson on June 6, 1934. They had 3 children. He died Feb 9, 1987, in Minot, ND.

5) Edna Haga, twin, born Jun 5, 1911, married Merrell Bergrude on June 14, 1941. They had 3 children. She died Feb 20, 1997, in Minot, ND.

6) Esther Haga, twin, born Jun 5, 1911, first married Selmer Braaten on June 30, 1931. They had 5 children. After Selmer died in 1970, Esther married Raymond Bell in 1982. She died May 16, 1997, in Velva, ND.

7) Oscar Haga, born Aug 3, 1912, married Delores "Dutchey" Hohman on July 30, 1943. They had 2 children. He died Feb 12, 2000, in Billings, MT.

8) Carl Arnold Haga, born March 4, 1915, died March 12, 1915, in Bergen, ND.

My grandmother, Luella Haga, with 100% Norwegian blood, married a Swede -- Rudolph Helstedt. This was as bad as a Lutheran marrying a Catholic in those days! (In fact, the Bergen city cemetery has a dividing line and Norwegians are buried on the north side and Swedes are buried on the south side). Lue and Rudy had 3 children:

1) Robert Helstedt who married Ardella Weber. They had 2 daughters, one being me.

2) Audrey Helstedt who first married Vern Eslinger and had 4 children. She then married Art Hultman and they had 1 son.

3) Bonnie Helstedt who married Curt Feist. They had 4 children.

My grandmother Lue, was a fun, lively, wonderful lady who loved entertaining her children and grandchildren. After Rudy died in 1962, she sold the Helstedt farm and moved into the town of Bergen and later moved to Velva. She was active in the Lutheran church and the Senior Citizens group there. Grandma Lue was a wonderful cook. Christmas at her house always had lutefisk and lefse on the menu (a tradition carried on even today) and goodies like strøll, fattigmann and sandbakkels. The coffee pot was always on and friends and family were always welcome to visit – a true Haga trait.

One final Haga note – and again it took a Norwegian to connect the dots. Ole Gamme from Hadeland received an inquiry from a Sandra Haga Scott in Canada, inquiring about Hagas from Hadeland. He suggested she get in touch with me as he thought we were related – and there was the missing link of the Hagas that went up to Canada and settled in Vulcan, Alberta!

Sandra's grandfather was Albert Haga, born Apr 13, 1877, the son of Lars Haga (born 1845) and Ingeborg Eriksdatter Grua (born Jan 26, 1847, in Lunner). Albert had been with the group of 11 Hagas that headed west to Bergen, ND but he found Canada more enticing. Albert married Rose Brørby on June 23, 1914 in Northwood, ND and brought Rose up to Canada. Rose was born Oct 11, 1889, in Northwood the daughter of Ole Pedersen Brørby and Birthe Olsdatter Carls. Rose found Alberta to be desolate but she was a true woman of the frontier and raised 9 children on the prairie during the Depression and Dirty 30's. Albert died Mar 7, 1938, in Vauxhall, Alberta. Rose died June 16, 1963, in Vulcan, Alberta. Their family remains in Canada.

In discovering my Norwegian roots, I cannot describe the joy of having met long-lost relatives, not only in Norway, but also in the United States and Canada. It has been wonderful to discover these relatives and make new friends. I think of how pleased my grandmother Lue would be to know that the Haga family now is in contact with each other "across the pond" via the internet and enjoying trips to visit one another. Being able to visit the land of my ancestors in 2005 and 2010, and learning more about their traditions and where they came from, has been such a rewarding experience. This journey would have been much more difficult if not impossible for me without all the help from members of the Hadeland Lag, including the great articles they publish in the Brua. I have been able to fit many of the Haga family puzzle pieces together, but it seems the picture keeps expanding and there's always more to learn. I have discovered that my ancestors Gudmund Johnsen Haga and Eli Halvordatter Rÿa were true immigrants and pioneers who endured incredible hardships as they settled the land, but they worked hard and found great prosperity in the United States. I am proud to be one of their many descendants.

Jens Ingwell Finnerud

previously unpublished   Form 87,88   *Carol Pendretti*

Ingvold and Karen Finnerud are the author's great-great-great-grandparents and their son Jens and his wife Mari are her maternal great-great-grandparents.

Lunner Church, part of Jevnaker parish until 1906 Johan Jorgen Lange was sogneprest (parish pastor) from 1792-1814. Ole Rein served from 1768-1792, and Ludvig Lunholtz from 1832-1834.

Ingvold Olson Finnerud was baptized in Lunner Church in 1803. His father, Ole Engvalsen Mellerud had been baptized in Jevnaker Church in 1774. Ingvold and his wife Karen Jensdatter's son Jens was baptized in Lunner Church in 1834.

On April 14, 1853 the Ingvold Olson Finnerud family received permission to leave for America. The church records lists Ingvold and Karen and their three sons and two daughters. Jens was listed separately. The family traveled to America on the sailing ship *Good Hope*. The Finneruds stayed with the Ingvold Olson Midlilien family in Argyle, Lafayette County, Wisconsin. Mrs. Midlilien was Ingvold Olson Finnerud's sister.

Ingvold Olson Finnerud (1794-1865)

Ingvold and his wife Karen soon bought some farmland in the Township of Blanchard where they built a log house. Later a little white house was built, which became the cook shanty when Jens, who took over the farm and built the current house. Ingvold and Karen lived with Jens and his family until their deaths.

When the Finnerud family came to Wisconsin, the railroad went as far as the east side of Wiota. Jens went to Janesville and worked at harvest time for 50 cents a day. He worked as a wood chopper and farmhand. He chopped railroad ties and did other work on the Mineral Point railroad. The contractor supposedly failed and cheated the men out of their summer wages. Jens received a large grindstone for his work. He began farming with his father and bought land for $1.25 an acre. He increased his land holdings to 440 acres, paying for it by cutting down trees and selling barrel staves.

Jens married Mari Erichsdatter Gjesleberg in 1856. They had thirteen children, including Gusta Avilde who married Martin Paulson Toen. Jens was a Town of Blanchard pioneer and a

Jens Finnerud Family
Jens is seated in the middle. His daughter Gusta is on the far right.

public-spirited man. He was instrumental in getting the Yellowstone Church built. He held the positions of town chairman, town clerk and supervisor and helped get school district #7 – Blanchard and Moscow – organized. He was an earnest reader of *The Skandinavan* and was interested in politics. Jens lived to see his county grow from a wilderness to one of the best dairy areas of Wisconsin, with the price of land increasing from $1.25 to $200.00 an acre.

In his religion Jens was rather moderate. The Finnerud's old log house was the site of religious meetings in the neighborhood. At one time nine children were baptized there after Jens walked to Wiota to get the pastor, Johan Munch.

In the 1870 Wisconsin Agriculture Census, James Ingwell is listed as owner of 80 acres of improved land, 5 acres of woods and 120 acres of unimproved land in the Township of Blanchard, Lafayette County. He owned 3 horses, 4 milk cows, 11 other cattle, 15 sheep and 17 swine. He produced 500 bushels of wheat, 300 of corn, 30 of barley, 150 of potatoes, 200 pounds of butter and 20 tons of hay.

Gusta Finnerud Toen

Jens lost one eye while hammering a plow share and lost the sight in his other eye two years before his death in 1920.

Mari's family

Jens' wife Mari was the daughter of Erich Erickson Gjesleberg and Else Pedersdatter Biorge. Mari's parents were married in November of 1832 in Gran. Erich's father was Erich Hanson and his mother was Aaste Torgersdatter. Else's father was Peder Guttormson.

Erich Erickson and his four daughters: Annie, Carrie, Marie and Caroline came to America in 1853. They made the voyage on the ship *Good Hope* that also carried the Finneruds. Else's name did not appear on the passenger list, so it is assumed she died before her husband

Erich Gjesleberg

and daughters left Norway. Carrie died at an early age. Anne married Jens' brother Andreas Ingwell, and Caroline married Embret Harestua Thompson.

We were not able to locate a farm in the Gran, Hadeland area named Gjesleberg, nor do we know exactly where the Gjesleberg family lived when they came to the Blanchardville area.

Gulbrand and Marte Vinger

previously unpublished　　　　*Forms 422, 224*　　　　*Carol Pendretti*
Gulbrand and Marte Vinger are the author's paternal great-great-grandparents

Gulbrand Vinger Family
First row: Gulbrand, Gustave, Mathilda, and Marte
2nd row-Caroline, Brede, Christian, Theodore, and Edward
Top row-Henry, Lauris, and Oliver

Gulbrand Oleson Roisum and Kjerstie Gulbrandsdatter Roisum were married in 1821 in Gran Parish. The family lived on the Roisum farm in Brandbu. (This farm is now used as a school for epileptics and is called *Roisumtunet.*)

Gulbrand died in 1838. Kjerstie and their children Ole, 11; Gulbrand, 8; Mari (Enga), 18; Kari, 16; and Berthe, 15, went to live at the Vinger farm.

On September 1, 1850 Gulbrand Gulbrandson Roisum Vinger arrived in New York harbor on the *Vesta*, a brigantine, with Captain Frederich J. Schroater at the helm. The ship's register lists him as Gulbrand Gulbrandson, age 20. The ship had 100 passengers, many from Hadeland, and took 10 weeks to cross the Atlantic Ocean. From New York Gulbrand travelled up the Hudson to Albany on a steamboat. He transferred to a canal boat drawn by horses on the Erie Canal to Buffalo. He crossed the Great Lakes by steamboat, arriving in Milwaukee on September 14. Gulbrand continued on by oxen, first to the Norwegian settlement of Koshkonong, then on to Muskego. The Hans Framstad family continued to live in Muskego for several years, but Gulbrand, Ole Phillipson, Molen, Halvor and Anders Sandbakken

416

soon started for the Hadeland settlement in Yellowstone by horse and buggy. Gulbrand stayed at the home of Martha Rosta (Mina Olson Vinger's great-grandmother) there. Gulbrand had two sisters and a brother who also came to America later and a sister who stayed in Norway.

At this time Green County was being settled and he bought some land for $.75 per acre and some partially improved land for $1.25 per acre, for a total of 200 acres. He then started to clear the land. He built a log cabin and the first summer after it was ready, four families and two bachelors moved into it also! It was difficult to get employment and wages were so small that it was impossible to save any cash.

Gulbrand tried the shoemaking trade and worked on a farm chopping wood in Mineral Point. He went north to the lumber camps of Wisconsin Rapids. Later he and some of his friends went to work in a pinery in the Stevens Point area. He also worked in Portage with a shoemaker. He worked in the sawmills in northern Wisconsin and then was offered $80 to float timber down the Wisconsin River and on the Mississippi River to St. Louis, Missouri. After this trip, he went back to Green County to his farm in York Township, and began to clear and cultivate the land with oxen.

In November 1854 Gulbrand married Marte Carlson, who had come from Norway with her siblings and parents in 1852. I have found several stories about Gulbrand and Marte's wedding. One says that they went to the Justice of the Peace at Argyle with another couple who were getting married and they also decided to be married. Another story says that they were married in a triple ceremony by her father, Lars Carlson with Erik Myren and Maren Linstad, and Hans Stomne (Emberson) and Else Linstad. Yet another story says that Gulbrand ordered *vadmel* (homespun cloth) from Norway for a new suit of clothes. This material was of the finest wood, dyed, woven, steamed and pressed by experts in the clothing business. The bride was a seamstress, so evidently she looked as chic as the groom.

Everyone else moved out of Gulbrand's cabin when Marte moved in, and the couple lived on the farm for 40 years and raised their 12 children there.

The 1870 Agriculture Census lists a farm belonging to George Gilbertson (a name Gulbrand also used) as having 400 acres with 80 of that in timber with a value of $9,600. He had 9 horses, 8 milk cows, 3 other cattle, 28 sheep and 5 swine. He produced 600 bushels of spring wheat, 500 bushels of corn, 100 pounds of wool, 200 bushels of potatoes, 400 pounds of butter and 40 tons of hay.

When Oliver left home to work at Rossing store, Gulbrand had 440 acres. Then he bought farms for Chris and Gus at $32-$35 an acre. Theodore's farm was acquired for $26 an acre, and Henry's cost $75 an acre. The farm that became Edward Vinger's was purchased in 1880. In 1894 Gulbrand and Marte moved to the Theodore Vinger farm. They lived there for 3 years, and then bought a house in Argyle from a Sardeson. Later they built a new house there. Marte died in 1911 and after Gulbrand broke his hip, he lived with his daughter, Matilda Nelson, until his death in 1924 at the age of 94.

Gulbrand Vinger was a soldier in the Civil War. He enlisted in February 1865 and left Marte to run the farm with 4 little boys. Son Christian was born while he was gone. Gustav, the oldest at 10, remembered memorizing his Catechism lessons as he was doing the plowing that spring. Here is the information that can be found from the Department of the Interior, Washington, D.C. – Gulbrand G. Vinger, alias George Gilbert, Stewart, Wisconsin

> Height – 5 feet, 5 inches   Eyes – Blue
> Enlisted February 28, 1865 at Moscow, Wisconsin
> Served in 46 Wisconsin infantry, Company "A"
> Discharged – September 27, 1865 in Nashville, Tennessee

John Monson has written in more detail about Gulbrand's service in the Civil War section of this book.

Edward Vinger was born in 1861 and in 1888 he married Oleanna Moen. They lived on the first farm on the right on VW Road, which Gulbrand had purchased in 1880. This is the farm on which Oscar, Mabel and Viola were born. Oleanna died at the age of 32 in her home on Saturday, March 24, 1900. On March 16, 1903 Edward married Laura Farmer and they had two children, Lawrence and Olga.

Mabel went to a Norwegian high school in Fargo-Moorhead, Oak Grove Ladies Seminary, where she boarded and then on to nursing school in Freeport, Illinois. In 1918 Mabel married Ingwell Peterson.

Oscar attended Augsburg College for a short while with the intention of becoming a minister.

Marte's Family

Lars Carlsen was born on the Voien farm in Gran in 1804, and his wife Mari Hansdatter was born on Rækken in Tingelstad in 1805. They were married in Lunner on April 8, 1833. They had five children:

- Maren was born in 1832 and died in 1834 on the Voien farm
- Kari was born 2 July 1835 at a cotter's place on the Helgeland farm in Lunner.
- Marte was born at a cotter's place on the Kraggerud farm in Lunner on 25 September 1837
- Maria was born 8 January 1841 on Kraggerud
- Hans was born 31 August 1843 on Kraggerud

On April 5, 1852 Lars and Mari and their 4 living children emigrated from Kraggerud to the Yellowstone area in Lafayette County, Wisconsin and joined a large settlement of Hadelanders. Maria and Hans married and remained in Lafayette County. Kari and Torgrim Larsen Bilden raised their family in Clayton County, Iowa.

418

Ole Olesen Tokerud and Kari Avtjern

previously unpublished   *Form 450*   *David Gunderson*

The west side of the Randsfjorden, in the Bjoneroa, is a very beautiful area of Hadeland. From a historical perspective, this area appears to have been settled very largely with folks from Ådalen in Buskerud. In the case of my family, my great, great, great, grandfather, Ole Andersen

Putten farm c. 1996

came from Ramberget Farm on the west side of Lake Sperillen. Ole's ancestry is well-documented – it can be traced back to Harald Sorum in Sør Aurdal, who was born about 1570. Ole's wife, Anne Olsdatter Haugen shared this same ancestor – she was Ole's 3rd cousin once removed. By 1801, Ole Andersen was living at Putten with his wife and 4 children. Despite continuing to live at Putten, he apparently was always known as Ole Andersen Ramberget. In December 1804, Ole Andersen finalized the purchase of Putten. Today, the farm remains in the family. It is owned by

my 4th cousin, Kjell Putten. Ole Andersen had twelve children. In about February, 1805, my great-great grandfather, Ole Olsen Putten, was born. As a younger son, he could never inherit. The original farm house on the Putten Farm burned about 1996 and was replaced by a brand new home with metal siding. The picture above shows the original house.

Avtjern, Bjoneroa

My great-great grandfather, Ole Olsen Putten, married Kari Nilsdatter Avtjern October 17, 1830 in Gran. Kari's parents were Nils Guldbrandsen Jønnes and Elene Gudbrandsdatter Kalvskinn. They married November 21, 1796 in Gran. Again, Kari's ancestry can also be traced back to the 1500's. Avtjern is very close to Putten. The house was purchased years ago to be made into a summer cabin (*hytte*). Nothing was done with it and it certainly looks abandoned. Kari-Mette Avtjern provided this photo to me. It is very small, but it still has the classic floor plan of a 200 year old Norwegian farm house.

Their 1st child, Ole Olsen Putten was born January 2, 1831. Their 2nd child, Nils Olsen Putten was born September 19, 1833 and died August 15, 1834. Their 3rd child, Helene Olsdatter was born August 18, 1835 and died September 20, 1835 at Brunstad. I did visit Brunstad in 2005.

419

Nothing remains of the landlord's house. There is a relatively new home there. In the back of the pasture, you could see a classic 18th or 19th century Norwegian cotter. On August 23, 1836, my great grandmother, Elene [Elena] Olsdatter was born at Brunstad. The next child, Nils [Nels] Olsen was born at Hollingdalen in Søndre Land on February 28, 1840. The next child, Anders [Andrew], was born September 25, 1843, also at Hollingdalen. The final child, Ingeborg [Emma Isabelle] Olsdatter was born at Tokerud July 6, 1847, probably at the Grytebækken cotter. This cotter was apparently named for a small stream that flows into the Randsfjorden. In 2005, I visited the site of Grytebækken. There is a relatively new home there. I was told that when they decided to build the new house, you could still see that foundation for the old cotter.

On May 17, 1860, my great grandmother gave birth to a son, Peder Ellingsen at Grytebækken on Tokerud. The father was Elling Pedersen, from Søndre Land. He did not marry my great grandmother.

My great, great uncle, Ole Olsen Tokerud married Anna Jacobsdatter Bakke on February 22, 1855 in Gran. She was born July 22, 1832 at Bakke, Sør-Aurdal. By 1861, the decision was made to emigrate to the United States. The party included Ole Olsen Tokerud and his wife Anna Jacobsdatter Bakke, her sister Inger Jacobsdatter, all from the Malkjærn Farm. I visited this farm in 2005. It had a huge landlord's house. Inside the dining room, the family's genealogy was painted on the wall! In addition, Nils Olsen Tokerud joined his brother for the trip from the Tokerud Farm. A large group from Hadeland walked to Christiana. At this time, the passengers were required to bring their own food. The ship was the *Drøbak*. In 1858, this ship made to trip to Quebec in 45 days. In 1859, it took 41 days. In 1860, it took 73 days. In 1861, the Drøbak left Christiana on April 20, 1861 and arrived in Quebec on July 6, 1861. It had run into heavy storms. The passengers ran out of food! Apparently 12 died on the ship, almost all children. The first child of Ole Olsen Tokerud was born and died at sea. Ultimately, Ole Olsen Tokerud and his wife Anna had 9 children, only three of whom lived to adulthood. The path of immigration was often marked with too many small graves. They settled by Yorkville, Wisconsin.

In 1864, the youngest brother Anders Olsen came to the United States. I have never found any record of him in the "out-migrant's index." On August 20, 1864, Anders joined Company K, 2nd Wisconsin Cavalry. His unit served in Tennessee and Missouri. He was frequently ill with "fevers". He was discharged June 14, 1865 at Memphis. I'm sure his enlistment bonus helped pay for the rest of the family to leave for the United States. More details of his service can be found in the Civil War section of this book.

On March 17, 1866, Ole Olsen Tokerud [age 61]; his wife Kari Nilsdatter [age 60]; his daughters Elena and Ingeborg, and his grandson Peder Ellingsen, show up in the "out-migrant's" index as leaving Hadeland. Their ship was the *Nordlyset*. They left Christiana on April 18, 1866. They arrived in Quebec on May 24, 1866. Their surname was shown as

"Gryptbakken". They travelled to the Decorah, Iowa area when they were reunited with the rest of their family. Unfortunately, Anders Olsen Tokerud died November 3, 1867, and is buried at Washington Prairie Lutheran Church.

Ole Olsen Tokerud and Kari Nielsdatter Avtjern

By July 11, 1868, Ole Olson Tokerud had moved to Hayward Township, Freeborn County, Minnesota with his wife, his daughter Elene and her son Peder Ellingson. He purchased an 80 acre farm from Joseph McCutchum for $400.00. This parcel of land is described as follows: Township 102 North, Range 20 West, west ½ of the Southeast quarter, Section 4.

On October 19, 1869, Ole Olsen Tokerud, the father, sold 40 acres of his farm to Anton P. Hanson, retaining the Southwest quarter of the southeast quarter. On May 1, 1878, Ole Olsen Tokerud sold his 40 acre farm in Freeborn Co., Minnesota for $560.00., and moved with his wife Kari to Mt. Valley Township, Winnebago County, Iowa to join his daughter Elene and her family. Kari Nielsdatter died May 27, 1880 in Winnebago County. Her husband, Ole, died in the last half of 1894 at the age of 89. They are buried at Winnebago Lutheran Church.

Ole Olsen Tokerud and Anna Jacobsdatter Bakke

Ole Olsen Tokerud, the son, also bought an 80 acre farm by Hayward, MN. However, by early 1872, he had moved his family to a 160 acre homestead on the southwest corner of what became Rothsay, MN. He later sold his 80 acre farm in Freeborn County. Ole became a United States citizen in November, 1877. The three children that survived to adulthood were Caroline [Mrs. Peder Nordrum][Mrs. Martin Thorsen Aas]; Anne Julia [Mrs. Amund Nilsen Nordrum]; and Olavus [Ole]. In December, 1879, tragedy struck the family. The closest store was at

Caroline Aas, Anna Haugtveit and Julia Nordrum

Manston, Minnesota, west of Rothsay. Ole Olsen Tokerud went there by sleigh for supplies. On the way back a blizzard arose, Ole got lost and froze to death. He was buried at Hamar Lutheran Church Cemetery in April, 1880. His widow Anna married Ole's cousin Erich Hansen Haugtveit [Furua] on November 13, 1880. They had a 40 acre farm northwest of North Immanuel Lutheran Church. It is now part of The Nature Conservancy land there. Anna Jacobsdatter Bakke Haugtveit died January 20, 1914. Erich Hansen Haugtveit died August 2, 1920. They are buried at West North Immanuel Lutheran Church.

Elene Olsdatter Tokerud and Olaus Gundersen

In 1869, romance also bloomed for my great grandmother, Elene Olsdatter. She met Olaus Gunderson in Hayward Township. He was born February 3, 1840 in Glemmen, Østfold, Norway, the son of Gunder Olsen and Inger Nielsdatter. On August 4, 1869, Elene and Olaus had a son, Anders Gundersen. They ignored Norwegian naming customs and named the child after Anders Olsen Tokerud. On December 11, 1869, Elene and Olaus married at East Freeborn Lutheran Church. Including Anders, they ultimately had 6 children: Guldbrand [Gilbert], Inger Marie [Mary], Ole Christian [Christ], Clara, who died when less than 2 months old, and Ludvig. Guldbrand was my grandfather. Anders died in 1887.

Olaus Gundersen was a good businessman and farmer. He ultimately owned 320 acres of prime land. In the winters, they cut firewood and hauled it to Forest City, Iowa for sale. Olaus died October 11, *1905*. Elene died May 14, 1908. They are buried in Mount Valley Lutheran Cemetery in Winnebago County, Iowa.

Peder Ellingsen Tokerud [Peter Tucker]

Peter Tucker ultimately ended up in Waubay, South Dakota. He was a farmer and a mason. With his first wife, Mathea Monsdatter, he had 3 sons named Clinton, and one daughter Bessie. As each son died young, the name Clinton was reused.

Peter Tucker and children

In contacting descendants, they were astonished to learn of their Norwegian ancestry – they thought it was English!

Peter's first wife died September 17, 1904. Thru his Uncle Nils Olsen Tokerud in Manistee, Michigan, he was introduced to Hannah Sorensen, who became his 2nd wife. Peter died February 23, 1931. His 2nd wife died December 19, 1973. Peter had 5 grandchildren.

Nils Tokerud Family c. 1873

Nils Olsen Tokerud [Nels Olson]

After his arrival in the United States, Nels worked in northwestern Iowa and many areas in Wisconsin. On April 15, 1872, he married Emma Frances Bugg Cubitt in Manistee, Michigan. She was born October 27, 1848 in France to English parents. They had 6 children: George Nels; William Sam; Carrie Emma; Nora; Florence Hazel; and one more child who died at birth.

Nels was a farmer. In his later years, he was in very poor health. Nels died April 6, 1914, his wife Emma died May 19, 1933, both in Manistee, Michigan.

Emma Isabelle [Ingeborg Olsdatter Tokerud]

Emma Isabelle married David Andreasen Scott [Kath] January 17, 1871 in Racine, Wisconsin. He was born January 21, 1845 in Modem, Buskerud. They started out in Ludington, Michigan but later moved to Alexandria, Minnesota. They had five children: Andrew Olaf; John; Conrad Milton; Ida Manvella; and Anna Bertha. Mr. Scott had a bit of a drinking problem. Emma Isabelle divorced him and moved to Northwood, North Dakota with the children. She ran a rooming house there. David Scott died February 4, 1904 in Nelson, Minnesota. Emma Isabelle died December 29, 1936 in Williston, North Dakota.

Emma Isabelle

423

The Bjone Brothers

previously unpublished   *Form 15*   *Judith Bjone Liebelt*

The author is the daughter of Gil Bjone and granddaughter of Lars C. Bjone

Bjone Farm in Hadeland Today

America became the "Land of Opportunity" for the Bjone brothers---Lars C., Gilbert, Hans, and Simen.

My story begins with Lars, my grandfather. Lars C. Bjone married Rasmina Malene Karoline Olson Engelstad. She was born in Sogn og Fordane, Norway. Lars and Rasmina were married at Fort Ransom, North Dakota, on November 22, 1894. Six of their seven children were born in the United States---Christ, Melvin, Ralph, Olga, Laura, and Clarissa.

Rasmina and Gilbert's wife Abilena were sisters. Their family had immigrated to America when the sisters were young. Their family came to Kindred, ND, but later moved to Litchville, North Dakota, fifty miles to the west. Their father was killed by lightning and their pregnant mother walked to Litchville with her children.

Lars was legendary in Bjone and Hadeland. He traveled back and forth nine times from America to "the old country". After they went back to Norway, he would disappear from the farm at Bjone and Rasmina would hear from him in Oslo saying that he was getting on a ship to the U.S. He was an immigrant guide many times and in New York City he was referred to as the 'Norwegian Fox' because he would never stay in a hotel room that was lower than the 2nd floor. He had heard that robbers would climb in the lower windows and make off with the unsuspecting person's money. He could speak both Norwegian and English very well.

Lars C. Bjone, age 24

On one trip back to Norway, he smuggled some gold back to help his mother and the Bjone estate. Lars and his sister-in-law, Abilena, came up with a plan for getting the gold home to Norway. They sewed it into the lining of a heavy buffalo coat. The coat had to be worn every minute during Lars's summer trip. Of course, it was a bit strange for someone to be wearing a buffalo coat in the heat of a New York summer, so Lars pretended

On one of his crossings Lars acquired this farm at Sharon, ND, farm in a poker game aboard ship.

that he was a demented person and isolated himself out on the ship's dock. His crazy man's rantings successfully kept people away! That successful trip kept the Bjone farm in Norway intact for years to come through World War II and its economic difficulties and the resulting world depression. It also paid for his family's final move back to Norway.

Lars Bjone farm – Litchville, North Dakota

While they were living at Litchville, North Dakota, his father passed away. Lars was in line to inherit the Norwegian farm because of the law of progeniture. At the time of his father's death, he was the only Bjone brother who had children, and his other three brothers were not interested in moving back to "the old country." He, however, wanted to claim that inheritance.

Rasmina did not want to leave America. She would be leaving behind her family and all that she knew and loved. She consented to his iron will, but she wanted her McCall's magazine subscription, her cast iron parlor stove and her piano. He carried out her wishes. The stove and piano were still in use 25 years ago.

Lars and Rasmina's youngest son, Gil, was born in Norway. He emigrated to the United States in October 1933 at the age of 19. He had been the subject of untrue rumors that Lars had believed. In order to protect his land and income, Lars made arrangements with a ship's captain to send Gil to America. Lars was very connected politically, socially and dramatically whenever necessity and the occasion suited his thoughts or needs. Gil later met his wife,

Bertha, at Kindred, ND. They had four girls---Judith, Sandra, Linda and Clarice. He went back to Norway once to visit after his father Lars died.

Lars and Rasmina are buried in the Sorum church cemetery at Bjoneroa.

Gilbert's and Hans's stories are told in "History of North Dakota."

Gilbert C. Bjone was actively engaged in farming in LaMoure County. He was born in Norway, August 6, 1862, to Christian and Kjersti Sorum Bjone. His father had been a farmer also.

Lars' son Gil Bjone

Gilbert was indebted to the public schools of Norway for the educational opportunities that he enjoyed. The reports which reached him concerning the opportunity of the new world he was determined to try his fortune in America and in 1881, at the age of 19, he left his native land and sailed for the United States. He did not stay in New York, but continued to Fergus Falls, MN, where he worked for an uncle for a year. In 1882, he moved to Kindred, ND, where he spent a year and in 1883, he arrived in LaMoure County, where his brother Simon was then living. In four years he purchased his first section of land and in 1891, he bought his brother's homestead. He continued to purchase land until his holdings were 960 acres of some of the best farmland in the state. He was numbered among the most successful agriculturists and substantial citizens of his county. His farm home had the amenities of a city home with hot water heat and gas lights. His barn was one of the largest in the state and sheds and other outbuildings had ample storage for grain, stock, and farm machinery. He used only the latest improved agricultural implements and he used only the most progressive farming methods. He and his brother, Hans C. Bjone, organized the Farmers & Merchants State Bank of Verona, of which Gilbert was the president.

In 1889 Gilbert C. Bjone and Abilena Olson, also a native of Norway, were married. They had one child, whose name was Hannah. He never regretted his decision to come to try his fortune this side of the Atlantic. His life record indicates what may be accomplished when there is a will to dare.

Hans C. Bjone, was born in Norway September 29, 1873, to Christian and Kjersti Sorum Bjone. Hans C. was just fourteen at the time of his father's death. He acquired his education in his native land and in 1893 came to America to live with his brother Gilbert. He worked for his brother for several years, and was very careful to save his earnings until he was able to purchase six hundred and forty acres of land. In 1908 he built a modern nine room house with all the modern conveniences as had his brother. His land was wild and undeveloped when it

426

came into his possession but he set about at once to successfully improve the land. He also became one of the organizers of the Farmers and Merchants State Bank of Verona, of which he was vice president. Gilbert and Hans opened the bank on Saturday, August 19, 1916, with their nephew Hans Bjone as cashier.

Tuesday, March 1, 1927, about 11:00 a.m. the dead body of H.C. Bjone, the nephew of Gilbert and Hans C., and the cashier of the Farmers and Merchants State Bank of Verona was discovered by citizens of Verona in the bank vault. Four bullet wounds in his head told the story of one of the most atrocious crimes ever committed in LaMoure County or the state of North Dakota.

Mr. Bjone was last seen alive between 4:00 and 5:00 Monday afternoon, when he had visited a local restaurant to eat a light lunch. No one suspected anything when he did not appear for supper. Even his not appearing for breakfast caused nothing more than a passing comment.

Persons who visited the bank building on Tuesday morning found the door locked. The passersby forced the door open. Nothing seemed out of place inside the bank. The vault was found shut, which seemed rather odd. A former employee who had once known the combination tried to open the vault, but to no avail as the combination numbers eluded his memory. The searchers then decided to dig their way through the more than a foot of brick wall into the vault, but while that work was going forward, Mr. Sather succeeded in solving the combination and the vault door was opened.

Inside the vault, they found the body of the murdered cashier with the upper portion of his body lying in a pool of blood. Four bullets had been fired into his head, one under the left ear, two in the right temple, and one on the right side of his head. The first bullet fired---the one under the left ear---had passed completely through the brain, and must have caused instant death. Two other bullets also passed through his head, while the fourth remained inside his skull.

Reconstructing the scene, as nearly as it would seem, it was concluded that Mr. Bjone, after eating lunch, returned to the bank, entered the vault, took a seat on a stool, and proceeded to sort over the checks which had been handled during the day. While thus engaged, someone entered the bank, passed through a low swinging door leading into the office, discovered Mr. Bjone in the vault, and immediately shot him. Mr. Bjone toppled off the stool to the floor, after which his assailant fired three more bullets into the cashier's head.

The murderer closed and locked the vault door and then nailed the front door. One nail was driven at the base of the door and two along the side. Escape was then made by way of a back door.

The time of the crime was fixed about 5:00 p.m. because at that time a gentleman passed the bank and heard the sound of pounding within. It was almost certainly the time the murderer was nailing the door shut. The gentleman was going to have stopped to investigate, but concluded he would stop by instead on the morrow.

The county coroner, states attorney, and sheriff along with finger print experts from Aberdeen, South Dakota, were summoned to Verona to investigate, but so many people had entered the bank and vault before their arrival that their efforts were fruitless.

The authorizes suspected that the gun used for the crime was Mr. Bjone's own revolver. They surmised that the murderer may have found the cashier's pistol lying on the bank counter, and that he used the weapon to end the life of its owner. Hans was known as an expert marksman and was said to carry a gun at all times.

The robber got away with between three and four thousand dollars. For some reason he did not take the silver or gold coin that was fully exposed in the vault. A reward of $500 was posted for the capture of the murderer and robber.

The authorities eventually found the culprit--- Francis Tucker. He was convicted and was given a life sentence at the state penitentiary at Bismarck, ND. He was released 17 ½ years after he began his sentence for first degree murder. After the murder Tucker had unusually large amounts of cash in his possession, but he claimed he was innocent.

Because many bank customers lost money from the robbery, Gilbert made their losses good from his own account. After the funeral of his nephew, he and his wife left town in the night, never to return to Verona. They resettled in Oregon where they later died and are buried.

Hans Bjone continued to farm, raising his children in the home he had built. Later his son Christ farmed the land. At the time of this writing, his grandson Hans lives on the farm, but cash rents the land. He is buried in a cemetery near Fort Ransom, ND.

Hans C. Bjone Family

Simen Bjone made his home at Sauk Center, MN, where he owned and operated a general store. His wife, Sophia, stayed home and took care of the family. Their final resting place is in that area.

All four of the Bjone brothers were grateful for the opportunities that had been afforded them in America, the "Land of Opportunity."

Peder and Kari (Wirstad) Lunder

previously unpublished   *Form 432*   *Karen Lynnes Kruse*
The author is Peder and Kari's granddaughter

Peder Erickson Lunder was born to Erick and Maren Lunder at Lunner Toppen, Norway on April 30, 1870. He was the youngest of three siblings. At this time Oslo was still known as Christiania. Sweden ruled Norway, and King Oscar was the named reigning monarch of both countries.

Peder liked adventure and served in the King's Guard. There were Norwegian and Swedish guards posted along the border. Peder remembered that it was a peaceful time and the guards on the border were friendly and greeted each other as they met. They would often sit together and play cards to pass away the time.

1899 chalk drawing of Kari Wirstad in the mountain pasture

In 1893 Peder emigrated to the United States. There he found work on his uncle Hans Lunder's farm near Canton, South Dakota. After a period of time, he returned to Norway and connected with his sweetheart Kari (Thron's daughter) Wirstad.

Kari was born on October 25, 1876. She was one of the ten children born into the Wirstad family. As a young maid she spent her summers as a *seter jente*. She lived in a shack in the high pasture where she milked cows and made cheese and butter for the family at the Wirstad *gård*. Kari was 10 years old when her mother died giving birth to her sister Martha.

December 15, 1889 was the date of Kari & Peder's wedding. It took place in Lunner Church. a twelfth century stone church at Lunner Toppen. The church has been restored and is a popular place for worshippers and tourists in this twenty-first century.

A baby daughter, Karen Marie was born to Peder and Kari Lunder on June 6, 1900. That summer much planning and soul searching took place as the couple prepared to emigrate together. Brother Gudmund had inherited the home farm which was the tradition at that time. Peder was once again eager to travel back to the United States with the promise of a bright future. A large trunk was packed with clothing, linens, and the belongings they most cherished.

A glass-stemmed bowl with the initials KTDW etched on the side was left with sister-in-law Mrs. Gudmund Lunder. When I visited Norway in 2000 on a trip with the American Hadeland

Lag, the bowl had been identified by Hans Gudmund and Jorun Lunder and to my surprise I received it as a going away present! After 100 years at Lunner Toppen, Kari's confirmation gift came home to America!

Peder was given a family heirloom, an *ol krus* (tankard/mug) with a silver cover. It had been in the family nearly two-hundred years. The family insisted that he take it with him. There was one problem. There were rules in Norway about taking silver out of the country. Peder removed the silver cover and stuffed it into his sock so they were able to walk through customs without a problem. That mug has been and will always be a conversation piece in the Lunder family.

Peder, Kari and their daughter Karen left by train from the Roa station. A brass band had assembled on the platform and was playing when the couple rode up in a horse-drawn carriage. They presented Peder with a large silver spoon and said their farewells. Peder had

The 200+ year old tankard

been a member of that band. The spoon is still in the family. It is now in the possession of granddaughter Karen Lunder Hagen.

They traveled to Christiana (Oslo) and boarded a boat for England. The reason for this was that England had more sea-worthy passenger ships. After arriving in England, they were booked on the passenger vessel *Oceanic* owned by the White Star Line (builder of the Titanic).

The trip was long and tedious. They traveled by rail across the country to Fairview, South Dakota where they purchased 80 acres of land which turned out to be too wet and muddy for the milk cows. The cows had to be washed down each time they were milked. They also had chickens and pigs. Three more children were added to the family, Emma in 1902, Magnhild in 1905 and Edwin in 1908. Later in 1908 they gave up their South Dakota farm.

The lure of homesteading led Peder to file a claim on the southeast quarter of section 14 in St. Croix Township, ten miles northeast of Regent, North Dakota. Regent had just acquired the railroad and with immigrants arriving weekly, it was becoming a boomtown. Peder left ahead of the family to build a small two-story house on the claim.

Kari arrived by train with the four children only to find that Peder was not at the depot to meet them as planned. There had been a misunderstanding. Peder had been at the depot earlier and had given up and made the long trip home with horse and buggy. Kari waited until late and finally decided to feed the children and get a hotel room. She had all of the children in bed with her when rain came, the roof leaked, and the bed got wet. After waiting three days and with a baby in diapers, she was running out of money and decided she had to hire a buggy to drive them out to the homestead. On the road they met Peder who was on his way to meet them. What a great reunion for the family!

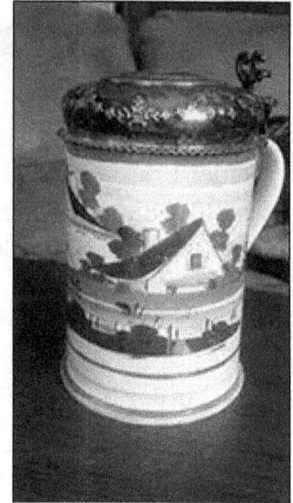

The Lunder family spent some time with the Iver Haakenstad's, Kari's cousin from Hadeland, Norway, until the house was finished. Peder did most of the work himself.

A lot of hard work went into building a new farmstead. Lumber was hauled by wagon and horses from Gladstone which was a two day trip. There were sheds and barns built. A new well was dug; that was a dangerous job because of the gases in the soil.

The Lunder Homestead in Regent, North Dakota c. 1912
Left to right: Karen, Emma, Peder with baby Edwin,
Martha Wirstad, Magnhild, Kari, and Ida.

Wagon loads of rocks were picked off the fields so the land could be tilled. Some of the rocks were used to dam up a small creek so the cattle could get water during the dry season.

Three more Lunder children were born on the homestead; Ida in 1910, Clara in 1913, and the youngest, Thron in 1915.

In March of 1910, Kari's youngest unmarried sister Martha arrived from Norway and filed on a homestead near the Lunders on the northwest quarter of section 14 in St. Croix Township. One can only imagine the excitement and joy the two sisters had to see each other after being apart for ten years! A sod shanty was built on the land about a half mile west of Lunders. Peder rented her farm land. Martha had to sleep in her shanty so many nights in a month to prove her claim. One of the Lunder daughters always slept with her because she was afraid to sleep alone. Martha was great help to sister Kari rearing a large family.

As a small child Martha had attended a political rally with her father Thrond Wirstad, and she had the honor of being seated in the lap of King Oscar!

Martha was trained as a midwife. She worked with Dr. Hill, Regent's country doctor. Horseback was her means of transportation as she traveled to assist the mother giving birth.

Iver Haakenstad's sister Martha emigrated from Hadeland in September of 1910, and filed on a homestead at Mott, North Dakota. Martha Wirstad and Kari Lunder were cousins of Iver and Martha Haakenstad. They clung together like siblings because they had no other family in America. This relationship lasted a lifetime.

The Marthas enjoyed being together and often rode horseback. On a Sunday evening they rode along the Cannonball River. The scenery was beautiful. After riding a few miles, they decided that it was time to retrace their path home. As the sun was setting they became lost and afraid. Riding a little farther they noticed a light. They proceeded to it and found a cabin. They hesitatingly knocked on the door. Soon a tall bewildered man appeared. The two girls explained they were lost. They asked, "Do you know where Lunders live?" The man answered, "Yes, I know where Lunders live!" The man's name was Anton Salle, a homesteader. Mr. Salle rode his horse with the two girls and they soon arrived back at the Lunder homestead.

Kari was happy to see the girls at home again and invited Mr. Salle in for food and conversation. Mr. Salle was invited to spend the night at Lunders. That was the beginning of a beautiful courtship between Martha Haakenstad and Anton Salle.

The couple was married in 1914 in the home of Iver Haakenstad. During the wedding celebration the neighbors came to shivaree the new couple. A shivaree is a noisy mock serenade to newlyweds. The neighbors were also looking for fun, refreshment and excitement. Someone got on the roof and covered the chimney with a blanket. The house became filled with smoke. The visiting party banged on the door and windows. A window was broken and Martha Wirstad's arm was cut by flying glass. Iver Haakenstad opened the door and shouted to the revelers, "Look what you've done! The house is full of guests. You must return at a later date." At last the crowd dispersed.

Martha Wirstad was friendly and outgoing. She soon met a bachelor homesteader, Alfred Romsos, who lived only three miles away. The Lunder children teased their aunt by saying, "Do you love rum? Do you love sauce?" Well, do you love ROMSOS?"

The couple was married in 1915. They had four children. Ted, Ida, Art and Helen. In 1924 they boarded the train at Regent and moved the family to Portland, Oregon.

The neighbors in the area bought a mine nearby and dug lignite coal for the winter. It was a decision within the group to give the Igaard family coal for the winter because they could not afford to buy into the group. One man, Mr. Johnson, was very opposed to this deal. One day the two men met on the road. Mr. Igaard had a load of coal. Mr. Johnson was on horseback and was carrying a shotgun. He shot Mr. Igaard right out of the wagon in cold blood! What a terrible Wild West tragedy! Then, worst of all, two families were without husbands and fathers. Mr. Igaard was dead and Mr. Johnson went to jail. The children of the two families had to face each other each day in the same school.

Cherry Butte School was the first consolidated school in Hettinger County. It was a two room school with a teacherage that opened in 1913. The Lunder children were privileged to attend this new school. Emmet Dorgen was one of their classmates. He was the father of US Senator Byron Dorgan.

There were lots of fun times, including picnics, farm meetings, birthday parties, and school gatherings. The children enjoyed running in the hills, playing Hide and See, Anti-I-Over, and

Tag. Peder Lunder ordered a new Piano through the Sears Roebuck catalog and several of the girls learned to play. There were many happy times spent around the piano.

The years on the homestead brought many hardships. Hot winds, grasshoppers and army worms destroyed the crops and hay land. Friends and neighbors were moving to other places. The church was hard to keep going. Worship and a Christian education was important to the Lunders.

Peder found what he was looking for in the Red River Valley at Kindred, North Dakota. In the fall of 1919 railroad cars were loaded with furniture, machinery and livestock. (The cows were milked on the train.) Peder and eleven year old Edwin and a friend Matt Olson (had a girlfriend in Kindred) rode in the cars with their stock and goods. The trip took at least two full days. Meanwhile nineteen year old daughter Karen had learned to drive the 1916 Ford. She was the sole driver on the trek to Kindred. Kari never drove a car, but she did keep everyone together with a positive attitude on the trip. Emma had gone with her sweetheart to South Dakota to leave more travel room for the younger siblings. A folded blanket was placed on the floor of the car so three year old Thron could nap.

The children were in awe when they arrived at the Missouri River. They had to cross from Mandan to Bismarck. There was no bridge! They drove the car unto a ferry and crossed by that means. They were so relieved when they came to the other side. The family continued to Steele, ND where they spent the first night. The second night was spent at a hotel in Mapleton since they had heard the accommodations were not good in Kindred. The next morning they drove to Kindred where they met the train with Peder, Edwin and Matt Olson. The cargo was unloaded and they made their way to a rented farm place.

Another disappointment was to upset them. The farm was contaminated with TB and the milk cows had to be sold. After a couple of moves in the Kindred area, the family purchased a farm about one mile North of the West Prairie Lutheran Church just off Highway 18 & 46. The year was 1926.

Peder died after a lengthy illness in 1937. Kari lived with Edwin on the home farm during World War II and spent time with her daughters until a small home was built for her on the Lynnes farm in 1948. Kari died in 1954 after a long battle with cancer.

My grandmother Kari and I were very close. She continued to talk about the nice modern home they had in Norway. They had electricity and water piped into the home. She reminded me that she was from *"stor folk i Norge."* I heard that more than once. How could that be? It never made sense to me because she was so frugal in the way she lived. She darned the socks and patched the bed sheets. Jewelry and frills were not important. My mother told me that Kari had pierced ears and wore gold earrings at one time! Really??

In 1977 Hans Gudmund and Jorun Lunder came to America with the KK Men's choir. I asked Hans Gudmund, " Is it true that my grandparents were *"stor folk?"* Hans Gudmund's answer was, "Yes, yes, of course, because they were land owners!" That statement answered my question.

The Lunder Family
Standing: Karen, Edwin , Thron, Emma and Magnhild. Seated: : Ida , Peder, Kari and Clara

All of Peder and Kari's children went to school, grew up, and found their partners while living on the Kindred farm north of West Prairie Church.

1. Oldest daughter Karen married Norris Hagen of Kindred on January 9, 1922. Norris was a farmer. The reared six daughters. Myrtle, Inez, Norma, Eileen, Arla Mae and Pauline. All were married and fifteen grandchildren were born. Teaching, office work, nursing and farming were their vocations. Karen died in 1968 of Parkinson's Disease and chronic arthritis. Arla Mae Discher of Clinton, Minnesota is the only surviving daughter. The other five girls died rather young.

2. Second daughter Emma was the first to marry. She wed Albert Loken of Fairview, SD on April 15, 1921. (Albert's parents had emigrated from Hadeland.) They reared three sons. Palmer and Eugene were Lutheran ministers and Merle was a medical doctor at the University of Minnesota in Minneapolis. He established the department of Nuclear

Medicine and became its director. All of the boys married and each had five children. Emma died in 1964 of Alzheimer's disease.

3.   The author's mother is Peder and Kari's third daughter, Magnhild. She was a country school teacher and a care giver. On November 26, 1936 she married Peter Lynnes, a farmer of Leonard, North Dakota. They farmed and reared a daughter and a son. Karen (the author) became a teacher and later worked in retail. She married a farmer at Kindred and had two children and four grandsons. The couple now reside in Fargo. Brother Carman became an Agriculture Engineer and is married and has four children and twelve grandchildren. He makes his home in Minnesota and Arizona. Magnhild died in 1999 after living over nine years in a nursing home.

4.   Edwin married Synora Nelson in Viroqua, Wisconsin on November 1, 1945. They had no children. They lived on the home farm at Kindred and raised cattle and grain until Edwin was stricken with Parkinson's disease. Edwin died in a Fargo nursing home in 1972. Synora moved back to her family in Wisconsin and died there in 1992.

5.   Ida married Harold Braaten on June 9, 1940. Harold farmed at Mayville where Ida went to teach school. The couple had two girls, Marlene who was a teacher and married a farmer/teacher. They lived in Portland and Fargo, ND. They have one son and one granddaughter. Alice was a hairdresser, crafter and worked in retail. She married a banker from Fargo. They have two married daughters and five grandchildren and live in Arizona. Ida died in1989.

6.   Clara married a local Kindred farmer, Thorvald Anvik on November 9, 1941. They had two sons, John Peter who has a degree in engineering and also a farmer. He was a pilot with the air guard in Fargo and also did crop spraying at one time. He is married and has adopted children and one grandchild. Stanley Wayne was a farmer, trucker, carpenter and handy man. He has one daughter and several adopted step children. He also has six grandchildren. Clara was in ill health after the boys were born. She developed debilitating rheumatoid arthritis. After a lot of medical treatments and suffering she died on Christmas Eve in 1960 at the age of forty-seven. The boys were twelve and fourteen years old.

7.   Thron married Louise Nelson from Viroqua, Wisconsin on November 20, 1947. She is a cousin of Synora Lunder, Edwin's wife. Thron served in World War II and saw action in England, France and Germany. He was an airplane propeller mechanic behind the front lines. The couple has two sons. Peter Marcus is a high school teacher. His field is math and computer science. He is single. Wayne was a farmer at Kindred. He lived on the Lunder farm. He now works in manufacturing. Wayne and his wife sold the Lunder farmstead at Kindred and moved to Ulen, Minnesota in 2013 to live near their daughter

Rachel Haugen and her husband. The couple has a married son in Arizona. They have two grandchildren. Thron died in 2002.

We grandchildren have been able to live the American dream due to the efforts and sacrifices of our parents and grandparents who paved the way for us.

Iver and Ida (Mathison) Haakenstad

previously unpublished   *Form 365*   *submitted by Karen Lynnes Kruse*
written by their daughter Hilma Haakenstad Stengel
Hilma died in March of 1998

Iver L. Haakenstad was born near the town of Roa in Hadeland, Norway on October 11, 1878. He was fourth in line of a family of ten children. His parents were Lars and Helene (Wirstad) Haakenstad. He was baptized and confirmed in the Lutheran faith in Lunner Church by Reverend Stub. He received his formal education in Norway, attending high school and business college in Oslo, Norway.

As a young man of twenty-one years, he decided to leave his homeland and go to America in September of 1900. His destination was Canton, South Dakota; here he worked as a farm laborer for two years. This was on the Hvattum farm northeast of Canton. Then together with a friend, a relative of the Schiager family, he rented a farm north of Canton (I believe this is the farm where Clarence Knutson now lives). He lived there until 1905.

During these years in the Canton vicinity, he met and courted Ida Mathison. Ida was born on the Mathison homestead on February 23, 1880, the youngest of the six children of Isak and Karen Mathison. She was only a few months old when her father died, leaving her mother to raise and care for the family, plus the responsibility of the farm.

Iver decided to respond to the lure of acquiring homestead land in St. Croix Township, Hettinger County, North Dakota. He settled on a quarter of land about seven miles northeast of Regent, North Dakota. This was in April of 1905.

Ida Mathison and her friend Susanna Gilbertson also went to North Dakota and took homestead claims on the township just east of St. Croix.

Iver and Ida were married September 1, 1906 by Rev. Wolf of the German Lutheran church near Mott, North Dakota. Iver had built a two-room sod house on his land and to this house he brought his bride. Lumber for the floors and roof was hauled by team and wagon from Richardston, North Dakota, a distance of about 40 miles. The inside walls of the sod house were plastered with gumbo and painted with calcimine. In the house their only daughter, Hilma, was born in August of 1908.

While in North Dakota their home was often a "stop over" for weary travelers. Lutheran pastors, while ministering among the Lutheran families in the area, often stayed in the Haakenstad home. They were charter members of the Cherry Butte Lutheran Church organized on June 30, 1907. In the fall of 1917, because of Ida's failing health, the Haakenstads

437

moved back to Canton, South Dakota. They rented the farm of Ida's brother Jacob Mathison. Jacob made his home with them for several years.

The following story serves as a special insight into the character of Ida and Iver. Imagine – learning about a baby in need of a home at 11:00 a.m. and a few hours later bringing him into your home to love and nourish as your son. This is what happened to the Haakenstad family on October 21, 1921. On that day, a Lutheran social worker from Minneapolis brought a three-month-old baby boy, intending to place him with a certain family in Canton. Upon arrival, she learned that serious illness in the family made it impossible for them to continue adoption proceedings. She then brought the baby to the Lutheran parsonage to seek the advice of the Rev. H. E. Rasmussen. The pastor knew the Haakenstads had spoken of their wish to adopt a child. He called them, explaining the situation. This was at eleven o'clock in the morning. Before noon Ida and Iver were on their way to Canton. Ida often said, "As soon as I held Donald in my arms, I knew he had to be our baby." Pastor Rasmussen presented such a positive recommendation of them as prospective parents the social worker agreed to leave Donald LeRoy in their care. A few months later he was their legal son. Ida, Iver and daughter Hilma were very proud of Donald. He grew to be a fine young lad, but on April 28, 1936, he died of a brain aneurysm at the age of 14 years. He was laid to rest two days before he was to have been confirmed into the Lutheran faith at Canton Lutheran Church.

In 1943 the Haakenstads together with their daughter and son-in-law Ernest W. Stengel, bought the farm. This farm belonged to the estate of Ida's brother Jacob Mathison, who died in 1925. The Stengels moved onto the farm and Ida and Iver moved into their house at 118 West Maple, Canton.

A big event in their lives was the celebration of their Gold Wedding Anniversary in September of 1956. Less than a year later, on August 2, 1957, Ida Mathison Haakenstad died. Iver died 10 years later on August 24, 1967.

Iver was always interested in community developments. After returning to South Dakota he served in various capacities on the school board of Schiager School District #8. He also served on the board of deacons and the board of trustees at Canton Lutheran Church. He was very much interested in cooperative businesses, maintaining that farmers could do much for themselves if they worked together. He served two terms in this capacity. This was during the time Sigurd Anderson was governor of South Dakota.

The Haakenstads lived through both good and hard times in the span of their lives but never did they lose faith in God or mankind. Certificates of commendation from governors of both North and South Dakota attest to the respect and honor the state and community held for them. God bless their memory.

Iver and Ida's granddaughter Merryll Stengel and her husband Mark Borg were living in England while Mark attended Cambridge in 1965. They visited Norway at Christmas. This special picture was taken of Merryll with her great aunts and uncles at the Haakenstad farm Christmas Eve.

Left to right: Lena, Berta, Mark, Hans, Merryll, and Ingeborg.

Gulbrand Gulbrandson and Kari Olsdtr

previously unpublished   *Form 218*   *Linda Weidenfeld*

Gulbrand Gulbrandson Daehlan was born on October 16, 1820 in the area of Brandbu in Gran *Prestegjeld*, Gran *Kommune*, Hadeland Traditional District, Oppland *fylke*, Norway. Daehlen was the name of the *gård* they lived on when Gulbrand was born. He was the son of Gudbrand Olson Egge and Johanna Nielsdatter Naest. His paternal grandparents were Ole Olson and Marthe Rasmundsdatter. His maternal grandparents were Niels Hanson and Berit Olsdatter. Gulbrand was baptized on October 22th at the Nes/Naes *kirke*. On October 26, 1846 Gulbrand married Kari Olsdatter in Gran Parish. They raised their family on the gård Gundalen near Nes/Naes *kirke*. He immigrated to America on May 5, 1882 with his two youngest daughters. Gulbrand died March 15, 1896 in Hollandale, Iowa Co, WI and is buried in the Hollandale Cemetery.

Kari Olsdatter Egge was born on October 11, 1822, in the area of Brandbu in Gran *Prestegjeld*, Gran *Kommune*, Hadeland Traditional District, Oppland *fylke*, Norway. Egge was the name of the *gård* they lived on when Kari was born. She was the daughter of Ole Bjornsen Hansen and Bertha Ellingsdatter. Her paternal grandparents were Hans Pedersen and Ragndi Olsdatter. Her maternal grandparents were Elling Bastiansen and Mallene Hansdatter. Elling was the son of Badstian Ellingsen and Aasa Andersdatter. Kari was baptized on October 20th at the Nes/Naes *kirke*. Kari's *dodsdatum* (date of death) was on April 21, 1882 just weeks before they were to emigrate. Her *Nar Begravet* (funeral service) was April 27th and her *Jordfestet* (internment) was April 30th. Her death record states she was born on Bjornshagen on Egge and her residence at death was on Egge. Her cause of death was *lungebetennelse* (pneumonia).

Gulbrand and Kari had ten children all born in Gran Parish:

Johanna Gulbrandsdatter Gilbertson	b. Aug 29, 1846	d. Nov 3, 1936
m. Jun 15, 1871 to Torsten Paulson	b. Oct 23, 1846	d. Mar 31, 1898
Karen Gulbrandsdatter Gilbertson	b. Apr 11, 1848	d. Mar 31, 1896
m. Oct 24, 1880 to Ole Olson Lee	b. Oct 19, 1838	d. Mar 6, 1901
Marthe Gulbrandsdatter Gilbertson	b. Dec 18, 1850	d. Feb 18, 1919
m. Nov 25, 1873 to Iver Pederson	b. Jul 25, 1851	d. Feb 2, 1932
Gulbrand (Gilbert) Gulbrandson Gilbertson	b. Jul 31, 1853	d. Apr 10, 1930
m. Dec 28, 1873 to Caroline Olsdatter	b. Aug 14, 1854	d. Jul 4, 1925

Birthe Gulbrandsdatter Gilbertson	b. Jan 22, 1856	d. Mar 27, 1860
Ingeborg (Isabelle) Gulbrandsdatter Gilbertson	b. Apr 2, 1858	d. Dec 25, 1920
m. Oct 18, 1882 to Erick Nielson Thompson	b. Nov 11, 1852	d. Apr 30, 1922
Birthe (Berthe) Gulbrandsdatter Gilbertson	b. May 19, 1860	d. Feb 10, 1947
m. Jan 3, 1885 to Edward Thompson	b. Jun 25, 1860	d. Nov 16, 1946
Ole Gulbrandsen Gilbertson	b. Oct 13, 1862	d. May 14, 1937
m. May 25, 1889 to Anna Olson Westlund	b. Apr 30, 1859	d. Dec 2, 1925
Anna Gulbrandsdatter Gilbertson	b. Apr 21, 1865	d. May 27, 1933
m. May 25, 1889 to Chris Hanson	b. May 1863	d, Mar 22, 1930
Kari (Carrie) Gulbrandsdatter Gilbertson	b. Nov 28, 1868	d. Nov 12, 1959
m. Dec 31, 1888 to Thomas Halverson	b. Jun 7, 1857	d. Dec 17, 1915

Gulbrand and Kari grew up near each other in the same region and parish in Gran. Their families knew each other and were all tenant farmers on the larger gård, Egge. The Gran *Kirkebøker* (parish register) records their marriage as the *ungkarl* (bachelor) Gulbrand, age 25 married the *pige* (maiden) Kari, age 21 on October 26th, 1846. He was the son of Gulbrand Olson and she was the daughter of Ole Bjornson. They both had residence on Eggeiet (part of the larger gård Egge). The record states that the *lysing* (public announcement of upcoming marriage) was given in church on three consecutive Sundays of September 13th, 20th and 27th. They raised their ten children on the gård Gundalen near the Nes/Naes *kirke* in Gran parish. Their fifth child Birthe died at age four in March of 1860 and their seventh child Birthe was born two months later and named in her memory.

The Oppland 1865 census lists Gudbrand Gudbrandson, age 44 and his wife Kari Olsdatter, age 43, living on Gundalen gård, in Naes local parish within Gran parish in the Mjonvald school district with seven of their children: Johanne age 20, Marthe age 16, Ingeborg age 7, Berthe age 5, Anne age 1, Gudbrand age 14 and Ole age 3. Their daughter Karen was living on Egge Ovre gård with the John Pedersen family as a *tienestefolk* (hired help). Gudbrand was listed as *Husmand med Jord* (renter of house w/small piece of land on larger farm).

Three of their children married in Gran parish. Johanna married Torsten Paulson in June of 1871, Marthe married Iver Pederson in November of 1873 and Gilbert married Caroline Olsdatter in December of 1873. The first child in this family to emigrate was Johanna and Torsten with their son in April of 1876. The next to leave Norway were their single daughters; Karen emigrated at the age of 19 in April of 1877 followed by Ingeborg, age 21 in April of 1879 and Birthe, about 20 around 1880. Martha and Iver and their two daughters emigrated on April 1st of 1881 and Ole, age 18 followed on April 28th of the same year.

On April 5, 1882, Gulbrand, age 55 along with his wife Kari, age 50 and their daughters, Anne age 11 (actually 16) and Kari age 10 (actually 13), contracted with A. Sharpe shipping line on the feeder ship *Rollo* to immigrate to America. Their destination was Monroe, Wisconsin. Kari became ill and died on April 21st with pneumonia, delaying their trip. Gulbrand left Norway on May 5th with his two daughters, Anne and Kari. They traveled from Christiania (Oslo) to Hull,

England and then on another ship to America. He joined his son, Ole who had immigrated the year before, and he lived in the Hollandale and Blanchardville area in Iowa County near his children.

The last child in this family to immigrate was Gilbert and Caroline with their five children, who immigrated in March of 1884. They settled near Blue Mounds, Wisconsin in Dane County.

Gulbrand and Kari's family all arrived in Wisconsin. Karen, Martha and Anna settled in St. Croix County in north east Wisconsin in Star Prairie and New Richmond. Johanna, Ole, Gilbert and Bertha all settled in close proximity in southern Wisconsin in Lafayette, Iowa, Green and Dane counties. Ingeborg moved to Soldier in Monona County in NW Iowa and Kari lived in Soldier, Iowa and Obert, in Cedar County in north east Nebraska.

Gulbrand lived near Hollandale and died March 15, 1896 at the age of 75. He is buried in the Hollandale cemetery and his grave marker is in the first row along School Road/County Road K.

The Children of Gulbrand and Kari:

Johanna, Peter, Gena, Bennett, Torsten and Carl Paulson

Johanna Gilbertson was born August 29, 1846 in the area of Brandbu in Gran *Prestegjeld*, Gran *Kommune*, Hadeland Traditional District, Oppland *fylke*, Norway on the Eggeiet gård. She was baptized on September 15th, the daughter of Gulbrand Gulbrandson and Kari Olsdatter. Johanne married Torsten Paulsen (Tom Paulson) on June 15, 1871. They immigrated on April 27, 1876 with their two year old son Peder with the shipping line Allen Brothers on the ship *Angelo.* They were listed on the ship manifest as Torsten and Johanne Paulsen Bronsaas (Brynsaas was the farm they were living on). They were both thirty years old and their destination was Monroe, Wisconsin. Johanna was the first in this family to immigrate to America. On the 1880 US census they were living in Adams Township in Green County, WI with their 6 year old son Peter and 8 month old daughter Gina B. The 1895 Wisconsin census lists a Thorson Paulson in the Township of Moscow, Iowa County. The record states 5 males and two females living there. A 4th male would be another child never recorded and there is a Torstin Paulson death record on March

442

31, 1898 in Iowa County. (Never verified). Tom died March 31, 1898 at the age of 51. In 1900, the widow, Johanna Paulson was living in Moscow Township, Iowa County with her 16 year old son Carl. This census record states she had four living children and had six children total. There is a record of a Leo B. Paulson death in Iowa County on June 17, 1894 that could be their 6th child. In 1910 she was still living in Moscow Township with Carl, age 25. In 1920 and 1930 she was living in York Township, Green County with her son Bennet and his wife Alma and five of their children. Johanna died November 3, 1936 at the home of her son Bennett at the age of 90. Johanna and Torsten are buried in the Hollandale, WI Cemetery.

Torsten (Thorston) Paulsen Hvaleby was born October 23, 1846 on the Hvaleby farm in Gran, Hadeland, Norway. He was the second son of Povel (Paul) Gulbrandsen Helgager and Birthe Torstensdatter Hvaleby. His brother immigrated in 1870 and his parents immigrated in 1877 with the rest of their eight children.

Johanna and Torsten's children:

Peder Tostensen Paulson	b. Oct 12, 1873	d. Mar 3, 1946
m. Mar 30, 1898 to Marit Oline Lee	b. Jun 17, 1875	d. Feb 15, 1901
Children: Beulah Jeannette	b. Jun 14, 1889	d. Feb 13, 1982
Marit Oline (Mayme)	b. Feb 1, 1901	d. Mar 15, 182
m. Jan 4, 1904 to Olea (Ollie) Anderson	b. May 3, 1874	d. Mar 3, 1965
Children: Tilman Conrad	b. Jul 19, 1904	d. Dec 15, 1905
Tilman Conrad	b. Apr 21, 1906	d. Feb 10, 1987
Gifford Palmer	b. Jul 1, 1908	d. Mar 28, 1988
Gerald Julian	b. Dec 9, 1910	d. Jul 17, 1967
Howard Ansel	b. Aug 29, 1916	d. Jul 21, 1960
Gina Bertina Paulson	b. Sep 6, 1879	d. Jun 22, 1908
m. Nov 15, 1898 to Gabriel O. Lee	b. Feb 16, 1873	d. May 12, 1946
Children: Orville Thomas	b. Mar 24, 1899	d. Dec 17, 1974
Julia Belinda	b. Jun 15, 1902	d. Sep 6, 1938
Marit "Mary" Oline	b. Sep 13, 1903	d. May 23, 1988
Raymond Conrad	b. Dec 12, 1907	d. Dec 2, 1986
Obert Gerald	b. Jan 24, 1908	d. Mar 28, 1976
Bennett Tosten Paulson	b. Oct 31, 1881	d. Aug 27, 1960
m. Mar 9, 1904 to Elma Julia Erickson	b. Mar 9, 1884	d. Apr 19, 1973
Children: Infant	b. Dec 20, 1905	d. Dec 20, 1905
Talmer Orion	b. Oct 13, 1907	d. Jun 22, 1980
Jennie Elvina	b. Jan 14, 1910	d. Oct 30, 1998
Edna Viola	b. Jan 28, 1912	d. Jun 1, 2000
Alvin Clifford	b. Mar 15, 1914	d. Mar 25, 1975
Irene Lillian	b. Jul 28, 1916	d.
Dorothy Evelyn	b. Jun 6, 1922	d.
Everett Byron	b. Jun 2, 1925	d. Jun 23, 1925
Carl Melvin Paulson (Rev.)	b. May 20, 1884	d. Aug 9, 1953

m. Oct 3, 1917 to Clara Jackson	b. Oct 15, 1886	d. Jun 8, 1976
Children: Anna Johanna	b. Jul 5, 1918	d.
Thelma Ruth	b. Nov 7, 1921	d. Aug 29, 1979
Carl Perry	b. Sep 14, 1927	d. Sep 9, 1932

Karen Gilbertson was born April 11, 1848 in the area of Brandbu in Gran *Prestegjeld*, Gran *Kommune*, Hadeland Traditional District, Oppland *fylke*, Norway on the Eggeiet gård. She was baptized on April 23rd, the daughter of Gulbrand Gulbrandson and Kari Olsdatter. Karen registered with Gran parish to leave the church and immigrate on April 30, 1877 at the age of 25. She settled in York Township, Green County, WI near her sister Johanna Paulson. On the 1880 US census she is living with Gilbert and Bagnil Thornason in York, Green County as a servant with her 3 month old daughter, Gusta. Karen married Ole (Olsen-Helgesen) Lee on Oct 24, 1880 in Polk County. Their marriage registration listed Karen Gilbertson and Ole Helgesson. They settled on a farm on the St. Croix-Polk county line in the town of Star Prairie near New Richmond, WI. The 1900 census lists Ole and Caroline Lee with their children; Ole G. age 18, Charles age 17, Elmer age 15, Lena age 14 and Clara age11 at Star Prairie, St Croix Co. Gusta married in 1899 to Gustav Erickson and was living in Stillwater, MN. Ole Lee died March 6, 1901 at age 62. In 1905 Karen was living on the family homestead with her five youngest children. In 1920 and 1930 she was living with Helmar and Ole on their farm. Karen died June 19, 1932 at age 84 on their family farm. Ole and Karen are buried at Oakland Cemetery, St. Croix County, Star Prairie, WI.

Ole Olsen Lee was born October 19, 1838, the son of Ole Helgesen Bergsundlia and Kari Syvertsdatter Aasterud from Benterud, Odalen in Hedmark County, Norway. Ole immigrated in June of 1871. He died in Star Prairie, St Croix, WI on March 6, 1901.

Karen and Ole's children:

Augusta Gilbertson Lee	b. Dec 15, 1880	d. May 18, 1960
m. Mar 16, 1899 to Gustav Pedersen Erickson	b. May 10, 1871	d. Jan 8, 1956
Children: Peter Oliver	b. May 18. 1901	d. Aug 17, 1985
Edith Violet	b. Apr 21, 1902	d.
Cora Rugna	b. Nov 21, 1903	d.
George Edwin	b. Jul 10, 1905	d. May 1982
Laura Geneva	b. Apr 28, 1909	d. Jan 8, 1956
Julia Esther	b. 1913	d.
Ole Gabriel Lee	b. Nov 21, 1881	d. Jul 9, 1955
Charles Edwin Lee	b. Dec 25, 1882	d. Aug 21, 1955
m. Nov 7, 1911 to Rose Boucher	b. Mar 28, 1892	d. Jan 27, 1932
Children: Viola Esther	b. Sep 11, 1912	d. Aug 27, 1980
Gladys Florence	b. Sep 12, 1914	d. May 1, 2002
Dorothy B	b. Apr 18, 1917	d. Sep 1993

Charles Victor	b. Aug 16, 1924	d. Jan 21, 2009
Katherine Elaine	b. 1930	d.
Helmar Julias Lee	b. Dec 23, 1884	d. Jan 15, 1936
Lena Lee	b. Feb 8, 1886	d. Nov 4, 1972
m. Sep 19,1912 to Valentine Nelson	b. Mar 9, 1886	d. Oct 24, 1962
Children: Raymond Adlorr	b. Jun 29, 1913	d. Apr 17, 1985
Bernice Vivian	b. Nov 26, 1914	d. Mar 26, 1999
Lois Elizabeth	b. Dec 4, 1917	d. Jan 14, 1990
Virginia May	b. May 15, 1919	d. Jul 28, 2005
Clara Lee	b. Jun 16, 1889	d. Dec 11, 1979
m. Nov 9, 1910 to Edwin Erickson	b. Sep 8, 1888	d. May 23, 1979
Children: Clarence Edwin	b. Apr 16, 1911	d. Aug 7, 1991
Edith Bernice	b. Apr 5, 1913	d. Oct 3, 1997
Earl Raymond	b. Aug 11, 1922	d.
Donna Mae	b. Jan 13, 1929	d. Jul 22, 2005

Ivar & Martha Pederson Family
Kari, Gena, Ida, Charles, Melvin, Peder

Marthe Gilbertson was born December 18, 1850 in the area of Brandbu in Gran *Prestegjeld*, Gran *Kommune*, Hadeland Traditional District, Oppland *fylke*, Norway on the Eggeiet gård. She was baptized on December 26th, the daughter of Gulbrand Gulbrandson and Kari Olsdatter. Marthe married Iver Pederson Blegeneiet on November 20, 1873. They registered with Gran parish on March 31, 1881 to leave the church and they emigrated April 1st. They contracted with the shipping line *Fr. Lie* on the ship *Hero*. They were listed on the ship manifest as Iver and Marthe Pedersen Eggebratten from Brandbu with their children, Kari age 6 and Gina age 2½. They were both thirty years old and their destination was Menemonee, WI. They lived in Menomonee for a year before they settled in New Richmond, WI near her sister Karen and Ole Lee. Iver was a shoemaker and a long time, well respected businessman and citizen of New Richmond. The US census in 1900 lists them in New Richmond, St Croix County as Iver, a shoemaker, age 48, Martha age 49, Carry age 25, Junie age 21, Charley age 16, Melvin age 14, Peter age 12, Ida age 9 and Viol0a age 2. In the Wisconsin 1905 Census Ivar was 53, Martha age 54, Gena age 25, Charles age 21, Melvin age 19, Ida age 15 and Viola age 7. In 1910 the same five children were still at home. Martha died on February 18, 1919 at age 69. Iver, age 68 was listed in 1920 as a cobbler with his own shop living with Gena age 40, Peder age 35 and Viola age 23. In 1930 he was still a cobbler at 78 and living alone. Iver died February 2, 1932 at age 80 years, 6 months and 7 days.   Martha and Ivar are buried in the New Richmond Cemetery, St. Croix County.

Iver Pedersen was born July 25, 1851 on a small farm called Dahlberg on Blegen gaard, in Brandbu, Gran, Oppland, Norway.   He was son of Peder Pedersen Blegeneie and Kari Ivarsdatter Kjoseiet. They immigrated in 1883 and joined their son in New Richmond, St. Croix, WI.

Martha and Iver's children:

Kari Pedersen	b. Oct 2, 1874	d. Mar 25, 1951
m. Jan 10, 1901 to Lars P Melbostad	b. Apr 15, 1870	d. Oct 4, 1949
Children: Irving Adolf	b. May 25, 1902	d. Feb 1, 1986
Stella Marion	b. Jun 29, 1904	d. Oct 23, 1995
Lottie A	b. Nov 6, 1906	d. Nov 1, 1965
Loren Kermit	b. Jul 1, 1909	d. Feb 15, 1976
Howard William	b. Dec 26, 1911	d. Mar 31. 1995
Esther Dorothy	b. Sep 20, 1913	d. Apr 27, 1973
Caroline Geraldine	b. Apr 6, 1916	d. Jun 9, 1992
Merton Donovan	b. Apr 23, 1919	d. Feb 11, 1994
Peder Pedersen	b. Dec 6 1876	d. Feb 1877
Gena Pedersen	b. May 3, 1881	d. 1883
Charles Peder Pedersen	b. Mar 14, 1884	d. Sep 24, 1964
m. Amanda Brummeier	b. Mar 1900	d. Aft 1946
Children: Robert Clinton	b. Apr 24, 1918	d. May 14, 1989
Loretta Gena	b. Oct 25, 1921	d. Jul 21, 2010
Charles P	b. May 1, 1922	d. Mar 21, 2003
Melvin Pedersen	b. Feb 16, 1886	d. Sep 18, 1968
m. Oct 8, 1905 to Clara Louise Bottolfson	b. Dec 25, 1884	d. Mar 13 1975
Children: Irving Arthur	b. Mar 19, 1906	d. Jun 3, 1987
Earl Mason	b. Apr 3, 1907	d. May 30, 2001
Ronald Leroy	b. Jul 28, 1910	d. Mar 12, 1975
Gordon Willard	b. Nov 25, 1915	d. Apr 28, 1989
Jane Marie	b. Jul 11, 1925	d. Aug 15, 2006
Peder Pedersen	b. Feb 16, 1888	d. Jul 22, 1961
m. Jan 8, 1927 to Grace Louisa Ryder	b. Jan 9, 1901	d. Mar 14, 1950
Children: Marilyn J	b. Apr 9, 1929	d.
Donald V	b. 1930	d.
Ida Melia Pedersen	b. Aug 5, 1890	d. Oct 31, 1946
m. Jun 7, 1911 to Hjalmer Peter Thronson	b. Aug 18, 1885	d. May 1967
Children: Marian Adelaid	b. May 18, 1912	d. Sep 4, 1985
Robert Randolph	b. Apr 24, 1915	d. Jun 17, 1983
Carl Frederick	b. Jun 25, 1922	d. Mar 1965
Howard	b. 1928	d. 1928
Viola Almida Pedersen	b. Sep 4, 1897	d. Jan 12, 1992

Gilbert Gilbertson and Caroline Olsdatter
Back: Ole, Gilbert, Kristi, Emma, & Kari Front: Mabel, Anne, Caroline, Lena, Gilbert & Otto

Gudbrand (Gilbert) Gilbertson was born July 31, 1852 in the area of Brandbu in Gran *Prestegjeld*, Gran *Kommune,* Hadeland Traditional District, Oppland *flyke,* Norway on the Eggeiet gård. He was baptized on August 21st, the son of Gulbrand Gulbrandson and Kari Olsdatter. Gilbert married Caroline Olsdatter on December 28, 1873. They migrated on March 20, 1884 with their five children: Kari age 10, Kjersti age 8, Ole age 5, Gilbert age 3 and Anna age two months. Anna died a few months after they arrived of pneumonia. They settled near Blue Mounds in Dane County. They were listed on the U.S. Census of 1900 as Gilbert Gulbrandson, age 46 and Carolina, age 45 with their five children: Anna age 13, Emma age 11, Maybell age 7, Lena age 5 and Otto age 2. The Wisconsin 1905 census lists Gilbert Gilbertson and Caroline with children; Mabel, Lena and Otto. In 1910 Ole age 31 was listed as the head of the household with his parents, Gilbert and Caroline, his 16 year old sister Lena and 13 year old brother Otto and sister Emma age 21 with her 2 month old daughter Clara. In 1920 Gilbert, age 68 was listed as head of household with his wife Caroline, age 67, their sons Otto age 23 and Ole age 42 and their daughter Mabel age 27 with her 5 year old son William Frame. Caroline died July 4, 1925 at the age of 70. In the 1930 Census, Gilbert, age 77 was living with his son Ole age 50, his son Otto age 33, his daughter Mabel age 35 and her son William Frame age 13. Gilbert died April 10, 1930 at the age of 77. They are buried in the Perry Lutheran Cemetery at Daleyville.

Caroline Olsdatter was born August 17, 1854, the daughter of Ole Borgersen and Kirstine Nilsdatter of Helgedalen in Tingelstad Parish in Gran, Oppland, Norway.

Gilbert and Caroline's children:

Kari Gilbertson	b. Mar 22, 1874	d. May 10, 1946
m. Sep 18, 1893 to Theodore B Lund	b. Apr 25, 1869	d.1946
Children: Alvin Lloyd	b. Jun 23, 1895	d. Oct 23, 1951
Ida May	b. Jan 27, 1899	d. Aft 1941
Clara Irene	b. Dec 14, 1901	d. Jan 1, 1984
Arthur William	b. May 25, 1902	d. Dec 14, 1983
Obert Raymond	b. Jul 24, 1905	d. Mar 31, 1970
Marvin Gilman	b. Dec 9, 1907	d. Aug 20, 1994
Viola Marvita	b. Apr 6, 1912	d. Apr 3, 1989
Ruby Christine	b. Jan 27, 1916	d. Aug 17, 1942
Kjersti (Christine) Gilbertson	b. Mar 6, 1876	d. Jul 23, 1914

m. Nov 8, 1905 to Nicolai Ben Lund	b. Jul 21, 1863	d. Nov 25,1948
Children: Beulah	b. Aug 18, 1906	d. Apr 13, 2001
Mildred Charlotte	b. Feb 14, 1908	d. Mar 30, 1986
Edna Laucerne	b. Jul 28, 1913	d. Jan 13, 1990
Ole Gilbertson	b. Aug 30, 1878	d. Aug 1, 1959
Gudbrand (Gilbert) Gilbertsen	b. Aug 21, 1880	d. Nov 12, 1942
m. 1901 to Rosena Anderson	b. Apr 3, 1877	d. Nov 6, 1929
Children: Milo Roy	b. Aug 1, 1904	d. Sep 5, 1991
Lila V	b. Sep 19, 1907	d. Apr 2, 1989
Bernice Luella	b. Oct 14, 1912	d. Mar 10, 1990
Alta Bernice	b. Aug 31, 1916	d. Jul 4, 1987
m. Helen Dorine Harvey after 1930	b. Nov 6, 1903	d. Nov 7, 1985
Children: David	b. Oct 3, 1939	d.
Joseph	b. Oct 3, 1939	d.
Anna Gilbertson	b. Jan 9, 1884	d. 1884
Anna Gilbertson	b. Sep 20, 1886	d. May 30, 1955
m. Sep 20, 1907 to Theodore O Topper	b. Dec 1, 1884	d. Feb 21, 1937
Children: Gilman	b. Jan 31, 1908	d. Jun 28, 1986
Mildred Viola	b. Jan 30, 1910	d. Aug 6, 1977
Hazel Marida	b. Aug 15, 1912	d. Nov 18, 1981
Marvin Clifford	b. Mar 7, 1913	d. Mar 22, 1987
Esther Elenore	b. Jun 19, 1916	d. Oct 21, 1998
Ruth Bernice	b. Feb 24, 1919	d. Apr 5, 1919
Ruth Bernice	b. Jan 2, 1920	d. Dec 1, 2012
Clifford Tillman	b. Sep 2, 1921	d. Mar 9, 2001
Donald Richard	b. Oct 27, 1924	d. Feb 7, 1985
Emma Gilbertson	b. Oct 3, 1888	d. Mar 22, 1967
m. Jan 18, 1916 to Ole Swingen	b. May 3 1882	d. Jun 24, 1969
Children: Clara Geneva	b. Mar 17, 1910	d. Nov 19, 1993
Wallace Melvin	b. Nov 12, 1916	d. Dec 22, 1989
Endelien (Ann)	b. Jun 17, 1919	d. Jun 23, 2004
Alvida (Eleanor)	b. Sep 14, 1921	d. Mar 18, 2004
Doris Arlene	b. Nov 29, 1924	d. Sep 26, 1996
Gaylord Milo	b. Jan 13, 1928	d. Jan 17, 2000
Mabel Thilda Gilbertson	b. Dec 31, 1893	d. Dec 31, 1936
m. Aug 5, 1935 to Olin Nelson	b. Sep 23, 1899	d. May 19, 1953
Children: William V Frame	b. Apr 3, 1915	d. May 4, 1975
Lena Gilbertson	b. Aug 10, 1894	d. Oct 17, 1987
m. June 10, 1914 to Melvin Bonner	b. Nov 27, 1892	d. Nov 4, 1918
Children: Alvin Robert	b. Jan 14, 1914	d. Mar 18, 1931
Melvina Lillian	b. May 17, 1919	d. Jul 2, 2006
m. May 15, 1924 to Carl William Radel	b. May 2, 1895	d. Oct 20 1959
Otto Gilbertson	b. Jul 2, 1897	d. Sep 7, 1972

Ingeborg (Isabelle) Gilbertson was born April 2, 1858 in the area of Brandbu in Gran *Prestegjeld*, Gran *Kommune*, Hadeland Traditional District, Oppland *flyke*, Norway on the Eggeiet gård.

She was baptized on April 25th, the daughter of Gulbrand Gulbrandson and Kari Olsdatter. Ingeborg immigrated in April of 1879 at the age of 22 on a Star Line steamship and settled near Monroe, WI. She went to work on the farm of Nils Paalserud and Anne Stenrud where she met their son, Erick (Nielsen Paalserud) Thompson. They married on October 18, 1882 in Darlington, WI on the way to their future home in Iowa. They settled on a small farm near Soldier, IA and were listed on the Iowa Census of 1885 as Erick age 28, Belle age 24 with their daughter Anna age 1. Annie died at the age of two. They purchased a farm in Jordan Township, Monona County near Moorhead, Iowa and were on the U.S. Census in 1900 with their six children: Nels age 14, Annie age 11, Emma age 9, Cora age 7, Ida age 5 and Oliver (Elmer) age 1. On the 1910 census they were still in Jordan Township with Nels age 24, Emma age 19, Cora age 17, Ida age 15 and Elmer age 11. They were living in Soldier, Monona County, IA in 1915 according to the Iowa census, Eric was 62 and Isabelle was 56. They bought a house in Soldier in 1918 and their daughter Ida helped care for them until their death. Ingeborg died at their home in Soldier, IA on December 25, 1920 at the age of 67. Erick died April 30, 1922 at the age of 69. They are buried in the Soldier Valley Cemetery in Monona County, Iowa.

Erick Nielson Thompson was born on November 12, 1852 on the Framstad gård in Gran Municipality, Oppland, Norway. He was the son of Nils Paalserud and Anne Stenrud Rosendaleiet. They emigrated in 1853 when Erick was a baby. Erick died April 30, 1922 in Soldier, Monona, IA.

Ingeborg and Erick's children:

Anne Thompson   b. May 10, 1884 d. Aug 12, 1886

449

Nels Gilbert Thompson	b. Nov 1, 1885	d. Sep 13, 1971
m. Jan 17, 1927 to Violet Olina Kline	b. Jul 16, 1896	d. Dec 27, 1968
Children: Virginia Nell	b. Oct 15, 1927	d. Jan 23, 2007
Naomi Colleen	b. Sep 14, 1929	d. Feb 13, 2010
Delores Ilene	b. Oct 24, 1932	d. Mar 27, 2009
Carol Elaine	b. Jan 22, 1934	d. Apr 15, 2007
Elmer Nel	b. Apr 22, 1939	d.
Annie Thompson	b. Jun 15, 1888	d. Jan 5, 1923
m. Oct 10, 1906 to Elmer C. Lee	b. Oct 5, 1885	d. Oct 3, 1974
Children: Palma Irene	b. Mar 13, 1907	d. Mar 13, 1988
Elliott Clayton	b. Nov 15, 1920	d. Sep 15, 2008
Emma Thompson	b. Aug 30, 1890	d. Jan 28, 1962
m. Jan 28, 1914 to Erick Tilman Erickson	b. Aug 21, 1887	d. Oct 10, 1951
Children: Earl Tilman	b. Dec 7, 1914	d. Jul 6, 1979
Leroy Clayton	b. Jun 14, 1916	d. Feb 28, 1992
Evelyn Cora	b. Jun 10, 1919	d. Mar 20, 1985
Erling Elliott	b. Aug 27, 1923	d. Feb 12, 1997
Cora Thompson	b. Jan 24, 1893	d. Feb 19, 1919
m. Dec 10, 1913 to Marvel M. Lee	b. Feb 28, 1891	d. May 20, 1966
Children: Marion Ellsworth	b. Sep 25, 1914	d. Dec 11, 1914
Everett Marvin	b. Sep 29, 1915	d. Apr 20, 1995
Ida Thompson	b. May 15, 1895	d. Aug 8, 1972
m. Feb 8, 1922 to Marvel M. Lee	b. Feb 28, 1891	d. May 20, 1966
Children: Marjorie Elaine	b. Nov 14, 1922	d.
Myrlin Clair	b. Mar 17, 1925	d. Apr 12, 2008
Elmer (Tommy) Grant Thompson	b. Mar 13, 1899	d. Jun 17, 1938
m. Jun 23, 1928 to Johanna Newbaum	b. Jul 28, 1909	d. Aug 24, 1974

Birthe (Bertha) Gilbertson was born May 19, 1860 in the area of Brandbu in Gran *Prestegjeld*, Gran *Kommune*, Hadeland Traditional District, Oppland *flyke*, Norway on the Eggeiet gård. She was baptized on June 3rd, the daughter of Gulbrand Gulbrandson and Kari Olsdatter. Birthe immigration about 1880 and settled in the same area as her sister Johanna in Green County, Wisconsin. Berthe married Edward A. Thompson on January 3, 1885. They lived in Adams Township a few years before moving to York Township in Green County. The 1895 Wisconsin Census records Edward Thompson living in York, Green County with 4 males and 3 females in the household. In the 1900 U.S. Census they were in York, Green County with all seven of their children. Their son Selmer died in January of 1903 of strep infection and was buried in the York Lutheran Cemetery. They were still in York, Green County on the 1905 and 1910 census with their six children. Their son Clarence took over the farm in 1918 and they retired from farming and moved to Blanchardville, WI. The census for 1920 and 1930 records

them living in Moscow Township, Iowa County in Blanchardville. They were living with their daughter Emma and her husband Andrew Ayen in their final years. Edward died November 16, 1946 at home at the age of 86. Bertha died a few months later on February 10, 1947 at the age of 86. They are buried in the York Lutheran Cemetery.

Edward Thompson was born June 25, 1860 in Adams Township, Green County, WI, the son of Embert (Harestua) Thompson and Caroline Gisleberg (Ingwall) from Gran, Norway. They emigrated in 1852.

Bertha and Edward's children:

Gilbert Thompson	b. Aug 9, 1883	d. 1955
Emeline Emma Thompson	b. Oct 9, 1886	d. Nov 17, 1982
m. Dec 8, 1935 to Andrew Ayen	b. Aug 25, 1888	d. Nov 21, 1988
Clarence Thompson	b. Sep 4, 1889	d. Sep 6, 1947
m. Mar 1, 1922 to Mabel Clara Lund	b. Feb 1890	d. Jun 6, 1962
Children: Dean Lavern	b. 1930	d. 1931
Clayton Myron	b. Jan 24, 1924	d. Mar 17, 1993
Richard Dean	b. Jun 4, 1932	d. Jan 13, 2005
Edward Bernard Jr. Thompson	b. Sep 19, 1892	d. Apr 11, 1985
m. Dec 27, 1916 to Mary Rosella Anderson	b. Dec 25, 1891	d. Oct 22, 1984
Children: Vivien Evangeline	b. Oct 25, 1917	d. Aug 14, 2009
Paul Luther	b. Feb 13, 1921	d. Jul 22, 2004
John Edward	b. Dec 30, 1923	d. Apr 15, 2007
Robert Donald	b. Jul 18, 1925	d. Jun 29, 2007
Clara Mabel Thompson	b. Nov 4, 1894	d. Aug 1953
m. 1921 to Oscar Vamstad	b. Jan 24, 1896	d. Jul 17, 1969
Children: Everett Orlando	b. Dec 15, 1922	d. Jan 16, 1998
Doris Mae	b. Aug 15, 1925	d.
Oscar Luther	b. Oct 24, 1930	d.
Annie Mathilda Thompson	b. Jul 21, 1898	d. 1953
Selmer Thompson	b. May 5, 1900	d. Jan 28, 1903

Ole Gilbertson was born October 13, 1862 in the area of Brandbu in Gran *Prestegjeld*, Gran *Kommune*, Hadeland Traditional District, Oppland *flyke*, Norway on the Eggeiet gård. He was baptized on November 9th, the son of Gulbrand Gulbrandson and Kari Olsdatter. Ole died May 14, 1937 at the age of 74 near Hollandale, Iowa Co, WI and is buried in the Hollandale Cemetery.

Ole emigrated on April 28, 1881 at the age of 18 on the ship *Rollo* out of Kristiania (Oslo). He contracted with the ship line A. Sharp and his destination was Monroe, WI. Ole joined his sister Johanna Paulson and her family in Adams Township, Green County, WI. He settled in Moscow Township in Iowa County and married Anna (Olsdatter) Westlund on May 25, 1889 in Blanchardville, WI at the Lutheran Church. Tosten and Inger Paulson were their marriage witnesses. The 1895 Wisconsin Census lists the family in the Town of Moscow, Iowa County with 3 males and 3 females. The 1900 Federal Census lists Ole Gilbertson age 36, in Moscow Township, Iowa Co, WI with his wife Annie age 41, and their children; Selma P, age 13; Martin G, age 10; Christina A, age 6; Elmer O, age 4; and Ellen M, age 1. In the June 1, 1905 Wisconsin Census they were in Moscow Township listed as: Ole, age 42; Annie, age 45; Selma, age 18; Martin, age 15; Christina, age 13; Oliver, age 9; Ellen, age 6; and Raymond, age 4 months.

Ole Gilbertson purchased land south of Hollandale from Martin Bollerud on September 4, 1907 for $8,615.00. The Iowa County Abstract Warranty Deed stated the N½ NW¼ of Section 4-4-5, except right of way of Railroad Company and except ½ acre adjoining right of way sold to Railroad Company, containing 83.08/100 acres. Also the SW¼ NW¼ of Section 4-4-5, containing 40 acres. He sold the land to his son Oliver E Gilbertson for $12,300.00 on March 1, 1924.

Ole Gilbertson & Anna Westlund Family Selma, Ole, Oliver, Christine, Ellen, Anna, Raymond & Martin

The 1910 Federal Census records this family in Moscow Township with Ole age 47, Anna age 51, Martin age 20, Oliver age 14, Ellen age 11 and Raymond age 5. Selma age 23, was living in Chicago as a servant with Clesson and Julia Phillips. Christine age 17, was also in Chicago with Robert and Ida McCleary working as a servant. Christine married Selmer Lien in 1913. Selma married Tim Burns in 1914 and Martin married Nellie Vamstad in 1914. The 1920 census lists Ole age 58, Annie age 60, Oliver age 23, Raymond age 15 and Ellen age 21. Ellen married Henry Hendrickson in 1921. Anna died December 2, 1925 at age 67. Oliver married Florence Stoker about 1925 and Raymond married Leta McCoy in 1927. In 1930 Ole age 67, was living with his son Oliver age 34, his wife Florence and their 3 year old son James. Ole died May 14, 1937 at the age of 74. He is buried in the Hollandale Cemetery.

Anna Olson Westlund was born April 30, 1859 in Sunne Parish, Sunne municipality, Varmland County, Svealand Province, Sverige (Sweden). She was the daughter of Olof Larsson Toneby and Kajsa Jonsdatter Stopsjon. Anna died near Hollandale, Iowa Co, WI on December 2, 1925 at the age of 67 and is buried in the Hollandale Cemetery. Anna was the youngest of eight children, six boys and two girls. She was born on Westanjo farm and took the name Westlund when she immigrated alone in 1882. She settled in St. Croix County near New Richmond and became acquainted with either Anna Hanson, Karen Lee or Martha Pederson, sisters of Ole. She had a daughter, Selma born in New Richmond in 1887. She settled in Iowa County, possibly with Johanna & Torsten Paulson where she met and married Ole Gilbertson in 1889.

Ole and Anna's children:

Selma Pauline Gilbertson	b. Feb 23, 1887	d. May 7, 1958
m. Jan 27, 1914 to Timothy Francis Burns	b. Nov 2, 1888	d. Jul 1, 1970
Children: Mildred	b. 1912	d. Sep 30, 1943
Francis	b. 1914	d. 1921
Paul Jerold	b. Sep 17, 1916	d. Mar 5, 2008
Robert T	b. Jul 26, 1918	d. Oct 18, 2000
Arlene Mary	b. Feb 3, 1921	d. Mar 17, 1946
Francis Celestine	b. Sep 5, 1923	d. Sep 11, 1977
Lorraine Anne	b. Oct 5, 1925	d. Mar 1, 2004
Timothy Raphael	b. Aug 11, 1928	d. May 20, 1968
Cyril Benedict	b. Mar 21, 1931	d. Jun 14, 1999
Mona Patrice	b. Aug 11, 1932	d.
Martin Gilbert Gilbertson	b. Mar 30, 1890	d. July 13, 1970
m. Apr 8, 1914 to Nellie M Vamstad	b. Mar 31, 1892	d. May 5, 1972
Children: Orrin Alton	b. Jan 19, 1915	d. Oct 2, 1978
Malcom Burnell	b. Mar 17, 1917	d. Jul 17, 2002
Girl died at birth	b. 1920	d. 1920
Otis Leroy	b. Jan 8, 1926	d.
Martin Laverne Jr.	b. Jan 21, 1934	d. Jan 11, 2005
Christine Amelia Gilbertson	b. Jun 29, 1892	d. Oct 13, 1957
m. 1913 to Selmer C Lien	b. Dec 1, 1889	d. Sep 27, 1978
Children: Crystal Amy	b. Dec 13, 1914	d. Jul 18, 1997
Sylvia C	b. Feb 1, 1916	d. Feb 2, 1984
Kermit	b. Sep 10, 1917	d. Mar 6, 1968
Howard	b. Sep 10, 1919	d. May 28, 1978
Dorothy Mae	b. Apr 23, 1923	d. Sep 7, 1995
Otis Cyrus	b. Apr 15, 1925	d. Apr 8, 2003
Oliver Elmer Gilbertson	b. Jan 31, 1895	d. Aug 2, 1968

m. to Florence Myrtle Stoker	b. Oct 14, 1906	d. Jun 8, 1993
Children: Robert James	b. Oct 6, 1926	d. Dec 26, 2005
Gerald E	b. Aug 21, 1930	d. Nov 6, 2006
Francis A "Pete"	b. Aug 28, 1931	d.
Mary Ann	b. Sep 17, 1934	d.
Selma Lucille	b. Oct 29, 1937	d.
Sharon Lea	b. Nov 7, 1939	d.
Ellen Marie Gilbertson	b. Aug 28, 1898	d. Oct 23, 1973
m. Feb 22, 1921 to Henry Hendrickson	b. Jul 19, 1899	d. Feb 10, 1950
Children: Anna Karine	b. Aug 19, 1921	d. Jun 28, 2009
Joan Elaine	b. Jul 8, 1924	d.
Orlene Mae	b. Apr 25, 1926	d. Dec 6, 1988
Eleanor Marie	b. Nov 25, 1930	d. Jul 8, 2010
Henry Delano	b. Mar 2, 1933	d. Oct 6, 1982
Dean Eugene	b. Nov 17, 1935	d. Sep 2, 2006
Marilyn Patricia	b. May 13, 1938	d. Dec 13, 2005
Raymond Alvin Gilbertson	b. Mar 17, 1906	d. Oct 2, 1969
m. Jun 29, 1929 to Leta Francis McCoy	b. Dec 17, 1908	d. Jan 16, 1980
Children: Betty Jean	b. Dec 7, 1929	d.
Carole Rae	b. Nov 16, 1930	d.
Dorothy Ann	b. Dec 12, 1933	d.-

Anna Gilbertson was born April 21, 1865 in the area of Brandbu in Gran *Prestegjeld*, Gran *Kommune*, Hadeland Traditional District, Oppland *flyke*, Norway on the Eggeiet gård. She was baptized on May 7th, the daughter of Gulbrand Gulbrandson and Kari Olsdatter. Anna immigrated with her sister Kari and her father, Gulbrand Gulbrandsen on May 5, 1882 on the ship *Rollo* at the age of 16. The ship contract stated her age as 11 1/2. Anna's mother had died shortly before they left Norway. They joined her brother, Ole in Moscow Township, Iowa County, Wisconsin and/or her two sisters, Johanna Paulson and Bertha Thompson both in York Township, Green County. Two of her sisters, Karen Lee and Martha Pederson settled in New Richmond and Star Prairie in St. Croix County and Anna joined them where she met and married Chris Hanson on May 25, 1889.

The 1900 U.S. Census lists them in New Richmond, St. Croix County, WI as Christon Hanson, age 37, Anna Hanson, age 32 with Harry, age 8; Korra, age 5; and Lagoter, age 9 months. Christ was a saw mill worker and they had a 16 year old servant, Christine Damm and ten men living with them, listed as boarders who all worked at the saw mill. The 1905 Wisconsin Census has Chris and Anna living next door to her sister, Martha and Ivar Pederson in New Richmond. The listing had Chris, age 42 as a Saloon Keeper with Anna, age 36; Harry, age 12; Cora, age 10; Gertie, age 5; and Carl, age 2. The 1910 Census lists Chris, age 47, a Saloon Keeper with Annie, age 43; Harry, age 19; Cora, age 16; Legarthe, age 10; Carl, age 7; and Aunker, age 4. The record states Annie had 6 children with 5 living. Her obituary lists a son Edward who died in infancy. (There is a child in the New Richmond cemetery named Chris Hanson who died November 2, 1898 at one month old.)   In the 1920 Census H.C. Hanson was listed as the proprietor of a Pool Room at age 55 with Annie, age 52; Carl, age 17; and Marcus A (Aunker?), age 12. Chris died March 2, 1930 at the age of 68.   The 1930 Census lists an Anna Hanson, age 63 in Star Prairie, St. Croix County in a nursing facility with several elderly people. Anna died May 27, 1933 at the age of 68 in Mendota, a Madison Hospital. She is buried in the New Richmond Cemetery, St. Croix County, WI.

Hans Christian "Chris" Hanson was born in Frederiksstad municipality, Ostfold County, Norway in May of 1861. He died March 22, 1930 at age of 68 years in St. Paul, MN. He is buried in the New Richmond Cemetery, St. Croix County, WI.   Chris immigrated about 1883 at age 21. He settled in the New Richmond area and married Anna Gilbertson in 1889. He was employed by the Willow River Lumber Company for 17 years. He owned and operated his own business, a pool hall and saloon in New Richmond for 18 years. The last few years of his life he farmed near Cedar Lake. He died at St. Luke's Hospital in St. Paul after a long illness. In census records he was listed as Chris, Christon, Christ and H.C. His death record in the New Richmond Cemetery lists H.C. Hanson of Star Prairie died March 22, 1930 at age 68 years, 10 months and 19 days.

Anna and Chris 'children:

Harry George Hanson	b. Mar 28, 1892 d. Apr 11, 1975	
m. Aug 20, 1914 to Betty Erickson	b. 1882	d. Sep 5, 1972
Children: Mabel Adeline	b. 1915	d.
Harold W	b. 1919	d.
Cora L. Hanson	b. Sept 22, 1894 d. Aug 22, 1963	
m. Mar 2, 1912 to Charles L Bell	b. Aug 4, 1889 d. Sep 13, 1913	
Children: Charles L. Bell/Dean	b. 1914	d.
m. Oct 9, 1919 to George James Dean	b. Jul 1, 1888	d. Aug 4, 1960
Edward (Chris) Hanson	b. Oct 1898	d. Nov 2, 1898
Legartha Edvine Hanson	b. Mar 27, 1900 d. Nov 7, 1970	
m. Dec 31, 1919 to Edward H. King	b. Oct 3, 1893	d. Sep 29, 1963
Children: John E.	b. 1921	d. Mar 14, 1944
Richard Russell	b. Nov 10, 1926	d. Apr 6, 2010
Edward Carl	b. May 12, 1929 d. Sep 15, 1997	
Carl John Hanson	b. Jul 12, 1902	d. Jul 11, 1961
Aunker Marcus Hanson	b. Apr 30, 1906 d. Apr 3, 1931	

Kari (Carrie) Gilbertson was born November 28, 1868 in the area of Brandbu in Gran *Prestegjeld*, Gran *Kommune,* Hadeland Traditional District, Oppland *flyke*, Norway on the

Eggeiet gård. She was baptized on December 25th, the daughter of Gulbrand Gulbrandson and Kari Olsdatter. Kari emigrated with her sister Anna and her father, Gulbrand Gulbrandsen on May 5, 1882 on the ship Rollo at the age of 13. The ship contract stated her age as 10. Gulbrand and his two young daughters joined his son Ole in Moscow Township, Iowa County, Wisconsin. Kari met Tom Halvorson and moved with his family to Iowa where they married on December 31, 1888 in Onawa, IA. On the 1900 U.S. Census they were living in Soldier, Monona County, Iowa with children: Helmer age 5, Guy age 5 and Effa age 10 months. They were also living with Tom's mother, Carrie Halverson age 70 and his brothers John age 31 and Ole age 30. In 1910 they were living in Cedar, Nebraska with Helmer age 18, Guy age 15, Effa age 10, Clara age 8 and Mabel age 5. Tom died on December 15, 1915 at the age of 58 and was buried in New Castle, Dixon County, NE a suburb of Sioux City, IA. In 1920 the widow Carrie, age 52 was living in Daily, Dixon County, NE with her children Helmer age 28, Guy age 25, Effie age 20, Clara age 17, Mabel age 15 and Henry age 7. The 1925 the Iowa Census lists Carrie age 56 in Sioux City, Woodbury County, Iowa with her children: Guy age 28, Effie age 24, Mabel age 19 and Henry age 13. In 1930 Carrie was living in Sioux City, Woodbury County, Iowa with Guy age 32 and Henry age 18. Kari died November 12, 1959 at the age of 91 and is buried in Sioux City, IA.

Carrie Gilbertson and Tom Halvorson

Tom Halvorson was born June 7, 1857 in the Hadeland area of Norway, the son of Halver Halverson and Kari Paulson. This family emigrated in 1871 and was listed in the 1880 U.S. Census in Fayette, Lafayette County, Wisconsin. The Head of Household was H. Holverson age 28 with his wife Maria, and they were living with his widowed mother, Cary age 50 and his brothers Thomas, John, Ole and Gilbert and his sister Rhoda. Carrie Halvorson was living in Obert, Cedar County, NE in 1920 with her son Ole age 46 and her daughter, Rhonda Works and her family.

Kari and Tom's children:

Helmer Halvorson	b. Jul 3, 1891	d. Oct 5, 1965
m. 1922 to Vera Ion York	b. Nov 2, 1902	d. Apr 27, 1981
Children: Harold Vernard	b. May 15, 1923	d. May 13, 1990

Lyle William	b. Feb 12, 1925	d.
Shirley June	b. Jun 1, 1926	d. Jun 29, 2010
Wendell J	b. 1929	d.
Clara Bernice	b. Jun 16, 1932	d. Feb 24, 2013
Darrell Wesley	b. Aug 5, 1934	d. May 5, 1937
Lois Arvilla	b. Apr 22, 1938	d.
Delores (Dee)	b. Jul 9, 1943	d.
Guy Halvorson	b. Oct 5, 1894	d. Oct 1970
Effa "Effie" Halvorson	b. Jul 31, 1899	d. Oct 29, 1974
m. Mar 1, 1926 to Frank Vernon Clay	b. Jun 29, 1901	d. Jan 18 1975
Children: Frank Vernon	b. Sep 19, 1926	d.
Vernon Irvin	b. Mar 31, 1928	d.
Richard Dean	b. Apr 17, 1930	d. May 15, 2006
Betty Jean	b. Dec 18, 1932	d. Sep 20, 1952
Norman Leroy	b. Sep 19, 1934	d.
Donald Lee	b. Nov 4, 1936	d. Aug 25, 2005
William Henry	b. May 12, 1943	d. Jun 14, 1993
Clara Halvorson	b. Feb 7, 1902	d. Jan 7, 1992
m. Jul 5, 1923 to Sydney (Pete) Rasmussen	b. Jan 18, 1899	d. Dec 18, 1976
Children: Albert	b. Apr 10, 1925	d. Dec 1928
Mary Yvonne	b. Jun 6, 1927	d. Jan 15, 2013
Elaine	b. Feb 3, 1929	d. Mar 13, 1991
Thomas P	b. May 31, 1931	d. Jul 11, 1975
Robert C	b. Jul 19, 1932	d. Sep 29, 2013
Glynn H	b. Jan 21, 1935	d.
William D	b. Dec 8, 1936	d.
Russell Lee	b. Sep 5, 1938	d. Jun 5, 2010
Delores	b. Feb 6, 1940	d.
James F	b. Jun 17, 1941	d. Nov 15, 2001
Deanna Faye	b. Apr 10, 1944	d.
Dennis E	b. Sep 24, 1946	d.
Mabel Nadine Halvorson	b. Aug 9, 1905	d. Jan 5, 1999
m. Apr 4, 1925 to Wesley John Hansel	b. May 2,1905	d. May 31, 1983
Children: Pauline Phyllis	b. Oct 10, 1925	d.
Henry (Hank) Halvorson	b. Jan 9, 1912	d. July 7, 2002
m. Nov 30, 1945 to Vera Augusta Sulsberger	b. Jan 3, 1916	d. Jul 29, 1996
Children: Carrie H	b. Sep 28. 1946	d.
Julie Ann	b. Sep 24, 1949	d.
Joan	b. Mar 21, 1951	d.

Gilbertson sisters l-r: Johanna Paulson, Bertha Thompson, Karen Lee, Annie Hanson and Martha Pederson

The Wamstad Brothers

published February 2015   Forms 529, 530, 531   *Larry Shoger*

Andreas Torsteinsen Hvamstad was born 28 February 1882 at Hvamstad, Tingelstad, Gran, Hadeland. His parents were Torstein Olsen Hvamstad and Elina Torstensdatter Helmen. He was the eighth child of nine siblings. In 1899, Andrew immigrated to America when he was 17 years old and shortly thereafter changed his name to Andrew Thomas Wamstad. He had heard of the good fortunes of America from his two older brothers, Lars Thorstein Wamstad and Carl Adolph Wamstad, who had immigrated to America in 1889. Andrew settled in Cedar Township, Mitchell County, Iowa where his brothers were living. It is important to note that Lars T. Wamstad and Carl A. Wamstad immigrated to America after hearing about the accounts sent to them by their aunt and uncle, Anna Olsdater Hvamstad and Gulbrand Gulbrandson Lundberg who had immigrated to America in 1865 and settled in Cedar Township, Mitchell County, Iowa and his two uncles, Anders Olsen Wamstad and Brede Olsen Wamstad, who had immigrated to the same area in 1887.

The 1900 Federal Census shows Andrew living with his uncle and aunt, Ole and Carrie Wamstad, and their four children in Cedar Township, Mitchell County, Iowa.

Cpl. Wamstad's uniform, found on E-Bay

Andrew enlisted in the U.S. Army in 1903 and served until 1906. He enlisted at the age of 21 yrs, 10 mos, was 5'10 1/4" tall, had brown hair and brown eyes. He was assigned to the Coast Artillery unit in Washington state. He was honorably discharged on March 23, 1906, at Fort Flagler, Washington, at the rank of Corporal.

In 2011, Diedre Olsen Badker and I were contacted by Carol Maki of Port Ludlow, Washington concerning a military uniform the historical society had found on Ebay. The uniform was described as procured at a Minneapolis/ St. Paul, Minnesota estate sale with the 106th Company collar insignias, and a gunnery medal with the name A.T. Wamstad inscribed on the back. So Carol Maki did some research and found Diedre had posted some information online about the Wamstad family. Carol then contacted Diedre who in turn contacted me, since Andrew T. Wamstad

459

had married into my Shoger family. It turns out that this uniform was in fact Andrew's and it brought more details of his military service to light.

After his service, Andrew returned to Iowa. In 1908, he moved to Minneapolis, Minnesota. The 1910 Federal census lists him living in Ward 2, Minneapolis and working as a motorman for the railway. He attended college in St. Paul, Minnesota.

On October 25, 1916, Andrew married Mathilda Shoger at Rock Creek Lutheran Church, Meroa, Iowa. Mathilda was the daughter of Andrew and Betsy (Larson) Shoger. Her parents were both born in America and their parents were immigrants from Norway. Mathilda's grandparents, Christian and Anne Shoger, were from Land, Oppland, Norway and Bastian and Anne Larsen were from Fjeldberg, Hordaland, Norway.

Marvin Wamstad

David Wamstad

Andrew and Mathilda lived their entire married life together in St. Paul, Minnesota. They had three sons - Telford, Marvin and David. Andrew worked as a mail clerk for 44 years. He was a charter member of St. Anthony Park Lutheran Church, and was an active member of his church and the local Sons of Norway Lodge, as well as the Retired Postal Clerks Association.

Andrew passed away on October 17, 1963 at the Mounds Midway Hospital in St. Paul. His wife Mathilda passed away on May 2, 1973 in St. Paul. Andrew and Mathilda are buried at St. Paul, Minnesota.

The following information is from several newspaper accounts of a serious accident which involved Andrew T. Wamstad while he was in the service. The first one is from the November 5th, 1905 edition of the *Port Townsend Daily Leader:*

MAN INJURED AT FLAGLER YESTERDAY
CORPORAL WAHMSTEAD OF THE 106th Co THE VICTIM

Fort Flagler, across the bay from here, was yesterday the scene of a serious accident which, so far as meager reports and restricted telephonic advices were obtainable last night, would indicate that they will probably result in the death of the victim.

Under command of Lieutenant Margetts, the men of the 106th Company were engaged in regular autumn firing with the 12-inch guns and the practice had proceeded without incident beyond the display of superior marksmanship until a squad under Corporal Wahmstead was taking its turn. As stated, information from the scene is limited, but as so far as can be learned, the heavy carriage was returning to its position, a defect in the mechanism caused a break, and a heavy piece of steel casting was precipitated upward and outward, striking Wahmstead in the side of the head and hurling him violently to the ground. Firing was at once suspended and every possible assistance was rendered the injured man. It was plain to be seen that he was seriously hurt and examination made later developed the fact that the unfortunate corporal had sustained a fracture of the left side of the cranium, his shoulders were badly wrenched, and it is believed that he has suffered internal injuries.

That the accident to the gun itself was of a serious nature is shown in the fact that the commandant yesterday wired East for new parts to replace the damaged portions. Had the break been of minor importance, repairs could have been made either by the company machinist, or at least in one of the big repair shops up-Sound.

As is usual in such cases, the accident will be made the subject of an official investigation, and until this is held and the findings have been sent to the war department for approval and publicity, the reading public will be in the dark as to the real cause of the mishap.

The present is the first serious accident which has occurred at any of the forts in the Puget Sound artillery district since its organization. An accident happened at Flagler some years ago, but this was as small arms practice. Through it, one of the men detailed to mark the shots exposed himself as a shot was fired and the bullet pierced the unfortunate soldier's skull, killing him instantly.

Owing to the fact that careful inspection is made of all preliminaries to the big gun practice, it can be stated with all but absolute positiveness that the accident of yesterday was resultant from defective construction in the gun in use and not through any carelessness on the part of the officers or men engaged in the firing.

Note: The individual that the article mentions being killed during small arms practice was Pvt. Everett Frazee.

This was followed up in the November 10th edition of the *Port Townsend Daily Leader:*

NO RESULTS ATTAINED IN FLAGLER ACCIDENT INJURY INQUIRY
DESPITE HIS SERIOUS WOUNDS CORPORAL WAHMSTEAD IS
RECOVERING

The official investigation which followed the accident occurring to a 12-inch gun at Fort Flagler on Tuesday last failed to develop any defect or deficiency in the construction of the metal parts of the heavy ordnance and leaves the causes as much a matter of speculation as it was when Corporal Wahmstead received his serious injuries.

Wahmstead, it appears, was detailed to sight the gun, and was standing on the sighting platform elevated about eight feet from the ground, with his eye glued to the telescope. The gun had been fired and was returning to the emplacement, and it was while this act of the mechanism was in progress that the buffer of the sighting support was struck. The force of the blow was communicated directly to the forehead of the unfortunate corporal, with the result that the skull above the right eye was badly shattered and the face torn open through the check to the mouth. Nor is this all. The force of the blow precipitated the unconscious man violently to the concrete floor of the emplacement, fracturing his collar bone, dislocating his shoulder and his left thumb as well as causing a great concussion at the back of his head. It was feared that this part of Wahmstead's injuries might prove the most serious as ordinarily concussion of the brain would result from such a jar.

The unlucky soldier was not entirely deserted by luck, however, for as stated he escaped concussion of the brain but also escaped the loss of sight of the eye, although the forehead and cheek-bones were badly shattered. According to reports last evening, under the efficient care of Post Surgeon Maybe, Wahmstead was resting easy and unless unforeseen complications set in is sure of recovery, although he will be badly disfigured as a result of his accident.

From *The Daily Colonist,* Victoria BC, Nov 8th 1905

Port Townsend, Nov. 7

During heavy target practice with the 12-inch guns at Fort Flagler this afternoon, an accident to the gun injured Corporal Wahmsted of the 106th Company so seriously that he may die. Wahmsted was a member of the firing squad under Lieut. Margetts. At the time of the accident the unfortunate man was working immediately behind the disappearing carriage of gun No. 1.

As the gun was fired a chunk of metal as large as a loaf of bread snapped loose from the carriage and struck the corporal with tremendous force over the left eye, fracturing the skull and rendering him unconscious. An operation was performed this afternoon and Wahmsted is still alive. He is a Minnesotan and has been a soldier two years. The seriousness of the damage to the gun may be seen from the fact that telegraphic orders for repairs to the carriage were sent East immediately after the accident.

From *The Los Angeles Herald;* Nov. 8th, 1905

SOLDIER FATALLY HURT
CORPORAL WAHMSTEAD INJURED DURING
ARTILLERY PRACTICE AT PORT TOWNSEND

By Associated Press

Port Townsend, Wash., Nov 7

Corporal Wahmstead of the 106th company, coast artillery, was seriously and probably fatally injured in an accident which occurred at noon today at Fort Flagler.

Practice with 16-inch guns was in progress when a defective carriage mechanism blew out a piece, striking Wahmstead, who was in charge of the firing squad, fracturing his skull and dislocating his shoulder.

An official inquiry will be commenced tomorrow to ascertain the cause of the accident.

Lars Thorsteinsen Hvamstad was born August 15, 1878 at Hvamstad, Tingelstad, Gran, Hadeland. His parents were Thorstein Olsen Hvamstad and Eline Thorstensdatter Helmen. He was one of three siblings who immigrated to America. On March 1, 1889, Lars set sail for America and traveled to Nora Springs, Iowa, which was located within walking distance of his three uncles' farms. He changed his name to Lars T. Wamstad.

Carl Adolph Thorsteinsen Hvamstad was born July 31, 1880 at Hvamstad, Tingelstad, Gran, Hadeland and came to America in 1890. Carl settled in Cedar Township, Mitchell County, Iowa where his brother, Lars T. Wamstad was living. Carl also changed his last name to Wamstad.

Lars and Carl worked for their uncles - Ole Wamstad, Andrew Wamstad and Gulbrand Gulbrandson on their farms in Cedar and Rock townships, Mitchell county, Iowa.

In 1891, Lars and Carl bought 95 acres of land from Paul Berge who had moved to North Dakota. This land was located on section 3, Cedar Township, Mitchell County, Iowa. There were no buildings on the land so they moved an old five-room house from the Ole & Ellen (Knutson-Shoger) Dahley farm and a building from the Sponheim farm which they used for a barn on their land site. A few years later, Andrew T. Wamstad joined his two brothers and helped work their farm land.

Interestingly enough, Andrew T. Wamstad later married Mathilda Shoger who grew up on the farm next door to this farm. Andrew T. and Mathilda Wamstad's story is told above.

On December 16, 1906, Lars married Caroline Enger Iverson at Rock Creek Lutheran church in Meroa, Mitchell County, Iowa. Caroline was born March 4, 1883 in Cedar township,

Mitchell county, Iowa. They became the parents of four children – Ethel (Mrs. John Robinson), Clifford, Tennes, and Georgia (Mrs. Orville Berg).

Around 1906, Carl moved to St. Paul, Minnesota. He died on October 10, 1918 in St. Paul from Spanish influenza. He is buried at Rock Creek Lutheran Cemetery, Meroa, Mitchell County, Iowa.

Lars became a naturalized citizen on 11 Mar 1913 at the Mitchell County Courthouse in Osage, Iowa.

Lars and Caroline continued to live on the farm until they retired in 1943 when they moved into Osage, Iowa. Lars passed away on December 30, 1971 and Caroline passed away on January 9, 1975. They are both buried at Rock Creek Lutheran Cemetery, Meroa, Mitchell County, Iowa.

Anna, Ole, Andrew and Brede Wamstad

published May 2015   *Form 209*   *Larry Shoger*

Anna, Ole, Andrew and Brede were cousins of the Wamstad brothers

These four siblings were all born on the Hvamstad farm in Tingelstad, Gran, Hadeland. Their parents were Ole Larsen Hvamstad and Bertha Thorsteinsdatter Gagnum.

ANNA OLSDATTER HVAMSTAD GULBRANDSON

Anna Olsdatter Hvamstad was born on October 11, 1833 at Hvamstad. She was married to Gulbrand Gulbrandsen Lundberg on February 3, 1863 in Norway. Their first child was born December 2, 1863 in Norway. The family immigrated to America in 1865 or 1866, landing in New York and settled near Decorah, Winneshiek County, Iowa in the small community of Nordness. In 1868 the family moved to Mitchell County, Iowa where they settled on a farm in Cedar Township. Anna's brother, Ole Wamstad, came with them. Gulbrand and Anna changed their name from Lundberg to Gulbrandson shortly after arriving in America.

Anna and Gulbrand were the parents of six children, namely: Lars, Gillis, Martin, Olava, Martha, and Bertha.

1) Lars Gulbrandson, born December 2, 1863 in Norway. He died on November 9, 1950 at Mason City, Cerro Gordo County, Iowa. He married Anna Marie Thompson on December 9, 1894 at Rock Creek Lutheran church, Meroa, Mitchell County, Iowa. Lars learned the carpentry trade and became a manager of the Rudd Lumber Yard in Rudd, Floyd County, Iowa. He later purchased the Charles Duston Lumber Company in Nora Springs, Floyd County, Iowa. He sold the business and bought a farm located two and a half miles west of Nora Springs. They lived on the farm until March 1926 when they moved to Mason City, Iowa. He served as the Vice President of the First State Bank in Nora Springs, Iowa for 20 years. He owned the first car in Floyd County, Iowa. Lars and Anna were the parents of three daughters: Mabel, Ellen Mae (Mrs. Lloyd Snively), and Lenore (Mrs. Joseph Ludeman).

2) Gillis Gulbrandson, born February 13, 1867 near Decorah, Iowa. He died on October 17, 1959 at Northwood, Grand Forks County, North Dakota. He farmed 160 acres on section 17, Cedar Township, Mitchell County, Iowa. His farm was across the road from his uncle Ole Wamstad. In 1911 he moved to Northwood, Grand Forks County, North Dakota and farmed there for a number of years as a hired hand. He is buried at a cemetery in Northwood, North Dakota.

3) Martin Adolph Gulbrandson, born December 4, 1868 in Cedar Township, Mitchell County, Iowa. He died December 9, 1936 at Janesville, Rock County, Wisconsin. He married Olena Marie Borseth on October 25, 1905 at Calmar, Winneshiek County,

465

Iowa. Olena was born on July 24, 1885 at Decorah, Winneshiek County, Iowa. Martin and Olena farmed the family farm in Cedar Township for a number of years. They moved to a farm near Milton, Wisconsin, where they lived until 1928, when they retired from farming and moved into Milton. They purchased a large house and rented out rooms. Martin died on December 9, 1936 at Janesville, Rock County, Wisconsin. He is buried at Oak Hill cemetery in Janesville. Olena died on January 11, 1957 at Janesville and is buried next to her husband. They were the parents of five children: Anna (Mrs. Oliver Linsey); Alma (Mrs. Albert Hudson); Millie, an infant; Mabel (Mrs. Robert Suter); Minnie (Mrs. Roy Whitford); and Milo.

4) Olava Matilda Gulbrandson, born March 23, 1871 in Cedar Township, Mitchell County, Iowa. She died on June 28, 1962 at Milwaukee, Wisconsin. She married Tollef Dahlen in 1896 at Forest City, Winnebago County, Iowa. He was born in 1859 at Telemark, Norway. They lived in Forest City for fifteen years. They had four children: Alver, Alma (Mrs. John Kensrue), Myrtle (Mrs. Harold Champion) and Theodore. In 1930 the family moved to Osage, Iowa. Tollef passed away in Osage on May 26, 1931. Olava passed away at her daughter's home in Milwaukee.

5) Bertha Louise Gulbrandson, born April 26, 1874 in Cedar Township, Mitchell County, Iowa. She died on May 5, 1967 at Park River, Walsh County, North Dakota. She attended the Cedar Valley Seminary at Osage, Iowa and was a teacher in rural schools in North Dakota. She married Oscar Johnson on November 25, 1897 at Rock Creek Lutheran Church at Meroa, Iowa. They farmed in Fertile Township, Walsh County, North Dakota. Bertha also attended the University of North Dakota. Oscar and Bertha were the parents of eight children: Archie, Lillian, Victor, Elmer, Esther, Blanche, Florence and Olaf. They farmed until 1935 when they retired from farming and moved into the town of Park River. Oscar passed away on August 21, 1953 and Bertha passed away on May 5, 1967 - both at Park River, Walsh County, North Dakota.

6) Martha Marie Gulbrandson, born August 3, 1876 in Cedar township, Mitchell County, Iowa. She died on January 15, 1869 at Osage, Mitchell County, Iowa. She attended the Nora Springs Seminary at Nora Springs, Iowa. She married Martin Olson on November 8, 1894 at Rock Creek Lutheran Church, Meroa, Iowa. They farmed near Rudd, Floyd County, Iowa for fifteen years and then moved to a farm in Burr Oak Township, Mitchell County, Iowa. They remained on the farm until they retired in 1924 and moved into Osage. Oscar passed away on October 15, 1933 at Mason City, Iowa. Martha passed away on January 15, 1969 at Osage. They were the parents of seven children: Albert, Melvin, Mabel, Myron, Alfred, Louise and Roy.

Gulbrand passed away on October 9, 1902 at his farm home in Cedar Township. Anna passed away on a few days later on October 14, 1902. They are buried at Rock Creek Lutheran Church, Meroa, Mitchell County, Iowa.

OLE OLSEN WAMSTAD

The Ole Wamstad Family
Back: Milton, Carl, Lawrence, Henry
Front: Carriene, Clara, Ole

Ole Olsen Hvamstad was born on October 9, 1846 at Hvamstad. In 1864, Ole immigrated to America when he was 18 years old. He changed his name to Ole Wamstad. He first settled in Wisconsin, then moved to Minnesota, then settled in Iowa where he worked on farms in the summer and attended school in the winter. In 1869 he came to Mitchell County, Iowa with his sister and brother-in-law, Anne and Gulbrand Gulbrandson from Decorah, Iowa. On June 28, 1969, Ole purchased 80 acres of land on section 18 in Cedar Township, Mitchell County, Iowa. He was one of the early settlers of the west part of Cedar Township.

On June 2, 1872, Ole married Anne Karine Pedersdatter Rosland at Rock Creek Lutheran Church in Meroa, Mitchell County, Iowa.

Anne Karine Pedersdatter Rosland was born on October 14, 1846 at the Rosland farm near Kragero, Norway. She was the daughter of Peder Bjorn Olsen and Kari Isachsdatter Rosland. She immigrated to America in 1860 and settled in Michigan and Wisconsin, and later came to Mitchell County, Iowa in 1871. She changed her name to Carriene Peterson prior to settling in Iowa.

Ole and Carriene were the parents of six children: Berthe, Carl, Lawrence, Albert, Clara (Mrs. William Gaylan) and Milton.

1) Bertha Marie Wamstad, born May 23, 1873 and died August 29, 1874 at Cedar Township. She is buried at Rock Creek Lutheran Church cemetery, Meroa, Iowa.

2) Carl Oscar Wamstad, born March 13, 1875 at Cedar Township. He died February 27, 1949 at Long Beach, California. He married Nettie Elisabeth Carlson on June 8, 1899 at Rock Creek Lutheran Church, Meroa, Iowa. They were the parents of four children: Lucille, Kenneth, Henrietta and Charles.

3) Lawrence O. Wamstad, born December 22, 1876 at Cedar Township. He died November 25, 1946 at Parma, Canyon County, Idaho. He married Ethel Adelia Mathews on December 11, 1924 at Boise, Idaho. He attended the Nora Springs Seminary at Nora Springs, Iowa and in 1906 he moved out west to help turn the land into farmland.

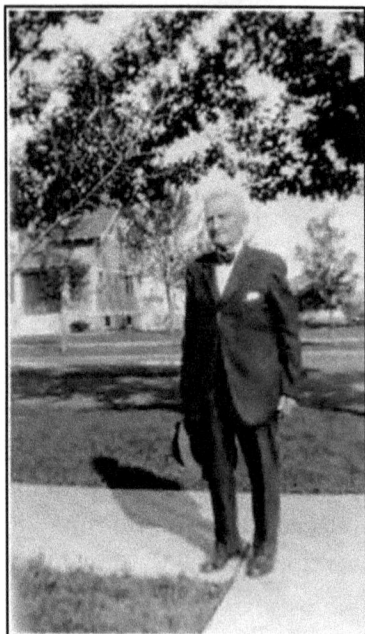

Ole in Osage, Iowa

4) Albert Henry Wamstad, born January 26, 1879 at Cedar Township. He died October 14, 1962 at St. Petersburg, Florida. He married Ella Josefine Eidness on May 4, 1916. After her death in 1934, he married Louise Justi on March 28, 1942 at Yuma, Arizona. He is buried at Rock Creek Lutheran Church cemetery, Meroa, Iowa.

5) Clara Olive Wamstad, born October 25, 1884 at Cedar Township. She died December 1, 1924 at Roswell, New Mexico. She married William Franklin Gaylan on February 26, 1916.

6) Milton Bernhard Wamstad, born February 3, 1889 at Cedar Township. He died July 14, 1962 at Osage, Mitchell County, Iowa. He married Mina Olive Field on June 10, 1914 at Rock Creek Lutheran Church at Meroa, Iowa. Milton took over the Wamstad farm after his father passed away. Milton and Mina were the parents of two children: Milton Eugene Wamstad and Adelaide (Mrs. Vernon Larson).

Ole and Carriene were very prosperous farmers and between 1895 and 1911, they farmed a total of 320 acres of land - 80 acres in Cedar Township, Iowa and an adjoining 240 acres (section 20) in Rock Grove Township, Floyd County, Iowa.

Carriene passed away on January 29, 1920 at her home in Osage, Iowa. Ole moved to Parma, Idaho where two of their children were living and remained there until his death. He passed away on October 13, 1941. Ole and Carriene are buried at Rock Creek Lutheran Church cemetery, Meroa, Iowa.

ANDREW OLSEN WAMSTAD

Andrew Olson Farm
Section 29, Cedar Township, Mitchell County, Iowa

Anders Olsen Hvamstad was born May 14, 1850 at Hvamstad. He was seventh of nine children. He immigrated to America in 1866 at the age of 16 and changed his name to Andrew Wamstad. He settled in Clayton County, Iowa and later moved to Mitchell County, Iowa. The 1870 Federal census lists Andrew Oleson, age 20, and his brother, Ole Oleson, age 30, living on the Gulbrand Lewison farm in Cedar Township, Mitchell County, Iowa - both listed as farmers.

Andrew married Mrs. Ingeborg Dynna on March 27, 1877 at Rock Creek Lutheran Church, Meroa, Mitchell County, Iowa. She was the widow of Lars Larsen Dynna who died on 25 Feb 1873 at Cedar township from an accident while checking to see of the logs were secure on his wagon. The chains broke and the logs rolled onto him, crushing his chest. Lars Larsen Dynna was born on June 7, 1839 at the Dynna farm, in Gran, Hadeland.

Andrew's wife was born Ingeborg Larsdatter Flatla, on November 28, 1840 at Lunner, Hadeland. Her parents died young, so she was raised by her grandmother. She married Lars Dynna on May 28, 1868 at Lunner, Hadeland, Norway. The couple immigrated to America on June 4, 1868. They came over on the boat *Peruvan* and landed at Quebec, Canada. They traveled to Rock Township, Mitchell County, Iowa where they lived with Lars' brother, Andrew Larson Dynna until their house was built. They had two children from her first marriage, namely Ludvig and Lise.

469

1) Ludvig Larsen Dynna, born October 27, 1870 at Rock township, Mitchell county, Iowa. He died June 15, 1910. The 1910 Federal census shows him living in Mason City, Iowa and working as the brick & tile plant. He also served as a Lieutenant in Company D, 1st South Dakota Infantry during the Spanish-American war in 1898. He never married.

2) Lise Marie Dynna, born December 2, 1872 at Rock township, Mitchell county, Iowa. and died February 1, 1926 at her home in Cedar township, Mitchell county, Iowa. She attended Cedar Valley Seminary in Osage, Iowa. On March 9, 1892, she married Herman Knudsen Klemesrud at Rock Creek Lutheran church in Meroa, Mitchell county, Iowa. They were the

Ingeborg (Flatla) Wamstad

parents of ten children - Kalmer, Livius, Alice - Mrs. Ingvald Sponheim, Helen - Mrs. Edwin Maakestad, Kalmer, Irene, Knud, Lars, Louise - Mrs. Stanley Dieterichs, and Herman. Lise's husband's parents were immigrants from Sor-Aurdahl, Hedalen, Oppland, Norway.

Andrew and Ingeborg farmed in Rock and Cedar townships until the Spring of 1915, when they moved into Osage, Mitchell county, Iowa. They were the parents of three children - Brede, Ingeborg, and Oline.

1) Brede Andreasen Wamstad, born April 17, 1878 in Rock Township, Iowa. He died October 15, 1971 at Osage, Mitchell County, Iowa. He married Inga Katherine Rone on June 29, 1905 at Northwood, Worth County, Iowa. They had one daughter, Constance Ingeborg (Mrs. Carlin Bucknam).

2) Ingeborg, born March 3, 1880 at Rock Township, Mitchell County, Iowa. She died June 16, 1963 in Northwood, Iowa.

3) Oline, born March 19, 1882 and died March 20, 1882 at Rock Township, Iowa.

Andrew passed away on October 28, 1928 and Ingeborg passed away on January 16, 1936 at their home in Osage, Iowa. They are buried at Rock Creek Lutheran cemetery in Meroa, Iowa.

BREDE OLSEN WAMSTAD

Brede Olsen Hvamstad was born December 11, 1856 at Hvamstad. He was married to Marie Tronsdatter Klastad in Norway. After his wife died, he immigrated to America in 1887. He attended the normal school at Madison, South Dakota and was employed by Cargill Inc., as a grain buyer and managed the elevators at Madison, South Dakota and Ramona, North Dakota. He was promoted to the main office in Minneapolis, Minnesota in 1916.

Brede married Christine Olson in 1891 at Rock Creek Lutheran Church, Meroa, Mitchell county, Iowa.

Brede died on July 18, 1938 and Christine died on April 23, 1944 - both at Minneapolis, Minnesota. They are buried at Rock Creek Lutheran cemetery, Meroa, Iowa.

Kjersti Nielsdatter Kjos Family

previously unpublished   *Form 880*   *Pam Solwey*

Back Row: Christian Kjos, Nels Kjos, Ole Milsten, Iver Kjos;
Front Row: Nicolai Nelsen, Kjersti Kjos Nelsen, Kjersti Nielsdatter Kjos, Anna Kjos Milsten
The individuals in this photo were identified by Albert Milsten, Saskatoon, Alberta, Canada

The name Kjos is fairly common in the North Dakota and Minnesota area. The farm, Kjoseiet or Kjos, is located in Gran, Brandbu Parish, Hadeland, in Oppland, Norway. My family did not originate from there, of course, because they were renters and not land owners. They took the name Kjos after they came to America. A great big thank you to Ole Gamme for information on the Norway segment which gave me clues for the whole story.

Kjersti Nielsdatter was born Oct 13, 1839, and baptized on Nov 24, 1839, in Gran Parish, in Oppland. She was the daughter of Niels Torgersen and Anne Andersdatter Rettrum. Confirmation records for Niels Torgerson at Gran Parish show that his birth record was burned in a fire at Biri Parish in Toten. Kjersti's mother, Anne Andersdatter Baalerud, was born Sept 4, 1803, recorded in the Gran Parish records. The marriage certificate for Niels and Anne shows

472

Nils Torgersen Gullerudsfjord and Anne Andersdatter Baalerud, 24 and 22, children of Torger Hansen Sinnerud and Anders Hansen Baalerud. Kjersti's family seems to have lived first at Gullerud and later for the births of the rest of the children, they were at Retterum or Rettrum as renters.

Kjersti's husband was Anders Christiansen Smedshammer. His birth and baptism are recorded in the Gran Parish records as April 3rd and 12th, 1830, as the son of Christian Ericksen and Ingeborg Andersdatter Smedshammer. For now I have not continued research on Anders parents. There seems to be two Christian Eriksens. Leslie Rogne, Genealogist for Hadeland Lag, in a 1993 letter to Marge Lundmark also refers to this problem. The parents of Anders appear to have lived mostly on Smedshammer as renters or *husmann*. At age 19, Kjersti married Anders. He was 28 and single. The marriage record shows: Dec 2, 1858, Anders Christiansen Smedshammer and Kirsti Nielsdatter Retrumiet with parents Christian Eriksen and Niels Torgersen. Anders and Kjersti had a daughter, Ingeborg, who was born Dec 21, 1858, with parents listed as Smedshammer. Unfortunately she died at age 2 ½ on July 30, 1861 at Rokeneiet.

The first son, Niels, was born on May 10, 1860, with parents listed as Anders Christiansen Retrumseiet and Kirsti Nielsdatter. The next son was my great grandfather, Christian. He was born June 7, 1862, with parents listed as Anders Christiansen Rokeneiet and Kirsti Nielsdatter. The third son, Iver, was born April 14, 1864, with parents listed as Anders Christiansen Rokeneiet and Kirsti Nielsdatter. The last child born to this couple was Anne, who was born on July 10, 1866, and her parents were listed as Anders Christiansen Kjosiet and Kirsti Nielsdatter. The common baptismal sponsors are Kari Jacobsdatter Smedhammer; Erik Christiansen Smedhammer (who was sponsor at all baptisms); Birthe Nielsdatter Rokeneiet and Alm; and Gudbrand Iversen Kjos.

The 1865 Norwegian Census for Gran Parish, Sylling farm, shows Anders Christiansen, husband, husmand with land, 35 years old, born in Gran, had 2 cattle, 1 sheep, ¼ barley, 6/16 mixed grain, 1/16 peas and ¾ potatoes. His wife is listed as Kjersti Nielsdatter, 33 years old and born in Gran. He has 3 sons: Niels Andersen, age 6, born in Gran; Christian Andersen, age 4, born in Gran and Iver Andersen, age 2, born in Gran. Anders Christiansen died at the age of 36 at Kjosiet on March 8, 1867, leaving Kjersti with 4 small children. This record states his birth and confirmation. What happened to Kjersti next is not known. I have a letter from the Statsarkivet I Hamar, 1971, that mentions the 1875 Census for Gran. It seems Kjersti was a widow living with son Nels ,at Elvestuen *"en plass under garden Kjos i Gran"*. I have not seen the 1875 Census for Gran. However there is an 1875 Census available for Vestre Toten that shows a Kirstie Nielsdatter , born in 1839, living with Johanne Nielsdatter (born in 1829) and husband. I believe that the two are sisters. Kirstie is called *"inderst"* which refers to renter or lodger. On July 18, 1880, Kjersti gave birth to her last daughter, Kjersti Olsdatter, at Kjosiet.

The father of Kjersti was Ole Iversen from Alm. On the 1865 Census for Gran, Norway, Kjersti's sister , Birthe, lived at Alm as a servant. Also on this farm was Ole Iversen, age 33, son of Iver Steffansen. I am supposing that is how they met.

The Nels Kjos Family
Standing in back: Ole and Albert
Front: Martha, Ida, Minnie, Selmer, and Nels

On May 20, 1880, at age 20, Nels Andersen Kjos is listed in the church book leaving for America. He was followed by Christian, at age 19, on May 5, 1881, and finally by Kjersti, age 44, and children: Kjersti, age 2 , Iver, age 19, and Anne, age 17, on June 5, 1883.

According to a biography written in <u>Northern Minnesota, A Compendium of History and Biography</u>, 1902, Nels went to Freeborn County, Minnesota. He was trained as a shoemaker in Norway and stayed in Freeborn County for three years. When he went to Norman County he drove an ox team and the trip took 21 days. They lived in a log house on Strand Township for eight years and then he moved to Sundahl Township as a farmer. He had over 360 acres. He married Martha Helgesen on July 14, 1882, in Winnesheik County where she was born on

August 8, 1860. They were members of St Olaf Lutheran Church at Faith, Minnesota, and are buried in the church graveyard. The 1885 Minnesota State Census for Strand Township, Norman County, Mn, shows Nels as age 25, born in Norway, with wife Martha, age 24, born in Iowa, and daughter, Mina, age 2, born in Minnesota . Kjersti Kjos, age 46, born in Norway and Kjersti O Kjos, age 4, born in Norway are also in the household of Nels. In the <u>History of Clay and Norman Counties</u>, 1918, there are land office entries for Strand Township that shows Nils A Kjos in Sec 8, January, 1887. Nels and his cousin, Jacob Milsten, also invested in the Faith Flour Mill in about 1901. <u>The Twin Valley Community Saga</u>, 1986, has several pages about Faith, Minnesota, and the flour mill which has been placed on the National Register of Historic Places. There is a photo of Mrs Nels Kjos being carried across the flooding Wild Rice River in a cable box in 1909. Nels and Martha had 6 children, 5 that survived to adulthood. All were born in Norman County, Minnesota, except Mina who was born in Albert Lea. The following is based on Bible records of Mina's from 1965, online records from the Minnesota Historical Society, Find a Grave.com, and Family Search.

1. Mina Karolina was born on Dec 17, 1882, and married to Christian Carlson Berg on Nov 20, 1902 in Fertile, Minn. She died Aug 3, 1966, and is buried at Concordia Cemetery, Fertile, Minn. She had two daughters: Mabel Bertina and Nora Christine.
2. Albert Kjos was born June 15, 1886. Mina stated he had no children and that he died in 1942.
3. Ole N Kjos was born Sept 15, 1888 and married Amanda Norby on Nov 10, 1909. She died Dec 10, 1921; he married again to Viola Unknown. He had 3 children with each wife. His children were Millard, Lloyd, Norma, Donald, Betty, and Ronald. Ole is buried in Calvary Cemetery, Edinburg, ND.
4. Selmer Kjos was born Jan 20, 1893, and married Erna P. Wendt on Sept 22, 1926. He died in Mahnomen Minn. They had three children: Sylvia, Harold and Lois.
5. Ida N Kjos was born on Feb 25, 1895, and died the next day.
6. Ida Amelia Kjos was born June 22, 1898, and was married in 1920 to Albert Peterson. Mina stated that they had one child that died young. Ida died April 27, 1951 and is buried in Aspeland Lutheran Cemetery in Flom, Norman County, Minnesota

Unfortunately Nels died on May 12, 1905, which was about the time that his brother, Christian, was planning to move to Montana, his sister, Anna, died in 1905 and the Milsten family moved to Canada in 1906. Martha died Feb 7, 1921 and they are both buried at Faith

Minnesota in the St Olaf Lutheran Church yard. Martha was living with daughter Mina on the 1920 US Census.

The family of Christian and Caroline Kjos
Left to right is Alfred, Christian, Paul, Caroline, Anna. Thille is standing behind Paul. Emma is seated in front.

The next son of Kjersti's to come to America was Christian, whose Gran Church record states he left on May 4, 1881, and arrived at the port of Baltimore in June of 1881. Just where Christian landed is unclear. Family stories state that he worked in Minneapolis as an ice man and that was where he met his wife, Caroline Sandberg. She had emigrated in April of 1884 from Oslo and worked in Minneapolis.

On Dec 10, 1889, they were married in McIntosh, Polk County, Minnesota, and they lived in Lessor Township of Polk County where Christian was farming. Over the years he drilled wells, worked road construction, and custom combined. The first four children were born in Lessor Township and the last were born in Hill River Township of Polk Co, Minnesota. The 1895 Minnesota State Census for Hill River Township, Polk Co shows Christian as 37 years old, married for 11 years, born in Norway, June, 1862, came to US in 1881, farmer; Lena(Caroline) is shown as wife, 38, born in Norway in Oct 1861, married 11 years, had 5 children, 5 still alive, came to US in 1884 with children listed are Tillie, Anna, Alfred, Emma and Paul. Christian's brother, Iver, is listed as living with him.

Unfortunately Caroline died after childbirth on Sept 17, 1902, at age 40, leaving behind six young children. She is buried in the Olga (Salem) church yard in Polk Co, Minn. My grandmother, Thille, was the eldest and only 12 years old and the youngest, Paul, was 2 years old. The children of Christian and Caroline were:

1. Thille Christine, born Oct 4, 1890, married Martin Gonvick on Oct 27, 1907, and died on Sept 1, 1949. She had seven children: Clarence Mandel, Kermit Leroy, Clara, Kermit Ernest, Vernon, Irving, and Margerie. She is buried in Samhold Lutheran Cemetery, Gonvick, Minn.

2. Anna Josephine, born Sept 6, 1892, married Charles Johnson on April 14, 1914, and died on Jan 3, 1980. She had two daughters: Elvera and Marilyn. She is buried in Samhold Lutheran Cemetery, Gonvick, Minn.

3. Alfred Julius, born Sept 19, 1894, married Mabel Harrington on Aug 18, 1924, and died Sept 19, 1942. His grandson, Ken Harris, has written a detailed story about Alfred and Christian and it can be found at the Naeseth Library in Madison, Wisconsin. Alfred had four children: Helen, Robert, Betty, and Jane. He is buried in Conrad Memorial Cemetery, Kalispell, MT.

4. Emma Mathilde, born on Nov 27, 1896, married Jack Hartley, Sr, on Nov 10, 1952, and died April 22, 1978. She did not have any children but kept many family records and correspondence. She is buried in Miami Memorial Cemetery, Miami, Florida.

5. Paul Clarence, born April 22, 1900, married Lillian Eggin on July 4, 1920, and later Ann Hewitt on March 29, 1979. He had 5 children: Clayton, Bernen, Lois, Eileen, and Donald. He is buried in Pines Cemetery, Spokane, Washington.

6. Baby Boy, was born and died on Sept 17, 1902. I am wondering if he was buried with his mother.

These records came from many sources: Emma Kjos Hartley, Polk Co Courthouse, personal knowledge, Margerie Wood, Kjos family correspondence, Ken Harris manuscript about Christian and Alfred Kjos.

Christian remarried on Oct 17, 1903, to Hilda Paulson Olson. She was the widow of John Olson who farmed near the Kjos family and they had a daughter named Milla in April of 1898. Hilda was eight years old when her family came to America from Sweden. After she married Christian they lived at the home of Christian in Hill River Township where they had five children. On the 1910 U.S. Census for Hill River Township, Polk Co, Minnesota, Christian is listed as 47 years old, married twice, 6 years this marriage; Hilda is listed as wife, 42, born in Sweden, came to US in 1884, married 6 years. In 1910, Christian made an application for homestead in Montana with final proof papers on March 3, 1915 for residence at Grandview, Montana that he established his residence there on June 17, 1910, with himself, wife, 7 minor children and 2 adult children. The children of Hilda and Christian were:

1. Hilmer Clifford, born April 14, 1907, unsure if married, died May 28, 1949. He was twin of Pearl. He is buried in Grandview Cemetery, Bonners Ferry, Idaho.

2. Pearl Nina, born April 14, 1907, married Axel Berglund, and died in April of 1949. She had two children: Pearl and Milton. She is buried in Riverside Cemetery, Orofino, Idaho.

3. Elvin and Tina (twins) born June 17, 1908, and died Sept 21 and 24, 1908. They are buried at (Salem) Olga Cemetery in Polk Co, Minn.

4. Delia, born Sept 4, 1910, married Charles Falk, Nov 18, 1929, and died Jan 12, 1969. She is buried in Newport Cemetery, Newport, Washington.

This information came from Emma Hartley, Kjos family correspondence, personal knowledge and Find a Grave.com. Unfortunately, I do not have a picture of Christian and Hilda or their children.

The 1920 U.S Census shows Christian and Hilda now living in Bonners Ferry Pct, Boundary County, Idaho: Christian is listed as 54, married, Hilda is listed as 52, wife, and children are listed as Millie, Nina, Clifford, and Delia. The obit for Hilda states they came to Idaho in 1919. Hilda died April 21, 1949 and Christian died in a construction accident on Oct 17, 1943. They are both buried in Grandview Cemetery, Bonners Ferry, Idaho.

The third son of Kjersti and Anders was Iver. He left Norway with his mother and sisters, Anna and Kjersti ,on June 5th, 1883. According to the naturalization intent, they arrived through the port of Detroit in June of 1883. Iver never married but farmed and did own land in Polk County in Section 6 of Township 149 of 160 acres in August of 1891 and 160 acres on Township 151,Sec 34. He lived with his mother and siblings off and on and died Nov 3rd 1940, in Marshall Co, Minn. He was on the 1930 US Census living with his sister Kjersti and husband in Newfolden, Marshall Co, Minn. I don't know where buried.

The last child of Kjersti and Anders was Anna. She came over with her mother and family. According to the 1900 US Census, she married Christian H Milsten by 1891. I have had very little luck finding Christian in the Norwegian records. He is often listed as the son of Erick Christiansen Milsten but I can find no proof of this. There is an interesting account for Jacob E. Milsten in the History of Clay and Norman Counties that discussed his father Erick C. Milsten. Erick C. Milsten is the brother of Kjersti Kjos' husband, Anders Christiansen. He came to America to Norman County in 1878 and had a son, Christian E. Milsten. According to the way the Norwegian families were named – Christian H. Milsten would have had a father with the first initial H. The rest of the family continued to use the father's initial for their middle name in America. Jacob E. Milsten is identified as a cousin of Nels Kjos in the Twin Valley Community Saga .

Erik and Kari Milsten Family c. 1880
Back: Elise, Jacob E, Christian, Kari; Middle: Anna, Eric C. and Kari,
Ingeborg; Front: Marthe, Randine, Mari

In the translated version of <u>Norwegians in America, their History and Record</u>, 1907 and 1913, Christian E. Milsten is listed as living in Norman County. There is also a reference to a Halvor Milesten from Gran, Hadeland who emigrated to Wisconsin in 1847. He had a son Phillip Milestone who farmed in South Dakota. There is a Halvor Olsen on the *Utflytta* list from Milsten, Jevnaker, in 1848, with wife Else and children, Ole, Dorthe, and Lars. Gerhard Naeseth also refers to this Halvor Olsen Milesten. Christian H. Milsten lived in Norman County before moving to Saskatchewan where he is buried. There is a farm named Milsten in Norway and I am sure that Christian H. was from the area or related to someone from Milsten. I have not found that connection yet.

Christian H. and Anna are found living back and forth between Polk County and Norman County Minnesota. They are on the 1895 Minnesota State Census in Brandvold Township, Polk County with children Alma and Albert. Anna's mother Kjersti also lives with them. In 1899, Christian homesteaded 160 acres in Polk County. In 1900 they are still in Polk County, King Township, McIntosh Village. He is listed as 32, married for 9 years, came to US in 1883, born in Norway. On the 1905 Minnesota State Census they are in Fossum Township, Norman County, Minn, living next to Martha Kjos, wife of Nels. Nels died May 1905 and then his sister, Anna Milsten, died Dec 27, 1905. I believe that she is buried at Faith, Norman County but have not seen the record. Christian never remarried. In 1906 Christian and his children, Albert, Millie, Edith, and Clara, moved to Saskatoon District, Saskatchewan. On the 1921 Canadian Census, he is listed as living alone in Swanson village, Kindersley Dist, Sask, as a shoemaker. He is listed as a land owner in the Sask Homestead Index with the Sask Genealogical Society but I did not order the file from them. He died on July 12, 1950 in Vanscoy, Saskatchewan, Canada, and is buried in Woodlawn Cemetery, Saskatoon, Sask. Canada. Christian and Anna had six children. This information came from a letter from Gwen Hamilton, Saskatoon, who was the daughter of Millie Milsten Utigard, census records, and online genealogical records from Ancestry.com and Familysearch. They are:

1. Alma was born, May 1892, in Faith, Minn, and died in 1910 from tuberculosis .She is buried at Outlook, Sask, Canada.

2. Albert Henry was born ,August 4, 1894, in Polk Co, Minn, married Frankie Jackson in 1945, and died on July 1, 1980. He is buried in Woodlawn Cemetery in Saskatoon. They had no children. He was a good friend of my grandmother, Thille Kjos Gonvick, when they lived in Canada in the 1920's.

3. Millie was born, June 1896, in Polk Co, Minn, married Bert Utigard in 1916, and died on Sept 26, 1987. They had 10 children: Raymond, Laverne, Eunice, Roy, Vivian, Gwendolin, Lloyd, Ronald, Ken, and Lyla. She is buried in Woodlawn Cemetery, Saskatoon, Sask.

4. Mina was born, July 12, 1898, in Minnesota, never married, and died in Seattle, Washington, in January 1979.

5. Edith was born, April 7, 1902, in Minnesota, married Stanley Hunt, and died in 1953 in Calgary, Alberta, Canada. They had two children: Willard and Una. She is buried in Queen's Park, Calgary, Alberta.

6. Clara Amanda was born, July 6, 1904, in Minnesota, married Willard Vincent in 1916, and died in Regina, Sask, Canada on March 20, 1985. They had one son, Donald.

The last daughter of Kjersti Kjos was Kjersti, born July 18, 1880, at Kjosiet, Gran Parish, Norway. She came to America at age 2 ½ with her mother and siblings. When she was 18, she married Nicolai Nelson who was born at Baalerud, Gran, Hadeland, Norway on Nov 25, 1872. He was the son of Niels Olsen Baalerud and Agnete Andersdatter. Nicolai came to America in 1886 but I could not see who he accompanied since he was only 14 years old. Nicolai and Kjersti were married Feb 16, 1898, and farmed in Polk Co, Minn. BLM-Glo records show that Nicolai owned land in Clearwater County, Minn, on July 15, 1904. The 1900 US Census for Pine Lake, Beltrami Co, Minn (Clearwater was formed from Beltrami), lists him as 28,married for 2 years, born in 1871, came to US in 1886, and naturalized in 1896, and farming. Kjersti is listed as age 19, came to US in 1883, no children. They remained on the farm near Pine Lake on the 1910 and 1920 US Census records. In 1930 they are listed as living in Newfolden, Marshall Co. Minn with children Ingval, Edith, Earl, as well as Kjersti's brother, Iver Kjos. The census records on Ancestry.com have badly misspelled the names on every census. Kjersti's mother, Kjersti, was living with them on the 1910 US Census near Pine Lake. Nicolai died May 18, 1935, and is buried in Newfolden, Minnesota. In 1938, Kjersti remarried to George Tilberg. They lived in rural Clearwater County and Iver Kjos continued to live with them. Kjersti died Feb 25, 1959 and is buried in Samhold Cemetery in Gonvick, Minnesota. George died in 1970 and is buried in Clearbrook, Minn. Kjersti and Nicolai had 9 children. According to Nora Swanson notes, the first 5 were born in Polk County and the rest in Clearwater County. My information for the following children is from Nora Nelson Swanson, 1967, <u>Nelson Family History</u>, unpublished, by Janet Buness Dreyer, Kjos Family Reunion, 1993, and Find a Grave internet site:

1. Anna C was born August 13, 1901, and married Peter Svaleson on July 11, 1916. They had 4 living children: Henry, Luther, Lillian, and John. Anna married second, Karl Buness, on July 21, 1927. They had 6 living children: Donna, Beverly, Janet, Marilyn, Duane, and Bruce Karl. Anna married third, Herbert Janson, on April 12, 1974. Anna died August 23, 2001. She is buried in Seljord Lutheran Cemetery, Clearbrook, Minn.

2. Albert Norval was born Nov 11, 1904, and married Mabel Dennett on Dec 29, 1927. He died June 7, 1982, and is buried in Bell Memorial, Temple, Texas. They had 4 children: Phyllis, Alice, Gaylene, and Ronald.

3. Nora Christine was born August 8, 1906, and married George Swanson, Nov 16, 1927. She died June 15, 1999, and is buried in Morningside Memorial, Coon Rapids, Minn. They had 3 children: Elvina, Lyle, and Shirley.

4. Clara Amanda was born Sept 6, 1909, and married Chester Nelson on Nov 16, 1929. She died on Jan 9, 1974, and is buried in Opdahl Cemetery, Newfolden, Minn. They had 4 children: Evelyn, Doris, Ronnie and Betty.

5. Selmer was born Feb 16, 1912, never married, and died on Oct 11, 1982. He is buried in Opdahl Cemetery, Newfolden, Minn.

6. Engval was born April 16, 1913, and married Angela Charles on Oct 24, 1945. He died on Oct 6, 1980, and he is buried at Evergreen Cemetery, Big Falls, Minn. They had 4 children: Dennis, Sheila, Calvin, and Charlene.

7. Edith was born Oct 4, 1916, and married Emil Sorenson on Dec 31, 1935. She died in Aug of 1989 and is buried in Westaker Cemetery, Newfolden, Minn. They had ten children: Kenneth, Norman, Edwin, Lyle, Dolorise, James, Jerry, Linda, Roger, Richard.

8. Earl James was born Dec 21, 1921, and married Arlis Jacobson on Oct 19, 1947. She died Aug 17, 1985, and is buried in Tonseth Cemetery, Erhard, Minn. They had 2 children: Linda and James.

The photo on the next page was done by Emma Kjos Hartley and Julia Lundmark Vanatta. Emma had the wrong birth date on the photo which was done about 1908. While preparing this family story, I am aware that there were many family members that came to America from Gran, Hadeland. This is the story of only one. Kjersti Nielsdatter Kjos lived in America over 40 years. Family stories say that she was a midwife and a very resourceful woman. On Jan 14th, 1887, she appeared in the 11th Judicial Court and filed intent for citizenship. She stated that she

Kjerste Kjos 1834 - 1927

came through the Port of Detroit. She paid in full Aug 12, 1891, for 160 acres at the Crookston Land Office and had a homestead of 160 acres that was filed Feb 10, 1896, in the Crookston Land Office. Kjersti died on July 9, 1927, at age 88. Her obit states she was born in 1833 and was 90 which was a mistake according to the Norway records. She is buried in the Samhold Lutheran Church Cemetery in Gonvick, Minn.

Johan Erickson and Mari Larsdatter Lynne

previously unpublished   *Form 370*   *Peder Lynne*

Johan Ericksen was born on September 2, 1818 on the Gran farm in Gran, Hadeland, Oppland Norway. He was the oldest child of Erik Johansen and Anne Pedersdatter. Erik and Anne did not own a farm of their own and moved quite often early in their marriage. Three years later when their second child was born, the family lived on Woren, and by 1825 when their third child was born, they had moved to Lindstad where Anne had three more children. The family appears to have lived there until around 1844 when they moved to Lundehager (Lynnehagen). Hagen shows they lived as tenant farmers on the Lunde farm. The vital records use the spelling Lynne, while the census and maps use Lunde. All of these farm homes were quite close together. John's father and brother Peder remained on Lynnehagen, hence this would be thought of as the home farm after Johan married and emigrated. Anne died in 1848 at the age of 56. Erik died in 1866 at the age of 74.

Mari Larsdatter was born on Nov. 4, 1822 on Dammen, which is a small farm on the larger farm of Molden. She was the second of five children of Lars Jensen and Margrethe Olsdatter. Lars had been born on Molden, too. His father Jens had acquired this farm in 1785 from his first wife. The records passed down in America show Mari's surname as Dammen. Mari's father died in 1866 at the age of 73. Her mother died in 1880.

Johan was a carpenter and cabinetmaker. He married Mari on December 21, 1846. He was 28, Mari was 24. Their first child, Anne, was born on Dammen Nov. 25, 1847. A stillborn son came on Dec. 8, 1850, then son Lars on Jan. 17, 1852. The church records say Jan. 24! In March of 1853, Johan, Mari, Anne and Lars left for America. The reason was probably to obtain land of their own and make better lives for their children. In 1981, Mom, Dad and I went to Gran. We visited the main farm of Lunde Nordre and hiked up to Lynnehaugen as there was no road to the farm. The view was beautiful as the farm is situated on top of the mountain and overlooks the large valley below. As I stood there looking at the view, then at the farm which was small with little flat land and so inaccessible, I said to myself, "I can see why they left!"

Upon arrival in America, they took the last name Erickson and settled on 120 acres of land in Glenwood Twp., Winneshiek Co. Iowa, 8 miles northeast of Decorah. About 20 years later, while attending Luther College, son Lars decided there were so many Erickson, Olsons, Johnson, etc. that he had the family name legally changed to Lynne. Johan was among the early pioneers of this area and transformed a wild piece of land into a valuable farm. Four more sons were born here. The house had a beautiful yard with apple orchard, plums and willows. In early times they took their grain to Lansing, Iowa to be milled and sold, and they bought supplies. It was a day's ride each way.

Lynne Homestead near Decorah c. 1891

The booklet "Past and Present of Winneshiek County," states that Johan was "highly respected and esteemed by all who knew him. He was a public spirited man, interested in public affairs and successfully held various township offices." Johan and Mari were among the people who helped found the Washington Prairie Lutheran Church, one of the most beautiful rural churches in America. They always gave strict allegiance to this church. No card playing or dancing was allowed. The school for District #6 Glenwood Twp. was called the Lynne School because it was on the Lynne farm. In the first years, the teacher stayed at the Lynne house. Sometimes there were between 30 and 40 pupils - all the grades taught by one teacher.

Mari is said by her granddaughter Edna Lynne Erickson to have been a strong, capable and active woman. Mari's sister Siri Larsdatter and her husband Gulbrand Aarness moved near Decorah, and Johan's brother Gunder Ericksen Morstad came to Decorah in 1868 with his family (in 1874 they moved to Lisbon, MN), so there were relatives on both sides nearby.

Johan fell sometime around 1893. This paralyzed him and caused him to be bedridden for the remaining 13 years of his life. His son Edward had married in 1879 and took charge of the

484

farm in 1883. Johan and Mari continued to live on the farm with Edward and his family. Johan died at the age of 87 in 1906. Marie died in 1907 at the age of 84. Both are buried in the Washington Prairie Church cemetery. Edward sold the farm in 1912 and moved into Decorah.. Johan and Mari's children were:

1) Anne Lynne Dybvik (Nov. 25, 1847-Sept. 3, 1924) was born on the Molden (Dammen) farm. She was 5 when her parents emigrated. She married John Dybvik (1845-1919), son of Peder Johnsen and Gjøri Bottoldsdatter Dybvik of Fresvik (under Leikanger) parish Sogn og Fjordane. They farmed in Winneshiek Co. later moving to Harmony MN. They had 6 children: Peder Julius Lynne (1869-1957), Jeannetta Marie (Nettie) Pierce (1872-1959), Lizzie Amelia Natvig (1875-1963), Selma Gustine Noble (1878-1960), Alfred Melvin Lynne (1883-1982) and Wilhelmina Elizabeth (Ella) Mull (1886-1975). All were married.

John and Anne Dybvik Family
Back: Nettie, Lizzie, Julius, Selma
Front: Alfred, John, Anne, Ella

2) Lars Lynne (Jan 17, 1852-Feb. 13, 1939) was born on the Molden (Dammen) farm. He was one year old when he came to America. He attended Luther College in Decorah and the University of WI at Madison. He taught math at St. Olaf College in Northfield MN and came to Fergus Falls, MN in 1880 where he was a bookkeeper. On October 16, 1882, Lars married Josephine Norman (1858-1949), daughter of Alexander Norman (Aslak Olavsen Bekkhus from Vinje, Telemark) and Anne Olsdtr. (born 1823 in Rauland, Telemark) from near Stoughton WI, moving to St. Olaf Twp. Grant Co. in 1870. In September 1883, Lars came to Ashby, MN where he was the first bank teller of the bank there. He moved to Elbow Lake and was elected treasurer of Grant County. He held that position until 1935 when his daughter Edna took over. He was an accomplished musician and directed bands and orchestras and was church organist and choir leader at St. John's Lutheran Church. Lars and Josephine had 6 children: Justus Alexander Lynne (1883-1987), Agnes Marie Lynne (1885-1875),

Edna Margaret Lynne (1888-1965), Alfred Norman Lynne (1890-1975), Phillip Walter Lynne (1896-1899), and Victor Arnold Lynne (1900-1950). Justus, Alfred and Victor married. The elementary school in Elbow Lake was named the Agnes Lynne School, as Agnes taught first grade there for over 50 years and was very loved.

Lars and Josephine Lynne Family
Back: Agnes, Justus, Edna
Front: Lars, Alfred, Victor, Josephine

3) Edward Lynne (Oct. 3, 1855-Feb. 20, 1935) was born on the Iowa homestead. He took charge of the management of the home farm in 1883, added 40 acres and brought the land to a high state of productivity. He specialized in full-blooded Poland China hogs and a high grade of Guernsey cattle. He helped organize the first creamery in the area. In 1908 Edward rented the farm and moved into Decorah to go into the flour and feed business, and later the grocery business. He sold the farm in 1912. Edward served as township tax collector, assessor and trustee, as justice of the peace and president and secretary of the school board of Glenwood Twp. On May 6, 1879 he married Catherine Peterson (born 1855 died 1946), daughter of Gustav Peterson and Helen from Lisbon IL. They had five children; Clara Amanda Running (1880-1925), Milla Helene Ramsey (1883-1944), Gustav Julius Lynne (1886-1980), Arthur Conrad Lynne (1889-1970), and Edna Constance Erickson (1891-1986). All were married.

4) Johan Magnus (John) Lynne (Aug. 11, 1858-Sept. 1, 1927) was the only one in the family with brown eyes. He attended St. Olaf College in Northfield MN. He came to Ashby MN in 1883 and worked about six years as a clerk. He then put up a building and opened a general merchandise store. This building burned in 1893. He then formed a partnership with G. T. Hoff and continued

John Lynne

in the merchandise business for the rest of his life. John served on the village council and as village treasurer. He was county sheriff for a time, president of the local telephone company and one of the founders of the Pelican Lake Lutheran Church. On Nov. 20, 1899, John married Mary Axelson (Margit Aslaksen) (20 Jan. 1866-1947), daughter of Eivind Aslaksen and Gunhild Halvorsdtr. Kostvedt, Vinje Telemark (baptized in Rauland Telemark). John and Mary lived in Ashby. They had 5 children: Milla Evelina Hildahl (1892-1936), Gilfred Justus "Bob" Lynne (1894-1967), Roy Alexander Lynne (1897-1968), Walter Ferdinand Lynne (1900-1900), Gladys Marie Christianson (1903-). All were married.

5) Peter Lynne (March 25, 1861-May 19, 1945) was handsome and gallant, loved by his nieces and nephews. He was first a photographer in Crookston MN, and after catching gold rush fever, went to Alaska where he lived a rugged life. He went into the lumber business. He later settled in Tacoma, Washington where he had a grocery store and raised fruit. He was not married.

Peter Lynne

6) Olaus "Lavi" Lynne (Dec. 4, 1863-Jan. 20, 1936) married Feb. 19, 1896 in Winneshiek Co., Bramine Clara "Minnie" Nygaard (Oct. 27, 1867 IL-Apr. 22, 1941). Lavi was a rancher in El Campo TX. He was a very tall man with dark hair and wore a handlebar mustache and a wide brimmed Stetson hat. Lavi and Minnie had no children.

Olaus "Lavi" & Clara "Minnie" Lynne

Wagon Train 1875

previously unpublished   *Joy Sundrum*

Several family histories include ancestors who were part of a trek from Fillmore County, Minnesota, to Chippewa County, Minnesota, in 1875. Following is an account taken from several by Alfa Olson Rud and from information from her mother, Karen Marie Jerve Olson. She was the oldest child of Sivert and Kari Jerve who came with her family from Norway and walked with them across Minnesota in 1875. Added information is in italics.

   Having relatives in Chippewa County, many of the settlers near Rushford decided to go there so Jens Gilbertson was hired as a sort of foreman to organize a caravan to take these people to their new homes. There were ten covered wagons in all, five of which drove with horses and five with oxen. Of course they tried to bring as many of their possessions as possible. In all, eight families, totaling around forty people, started out. The youngest child was Jacob Nokleby who was only eight weeks old. The families were as follows:

   Ole and Lena *(Magdelena Andersdtr Falla)* Nokleby with Ragnhild & Jacob *(Form 140)*
   Abraham Presbraten Gilbertson (Gulbranson), his wife Kari Steffensdtr, with Jens
         and Anne (later Anne Byholt) *(Form 600)*
   Mrs. Maria Falla with Andreas and Helene (later Helene Myhre) *(Form 601)*
   Carl and Magrethe Falla with Mina *(Margrethe was the daughter of Abraham
         Gilbertson and Kari Steffesndtr listed above.) (Form 600)*
   Johannes and Ingeborg Stenhus *(Ingebor was pregnant.) (Form 1245)*
   Tosten and Marthe Jenson with Emil and Julia (later Julia Hanson) *(Form 1023)*
         Marthe was a sister of Kari Jerve (below).
   Syver and Kari Jerve with Karen, Hans, Gilbert, Anne, Carl, Sophia *(Form 927)*
         (Syver was a first cousin once removed of Mrs. Maria Falla.)
   Abraham and Karen Johnson with John, Carl and Dorthea *(Form 601)*
         (Abraham was a nephew of Mrs. Maria Falla.)
   Per and Tarina Myhre (Myrestua) with Ole, Sofia, Tosten, Peter & Andreas.
         *(Tarina/Inger Thorine was pregnant. Son Ole married Helene Falla in
         Chippewa County in 1885. Daughter Mina born 1880 married Jacob
         Nokleby in 1899 in Jevnaker Lutheran.)*

488

The distance from Rushford to Montevideo, Minnesota, was about 300 miles and Abraham Persbratten Gilbertson walked the whole way leading two young two-year-old colts. He led the whole caravan; next came the cattle that they drove along; then came the five oxen teams, while the five horse-drawn covered wagons brought up the rear. The trip took 21 days in rain and sunshine, over stones and rivers - there were no tarred highways in those days.

Mother *(Karen Jerve Olson)* told about when they were going across a river one of the young men's hat blew off and floated down the river; this was quite a loss as one didn't come by a hat easily in those days. The journey was long and food supply grew short so one time they stopped and baked bread on a stove which Kari Steffensdtr Gulbranson had brought along. Kari's husband, Abraham Gulbrandsen, 63 years old, brought two colts that he would not trust to anyone's care. He walked every step of the way, leading a colt on either side of him.

Mother *(Karen Jerve Olson)* was only twelve years old but had to walk and help drive the cattle along. After walking nearly a whole day in the rain, she was asked to ride in the wagon with Kari Steffensdtr Gulbranson who put dry clothes on her and put her to bed. She said, "I have often been weary and needed rest, but never had a rest seemed so good to me as then."

Finally on a Saturday evening they came to the journey's end, Montevideo, Minnesota, which was only a village then. They all stayed in the Windom Woods. Early Sunday morning they started out, came by what is now the Immanuel Church, past Rundhaugen (Norman Nelson farm) in a drenching rain. Then came to Gulbrand (Rapeshu) Gilbertson and stayed there three days, then on to the Johan Sandland home. They lived with the Sandlands until winter. The Sandland home was one room 10 x 14 feet with a lean-to shed on one side and a room upstairs just high enough to climb into, where they slept on flat beds. This low room had a small window with no screen. In this home lived the Sandland family with twin boys, one year old, all of mother's family (eight in all) and also Tosten (Vasjve) Jenson and wife and two children - 16 in all. Surely an example of "where there is heart room, there is house room". *"Hvis det er hjerterom, er det husrom."*

Another account says that they stayed in a bachelor's home. He had a one room log house, fourteen feet long. There was a low upper room with a half window. A ladder served the purpose of staircase. The two families and bachelor lived in this house until fall.

A third account added: In the fall the Jerve family built a dug-out *(sod house)*, borrowed a stove from Jens Gilbertson and moved in. There they lived until 1878. The Sandland family had 160 acres of land, but by law they could only keep 80 acres so Sivert got the other 80. It was necessary to keep your covered wagon on the land in order to claim it. Sivert Jerve filed on 80 acres and paid $800.00 for the land on the south side of the road. It was called railroad land.

A Wagon Train Reunion

In June 1935 a reunion of several original members of the wagon train and many descendants was held at the Carl Jerve farm on land that his father, Sivert Jerve, had homesteaded. Carl was a soon-to-be three toddler on the 1875 journey. The event was reported in the *Watson Voice* on June 6, 1935:

MORE THAN A THOUSAND PEOPLE ATTENDED
THE BIG BEND-MANDT OLD SETTLERS PICNIC
Twenty-one Surviving Members of the First Settlers Are Honor Guests

Twenty-one members of a company of Pioneers who came to the Big Bend-Mandt community sixty years or more ago were honor guests at an Old Settlers Picnic held at the Carl Jerve farm, eight miles north-east of Watson, on Memorial Day, where nearly two thousand people assembled in the afternoon and evening to pay their respect to those old pioneers and to hear the interesting story of pioneer building.

A large tent was erected in the attractive Jerve farmyard. The event was put on by the Jevnager church Ladies' Aid, who deserve credit for the fine arrangement and the interesting program.

Carl A. Johnson, one of the original settlers, presided over the program that started with "America" and "Ja vi elsker". It was the pioneer story of Norwegian settlers, so it was well also to remember the country that gave these sturdy men and women. "Luren," a men's quartette of many years standing offered two numbers, after which Knud Wefald spoke in the Norwegian language, and held his audience spell bound with his tales of Norse sturdiness and struggle to find and build new homes.

Musical numbers by the Mandt Male Octette and accordion selections by Virginia Johnson preceded the next speaker, Rev. P. Wee of Dawson who continued the story of building these prairies.

The Ladies' Aid served a very delicious dinner.

The evening program opened with selections by Mrs. Lofdahl's String Orchestra. Then a man's octet from the Buffalo Lake church sang. Mrs. Gust Holte of Montevideo offered a vocal number, and Rev. G. S. Froiland of Dawson held his audience with his many interesting episodes of pioneer life. Few can tell the stories as Rev. Froiland. One can readily hear they are not second hand. The pastor paid a glowing tribute to those sturdy men and women who could carry on in face of all thinkable obstacles. "There was no relief in those days to depend on," the pastor said, "although it many times was fifty to sixty miles to town, and no money or food at hand. It was to go through it, or die, and peculiar enough, most of them lived. Hard work and absolute honesty carried them thru," he said.

Most of the twenty-one surviving members of the first settlers were present and were called to the platform. They were: Mrs. Lena Nokleby, Mrs. Margaret Falla, Jens Gilbertson, Mrs. Karen Olson, Mr. and Mrs. Ole Myhre, Hans Jerve, Gulbrand Jerve, Tosten Myhre, Peter Myhre, Emil Jenson, Mrs. Julia Hanson, Carl Jerve, John A. Johnson, Dorthea Helgeson, Maria Laumb and Torvald Laumb.

They Came in 1875

Settlers began to come in to Big Bend-Mandt community some sixty years ago. Before 1875 there were six homesteaders in the locality. They were: T. E. Mandt, Peder Mandt, Jos Skogrand, John Skogrand, Lars Johnson and Martin and Arnt Lund.

But on June 21, 1875, forty-seven people came in one company. From Fillmore county they traveled slowly up the Minnesota valley in ten covered wagons, five drawn by horses and five by oxen. The 300-mile journey took them three weeks. Those in the company were: Ole and Lena Nokleby, daughter Randi and son Jacob; Syver and Kari Jerve and children: Karen, Hans, Gulbrand, Anne, Carl and Sophia; Tosten and Martha Vasie, daughter Julia and son Emil; Abraham and Kari Persbratten, daughter Anna and son Jens; Carl and Margret Falla and daughter Mina;; Per and Torina Myhre and children: Ole, Sophia, Tosten and Peter; Abraham and Karen Johnson and children, John Carl and Dorthea; Johannes and Ingeborg Stenhus; Mrs. Maria Falla, son Andreas and daughter Helma.

These nine families came all in one group. One week earlier a tenth family, Alaous Laumb, his wife Ellen, sons Jacob, Olaves, Torvald and daughter Maria had arrived.

Some additional information

There were 48 people counted in the nine families:

 4 were babies

 8 were toddlers, age 1-4

 9 were elementary-age children

 4 were teenagers

 4 were young adults

 19 were adults, including:

       3 were 54-64 years old

       2 women were pregnant

       9 married couples or 18 individuals

       1 widow

Of the eight Hadeland descended families, all had relatives in the group. Not every family was related to every other family, but every family was related to more than one of the other families. The ninth family, the Laumbs, married into the Hadelander-Americans when son Thorvald married Anna Karlsdtr.

The Wagon Train group arrived late June or early July 1875. On September 23, 1875 Kristie Olson was born to Peder and Inger Thorine Olsen Myhre, followed closely by Caroline Stenhus, daughter of Johan and Ingebor Olson Stenhus on September 27. On October 12, 1880, the confirmation class at Immanuel included those who were born to this group 1874-1876 (as recorded in the church record with "American" surnames in parentheses): Julia Mathilde Wasjo (Jenson), Mathilde Abrahamsen (Gilbertson), Clara Sophie Gjerve (Jerve), Jacob Nøkleby, and Dorthea Johnson. The first marriage from the group was Gustav Laumb in 1879 when he married a Valdres descendant. The marriage of two youngsters who were both in the wagon train was Helena Andersdtr. Falla and Ole Pedersen Myhre on 14 November 1885 at Immanuel Lutheran. (Jevnaker had not yet been built.)

Falla Family History

previously unpublished **Form 601** *Arnold Zempel*

The author is a descendant of Peder Hanson, his first wife, his second wife, and also of Gulbrand Jenson. This is a story of moving a family to America from Hadeland and of the families from so long ago with the courage to make such a dramatic move and succeed.

The trek to America began in 1849 with the first family members leaving the Falla farm in Jevnaker and going first to Argyle in Lafayette County, Wisconsin. One of the last left in 1901 and went to Mandt Township, the center of the new settlement in Chippewa County, Minnesota. This migration involved many family groups over several generations. The oldest (74 years) to emigrate was Gulbrand Jenson Falla born on Sogn farm in 1775. He didn't come to Minnesota but several of his children and descendants came to Mandt Township, Chippewa County.

To understand the family story we must go back to the latter part of the 1700s when three families were to become entangled by marriage and location and form the base of the story. First is Peder Hanson born 1768. Second is Gulbrand Jenson born 1775, and the third includes three sisters: Mari 1778, Margrethe 1780 and Kari 1782 Andersdtr. All of these people have descendants in the Mandt Township Settlement.

Peder Hanson 1768-1847, the third son of Hans Ellensen and Kari Fredriksdtr, married Berte Gudmundsdtr 1771-1812. Their children: Hans 1797, Karen 1799, Ole 1801, Marte 1805, and Berte, a twin, 1812-1813. They were on the Falla farm before Berte was born. Peder's wife, Berte, died in 1812 and Peder remarried Kari Andersdtr in 1813; their children born on Falla are: Anne 1815, Anders 1817, Berte 1820, and Kari 1823. Three of Peder's children have descendants in Mandt -- Ole, Martha and Anders.

The second family is Gulbrand Jenson's 1775, second son of Jens Olsen Sogn and Dorthe Gulbrandsdtr. In 1799 he married Mari Andersdtr 1778 in 1799; they had twins, Jens and Anders, born 1799. Other children followed: Dorthea 1802, Halvor 1804, Ole 1806, Gulbrand 1808, Abraham 1811 on Falla, Syver 1815, Martha 1818 and Maria 1821. Four of this group made the move to Mandt -- Dorthea, Abraham, Martha and Maria. Dorthea was a widow and 78 years old when she emigrated in 1880 to Mandt. She lived with her son Abraham Johnson who had come twelve years earlier.

The third family is the sisters Mari, Margrete and Kari Andersdtr. Shortly after Kari was born in 1782 her father, Anders Halvorsen, died in 1784 leaving her mother, Anne Christensdtr, a widow with the three little girls. Anne married again to Halvor Hanson and had five more children. Of the first three daughters, Mari, the eldest, married Gulbrand Jenson and Kari married widower Peder Hansen. Margrete married Johan Gunderson; grandson Syver Gunderson Jerve 1837 is also part of this story. Mari and Kari both emigrated in 1849 and lived

493

several years in Wisconsin. Kari moved to Minnesota in 1856 and Mari was in Iowa County in 1860.

From about 1810 both the Peder Hanson and Gulbrand Jenson families were on the Falla farm on the west side of the Randsfjord in Jevnaker. In 1842 Anders Pederson and Maria Gulbrandsdtr were married, binding these families even closer.

The journey to America began on 17 April 1849 when the following checked out of the Jevnaker parish to go to America:

Maria Gulbrandsdtr

Anders Pederson Falla	32 yrs
Wife,Maria Gulbrandsdtr	27
Anne	6
Peder	5
Mari	2½
Kari Andersdtr Falla, widow	67
Gulbrand Jenson Falla	74
Wife, Mari Andersdtr	71
Syver Gulbrandson	34

They boarded the brig *Vesta* from Christiania to New York, arriving on June 28, 1849, with 105 emigrants on board, nine of whom are the Falla family. Most, but not all, of the 105 are from Hadeland. The Falla family's next destination was Argyle in Lafayette County, Wisconsin, where they can be found in the 1850 census. From here Syver and his parents moved to Pulaski Township, Iowa County, Wisconsin. Syver married a widow with three children. They, along with his parents Gulbrand and Mari, are found in the 1860 census. Gulbrand Jenson and Mari, while well advanced in age at emigration, certainly prove emigration was not only for the young.

The Anders Pederson family preempted land in Norway Township, Fillmore County, Minnesota, in 1856 and moved the family to Minnesota where they remained for 19 years. While in Fillmore they were members of the Highland Prairie Church, Rushford. The family grew with Carl born in Wisconsin, then Magdalena, Andrew and Helene born in Minnesota. Daughter Mari died in Wisconsin and Anders' mother, Kari, died in Minnesota.

Anders expanded his land holding by going into debt so the economic crash in the early 1870s brought ruination. The family story is that Anders went to town one day and was never heard from again. There is no hard evidence, only an oral history handed down.

While in Fillmore the older children married and started their own families: Anna married L. H. Johnson, Peder married Martha Solem, Carl married Margrete Abrahamsdtr and Magdalena married Ole Nokleby. Other extended family joined them in Fillmore: Maria's brother Abraham

Gulbrandson and family, nephews Abraham Johnson, Johannes Olsen Stenhus, Peder Olson Myhre (picture below). cousin Syvert Jerve, and Tosten Jenson whose wife was a sister of Syvert Jerve's wife.

Gulbrand Abrahamson with his wife Anne (another sister of Syvert Jerve's wife) and family and L. H. Johnson and Anne with their family had moved to Chippewa County in 1873. With the financial problems and opportunity to homestead land in Mandt, other Hadeland relatives made the decision to move as a group to Mandt by wagon train in 1875 and begin anew on prairie land. The wagon train took three weeks to make the trip to Montevideo, Chippewa County. After staking their claims they had to go to Litchfield to file their claims at the land office.

Ole & Helena Myhre and ten children.

Helena was born in Fillmore County 1864, the youngest of seven children of Anders Pedersen and Maria Gulbrandsdtr. who emigrated in 1849. Ole and Helena's children were all born in Chippewa County.

There were nine families from Hadeland in the wagon train with 41 people in total. Eight of these families are related to the author.

Several more families related to wagon train members joined them in Mandt Township. Some names are Dahlrud, Christian Olsen, Rud/Larson, Abramson/Gilbertson, and Nokleby. Nieces of Kari Henriksdtr Jerve, wife of Sivert, a niece to Ole Nokleby, and Birthe Larsdtr Nelson arrived in the early 1900s. By 1900 over half of Mandt Township, Chippewa County, Minnesota, was related to the member of the Wagon Train of 1875.

A reunion of the wagon train of 1875 was held on the Carl Jerve farm (son of Sivert Jerve and born in Fillmore) in 1935, 60 years later with over two thousand people in attendance (newspaper report). Many of the original people were able to attend -- 20 out of 41. Both Margrete Falla and Magdalena Nokleby were young mothers with children in 1875.

Only Maria Gulbrandsdtr Falla 1821 was in both the 1849 emigration and the 1875 wagon train. Four members of the 1849 group lived beyond 1900: Syver Gulbrandson 1815, Maria Gulbrandsdtr 1821, her daughter Anna 1843 and son Peder 1844 who homesteaded in Brandt, South Dakota with his wife's family. Only Anna was still living when the reunion was held although she was not part of the wagon train after moving to Mandt in 1873 with her husband, L. H. Johnson, and children. She died in 1936, 93 years old; she had lived through all these events.

Mostly only family members who came to Mandt Settlement are mentioned here but there are many other descendants of Peder Hanson, Gulbrand Jenson, and the Andersdtr sisters in America.

Today the descendants have scattered across the United States and have engaged in a wide variety of occupations. Many have made trips to Norway to visit the home of their ancestors.

Reflections of Mrs. Falla

previously unpublished   *Form 600*   *submitted by Joy Sundrum*
written by Mrs. Clifford Koethe in 1941

Below are two articles published in the <u>American</u> (Montevideo, Minnesota). The Norwegian Digitalarkivet established the emigration date as 1868, not 1866 as noted in the following. Margrethe Abrahamsdtr Falla was the daughter of Abraham Gulbrandsen and Kari Steffensdtr. She was 91 when she was interview for the articles and died two years later.

MARKS 75ᵀᴴ ANNIVERSARY OF ARRIVAL IN AMERICA
Published April 18, 1941

Observance of the diamond anniversary of her emigration to America is the unusual pleasure afforded this month to a pioneer resident of Mandt township, Mrs. Margrethe Falla. Mrs. Falla came to America at the age of 18 years in 1866 on a sailing vessel and was among the early pioneers who traveled to this community by covered wagon in the summer of 1875.

"Ocean Voyage in 1866" is the title of the story of Mrs. Falla's migration to this country, prepared for the *American* by Mrs. Clifford Koethe.

Froken Margrethe Abramsdatter Falla was 18 years of age when she left her home in Randsfjorden, Hadeland, Norway. The emigrants sailed from Christiania (now Oslo) on the third day after Easter Sunday, 1866, on the sailship "Refondo" after delaying three days in the harbor of Drobak, waiting for a wind.

The passage cost was $60.00 per person. Mrs. Falla related how she borrowed $120.00 to pay for her own fare and her mother's. To pay back that sum she worked in the harvest fields binding sheaves at $1.20 per day. "And I kept up with the men" she said. Sometimes the work was rushed so she was allowed higher wages which made it possible for her to repay the debt after three summers in the New World. This farm work was done in Fillmore county where she lived until the summer of 1875.

Mrs. Falla enjoyed her voyage immensely and she did not suffer from seasickness. She and Abraham Bybedalen Johnson cooked for a group of seven people who all came from her own community. The cooking was done on an upper deck where there was a hut enclosing 12 stoves lined up six in a row. She remembered with glee the mad scramble they had for places at the stoves. The cooking was quite simple as it was usually a preparation of *grod* (mush) or soup and an occasional baking of lefse or rye bread.

The good kettle was the most necessary utensil and each family had brought their own. They were of cast iron to be used over a direct flame. The only food item supplied by the ship was water. Each passenger was allowed three pots of water daily. "Because we were so many in our group, " she says, "we had enough water to do a little washing."

497

The emigrants had their own food supplies consisting mainly of flour, salt, flatbread, lefse, dried beef, cured pork, dried peas, potatoes, barley rice (*byg gryn*) and whole milk, which was eaten in (sic) of which they had more than enough for the voyage. The left over flatbread had taken on a distasteful ocean flavor and was thrown to the hogs, she said.

Mrs. Falla gave the following sample menus for a day on shipboard: Breakfast - rye bread, butter, homemade cheese and coffee or sour milk; dinner - soup cooked from a bone of ham with dried peas, potatoes, barley rice added. Flatbread was eaten with soup; supper - usually "*vas graut*" or water mush. With this *grod* they ate dried beef and flatbread with klabbered milk.

This particular *grod* is one of the simplest of all *grod* recipes. It is made as follows: have the desired amount of salted water in kettle over fire. When it boils, begin adding flour by hand and beat vigorously (a wooden mixing implement especially intended for *grod* cooking). As the *grod* thickens add a few more drizzles of flour until it becomes of desired thickness.

Mrs. Falla recalled that in observance of Pentecost Sunday on shipboard, her family group had a very special dish called *smorgrod* which was made of melted butter, combined with flour and gradually thinned to proper thickness by addition of water.

The captain of the ship, Harris was his name, conducted devotions every morning for those assembled.

Two babies were born during the voyage, one of them was her nephew. Miss Margrethe was given full care of the infant as she was the only member of the family who was not sick. To enable her to provide for the baby's comfort, she was given special permission to use the steward's kitchen. As a result she became acquainted with some of the ship's officers and related her romance with one of them.

Her nephew was baptized on the ship with Miss Margrethe as a sponsor. She told of the captain's disappointment over the mother's refusal to name the baby "Harris" for the captain or "Refondo" for the ship. He was named simple "Anton," she said.

During the voyage 15 young children lost their lives in an epidemic of measles.

Mrs. Falla described several amusing incidents on shipboard. One which stands out especially in her mind happened one evening after a rain. The steps down from the cooking hut were slippery. As she started down with a kettle of *grod* she slipped and fell to the floor below but managed to hold on to the kettle and none of the group was spilled.

The passengers were entertained with dancing and dancing contests. Mrs. Falla won a prize with a "*springdans*" on one occasion. There was no orchestra but there were passengers who could play the violin or accordion.

After seven weeks on the ocean, they landed in Quebec.

PIONEER DESCRIBES LIFE IN THIS COUNTRY 65 YEARS AGO
Published April 25, 1941
Fillmore and Mandt townships are in Minnesota

Mrs. Margrethe Falla, who is this year observing the diamond anniversary of her migration to America, as told in last week's *American*, was a member of the group of ten families who came by covered wagon to Mandt Township in the summer of 1875. They covered the distance of 300 miles from Fillmore county in one month. She and her husband, the late Carl Falla, had one child. Their second child was born soon after they reached their new home.

They had sold their household goods at an auction, keeping only bedding, a few dishes and a cook stove, which had been given to Mrs. Falla by a lady for whom she had worked.

They also brought the two horses hitched to the wagon, three cattle and two hens that rode in a crate fastened on behind the wagon. Five wagons were drawn by oxen and five by horses. The young folks in the group, walking bared footed, helped drive the cattle.

Their provisions, sufficient for the entire trip, were chiefly flour, flatbread, dried beef and the milk which the cows gave daily. They slept in their wagons at night.

When someone in the group was out of bread, the whole party halted for a day to permit the lady to bake her bread. They had cook stoves in the wagons. Further historical details of this trip were recorded at the 60th anniversary of the arrival of these settlers in Mandt.

When they reached their destination, just before July 4, Margrethe and Carl Falla settled on the quarter section now farmed by Joseph Gilbertson. Their first homes were sod huts. As it was too late to put in crops, Mrs. Falla worked out as a harvest hand that summer. He also put up a good supply of hay from his own land.

Mrs. Falla recalls how the abundance of wild, tall grass made the prairie look like an immense body of water, like and ocean, she said. She called one species of grass "stall" grass. The word "stall" *(stål)* means "steel." This grass made exceptionally good fuel if cut and stacked before harvest, she said. It contained oil which seemed to be lost if the grass was cut late. This particular grass grew in low places and was also excellent feed for cattle and horses. Mrs. Falla used to leave the children alone all day to go haying with her husband, often seven miles from home. She tells how they would bring home two loads a day from the prairie northeast of their farm where land had not yet been claimed by anyone. They stacked up enough at home for fuel and fodder for the winter and had a great deal of it to sell besides. For eight years they used the grass for fuel.

When leaving Fillmore County, they had been warned of the terrible grasshopper ravages in this part of Minnesota and they found these stories had not been exaggerated. Mrs. Falla said their first three crops of oats were destroyed by grasshoppers.

But Mr. Falla was fortunate enough to obtain employment with Ole Nokleby who had brought a thresher from Fillmore County. They threshed until very late that fall for farmers all along

Chippewa River where the crops had been spared. In that way Mr. Falla was able to buy lumber for a frame house the first fall after they settled in Mandt. He hired Peter Myrestuen as carpenter.

Mrs. Falla told of an afternoon in the summer of 1877 when she and the children had walked over to her mother's home. In the late afternoon, her mother accompanied them home and they became puzzled over the strange appearance of the oats field. Upon coming closer they discovered the grasshoppers had cut the oats stems, beheading the grain. That crop was a total loss.

Finally they saved their grain in the following novel way, quite by accident.

In the spring of 1878, Mr. Falla. with the help of his relatives, who were also his neighbors, enclosed a piece of land with a sod fence. Mrs. Falla said it was a terrible job to find the cattle at milking time when they had wandered off in the tall dense grass. The young calves had to be hunted and carried home and the mosquitoes were enormous, she said. They were a terrible plague in those days when sloughs were not drained. Often, she said, they didn't get the milking done until noon. (Yes, we're coming to that grasshopper remedy.)

Being very resourceful, neighborly and cooperative, four families built a sod fence to be used as a joint pasture enclosure. It was a monument to pioneer patience and resourcefulness. It so happened that the grasshoppers that year arrived from the southeast. Mr. Falla's oats field was west of the sod fence. When the grasshoppers had completed their ruinations on the east side of the sod fence, they proceeded toward Falla's fields but could not hop the sod fence. Not only that but they fell back from the sod wall into the narrow trench by the sod removal where they perished helplessly. "That fall we had oats to sell," said Mrs. Falla.

Mrs. Falla experienced many severe winters but one which stands out in her memory most distinctly is the early blizzard of 1880. That fall brought an unusually heavy snowfall on October 14 and 15. Mrs. Falla said, "Our grain stacks could just barely be located and we could hardly crawl out of the house, up over the high snowbanks and down another snowbank into the barn. Threshing was not done until late fall but was finished before Christmas.

When Mrs. Falla was 42 years of age she had a family of ten children. Besides providing food for the family, butter, bread of which she averaged 24 loaves a week, all the meat which must be cured for the summer, there were clothes to be made. She prepared wood from their own sheep, spinning, weaving and sewing by hand. Linen, too, was woven at home. She sometimes wove enough cloth in one day for a dress. "I used to sit up until two in the morning to get my sewing finished," she said.

Just before Christmas, she would have to work night and day to prepare homemade clothes for Christmas gifts. She recalls how her oldest daughter would sit up at night to keep her company, plying her with questions about the meaning of Christmas when her mother was so tired she couldn't answer sensibly, but still sat sewing into the wee hours of the morning.

Jerve-Jorve Relatives, Jevnaker & America

previously unpublished   Form 218   *Joy Sundrum*

Fillmore County is in southeastern Minnesota. Chippewa County is in western Minnesota. Big Bend and Mandt are townships in Chippewa County. Rothsay is partly in Wilkin County, Minnesota and partly in Otter Tail County, Minnesota. The events of the ocean journey and settling in Chippewa County come from several accounts recorded by Alfa Olson Rud from her mother, Karen Marie Syversdtr Jerve Olson.

My great-grandfather Syver Gundersen from the Jørve place under Sogn in Jevnaker was granted homestead in Big Bend Township, Chippewa County in 1882. On land immediately east were his wife's sister and husband, Tosten and Marthe Jenson who were granted their homestead claim on the same day. These were only four of the many Hadelanders who settled in Chippewa County. It is hard to count how many they were related to.

The homestead record show the name Syver G. Jorve, but all his children spelled it Jerve while his brothers near Rothsay in Wilkin County were Jorve. In Norway it was Jørve or Gørve; most Norwegian records for the early 1800s and before show simply Sogn as the farm name. The Jørve family ancestry has been traced back to the beginning of the 1600s in Hadeland on farms in both Jevnaker and Lunner. They were cotters, often moving from farm to farm with their families, trying to provide for them.

There were seven children of Gunder Johansen and Kirsti Syversdtr. Gunder died in 1858 and Kirsti in 1874, both of them on Sognseie, land once owned by the Sogn or parish, and on their cotter's plot Gørve or Jørve. Of the seven children, five of them went to Minnesota and two remained in Jevnaker. All of them left after their father had died and two after their mother had died.

Johan Gundersen Jørve 1835-1899 was the eldest and the first to leave in May 1869 with his younger brother, Martin. Johan apparently didn't marry, died near Rothsay and was buried at Frelser's Lutheran church cemetery in Trondhjem Township, Otter Tail County. It is not known if he went directly to the area on arrival. If so, did he know Hadelanders there?

Syver/Sivert Gundersen Jørve/Jerve 1837-1891, the second oldest and the second to emigrate, married Kari Henriksdtr in 1862. She was one of the Jonsrud sisters listed in another article. They left in April 1870 for Fillmore County with four children: Karen Marie 1863, Hans Martin 1865, Gulbran 1867 and Anton 1869. Anton was born on 28 April 1869, died on board ship 15 May 1870 and was buried at sea, as noted on the passenger list.

Three more children were born in Fillmore County: Anna Matilde 1871, Carl Johan 1872, and Clara Sophie 1874. All these children with their parents were part of a ten-family wagon train that walked to Chippewa County in June 1875 with descendants of Sivert's Great-aunt, Mari Andersdtr. Falla. Mari and her husband, Gudbrand Jenson, emigrated from Falla to America in 1849, some of the early Norwegian emigrants. They traveled with their daughter, Maria, her husband, Anders Pedersen, and their three children plus Anders' widowed mother, Kari Andersdtr. who was also Maria's grandmother.

Karen, Sivert and Kari's eldest daughter, relayed her memories to her daughter, Alfa Olson Rud. She remembered they were on the ocean for eight weeks until they arrived in Quebec, Canada, where they slept one night on the ground. The following day was spent on a horrible boat until they were transferred to a train that was even less comfortable. There were only wooden plank benches; the train rocked and shook so much, the small children would fall onto the floor. Several days later they were transferred to a better train for the next six days and nights. In Rushford, Fillmore County, they were met by Gilbert Gilbertson (Gulbrand Abrahamsen), Syver's second cousin and his wife's brother-in-law. They lived in a sod house until fall when they moved into a log house, one room with about 140 square feet, two miles from the Gilbertsons. Syver/Sivert worked all summer for the payment of one cow and a little cash money.

Her memories continued: There were no luxuries. Fruit sauce was a luxury and was enjoyed only once while they lived near Rushford. The occasion was the arrival of the pastor to their home for the baptism of a baby girl. (*Clara Sophie in 1874.*) Clothes were at a minimum. Karen, the oldest daughter, had one dress during the first two years in Rushford. It was a sleeveless dress made of homespun material. On week days it was worn wrong side out, on Sundays the right side was out.

In 1875 a group of nine Hadeland families and a family from Nannestad, Akershus, trekked from Fillmore County to Chippewa County where there were other families from Hadeland, many in Mandt Township. Syver homesteaded in Big Bend Township in a sod house and built that fall. It was one room with a small entrance over the door in which they set up the stove. In the larger rooms were two beds, a box for a table and boxes for chairs. The following year a bedroom was added. The walls were whitewashed twice a year. The floors were "natural," soil. The first baby born in the sod house in 1876, named Anton after the son who died on the ocean journey in 1870, did not survive. Another Anton was born later.

Four children were born in Big Bend Township: Anton, 1876-1876; Anton 1877-1940; Louis/Lewis, 1880-1949; and Ole S., 1884-1941. Of all the children, Carl Johan lived the longest; he died in 1965 at age 93. Daughter Anna died in 1901, age 29, from tuberculosis, leaving a 7-year-old son who was raised by his aunts and uncles.

For several years after their arrival, there were grasshopper plagues that devastated the crops. (See *Pioneer Reflections of Mrs. Falla.*) Winters were brutally cold and summers plagued them with humidity and mosquitoes. Sivert and Kari's eldest daughter, Karen, looked after her siblings while her parents worked away from home--Kari doing housework for neighbors. Karen did not recall a time when she was hungry or that they were out of food. Both Sivert and Kari were blessed with relatives nearby: Kari had three sisters in two or three townships in

Sivert and Kari Jorve Family
Back: Carl, Gulbran, Karen, Anna, Clara, Sophie
Front: Hans, Sivert, Anton standing behind Ole, Kari, Louis

Chippewa County; there were 31 first cousins. Sivert had 16 second cousins (including once removed) who had 102 children (roughly counting).

Syver/Sivert and Kari's children and grandchildren married other Hadeland immigrants, many who were members of Jevnaker Lutheran in Mandt Township, Chippewa County. Surnames include: Gilbertson, Olson, Ellingson, Rud, Johnson, Frengen, Laumb, Thompson, and others.

Anders Gunderson Jorve, the third son of Gunder and Kirsti, was actually the last to emigrate in 1882 after both his wife and his parents had died. Two daughters, Karen and Hilda, and a son, Gulbrand, came with him to Wilkin County. The daughters did not marry; Gilbert (Gulbrand) was 42 when he married a widow with two children but he and Karen had no children. Anders and his children are buried in the Rothsay area.

The fifth brother of this Jorve group was Borger 1842-1922 who remained in Norway and gave the surname Borgersen to his descendants. He married Sigrid Eriksdtr born in Lunner, and they had nine children, three of whom emigrated. Borger was the first "Jørve" to work at the Hadeland Glassworks in Jevnaker and several of his sons, grandsons and great-grandsons followed him. A granddaughter and family and a great-grandson have warmly greeted Norwegian-American relatives who visit Jevnaker to meet relatives.

Borger's three children who emigrated were all associated with glassmaking. Sons Johan and Peter who emigrated in 1903 and 1905 had a glass shop in Chicago on Fullerton Avenue where they sold their handmade glass pieces. Johan became sole owner when Peter became a chiropractor. Johan married a Norwegian immigrant in Chicago where he died in 1957 with no children and an excellent reputation as a glass maker. Peter returned several times to visit his family in Jevnaker, died in Pennsylvania and was buried in Corning, New York, where his sister and her family had settled.

Borger's daughter, Mathilde Pauline, left Jevnaker with her brother Johan and her soon-to-be husband, Anton Isak Trondsen. Mathilde Pauline and Anton Isak left on 20 Mar 1903 and married 30 Jul 1904 in Corning, New York, where they raised seven children, all Trondsens. So--not a Jørve surname but she is a Jørve descendant.

Anton Isak worked at the Corning Glass Works in Corning, New York. He never learned to drive but got around on his bicycle when needed. All four of their sons (Tony, Olaf, Carl and John Trondsen) worked there also, and daughter Minnie married a Corning Glass Works executive. Trondsen descendants still live in the same area.

Another of Borger's children, Iver, left Norway on 9 Sep 1904 destined for Corning, New York, arriving after his sister's wedding, but perhaps he didn't intend to stay since he married in Jevnaker in 1913 and died in Jevnaker in 1958. Was he named after his Uncle Iver?

After Borger came Martin 1847-1904, Gunder and Kirsti's fifth child and fifth son, who was the first to emigrate in 1869 with his oldest brother, Johan. What prompted his decision?

504

How/Why did he end up in Rothsay in northern Minnesota? The same questions we often have for our ancestral relatives. He married a Norwegian immigrant and they had thirteen children, three of whom died as infants or toddlers. Sons Gilbert and Marius owned a hardware store in LaMoure, North Dakota. Ted had a grocery store and had six children. Martin's children married Swartwouldt, Haga, Bothun, Hammer, Nelson, Larson, Heden, and Berge spouses; Martin had 26 grandchildren. Martin, wife Eline and three infant sons are buried in the Scandinavian Evangelical Free Cemetery in Trondhjem Township, Otter Tail County, which is now at a rural intersection with no church.

Iver was Gunder's youngest son of six. Little is known about him. He was born in 1850 in Jevnaker and is buried (no year) in Hønefoss, Buskerud, a short drive from Jevnaker.

Gunder and Kirsti's youngest and seventh child was a daughter who was the third to emigrate, Birthe Marie, born in 1853, emigrated in 1881. She signed out of the Jevnaker parish on 13 May 1881, married Gulbrand Petersen on 14 May 1881 in the Jevnaker Church, and left on 20 May 1881 for Amerika. He may have lived on the Jørve plot because they had the Jorve surname in America.

Gulbrand and Birthe Marie Jorve Family
Back: Caroline, Ludvig, Peter, Axel, Idan, Gilbert
Front: Alma, Gulbrand, Calmer, Birthe Marie, Mina

They settled on a farm near Rothsay, where they raised nine children. Six of the nine never married; Caroline married Martin Marking and there were two daughters, Mina married Melvin Hammer and had two sons, and Gilbert married Alma Hansen and also had two sons. Calmer, the youngest and unmarried, lived for 106 years 1898-2004. Imagine the changes in his lifetime.

Even by the early 1900s the Jorve families from Jevnaker were living in both New York State and two areas of Minnesota where descendants still live--among many other places.

Andersdatter-Olson Family History

previously unpublished   *Forms 648,600*   *submitted by Joy Sundrum*
written by Alfa Olson Rud

This account was taken from several different short histories that Alfa Olson Rud wrote at different times. Her father was Ole C. Olson, mother Karen Marie Jerve, grandparents Ole Christian Olson, Randi Andersdtr and Sivert G. Jerve, Kari Syversdtr, all from Hadeland.

Christian Olson, born 1833 in Gran, married Rangdi Andersdtr, born 1834 on Vaterud, Jevnaker, in 1856 in Jevnaker, Hadeland. Ole died in 1896 at age 62 in Chippewa County, Minnesota. Rangdi died there in 1924 at age 90. Their three children: Martha, Ole and Caroline.

Christian Olson was a tenant farmer and carpenter on the 1865 Norwegian Census living on Moseby in Jevnaker. He and Rangdi Andersdtr. had married and had two children, Marte and Ole, when they all emigrated in 1868 to Iowa. In 1869 Rangdi's sister, Karen, and her husband, Lars Andreas Larson, with three sons left for McGregor, Iowa. Later they moved to Chippewa County. Karen's brother, Anders, left with them. Some years later in 1877 brothers Ole and Gulbrand Andersen also headed for America.

Christian Olson and Randi Andersdtr's son, Ole Christian Olson, was born December 8, 1861, on the Falla farm in Jevnaker, Hadeland. In 1868 he came with his parents and sister Martha to Clayton County in Iowa near a town called Claremont where Caroline Marie was born in 1871 and where they lived until 1876 when they moved to Chippewa County, Minnesota. Karen Jerve Olson was born in Jevnaker, Norway on February 2, 1863, and came with her parents, Kari and Sever Jerve and her brothers, Hans, Gilbert and Anton (who died on the ocean) to Fillmore County in southern Minnesota near Rushford, a place called Highland Prairie. In 1875 the family came to Chippewa County, Minnesota.

In 1876 Christian and Rangdi Olson, son Ole and daughter Caroline took the train to Benson, Minnesota, where they were met by relatives and taken to their home in Mandt Township, Chippewa County. They settled on the north half of Section 32. Daughter Martha had married in 1873 in Iowa to Martin Pederson, and they also moved to Chippewa County.

Karen and Lars Larson's three sons were Andrew Larson who married Cary Rear; they had five children: Ludwig, Gena, Henry, Caroline and Howard. The last three children died in infancy. Martin Larson Rud married Karen Gilbertson, a daughter of Hadelanders Gulbran Abrahamsen (or Gilbert Gilbertson) and Anne Henriksdtr Jonsrud. They had six children: Gustav, Lauris, Clara, Hannah, Melvin, and Conrad. The third son, Casper Larson Rud, married his cousin, Caroline Andersdtr; their children were Lawrence who married a Nokleby Hadeland descendant and "Willy" Rud who married his second cousin, Alfa Olson, also a Hadeland descendant whose documentation provided the family history for the Andersdtr-Olson family.

Christian Olson's brother, Peder and his wife, Inger Thorine Syversdtr, emigrated in 1873 with their five children, five years after Christian. They were part of the 1875 wagon train from Fillmore to Chippewa County that Karen Syversdtr Jerve was with and who married Peder's nephew, Ole, Son of Christian. So both Rangdi Andersdtr and Christian Olson from Jevnaker had siblings in Mandt Township, Chippewa County.

Christian Olson brought his skill as a carpenter with him from Norway; he built not only the Immanuel Church but also the seats, altar, communion rail, pulpit and the crown above the pulpit. He used a lathe he had made and stepped it with his foot. The lumber for that church was hauled from Benson, Minnesota, with oxen. It was a work of art. It was built around 1876-1882. He also built the Zion Church northwest of Watson. It was much like Immanuel, only smaller.

Interior of Immanuel Lutheran Church

Christian never did any fine woodwork until he was elderly. Then he decided he was going to try and he did very well. He made three grandfather clocks, a gun cabinet, tables, stools, picture frames, book cases, wall decorations, etc.

Christian Olson made coffins for most of the people in the area. He would buy wide boards and paint them black. Then when anyone needed a coffin, he was ready to make it. They would line the coffin inside with a cheap white material and make a pillow for the head. *His daughter-in-law, Karen Jerve Olson,* was often called on to go to the home where one had died and she prepared the body for the funeral. Friends and relatives were invited to the funeral for dinner on the day of the funeral, then there was a short service at home and on to the church for another service and back to the house for lunch. It took all day as all drove with horses.

I *(author, Alfa Olson Rud)* don't think those funerals cost over $5.00. Grandpa got $2.50 or $3.00. The neighbors dug the grave, filled it in again, etc. Same with weddings. Someone would drive from house to house to invite the people. No invitations, no phone calls. Some weddings were quite big, too. But, mostly they were married at their home. My parents were married in Immanuel Church *(Tunsberg Township, Chippewa County, Minnesota).*

Mother (*Karen Jerve Olson*) during the winter of 1876-1877 and a year after walking with the wagon train from Fillmore County to Chippewa County, lived and worked for a family while she went to confirmation classes at Immanuel Church. This arrangement was so that she would not have so long a distance to go to classes. She was confirmed in 1877, her dress was a brown calico with a deep black band at the bottom. She borrowed a scarf and shawl. Her father put new caps on her old shoes; she had no overshoes. As the oldest child she was often responsible for her siblings and doing housework when her parents worked away from home in the grasshopper plague years.

Mother *(Karen Jerve Olson)* and Dad *(Ole C. Olson)* were married July 4, 1885 by the Rev. O. E. Solseth in the Immanuel Church. The wedding reception was in the sod shanty. This had been cleaned up but during the night it rained so the mud ran down the windows in streaks. Grandma Jerve *(Kari Henriksdtr Jonsrud Jerve)* had to wash all windows again in the morning. The bridesmaids were Caroline Olson (later Falla) and Karen Gilbertson (later Rud). The best men were Hans Jerve *(brother of the bride)* and Martin Rud *(cousin of the groom)*. Gulbrand (Rapeshu) Gilbertson had bought a new surrey so he drove the wedding party to church.

Dad paid $1,000.00 for the first 120 acres with a small house and tiny stable. In this house they lived until Severin was born. The barn was built in 1911. The children born in this home were:

Ragna Karina 1886-1972   Married Jens Ellingson. 9 children
Conrad 1888-1911 (Died from tuberculosis.)
Severin 1890-1918 (Died from tuberculosis.) Married Aagot Kiland in 1915. 2 ch
Claudine 1893-1986   Married Joseph Gilbertson. 6 children
Alice 1896-1926   Married Samuel Gilbertson. 1 child
Alfa 1899-1991   Married Casper William "Willy" Rud. 4 children
Ella 1903-1993   Married LeRoy C. Johnson. 4 children
Alvin 1911-1993 (Foster son) Married Ingeborg T. Raffelson. 8 children

Dad was very civic minded. He was interested in all school, church and civic affairs. He held offices as treasurer, secretary or clerk of various boards. Although he had little formal education, he was an educated man due to his love of reading. He was Dist. 4 County Commissioner for eight years. Part of this time he was totally blind but continued his job with a keen interest.

Besides raising a big family, Mother cared for her Aunt Martha (Vasjve) Jenson for five years, for her mother, Kari Jerve, one year (Both these ladies were crippled.), and for her mother-in-law, Rangdi Olson. Dad's Uncle Ole Anderson, called Vesle Ole, *(brother of Ole C. Olson's mother)* stayed in our home for twenty-one years. Vesle Ole was blind. Besides these three, there were various other homeless and helpless people whom she cared for shorter periods of time.

Mother worked as a homemaker, mother, nurse, doctor, midwife, mortician and florist. She would often prepare bodies for funerals, including putting a silver quarter on their eyes, folding their hands and combing their hair in a becoming way. When her father-in-law had made the coffin, she would line it with white material and a pillow at the head. If no flowers were available, she would make a wreath of myrtle and white geraniums or other flowers.

In her last years Mother was quite sick and lived with her daughter, Claudine Gilbertson and family. She died on Christmas Day 1939 in the parlor of the Gilbertson home at the age of 76 of chronic valvular heart lesions from which she had suffered for ten years.

Dad died July 14, 1930. Mother died December 25, 1939. "Blessed be their

Ole and Karen (Jerve) Olson with Ragna and Conrad, 1888

memory." They are both buried in the Jevnaker Lutheran Church cemetery, Mandt Township, Chippewa County, Minnesota.

In October 1953 Ole and Karen Olson had 23 grandchildren and 31 great-grandchildren.

Jonsrud Sisters of Chippewa County

previously unpublished   *Forms 600, 927, 1023, 1024, 1025*   *Joy Sundrum*

In 1875 there were four Jonserud (Jonsrud or Johnsrud) sisters living in Chippewa County, Minnesota, and one in Lafayette County, Wisconsin. Although they were known in Minnesota as Jonsrud sisters, in Norway they were Henriksdatter. In America they assumed their husbands surnames and were Ann Gilbertson, Martha Jensen, Kari Jerve, Lise Hendrickson and Helen Fensand. All had married in Jevnaker and came to America at different times.

Their parents, Henrik Larsen and Anne Caspersdtr., both died a couple months apart in 1879 as *"fattiglem"* (paupers), at ages 74 and 66. In their married life of 46 years they had lived on Virstadeie, Rudseie, Kalvsjøieie, Kjørveneie and Bolkeneie. In 1865 the census they are on Bolkenjonserud, Jevnaker, and in 1875 on Jonserud under Bolken, which are different ways of saying the same place. During these ten years, three daughters emigrated from "Jonsrud."

Henrik's parents and grandparents had also died as paupers; his ancestry was mainly in Lunner, Hadeland, back to the mid-1650s. Not much is known about Anne Caspersdtr's father's family but her mother's can be traced to at least the early 1700s in Hadeland. The history of poverty in the mid-1800s probably made emigration a better option.

Henrik and Anne had nine children. The oldest, son Hans, remained in Norway. He married and had nine children. Surnames in Norway today include Kilstad, Andersen and Hansen. One daughter is known to have emigrated--Karoline Hansdtr married to Andreas Andersen left on October 9, 1902, destined for Iowa. Karoline died in 1961 and Andreas in 1909, both in Northwood, North Dakota. There were five children born in Norway and three in America. Karoline had five aunts and one uncle in America.

After Hans came four daughters who all emigrated, Anne, Marthe, Kari, and Lise, followed by son Peder who remained in Norway with Løvsgaard and Pedersen descendants. Then three more daughters, Helene, Maren, and Oline. Helene and three of Maren's daughters emigrated to Minnesota.

Between the births of the last two daughters, Maren and Oline, there was another son, Anders Henriksen, born to Henrich with another woman. This son also emigrated and died in Lafayette County, Wisconsin in 1934 where he married twice and had 13 children.

Lise, the fifth child and the fourth to emigrate in 1876 with her husband, Christian Engebretsen and four children went to Wisconsin. They established their home in Lafayette County where they raised nine children and took the surname Hendrickson, the patronymic of Christian's father. Their daughters married Wescott, Albertson, Ward, Hanshaw, Staver and Woodward men. There were more English descendants than Norwegian in their community!

Of the four daughters who were in Chippewa County, Minnesota, three first went to Fillmore

511

Lise Henriksdtr Jonserud Hendrickson Family
Back: Minnie, Ina, Babe, Henry, Sinda
Front: Carrie, Elmer, Lise and Christian, Nellie, Clara

County, Minnesota. The oldest daughter, Anne, and her husband, Gulbran Abrahamsen, were the first to emigrate in 1868, going to Fillmore County, Minnesota, with their two children, Karen age 4 and Abraham age 2. Son Anton Refondo was born on the ship; his middle name was the name of the ship. Captain Harris would have liked the baby to be named after him, but the parents settled on the ship's name. There were two more children born in Fillmore County and two more in Chippewa County; those four never married. Karen married Martin Rud in Chippewa County, had six children and moved to South Dakota where they both are buried. Abraham married twice (Ingeborg Svor and Laura Brun/Brown) and had nine children. He enjoyed recounting the trip in 1875 from Fillmore to Chippewa County where there are still many Gilbertsons. Anton married Karen Heim and had nine children, all with the Gilbertson surname. Anton and Karen are buried in North Dakota.

Why did Gulbran and Anne go to Fillmore County in 1868? Most likely because Gulbran's great-aunt Mari Andersdtr Falla, her daughter and son-in-law, Maria and Anders Pedersen, had emigrated in 1849 with a family group of eight Hadelanders to Lafayette County, Wisconsin, but had later moved to Fillmore County, Minnesota. In 1875 Maria was with her son Andreas and daughter Helen on the wagon train to Chippewa County.

Gulbran and Anne went to Chippewa County, Minnesota, in 1873. Gulbran's father's patronymic Gulbransen became the surname Gilbertson in America and of many families in Chippewa County, Minnesota.

Martha Henriksdtr, the second of Henrik and Anne's daughters, was the third to leave with

512

her husband and family in 1871, only one year after her younger sister, Kari. Marthe went with her husband, Tosten Jensen, and two sons, Julius and Emil. They had experienced the hardship of losing five infants while in Lunner, Hadeland. They joined Kari and her family in Fillmore County and were one of the families who trudged across Minnesota in 1875. Their surname was recorded differently more often than any of the other families. First they used the farm name Vasjø which appeared as Wadsjo, Wasea, Wasjve, Wasje, Vasjve, and Vashe before they settled on Jenson.

Martha's husband, Tosten Jenson, died in 1890 when their youngest child was not quite eight years old. In 1900 Martha and her two sons, Emil and Adolph, were living with her niece, Karen Jerve Olson, her husband, Ole C. Olson. The census record shows Martha had had twelve children, four of whom were living. Martha died on 30 March 1907. Son Emil 1870-1957; Adolph, Julia married to Anton Hanson, and Julius. The youngest son, Hjelmer, had died 2 March 1900, 18 years old, after appendicitis surgery. Martha died on 30 March 1907. Julia Mathilda 1875-1959 married Anton Hanson, 6 children; Julius 1877-1958; Henry Adolph 1880-1920 married Inga Opoien with ancestry from Nord- and Sør-Trøndelag, 6 children whose surname was Jenson; Hjelmer 1882-1900. Henry Adolph and Inga moved to North Dakota in 1905 where they died, but all their children returned at different times to Minnesota.

Kari Henriksdtr was the third daughter and the second to emigrate in 1870 to Fillmore County, following her sister Anne and her husband's relatives who had left in 1849. With Kari and Syver/Sivert were their children Karen, Hans, Gulbran and Anton who died just before his first birthday on board the ship. He was buried at sea as noted on the ship list.

Sivert and Kari left from the Jørve farm but the named evolved to Jerve in Big Bend Township, Chippewa County. Sivert was Jorve when he was granted his homestead in 1882, and on the next farm to the east was his wife's sister's family, Marthe and Tosten Jensen, who were granted their homestead on the same date.

Sivert and Kari's oldest daughter, Karen, never forgot the journey from Norway nor the journey across Minnesota. Karen's daughter, Alfa Olson Rud, was the family historian and recorded her mother's memories of this trek.

Karen, their eldest child, married Ole C. Olson who was born on the Falla farm in Jevnaker. Their eight children: Ragna married Jens Ellingson, 9 children; Conrad died at 22 from tuberculosis; Severin married Aagot Kiland but died at 27 from tuberculosis, 2 children; Claudine married Joseph Gilbertson, 6 children, Alice married Samuel Gilbertson, 1 son; Alfa married Willy Rud, 4 children; Ella married LeRoy Johnson, 4 children; Alvin (adopted) married Ingeborg Raffelson, 8 children. (Alvin is the father of DeLos Olson who was active in Hadelandlaget until his death in 2011.)

Karen was the oldest of nine children who grew to adulthood. Two Antons died - one at sea and one in Chippewa County. Karen's siblings were: Hans 1865-1944 married Ingeborg Berg,

7 children; Gulbran 1867-1947; Anna Matilde 1871-1901married Christian Frengen, 3 children; Carl John (1872-1965) married Ida Laumb, 12 children; Clara Sophie 1874-1952 married Oscar Laumb, 4 children; Anton S. 1877-1940 married Ragnil/Rachel Thompson, 11 children; Lewis 1880-1949; Ole 1884-1941 married Laura Laumb, 14 births/10 living children. Ole was only two years older than Ragna, his first niece born to his eldest sister, Karen Jerve Olson.

The fourth Jonsrud daughter and the last to emigrate, Helene, and her husband, Ole Fensand (Finsand), went directly to Chippewa County in 1881 with their two daughters, Berte Marie and Anna. Seven more children were born in Chippewa County. Berte Marie 1878-? married Adolph Nelson, 4 children; Anna 1879-1931 married Ole Hermanson, 3 children; Hans Peder 1882-1940 married Carrie Askim, 1 daughter; Ole 1883-1910 was killed in an accident; Emma 1886-1981 married Ingebret Olson, 3 children; Louis 1887-1974 married first Anna Berg, 4 children, 2nd married Mabel Nylen; Anton 1889-1928 married Alma Haugen, 1 daughter; Helmer 1891-1929 married Mary Tostenson, 4 children; and Alfa Lila 1897-1972 married Archie Williams, ? children.

Two daughters remained in Norway, Maren and Oline. Three of Maren's daughters came to America. Anna Marie Karlsdtr came in 1906 and married Thorval Laumb from Nannestad, Akershus in 1907; they farmed in Chippewa County. Helga Karsdtr came in 1909; she married Ellic Snyder and they settled in Iowa. Karen Karsldtr came in 1909 with her sister, Helga; she lived in Chippewa County until 1917 when she emigrated to Saskatchewan where she married Ole Egge from Valdres. They had seven children.

Jevnaker Lutheran Church
Mandt Township, Chippewa
County
Photo taken about 1939

"The Jonsrud Girls" were fortunate to have sisters, more relatives and other Hadeland immigrants nearby. In Chippewa County they first went to Immanuel Lutheran and later to Jevnaker when it was built to serve the expanding population. The Jevnaker name indicates the number of people in Mandt Township particularly who had emigrated from the Jevnaker-Lunner area of Hadeland.

Hard ocean crossings, limited supplies, grasshopper plagues, walking statewide to resettle, deaths of babies, new language and customs, parents and family remaining in Norway affected them all. They persevered and we are thankful!

514

A Family's Book of Revelation

previously unpublished   *Form 727*   *Allen Thoreson*

The author is the great-grandson of Christian Thoreson Kittelsrud and Anne Larsdatter Skolen and the current owner and steward of their family Bible.

We are who we are and where we dwell because of those who lived before us! Each of us stands upon the strong shoulders of ancestors. I exist and I am here in large part because of them. Each of us has a pair of parents, a double set of grandparents, eight great-grandparents, to say nothing of generations, layer upon layer, who lived prior to our time. Now and then something shakes us awake from the "nowness" and self-centeredness of the present, and reveals to us a deeper picture of where we came from.

Busy with the challenges and demands of the here and the now,   I unexpectedly received a treasury of information about a large part of my family background. This happened shortly after 1964 when I held in my hands, for the first time, a copy of a modest Norwegian Bible given to me following the deaths of my paternal grandparents, both of whom died that year, within months of each other. The Bible originally belonged to my grandfather's parents.

Given to me was a red, leather-covered volume, written in the Norwegian language and printed in nineteenth century archaic type-face. The book was not only a copy of Holy Scripture, it also conveyed unique and precious information regarding the family from which I and a host of others had sprung. On the blank end papers, inside the hard back and front covers, someone had scrawled hand-written notes. The pen-and-ink entries, in Norwegian, listed names, dates, and places regarding the Bible's original owners.

That family Bible belonged to an immigrant couple who, shortly after their marriage, left Hadeland, Norway for America. They were Christian Thoreson Kittelsrud and Anne Larsdatter Skoien. The inscribed notations recorded basic information regarding themselves, their origins, their trek to the new world, the finding of land for a farm home, and the births of their many children. Not only do readers have facts, they also can sense determination and pride of achievement. In addition, one reads of bewildering sorrow

Thore Kittelsrud, 1850s

in those simply inscribed entries.

Shortly after their marriage in 1854, at the Lunner Church in Hadeland, Christian Thoreson Kittelsrud, and Anne Larsdatter Skoien sailed for America. They journeyed deep into North America, via Canada, making their way to Iowa, and from there to Minnesota.

The farm they formed from the wilderness provided land to be cleared and plowed. It was nestled in the spring-fed Pine Creek valley, tributary to the Root River system of Southeastern Minnesota. It provided a supply of hard wood for fuel and building. A log cabin was constructed, later covered with clapboard siding and added rooms. The house still serves as the farm home of the current owner. Later a large barn was built upon a slope allowing easy entrance to the hay mow. Underneath was room for livestock and horses. Family legend says the barn was built of heavy beams brought by oxen from sawmills at Winona, Minnesota.

Anne Larsdtr Skoien Kittelsrud, 1910s

516

The land and farm were in Fremont Township, Winona County, on the line shared with Fillmore County. Other Norwegian pioneering immigrant families settled near them. From the mid-1850s, Christian and Anne worked hard to make a living and provide a home for themselves and their growing family. Fourteen children would be born to them over the course of twenty six years.

The final and fourteenth child was my grandfather Olaf Thoreson, christened with the number of his birth order in his name: "Olaf Titus Quartus Decimus" (Olaf Titus Four and Ten—a name which he, with embarrassment, tried to keep hidden all his life.). His mother was only a few days from her 49th birthday when he was born. Being so much younger than his older siblings, he hardly knew some of them as they, when young, scattered to the western frontier and elsewhere. Unlike Norway, where the eldest son generally received the farm, Olaf was given title to the family's farm following Christian's death in 1900. A provision of that arrangement was that Olaf and his wife, Minnie, were to take responsibility for his mother Anne, providing her with a house in nearby Rushford, Minnesota along with an annual stipend. She lived until 1923, to the age of 92. Though she dwelt in the new land for nearly seventy years, she stubbornly refused to learn English, of which she said (in Norwegian, of course), "I don't want to learn that new language!"

When Anne passed away, the Bible with its careful inscriptions passed on to Olaf and Minnie. When they died, both in 1964, their eight children, one of whom was my father, offered the Bible to me. As a Lutheran Pastor and one already possessing curiosity regarding family history, it was decided that I should have ownership of the old Bible that had belonged to my great grandparents Thoreson.

Opening that modestly appearing copy of the Norwegian Bible, with its' unique family record inside, one was able to read not only scriptural texts concerning the families of Old Testament Israel, and the Holy Family of the New Testament, one could also read the immigration saga of the Christian Thoreson Kittelsrud and Anne Larsdatter Skoien family.

By the 1960s, few, including myself, of the third and fourth generation of descendants, knew much of the family's journey from Norway and pioneering experience in America. Barely known was the fact that the original surname in Norway was Kittelsrud and not, as it became in America, Thoreson. Almost none knew there was in Norway an area called Hadeland, much less a Kittelsrud farm.

Fragments of information about the family had been passed along verbally. Most of this was not verifiable or documented. There was no coherent narrative of Christian and Anne's life. Some knew that after spending the first winter in Clayton County, Iowa, Christian had walked to Winona County, in Minnesota, to obtain land. They had heard that he moved Anne and their first-born child, a daughter born in December, 1854, to the new home the next summer.

An immigrant pastor, The Rev. U. V. Koren, provided spiritual care among the developing Norwegian settlements over a wide area of Iowa and Minnesota. It was he who baptized Christian and Anne's first child, perhaps at the Koren Parsonage, which today is preserved at The Vesterheim Museum in Decorah, Iowa. Such baptisms are written about in "The Diary of Elizabeth Koren", by Mrs. Koren. One of the congregations Rev. Koren established was North Prairie Evangelical Lutheran Church located a short 3 miles south of Christian and Anne's new home in Minnesota. An old and faded newspaper clipping, with Pastor Koren's photo, is pasted upon the title page of Christian and Anne's Bible.

Below, is my translation of the hand-written notes found in that Bible. I have supplied information and commentary which I feel is relevant to Christian and Anne's story. It is apparent that Christian writes in his own hand, except that death dates have been penciled into the Bible apparently at a later time.

"This Bible belongs to me, Christian Thoreson, born on the farm Kittlesrud in Gran Parish, in Hadeland, the 16th of November, 1834. I was baptized and confirmed in the same place." (Died the 1st of November, 1900.)

"My wife, Anne Larsdatter was born on the farm Skoien, the 7th of October, 1831 in Lynnes Annex in Jevnakers parish in Hadeland. Baptized and Confirmed in the same place." (Died the 19th of October, 1923.)

Note: Though Christian's father, Thoreder Andersen Kittelsrud, born to Anders Michelsen and Kari Toresdatter Sorum in 1803 is not mentioned in Christian's family Bible notes, his father is a part of this immigrant story. Thore's mother was Marte Jonsdatter Rustad, born in 1799 in Jevnaker, who died

*Christian and Anne Thoreson c. 1899
With daughter Anne Karine Swenson
and her son, Oskar Clarence*

in 1851. Thore, made the decision to turn over the Kittlesrud farm to his eldest son Anders, and to go to America with Margrethe Gudbrandsdatter Rustad, his new partner. They accompanied his second son Christian and Christian's bride, Anne. However, almost from the beginning of the journey, Thore, now in his fifties, found little to his liking.

Mons Grinager, also from Hadeland, whose letters to Norway were collected by Per Hvamstad, and translated by C. A. Clauson, were published in Norwegian American Studies. Vol

24, 1970, by The Norwegian American Historical Association, tells of Thore's unhappiness (pp. 54, 55, & 57), reprinted here by permission:

Grinager writes in May, 1855, **"I must tell you that during the Christmas season I paid a visit to a Norwegian settlement about twenty-five miles from here. A number of people from Hadeland live there... All of them were doing quite well and were free of worries except for Thore Kittlesrud who arrived there last year. This spring he set out on his return journey and by now is presumably nearing the Norwegian coast. He absolutely could not find satisfaction here in anything, no matter what it might be. Scarcely had he put to sea when he was seized by such homesickness that, without exception, everything that was a part of America was offensive to him. I have been told that he was willing to pay the captain a considerable sum of money to let him go ashore at Lindesnaes. This, the captain would not agree to do.**

I presume Thore will paint conditions in the New World in pretty dark colors when he gets to Norway. I suppose it is true that those who write home are either so intoxicated with the good things here that they speak only in superlatives, or else they hate this country so much that they cannot blacken her sufficiently. The latter, however, are few. As I gathered from a letter Thore had received from Norway, he was not guilty of praising America too much. I also learned that more attention was paid to Thore's letter than to all the other America letters put together, because his contradicted all the rest. There are not many who will picture both the bright and the shadowy sides of American life, and therefore two parties have arisen.

October, 1855, **"From your letter I also learn that you have spoken with Thore Kittelsrud, who after his troublesome immigrant trip has returned to his home community in Norway. I hope he will now have greater appreciation of the good things his fatherland has to offer, and that he will not again be lured to emigrate. I felt assured that he would criticize America in every respect--- as he did the time I talked with him. But now it seems that he is primarily criticizing the climate, the houses, and the food... I accept the situation as it is. Those who are not willing to forsake old customs and to begin life anew, so to speak, ought not go to America.**

Upon returning to Norway and the Kittelsrud farm, now owned by his eldest son Anders, Thore set up a blacksmith shop. The building still stands today, at the edge of the farm, Kittelsrud. An article on Thore appeared in "The Yearbook For Hadeland 1980" (p. 54), stating that he is remembered as a master blacksmith of Hadeland. Thore's descendants on the Kittlesrud farm today keep, in a *stabur* loft, a collection of tools and items fashioned by Thore. An anvil, made by Christian, who also did blacksmithing for a time, in America, remained in the family's possession for years. Unfortunately, not long ago, it was stolen.

Ironically, though Thore disliked the new land, he left strong traces of himself behind. It was not just the skill of pounding out red hot iron and making horseshoes on a blacksmith's anvil, but his name remained in the new country. A host of descendants, to this day, via Christian, and Anne, and their fourteen children, bear Thore's name, embedded obviously in the Thoreson surname. The original name, Thor is that of the Norse mythological god of thunder. The Vikings believed that Thor's hammer, *Mjolnir*, tossed in anger across the skies caused lightning and thunderous reverberation across the ice-topped mountains, and shadowed fjords of Norway. The farm home in Norway was named Kittelsrud. But as a name, it did not travel to America. Following the patronymic system, Christian and Anne claimed the name Thoreson for themselves and their children.

Lunner Church, Hadeland

We return to the hand-written entries in Christian's and Anne's Bible:

"**We were married in Lynders (Lunner) Church, the 10th of April 1854 and emigrated to America the 20th of April the same year, 1854.**"

"**We came here to America in July 1854, and lived for a year in Clayton County, Iowa, coming here to Winona County, the 10th of July, 1855.**"

"**Our Daughter Rangdi Maria was born the 21st of December, 1854 in Clayton County Iowa, baptized by Pastor U. V. Koren.**" (She married G.G. Gilbertson a farmer not far from her parents. She was called Mary. She died in 1930.)

"**Our son Thorvald was born the 8th of June, 1856 in Winona County, Minnesota, baptized by Pastor U.V. Koren**" (He anglicized his name to Thomas and lived near Wahpeton, North Dakota, later relocating to St. Paul, MN. He had nine children. He died October 31, 1914.)

"**Our son Lars was born the 1st of May, 1858 in Winona County, Minnesota, baptized by Pastor U.V. Koren.**" (He took the name Lewis and lived for a time in the Red River Valley area, relocating to Texas. He and his wife had ten children. He died June 7, 1934.)

"**Our son, Martin Julius, was born the 29th of September, 1859, in Winona County, Minnesota, baptized by Pastor H. E. Jensen.**" (He settled in South Dakota. He and his wife had five children. He died September 27, 1925.)

"**Our daughter Karen Heline Joneta, was born September 2, 1861, in Winona County, Minnesota, baptized by Pastor H. E. Jensen.**" (She married Peter Dahl. They lived in Minneapolis, Minnesota and had two children. She died January 13, 1942.)

"**Our son Anders was born April 20, 1863, in Winona County, Minnesota, baptized by Pastor H. E. Jensen.**" (He took the name, Andrew. He had two children and lived in Minneapolis, Minnesota. He died March 1943)

"**Our daughter, Anne Karine was born November 11, 1864 in Winona County, Minnesota, baptized by H. E. Jensen.**" (She lived in Hastings, Minnesota and married Ole Swanson. They had three children. She died December 9, 1948.)

"**Our son, Christian was born May 27, 1866 in Winona County, Minnesota, baptized by Pastor F. E. Clausen.**" (He married Irene Eagles with whom he had a family. They lived in the Eau Claire, Wisconsin area. He died February 21, 1936.)

"**Our son Ole Neal was born July 12, 1868 in Winona County, Minnesota, baptized by H. E. Jensen. He died September 2, a year and one month, and 18 days. God uses so many means to draw us men to repentance. This child's death likely was also a means by Him to draw his parents to Himself.**"

"**Our daughter Thina Oline was born the 22nd of March, 1870 in Winona County, Minnesota, baptized by Pastor Magnus. She died October 10th, 1877, 7 years and 7 months old. A human born of woman lives a short life and is of much trouble. He grows up as a flower or shadow and flees as a shadow and is remembered not.**" (For the first time in this family, the number of the child is in the child's name--- "Thina" for ten.)

"**Our daughter Nelley Elevine was born March 11, 1872 and died January 7, 1881, baptized by Pastor N. Magnus, in Winona County Minnesota. So thus also are the dead resurrected from corruption and raised to incorruption. So in honor, the resurrected are glorified--- planted in weakness but raised in power.**" (Note: the child lived to be nearly 9 years of age. Family tradition says she died of a horse riding accident. Her name included her number, "Elevine", eleven.)

"**Our son Nihel Tolven was born March 2nd, 1874 in Winona County, Minnesota, baptized by N. Magnus.**" (He died, July 2, 1927. The name "Tolven" indicates twelve. He and his wife had six children, locating to Augusta, Illinois.)

"**Our daughter Marthe Maria Tertine Decimine was born April 23, 1876 in Winona County, Minnesota, baptized by Christian Magelson.**" (Her death date is not in the Bible. Her name, "Tertine Decimine" indicates she is the thirteenth child. Her married name was Chilson. She and her husband had several children and they lived in the Preston, Minnesota area.)

"**Our son Olaf Titus Quartus Desemus was born September 27, 1880, Baptized by Pastor J. Krohn in Winona County.**" (He died in 1964. Two of his middle names, in Latin no less, meant "four and ten" or fourteen. He took over the family farm, which has a Peterson, Minnesota address. With his wife, Minnie Nisbit Thoreson, he had eight children.)

As the reader can easily see, there is much information yet to be uncovered and traced regarding this family and the continuing proliferation of Christian and Anne's descendants. Christian and Anne's children who died young are buried with their parents at the family grave-site at the North Prairie Evangelical Lutheran Church, Cemetery, rural Lanesboro, Minnesota.

North Prairie Church, Lanesboro MN

Because of the wide span of years from the eldest to the youngest, and the pull of the frontier upon the older siblings, this family was scattered over a wide area of the country. It has always been difficult across the years until the present time for the many descendants of Christian and Anne to remain in touch with each other. For many of those dependents, there is almost no knowledge at all, of the story of their forbearer's journey from Hadeland Norway, to America.

Thus, today, some 160 years after their arrival in America there are a great many threads of this family's tapestry that are hard to grasp, much less to be accurately woven into a fuller story. Now, well into the 21st century, there could easily be two thousand or more persons alive today, who are descended from Christian Thoreson Kittelsrud and Anne Larsdatter Skoien. Where are they? What do they know of this immigration story? Of course, the life-stream of this family has blended with the life-streams of many other families through marriage.

Though I have met but a few of these many now distant cousins, I have learned for sure that there are lawyers, doctors, dentists, pilots, clergy, a major league baseball pitcher, accomplished skiers, military officers, musicians, farmers, engineers, teachers, business owners, nurses, builders, archivists, computer analysts, factory workers, entertainers, missionaries, laborers, homemakers, managers, writers, etc., etc., who are descended from Christian and Anne Thoreson Kittelsrud. Many of these are totally unaware of this couple's saga, which began in Hadeland Norway in 1854 when they decided to cross the sea, enter the wilderness and make a home in a promised-land. We are, at least in part, who we are and where we are, because of their courageous choices and actions. We thank God for them and for the family's Bible, which revealed to us their old, old story.

Kari Gulbrandsdatter Vaterud
"Carrie Vatra"

previously unpublished   Form 417   *Sharon Sayles Babcock*

This article was written with my mother, Marlyn Johnson Sayles, who shared her many memories of Grandma Vickerman and childhood stories about growing up in the Big Woods of Fillmore County. Other details about Carrie's earlier life may never be known, as conversations and stories were not written down. The people who could share them are now long gone. Carrie was neither rich nor famous, but her immigrant story remains alive today and connects us to our past. Our Norwegian ancestors made difficult decisions and endured true hardships to create a better life for their children and grandchildren in America. We remember and are grateful for our "Carrie Vatra."

On 4 May 1877, the feeder ship *Hero* left Norway bound for Hull, England, with a cargo of wood pulp, canned milk, oats, old metal and silver, and 149 Norwegian emigrants in search of a better life. Among them were my Hadeland ancestors, Gulbrand Andersen Vaterud, his wife, Mari Gulbranddatter Greftegrev, and their three children, Anders, Kari and Karen. They were bound for "Amerika!"

The eldest daughter, Kari, was my great-grandmother, Carrie Gilbertson Vickerman. She was born Kari Gulbrandsdatter on 24 April 1866 in Jevnaker, Hadeland, Norway. Father Gulbrand Andersen was born 1831 on Hvaterud, Jevnaker to Anders Gulbrandsen Vaterud and Kari Torgersdatter Vaterud. Mother Mari Gulbrandsdatter was born 1832 on Greftegrev, Jevnaker to Gulbrand Olsen Grevtegrev and Kari Olsdatter Halvorsbøle. Gulbrand and Mari were married 3 January 1863 in the Jevnaker Church. Kari was baptized in the same church on 6 May 1866, as witnessed by Anders I Vaterud, Anders A Vaterud, Elling Vaterud, Kari Vaterud and Randi Vaterudseie. As the eldest, Kari was named in the traditional custom for her paternal grandmother. [Note: there are alternate spellings for both Vaterud and Greftegrev.]

The family is listed in the 1865 census as residing on Hvatterud Vestre, farm #223b. Also in the household at that time were his aging parents and sister, Ingebor Andersdatter. Gulbrand was *Selveier* and *Gårdmand* (owner and farm worker). His grandfather, a second son, had purchased a third of the farm from his own father in 1801. Mari was born on the nearby farm, Greftegrev, her great-grandfather having bought that farm in 1704. Leaving Jevnaker, the family emigrated from the port of Christiania (now Oslo) shortly after Kari's eleventh birthday on 4 May 1877. They would have changed ships in England, sailing from Hull across the Atlantic to Quebec. From there they would have had to take both rail and waterways to arrive at McGregor, Iowa, a landing on the Mississippi used by immigrants at that time. Their final destination was Monona, Iowa, which is in Clayton County, about 12 miles from McGregor.

Other Norwegians had already settled in this area, and the family's arrival would have been similar to and as welcome as previous arrivals.

"This was the time of the great Norwegian immigration and the picture of their coming, as given by the Times, is worth preserving... On Saturday last the Northern Belle delivered at McGregor nearly one hundred emigrants from Norway... They were composed of middle age and young men and women and children, very few of the company looked to be over 35 or 40 years of age. Boxes, wooden trunks and cases of all shapes and sizes, strongly banded with iron, painted and marked with hieroglyphics to us indecipherable, were carried from the boat to the levee until the wharf and road for several rods were completely blocked up. The appearance of some of the wooden trunks was very ancient, one of them we saw was marked 1707. There were others older in looks. The Norwegians are a most valuable accession to the state. They are frugal, industrious and honest; some of them are most talented business men, and scarcely one can be found that approaches, either from bad habits or imbecility, the condition of a pauper. They usually settle in neighborhoods, and a steady improvement of the country marks their footsteps. Iowa and Minnesota are receiving the best mental stamina of the eastern and middle states, as well as the most valuable physical and moral force of Europe ..." (from Memories of Clayton County)

The Andersen's stayed and farmed in Clayton County about 10 years, as noted in census reports. The entire family then relocated to a farm in Preble Township in Fillmore County, Minnesota, where they were members of the Highland Lutheran Church. The Vatrud's had many relatives in Iowa and Minnesota who had emigrated from Hadeland prior to their arrival. It is also not known what happened to Ole Watrud, Andrew's younger brother who immigrated with them to Iowa. We can assume there may have been letters back to Norway and to siblings in the U.S., but none were preserved. Many of the relatives continued the migration from Fillmore County to northern Minnesota and into the Dakota Territory.

Kari, however, remained in Fillmore County the rest of her life. She used the Americanized spelling "Carrie" and patronymic name Gilbertson on her marriage certificate, but always referred to herself as Carrie "Vatra." This name was spelled in various ways on Fillmore County census reports and documents, including *Watterud, Watro, Vaterud, Vathrow, and Vattera*. On the emigration ship's passenger list, it was spelled *Hvatterud*. Carrie attended seven years of country school in Iowa, and could read and speak English, as did her sister and brother. The parents spoke only Norwegian.

Another immigrant family, the Vickerman family, had settled in Fillmore County during this same time. John and Adele Vickerman arrived from Canada with their family of four sons and two daughters in about 1863. John was an English-speaking Anglo-Canadian, while Adele was

French-Canadian. After farming in Preble Township, John and his sons filed homestead patents in Tracy, Shetek Township, Murray, Minnesota. John returned to the Big Woods in Fillmore County with sons Isaac and William after a few years, as he "didn't like the prairie," leaving sons Robert and Thomas to take over the homestead in Murray County.

Carrie met neighbor William "Will" Vickerman, shortly after she and her family moved to Preble Township. Carrie and Will were married on 1 Sept 1889 and had two children, John Gilbert Vickerman, born 1891, and Mary Adelia Vickerman, born 1892. The children were named for their grandparents, following the Norwegian naming customs. Will was accidentally shot in the leg while coon hunting in 1893. He made a poor recovery from the leg wound and decided to go to a La Crosse, Wisconsin, hospital for an operation to remove the bullet lodged in his leg. The bullet was not to be found, and Will died at age 35 in August, 1894 as a result of an infected leg wound. He was buried in the Henrytown "English" Cemetery in Fillmore County.

Carrie, now a young widow with two small children, continued to live on the farm, which was near both her family and Will's large extended family. Robert, Will's older brother, had encountered disappointment and crop failure on the western Minnesota homestead as a result of devastating drought and grasshopper infestations. Murray County was among the southwestern Minnesota areas greatly affected by grasshoppers.

Will and Carrie Vickerman

"The grasshoppers were the worst set-back for the new settlers. These insects arrived in Murray County in 1873, but they were not as damaging as they were in the next three years following. They arrived in huge swarms and settled upon the green vegetation. About ten o'clock in the morning they started to fly and about noon they started coming down to the ground. Nothing green escaped them. Wheat fields over four feet high would be bent over with the weight of the grasshoppers. There were eight to ten grasshoppers on every stalk and the flint corn fields would have as many as fifty on each stalk. They spared nothing: wheat, flax, potatoes, and garden vegetables were bare stalks when night came. ...

The grasshoppers left as suddenly as they appeared. By 1875, they had all but disappeared, except in in 1877 when they appeared in large numbers. They were so thick at times that one could not see the sun." (From A History of Murray County)

Robert's first marriage to Ida Foster had ended in divorce. Disillusioned by poor crops and an unhappy family life, he sold his share of the homestead to his brother, Thomas, with whom he had homesteaded. Robert then returned to Fillmore County with his two sons, while his former wife and two daughters remained, eventually moving on to the Dakota Territory after Ida remarried. Robert and Carrie were later married in 1898, blending their families into one household in nearby Amherst Township in the Big Woods.

Robert, called Rob (which was pronounced "robe"), farmed and also operated a saw mill. He was a man of many talents and interests. He was a beekeeper, so the family always had sweet honey for their use. He also built a sorghum press that was used every year to supply sorghum for themselves and for neighbors in the community. He had a large vegetable garden and an orchard, in addition to the crops, livestock and poultry. He was referred to as an "engineer" on a census report, as he operated and repaired engines and machinery. Grandma Carrie was an excellent cook, making roast goose with all the trimmings, baking apple pies and desserts, and large, soft sugar cookies "with a raisin in the center" when the families would come to visit on Sunday. Nothing went to waste. In fact, she could also make a good stew out of coon meat! My mother remembers they always had *rullepølse* and *primost* cheese on hand.

Rob and Carrie had three children together: Roy (born 1900), my grandmother, Myrtle (born 1904) and Hazel (born 1906). Rob Vickerman froze his toes during the winter of 1937 and developed gangrene. He died the following June 1937 after an amputation of his leg, from which he had complications and infection. Carrie was again a widow.

Beginning with Will's death in 1893, Carrie experienced a series of losses in her family. Her mother, Mari Gulbrandsdatter Greftegrev had been bitten in the hand by a neighbor's dog and developed blood poisoning from the infection. Although she was taken to the hospital in LaCrosse for treatment, the doctors were not able to help her and she died 2 May 1900. Carrie's younger sister Carin died in 1904 at age 35 of a lung infection. Carin, or "Caroline," left a husband and six young children, including an infant daughter. Their father, Gulbrand Andersen Vaterud, died of "old age" on 7 Aug 1910 in Holt Township, Fillmore County, Minnesota. A widower, he had been living in the household of Caroline's surviving husband, John "Otto" Moger. The son, Andrew, never married and worked over the years for various farmers as a hired man or as a milk hauler. He lived alternately with either his father or with the family for whom he was working at the time. He apparently suffered from depression and committed suicide in 1910 by hanging himself in a neighbor's barn. Reflective of the attitude toward suicide in that time, he was not allowed burial in the church cemetery, but was buried in the nearby Poor Farm Cemetery. This death was never spoken of in the family thereafter.

This family rented, but did not buy the farms on which they lived. It is not possible to say where their paths may have led had tragedy not struck with the untimely deaths of Mari and Andrew and Caroline. Perhaps they would have continued "moving on," as did so many pioneers of that era. After marrying into a large English-speaking family, Carrie spoke mainly English in her daily life. In fact, she told her children and grandchildren that they were "American" now, and discouraged them from speaking Norwegian. When asked, she did not want to talk about the "old days." Both her parents and also Robert's parents died before her "second family" of children with Rob Vickerman were old enough to even remember their grandparents.

Carrie, having outlived two husbands, her parents and her siblings, lived to be 93 years old. She died of heart problems and old age in the Heaser Nursing Home in Lanesboro, Minnesota on 9 March 1960. She is buried in the Henrytown English Cemetery near Canton, Fillmore, Minnesota next to her second husband, Robert Vickerman and also near her first husband, William Vickerman. At the time of her death, Carrie was survived by two daughters, two sons, 21 grandchildren and 36 great grandchildren. She has many, many more descendants today.

CHILDREN OF CARRIE GILBERTSON VATRUD AND WILLIAM T. VICKERMAN:
1. John Gilbert Vickerman (1891 – 1974) married Clara M. Haugen in 1918. Children: Vernon Eldred (1918-1985) married Lucille Allhiser. Ernest (1921-1984), Grace Geneva (1923-1995) married Morris Pedersen; Donald A. (1927 – 1946) died in Korea. John Vickerman was a farmer in Fillmore and Houston Counties, MN.
2. Mary Adelia "Dele" Vickerman (1892 – 1956) married Lloyd Melvin Inglett in 1917. Children: Frederick Edward (b. and d. 1918); Harold Melvin (1921-1983) married Constance Garry; Lillian Mae (b. 1928) married Roy Hermanson. Mary and Lloyd Inglett lived near Canton, Fillmore, MN

CHILDREN OF CARRIE GILBERTSON AND ROBERT STANLEY VICKERMAN:
1. Roy Stanley Vickerman (1900 – 1994) married Dorothy Duff in 1942. Children: Stanley LeRoy (b. and d. 1949); Violet Mae (b.1951) married Neal Groth, Robert Nels (b. 1952), Hazel Irene (b. and d. 1954), Bonny Kay (b. 1955), and Pamela Sue Bjorge (b. 1960) married Leslie Wangen.
2. Hazel Vickerman (1904 – 1981) married Philip Gerard in 1922. Children: Milton (1923-2008) married Cora Thompson; Eldred (1925-1974) married Glorianne Nelson; Robert (b. 1927) married Ruby _; Phyllis (b. 1929) married Norris Sorenson; Richard (b.1931) m. _; Charles (b 1940) married Donna Hanson.

3. Myrtle Viola Vickerman (1906 – 1993) married Carl Johan Johnson in 1928. Children: Pernella (1927-2011); Marlyn (b. 1929); Dorothy (b. 1931), Janice (b. 1940), Irvin "Buddy" (b. 1943); Carol Joanne (b. 1947).

Marlyn Johnson is my mother, who married Wilbur Sayles (1925-2011) in 1949. Children:

1. Sharon (b. 1951) married Darrell Babcock, children Brent (b. 1974) married Nicole LeVasseur, their children Avery, Rowan, Paige; Ross, (b. 1979).
2. Beverly (b. 1954) married William Magoon (1948-2011).

Rob and Carrie's son Roy Vickerman

Rob and Carrie's daughter Hazel Vickerman and Philip Gerard on their wedding day in 1922, with half brother John and sister Myrtle Vickerman

Michael Johnson and Ingeborg Dæhlin

previously unpublished   Form 694   *Connie Ferris*

The author is Michael and Ingeborg's great-granddaughter. This is the story of an immigrant family and particularly two Hadeland emigrants, Michael (Jensen) Johnson and his wife, Ingeborg Olsdatter Dæhlin. Their stories begin, of course, with their parents, although their lives were shaped by generations of Hadelanders before them.

The Michael and Ingeborg Dæhlin Family in 1903

Michael's Parents: Jens Jensen and Karen Hansdatter

Jens Jensen was born 23 Aug 1820 in Lunner, the son of Jens Jensen and Kari Eriksdatter. Karen Hansdatter was born 2 Mar 1820 in Lunner, the daughter of Hans Jonsen and Marte Jensdatter. In 1844 Jens and Karen had their first child and then married 25 Mar 1845. They left Norway 19 Sep 1884, traveling with their granddaughter, Elise Hansdatter. In America their names became John and Carrie Johnson. John died 27 Feb 1891 and Carrie died 13 Apr 1896. They are both buried at East Wiota Lutheran Cemetery in Wiota, Wisconsin. They had eight children:

529

1. Jens Jensen was born 10 Jun 1844 in Lunner, probably on his mother's farm, Gulleneiet. He married Eline Hansdatter 16 Feb 1867 in Lunner. Eline was born in Lunner 30 Jul 1845. Jens and Eline had eight children, the first born onboard ship as they emigrated to America in May 1867. They settled in Wiota, Wisconsin where their names were Americanized to John and Ellen Johnson. John died between 1880 and 1900; his burial place is unknown. Ellen died in 1920 and was buried in East Wiota Cemetery. John and Ellen have 62 known descendants.

2. Hans Jensen, the second child, was born 19 Dec 1846 on the Vølla farm. He was one of perhaps two children who remained in Norway. Hans married 13 Apr 1882 in Lunner to Berthe Marie Paulsdatter and they had two sons. Hans died 27 Jun 1907 in Lunner. Over a decade before marrying Berthe, Hans and Karen Larsdatter had a daughter, Elise Hansdatter, on 26 Nov 1870 on the Jorstadvølla farm in Lunner. Elise immigrated to America with her grandparents Jens and Karen but nothing more is known about her. At this time, there is no information about Hans' two sons.

3. Kari Jensdatter was born 12 Apr 1849 on the Vølla farm in Lunner. She married a Swedish man, Johan Magnusson 27 Oct 1871 in Lunner. He was born 6 Jul 1844, probably in Värmland. Their first seven children were born in Norway in the Lunner area; one son died at age 4. Johan left Norway in 1884 and his wife, Kari left a year later with the six surviving children. They settled in Lafayette County, Wisconsin where two more children were born. In America their names were John and Kari Magnus. Kari died 10 Feb 1942 in Wisconsin and John died 10 Apr 1928 in Woodford, Wisconsin. They were both buried in East Wiota Cemetery. They have 159 known descendants.

4. The fourth child born to Jens and Kari was Iver Jensen. He was born 2 Apr 1852 on the Balangrudeie farm. He married Ingeborg Olsdatter on 21 Dec 1883 in Lunner. She was born 16 Feb 1860 in Flesberg, Buskerud, Norway. They had at least two sons born in Lunner. In both 1900 and 1910 censuses, the family is located on the Jorstadvolla farm. Nothing is known of this family after the 1910 census, but it is believed they remained in Norway.

5. Marthe Jensdatter was born 16 Apr 1855 in Lunner on the Balangrudeie farm. She left Norway 06 May 1881, traveling with her siblings, Lise Marie and Otto. Once in Green County, Wisconsin, her name became Martha Johnson. Martha operated a farm, later marrying Joseph Trosdahl (sometimes Throsdahl), who worked on the farm. They were married 13 Feb 1910 in Lafayette County, Wisconsin. Joe was born 11 May 1858 in Norway. Martha died 19 May 1929 in

Green County, Wisconsin. Joe died 18 Feb 1942 in Monroe, Green County, Wisconsin. They were both buried in East Wiota Cemetery. They had no children.

6. Michael Jensen, the sixth child, and subject of this article, was born 4 May 1858 on the Vølla farm in Lunner.

7. Lise Marie Jensdatter was born 27 Sep 1860 in Lunner on the Vølla farm. She left the parish 25 Apr 1881 to Oslo and then left Norway on 6 May 1881, along with her siblings Marthe and Otto. In America she used at various times "Eliza" or "Lizzie" Johnson as her name. She married Nels Ellefson 31 Jul 1889 in Jordan, Green County, Wisconsin. They had four children, all born in Wisconsin. By 1930 she and Nels were living in Campton, Kane County, Illinois. Eliza died 7 Oct 1944 in St. Charles, Kane County, Illinois. Nels died 28 May 1941. They were both buried in Whitney Cemetery in St. Charles. They have 26 known descendants, but there are probably many more.

8. The youngest child born to Jens and Karen was Otto Henry. He was born 18 May 1864 on the Vølla farm in Lunner. He left Norway with his sisters, Marthe (Martha) and Lise (Eliza), and lived for many years with Martha in Green County, Wisconsin. He never married and had no children. Otto died 10 Feb 1932 in Monroe, Green County, Wisconsin and was buried with Martha and Joe Throsdahl in East Wiota Cemetery.

Ingeborg's Parents: Ole Eriksen Dæhlin and Ingebørg Olsdatter

Ole was the second child of eight, born 24 Sep 1826 on the Dæhlin farm in Lunner, son of Erik Olsen Dæhlin and Kari Hansdatter. Ingebørg Olsdatter was born 23 Sep 1831 on the Bolken farm in Lunner. She was the middle child of at least three children born to Ole Hansen and Ingeborg Ingvaldsen. Ole Eriksen and Ingebørg Olsdatter were married 13 Nov 1854 in Lunner. Ole died 23 Dec 1903 and Ingebørg died 7 Jun 1906, both in Lunner. Their seven children were all born on the Dæhlin farm:

1. Kari Olsdatter, the oldest child, was born 19 Jun 1855. She married Matias Kimme Joakimson on 15 Aug 1896. He was born 13 Dec 1849 in Sweden. It is believed Matias and Kari may have emigrated to America sometime after the 1910 census in Norway. In America, the family may have used the surname Kime or Kimme.

2. Ingeborg Olsdatter, the subject of this article, was born 20 Aug 1857.

3. Edvard Olsen was born 17 Mar 1860, the third child of Ole and Ingebørg. He married Anne Marie Lukasdatter 20 Nov 1884 in Lunner and they had six

children. Ole, their oldest son, later emigrated to America. Edvard and Anne Marie both died in 1941 in Lunner. They have at least 73 descendants.

4. Ole Olsen (twin) was born 29 Oct 1862. He left for America in 1883 and settled first in Montgomery County, Iowa where his name changed to Ole Dahlin. He married Emma (maiden name unknown) and they had one son. Emma died 14 Nov 1913 in Minnehaha County, South Dakota. Ole married a second time to Karoline Nelsen on 14 Apr 1915 in Esmond, Kingsbury County, South Dakota. She was born 16 Jan 1877 in Norway. They had one son and may have adopted another. There are no known descendants from these three sons. Ole died in 1924 and Karoline died 2 Feb 1922 in Waddams, Stephenson County, Illinois. They were both buried in East Wiota Cemetery along with their two natural sons.

5. Anne Olsdatter (twin) was born 29 Oct 1862 and died 27 Aug 1863.

6. Hans Olsen was the sixth child born to Ole and Ingebørg, 16 Nov 1866. He emigrated to America 23 Aug 1883 where his name changed to Henry Daehlin. (He was most commonly just "H. O." but his middle name was sometimes given by family members as Otto and his surname was occasionally spelled Dahlen.) He married Anna Hansdatter Wang 16 Jul 1891 in Lafayette County, Wisconsin and they had two sons. Anna died 4 Aug 1927 and Henry married a second time to Alice Peterson, a widow with a young son. By 1940, although married, they were no longer living together. Henry died 10 Dec 1961 and he and Anna are both buried in East Wiota Cemetery. Only four descendants are known but there are probably others.

7. The last child in this family was Ingvald Olsen. He was born 23 Sep 1873. He left Norway 6 Jul 1894 and settled in Minnesota where he studied at a seminary and planned to become a missionary. He married Nicoline Dahl on 5 Jul 1898. They were sent to the mission field in China in the late 1890s. Nicoline died of tuberculosis on 5 Apr 1906 in Montevideo, Chippewa County, Minnesota and was buried at Saint Petri Cemetery in Cyrus, Pope County, Minnesota with the name "Daehlen." Ingvald returned to the mission field and sent for and married Emma Hasle on 30 Oct 1907. She was born in Norway on 23 Aug 1875. At some point their surname returned to the Americanized spelling of the Norwegian farm - Daehlin. This couple served for many years in China and all four of their children were born there. Ingvald died 25 Sep 1960 and Emma died 4 Jul 1951, both in Fergus Falls, Otter Tail County, Wisconsin, and are buried in Bethlehem Lutheran Cemetery there. They have 25 known descendants, but there are certainly more.

Michael Johnson and Ingeborg Daehlin Family

The Vølla farm was a humble place and too small to support all of Jens and Karen's large family. Michael worked for several years for Ole Eriksen Dæhlin on the large Dæhlin farm in Lunner.

Ingeborg was the second oldest of Ole's children. At an early age, a close friendship developed between Michael Jensen and Ingeborg. They most certainly knew each other at church, although they were not in the same confirmation class. Later, when Michael came to work for Ingeborg's father, the relationship grew more intense. Michael became Ole's right hand man in hauling and marketing timber, and tending the horses. Ole considered Michael almost as a son in the farm's business affairs. Some of Ingeborg's siblings criticized this relationship. They felt their father was showing too much trust in Michael, who was, after all, only a hired man. They were also concerned that he might be allowed to marry into the family. Two of the Dæhlin children did all they could to interfere with their courtship.

Twin cousins of Ingeborg's, Martha and Maria Pedersdatter Hoff apparently carried secret messages back and forth between the young couple. Eventually Michael left his employment at the Dæhlin farm and prepared to leave Norway, partially because he didn't want to take military training, but mostly to show the Dæhlins that he could make an adequate home for Ingeborg in America. Before he left the country Michael and Ingeborg were secretly engaged with the consent of her parents. Apparently, although a very pretty young woman, Ingeborg had had either an accident, disease, or birth defect that resulted in a significantly handicapped leg. She wore a "peg" below her knee, and perhaps because of this handicap, her parents were concerned that a more acceptable union might be difficult for her.

Michael arrived in New York from Liverpool, England, on the ship Nevada on 15 May 1879 (listed as "Michael Jensen, Denmark"). He traveled immediately to Wisconsin but no records have been found there prior to his application for citizenship in 1882 in Green County. By 1881 he had established himself on a farm and sent for his beloved Ingeborg.

Ingeborg left the parish 25 Apr 1881 and traveled with three of Michael's siblings, Martha, Lise and Otto, and Hans Pedersen Hoff, the brother of the twins who carried messages between Ingeborg and Michael. (Hans and his brother Ole Hoff became well known personages in Portland, Oregon.) Although their marriage date was handed down within the family as 18 Feb 1881, Ingeborg actually didn't arrive until

533

May. Regardless of the date, Michael and Ingeborg were married right after her arrival. Michael was always a loyal supporter of his adopted country and on 7 Nov 1882 he applied for citizenship.

Michael and Ingeborg lived on the farm in Lafayette County, northeast of Woodford for about fifteen years. All ten of their children were born on this farm. In 1907 the family sold the first farm and moved to another northwest of Wiota. From the very beginning the family attended the nearby East Wiota Lutheran Church and the children were all baptized and confirmed there. Many of the family were also buried there. Only one of their children, Ole, died in early childhood. The rest grew to adulthood and eventually married. Michael and Ingeborg were faithful members of their church. Ingeborg was a charter member of the local "Ladies' Aid," and maintained an interest in missions, both foreign and domestic, until her death. (One daughter, Ida Behrents, served in the mission field in China for many years.)

Michael died at his farm home on 2 Feb 1940; he was almost 82 years old. Ingeborg died 9 Feb 1943, at 85 years old. They were loving parents, good friends and neighbors, well respected and deeply missed. This happy couple has 161 known descendants and probably many more.

Michael and Ingeborg Johnson's children

1. Clara, born 19 May 1882, worked as a domestic for many years, living as a single woman in Chicago. At 48, she married 27 Nov 1930 John Due, a widower and family friend from the Wiota area. John died 1 Jun 1949 in Wisconsin and was buried with his first wife in Jordan Lutheran Cemetery in Jordan, Wisconsin. Clara lived near or with her sister Lena in Ottawa, Illinois until her death 16 Dec 1977. She was buried near her parents in East Wiota Cemetery. She had no children.

2. Ida, born 24 Jun 1884, started high school in Argyle, Wisconsin but she longed for a better education. She was encouraged by her uncle, Ingvald Daehlin, who was already active in the China mission field. Ida finished high school in Montevideo, Minnesota where she could help Ingvald as he cared for his dying wife, Nicoline. After graduation Ida started to train as a nurse at the Lutheran Deaconess Home in Chicago. She met Dr. Olav S. Behrents in Chicago, a Norwegian-American, on leave from the China mission field, and they were married 27 August 1908 in Wiota. Their journey by way of Norway and Russia back to the mission field was their honeymoon. After many years there, the family settled in Three Rivers, Michigan. Olav's heart was damaged by disease and he

died on his 64th birthday, 8 Dec 1936 in Chicago. Ida ran a boarding house for many years in Three Rivers and managed to put all five children through college. She died 29 Apr 1974 in Tucson, Pima County, Arizona where she was living with her daughter. She and Olav are buried in Mount Olive Cemetery in Chicago, Illinois. They have 50 descendants.

3. Hjalmer, the third child and first son, was born 1 Oct 1887. At 42, he married Alma Skogen on 18 Jun 1939 in Buffalo, Marshall County, South Dakota. Hjalmer worked with his father on the family farm and took it over after his father's death in 1940. He retired in 1948 and died 2 years later, on 13 May 1950, in Monroe, WI. Alma returned to Eden, South Dakota and died there 15 Dec 1969. They were both buried in East Wiota Cemetery. They had no children.

4. Ole was born 2 Jan 1890 and died 4 Jul 1891. He was buried with his grandparents, John and Carrie Johnson, in East Wiota Cemetery.

5. Anna was born 11 May 1892. She married Henry Johnson from South Dakota on 11 Feb 1915. Henry owned and operated a farm in South Dakota for many years. Both of their children were born in Plankinton, South Dakota. Henry died 8 Apr 1968 and Anna died 15 May 1971, in Davison County, South Dakota. They are buried in Immanuel Lutheran Cemetery in Mount Vernon, South Dakota. They have at least 42 descendants.

6. Helga (twin) was born 10 Dec 1894. She married George Olsen, a Chicago policeman, 2 May 1926 in Bloomingdale, Du Page County, Illinois. Both of their children were born in Chicago. George and Helga retired and lived in Florida until Helga's death 27 Jan 1979 in St. Petersburg. George returned to Illinois where he died 15 Dec 1987. They were buried in Acacia Park Cemetery in a Chicago suburb. They have seven known descendants.

7. Inga (twin) was born 10 Dec 1894. She married Conrad Holt, a farmer in the area, 5 Sep 1923 in Lafayette County, Wisconsin. They had one son and two stillborn daughters in Iowa County, Wisconsin, but farmed for many years in Blanchardville, Lafayette County, Wisconsin. Conrad died 3 Aug 1945 and Inga died 25 Jun 1964, both in Monroe, Wisconsin. They are buried in East Wiota Cemetery. They have five known descendants.

8. Morgan, the eighth child, was born 8 May 1897. He married Lillie Johnson in 1919 in Illinois and they had one son. They both died in De Kalb, Illinois, Morgan on 1 Aug 1981 and Lillie on 3 Nov 1995 and are buried at Fairview Park Cemetery in De Kalb. They have nine known descendants.

9. Lena was born 10 Dec 1899. She married Ervin Norem from Illinois on 29 Mar 1922 in Wiota. They had one son and lived for most of their lives in Ottawa, Illinois where Ervin owned a car dealership. They both died in Ottawa, Ervin on 12 Jan 1968 and Lena on 7

Feb 1988. Ervin and Lena are buried in Oakwood Memorial Park in Ottawa. They have 12 known descendants.

10. William, the last child born to Michael and Ingeborg, arrived on 15 Mar 1902. He married Evelyn Lynch on 14 Jun 1930 and they had four children. Later he married a second time to Marian Lucky. William was a doctor in Galesburg, Illinois and also had a farm there. He died 10 May 1973 in Galesburg and was buried there at Memorial Park Cemetery. He has at least 26 descendants.

Mary Solsten and Anders O. Lysgard

published November 2008   Form 1076   *Estella Johnson and Robert Brodin*

This was originally written in 1951 by Estella Johnson (1897-1994) in loving memory of her grandmother whom she attended and cared for until her death. In 1991, this was edited and presented on July 20 at the Solsten Family Reunion held at Luther College, Decorah, Iowa, by Bob Brodin, Mary's great-grandson and successor to their farm. Additional information was added for publication in the Brua.

Marit (Mary) was born in Ostre-Slidre, (Østre Slidre), Valders, Norway December 3, 1844 to Ole Bendickson (Bendicksen) (1819-1880) and Anna (Olsdatter Evenson) (1826-1903) Solsten who farmed on Solstenhaugen in Oppland Fylke at Ron, Valders, Norway. Their other six children, Ole Solsten 1848, Gertrude (Mrs. Knute) Stene 1852, Ingeborg (Mrs. George) Troe 1855, Bendick Solsten 1858, Astrid (Mrs. Gilbert) Nelson 1863, and Erick Solsten 1866, were born at Vestre-Slidre. She was baptized and confirmed in the Lutheran faith. Not long after confirmation, being the eldest of a family of seven, she went out to work, finally working for a family by the name of Gudbrand Hvattum for about seven years in Gran, Hadeland, Norway.   Letters came from America to friends in the homeland telling of America's golden opportunities. This gave "America fever" to many, much to the displeasure of those for whom they worked. But they could not resist America's call and

plans were made to leave the homeland.

On Good Friday 1867 Mary, with a group of friends including Anders Olson, left Gran for Christiania (now Oslo), Norway. On Easter Sunday, April 21, 1867, they sailed from Oslo for America, the voyage taking seven weeks. The trip was rough and hazardous, since the ship was only a sail boat. Some days they drifted backward and others were practically still. Many thought they would not see shore again. Landing in Quebec, Canada they and many others rode

537

uncomfortably on a freight train, in a cattle car, for several days on the first segment of their trip inland. From Norway, each family had to take along enough food for the voyage, which consisted of flatbread, lefse, salt pork, smoked meat, herring and some potatoes. Their provisions were getting rather low by the time they reached their destination.

According to information provided by Refondo passenger #88-Peter O. Stensven, age 24, from Vardals Parish: Two sail boats: the *Refondo*, with about 475 passengers, and the *Dagmar*, with about 396 passengers, left Christiania on April 21, 1867 for America and lacking enough wind they were both towed down the Oslofjord by steamboat to within one mile of Drobak where they encountered such a headwind that they 'laid-by' until the morning of the 22nd. A favorable wind then enabled them to sail speedily until they neared Faerder when they were forced by another strong headwind to sail back to Vallebo saltverk where they cast anchor. It was at seven o'clock on the morning of the 25th that a favorable wind gave them two days of good progress. Their journey to America, on their own, at last had begun. However, they would encounter more stormy days with changes of wind direction, as their ocean voyage continued. Stensven reported the deaths of fourteen children and four adults, as they occurred, on the *Refondo*'s month long trip across the ocean until they reached their Milwaukee destination." (With assistance from *Brua*'s editor, Verlyn D. Anderson and Ole P. Gamme of *Kontaktforum Hadeland-Amerika*, we have found websites pertaining to this trip. Stensven's report was contributed by Anne Dockwell, a relative, whose grandparents also came to Quebec on the Refondo.)

Stensven's account continues: "Sailing down the St. Lawrence Seaway they landed at Quebec, Canada and from there rode on a freight train in cattle cars, 'a most disagreeable conveyance,' for four days, as far as Sarnia, Ontario across from Port Huron, Michigan, where they waited for six days for their baggage, which had been delayed in Montreal, to arrive, be inspected and duty collected, and then wait also for their steamboat to Milwaukee to arrive. When it did, all baggage for about 1000 persons (from the two ships, at least) was packed on board and also the emigrants were packed in like herring in a barrel. In the next four days the steamboat traveled up Lake Huron and down Lake Michigan to Milwaukee where the emigrants disembarked to complete their journeys by trains which were then going in all directions."

Andrew's and Mary's train took them to Prairie du Chien, Wisconsin where they boarded a ferry to cross the Mississippi River coming ashore at McGregor, Iowa. From there they journeyed to Decorah, Iowa where they remained for three years. While there Mary worked at various places doing housework and often during the harvest season worked in the fields tying grain bundles and placing them in shocks.

Those first years were hard not knowing the language and getting adjusted to new surroundings. The loneliness for dear ones in the far-away homeland was hard to conquer. She often remarked how she would go off by herself and cry when others would sit down to eat. She vowed that as soon as she had enough money she would return to Norway, but this never happened.

Her parents and brothers and sisters came from Norway to Decorah, Iowa probably about six years after she had come. In later years her youngest brother, by 22 years, Erick Solsten told how when Mary was reunited with her family in Decorah, he thought it so strange that his mother would cry and hug a strange woman – his sister, Mary. It is said that tears came to his eyes as he told it.

In the fall of 1867 Mary was married to Anders Olson, the youngest of nine born January 1, 1836 in Gran, Hadeland, Oppland Fylke to Ole Olesen (Olsen) Stomne* from Opsahl farm who married Marte (Engebrettsdatter Mortviet) (Engebretsdatter Maurtvedteiet) Olson on 12/11/1817 and whose children were: twins, Ole & Engebret (died young), Goro 1820, Marie 1822, Ole 1824, Engebret 1828, Steffen 1830, Brede 1833, Anders 1836. This Olson/Stomne family attended the Lunner Church, while Mary attended one of the Sisters Churches while at Hvattums.

Ole Olesen Stomne was born about 1787 to Ole Anderson (Andersen) and Goro (Engebrettsdatter) Stomne. After Ole's death, Goro married Hans Ericksen of Flatla farm who took the widow Stomne's surname and their descendants also assumed that name. Anders Olson's brother, Steffen Olson immigrated in 1887 and assumed the Myrvold surname. Anders assumed the Lysgard surname about 1884. No other siblings immigrated. (In 2005 we visited the Torger Moldens in Gran, and learned there are still Lysgard and Myrvold farms there.)

Anders and Marit were married by the Rev. Ove Jacob Hjort, pastor of East and West Paint Creek Lutheran Churches of Waterville, Iowa, east of Decorah. Andrew had come to this country from Gran, Hadeland on the same boat as Mary, either on the *Refondo* or the *Dagmar*. The *Refondo*'s passenger list shows that most were from Gjørvik, Vårdal, Hamar, Toten, Aasnaes and Aker areas and the *Dagmar* list seems to be more from Jevnaker, Roa and Gran, Hadeland areas, although there are several pages on the *Dagmar*'s list with no identification of passengers. The two ships must have sailed closely throughout their voyage.

In the first part of May 1870 Andrew and Mary, together with two other couples, the Andrew Petersons and the Andrew Opperuds, came to Delafield Township, Jackson County, Minnesota by oxen team and covered wagon. This journey across the wild prairie, creeks and sloughs took six weeks. For this trip and their pioneer home they took with them such possessions as clothing, a small stove, a few dishes and pan, some food, a cow, one sheep, and last but not least their Bible, catechism and hymnbook. During their long trip they baked bread, milked the cow, churned butter and prepared daily meals. The covered wagon was their motel for the night.

Upon arrival in Jackson, Minnesota they secured a plat of Jackson County and picked their homestead. Trudging from there to Delafield Township, about 20 miles beyond, Andrew and

Mary settled on SW8. This was to be their lifelong home, Andrew's for 40 years and Mary's for 67 years.

The first task was to build their home, a sod house/dugout with two small windows and a door. The roof was of slough grass for, even by definition, this part of the Midwest was called "tall grass prairie." Here they lived three years, during which time their first daughter, Oline Marie (Mrs. Lars) Myrvold, was born May 20, 1871. Their first wood-frame house was built in 1873 and the lumber was hauled by Andrew from Lake Crystal (about 60 miles one way) taking three days by oxen team. This two-story, 14'x22' house, with low ceilings, consisted of a kitchen/living room, 14'x14', a small pantry and a very small bedroom downstairs. There were two small bedrooms upstairs with plastered walls and ceiling, separated by a vertical board wall and with a small window in each room. Here, their twin daughters were born August 9, 1874, completing their family of three daughters. This was the extent of their home for the next 18 years, until additions to the south and the north were added and later, a summer kitchen. But by that time, the early 1890s, two of their three daughters had married and moved away.

Lysgard home and Delafield Church at Fort Belmont, Jackson, Minnesota, about 2002

Andrew worked often on the St. Paul & Sioux City RR Co. railroad being built through here from Madelia to Sioux City (the Union Pacific since 1995), which also was laid through the

540

northwest corner of their farm. The grasshopper plague (1873-1877) was very discouraging and for two summers Andrew worked in Iowa to earn a little for living and also for seed to plant. Those were lonely days for Mary who remained at home with her daughters. One especially lonesome day, she climbed up on the sod roof and looked to the north, south, east and west to see if she could see any living being. To the east she happened to see a wagon load of hay drawn by a team of oxen, which brought some comfort. Another time when alone, she saw horse riders in the distance and feared, momentarily, that they were the notorious Jesse James gang of whom she had heard were in the area. And there was loneliness also because of lack of reading material with no mail. Mary told how she read and reread a paper which she had with her from Decorah (probably the *Decorah Posten*) until she almost knew it by heart. The Indian scares were pretty well gone when they had come. Only once did they and a few neighbors drive into Windom where there was a small fort because of a scare that the Indians were coming again – and that proved to be a false alarm. Worn paths from the Indian war dances were still seen about a mile east of the Lysgard place when they first homesteaded.

Andrew and Mary worked hard planting about twenty acres of trees, which gave them 80 additional acres as a tree claim. Most of this was hoed by hand with peas and beans planted between the rows. The trees were just small slips sent to them by the government. However, most of them grew and gave protection to the cattle from the hot summer sun and storms throughout the year. Wood was sawed and chopped in later years for fuel.

The pioneers did much exchange work during harvest. Mary, being strong and healthy, often worked equally to that of a man, walking to and from the neighbors before and after work. There was no limit, it seemed, as to how many hours she worked! The idea was to get the work done as soon as possible. Andrew, like most pioneer men, did not do the milking, so that was added to her day's work, as well. This was generally done outdoors in summer. There was no fly spray, but plenty of flies and mosquitoes to battle for both cows and the person milking. Since there were no cream separators or creameries, the milk was strained into large stone jars or crocks and the cream skimmed off the next day with a spoon.

In those early days there were no doctors or hospitals and Mary was called upon to act as mid-wife. As much as she dreaded this, she was thankful to God that she never lost a case.

She often spoke about how she had to butcher a sheep for meat, or ring the neck of a chicken, as her husband was not able to do this type of work. Shearing the sheep, washing and carding the wool, spinning it into yarn and knitting it into socks and mittens was most every pioneer woman's task, and Mary's also.

As more settlers moved into the community the loneliness faded away. Neighbors walked to each other's homes to visit and share each other's joys and sorrows. Knitting as they walked along was not an uncommon sight. As time went on, they prospered. God blessed their efforts and in not too many years Andrew and Mary were the owners of 200 acres of fine farmland, buildings and a home. All this in the land of opportunity – America! This they could not have acquired in their homeland.

Oftentimes in later years when Mrs. Johanna Opperud and Mary would get together they would talk about the time, when one hot summer day they had walked to Big Bend, a small trading post, with eggs and butter to trade or sell. They became very tired and thirsty and coming to a creek, they sat down to rest. They took off their shoes and each dipped her shoe into the creek to get a drink of water. There was no question of sanitation – they were thirsty! Finally they came to the Big Bend store. The grocer took the butter and poured it like water into a large jar that already had butter in it from other farmers. They would oftentimes laugh and cry as they reminisced over their past experiences.

Going to town in those early days was not a daily, weekly or even a monthly event. In the fall Andrew would drive to Jackson (20 miles) to get flour, sugar, salt, coffee and kerosene. This trip was not made again until early spring. Mary told about one winter she had ground some corn in the coffee mill in order to make some Johnnie cake to help stretch the wheat flour. Candles were used often for light and wood was their only fuel for heating. Andrew never failed to see that there was plenty of wood hauled and chopped. They and Opperuds had a 4-acre wood plot along the Des Moines River, now Kilen State Park, some seven miles from home. Some pioneers had to burn hay twisted into hard knots.

Three children were born to Andrew and Mary (Solsten) Lysgard: Oline "Lena" (Mrs. Lars) Myrvold, who was born May 20, 1871 and twins, Anna (Mrs. Charles A.) Johnson and Emma (Mrs. Edward A.) Hanson, born August 9, 1874. And at her death in 1937 Mary also had 16 grandchildren and 14 great-grandchildren.

Mary's husband, Andrew O. Lysgard, died at home October 18, 1910 at the age of 74 years. He will always be remembered by those who knew him as a very kind gentleman.

Mary continued to live in their home until the spring of 1912 when she rented out the farmland and buildings. She moved her furniture into two rooms of her 60' long house where she lived mostly during the summer months. The rest of the time she lived with her daughter and son-in-law, Lena and Lars Myrvold and also with her son-in-law, Charles A. Johnson and her granddaughters, Estella and Manda. Both Myrvolds and Johnsons lived in the same section which is adjacent to the section in which Lysgards lived, so she was close to home. Daughter Emma and her family lived in Sioux City and Minneapolis during those years.

In the spring of 1919 Mary fell and broke her leg. She was mending clothes, tripped and fell, causing a most painful break. She remained in bed for 13 weeks, but made a good recovery.

That decade, from 1910 to 1920 was a heavy one for Mary. Less than a month after her husband of 43 years died in October 1910, her daughter, Emma (Mrs. Ed) Hanson of Sioux City, with four children, was divorced, and the next April her other twin daughter, Anna (Mrs. Charles) Johnson with two young daughters, was institutionalized at St. Peter, Minnesota never to return home again. A few months after Mary broke her leg in the spring of 1919, her granddaughter, Mabel Hanson, died from appendicitis at age 17, and daughter, Emma Hanson died that November from heart failure, and daughter Anna Johnson died the next February from double pneumonia, both twin daughters at age 45. The joys in that decade for Mary were the births of three grandsons and five great-grandchildren.

In August 1933 at age 88, Mary again fell and fractured her hip. This time she was bedridden all winter and really never recovered to walk as before. Most of the time she was up was spent in a wheelchair. But she accepted it all with patience and cheerfulness. She was always interested in things around her and in her family. She spent much of her time knitting and reading. For example, during WWI she knitted 64 pairs of long, black socks for the servicemen. From early youth she had worked hard and to be able to be busy meant joy and satisfaction in her later years.

The rigors of those pioneer days added courage and stamina to this godly wife and mother. She left a heritage of memories which will inspire generations to come. Devoted in her faith she prayed earnestly for the furtherance of God's kingdom and for the salvation of her loved ones. Mary (Solsten) Lysgard died at her farm home March 6, 1937 at the age of 92 years, 3 months and 3 days, outliving all of her Solsten family, except brother, Bendick, who came from Chicago to attend her funeral.

Funeral services were held March 10, 1937 from her farm home and from her Delafield Lutheran Church. She was carried to her grave by five grandsons and one great-grandson. Burial was in the Delafield Cemetery, beside her husband, Andrew, and where two of their three daughters and ten of their sixteen grandchildren would also be buried.

Since 1958 when Mary's 91-year-old son-in-law, Charles Johnson, died, no one had lived in the Lysgard farm home, but it was furnished and maintained as a tribute to them by their grateful family. In 2000 the Lysgards' 60' long farm home and summer kitchen were donated and moved to Fort Belmont at Jackson, Minnesota, along I-90 and stand just yards from their beloved 2nd Delafield Lutheran Church whose congregation voted to disband and close the church in 1998, in its 125th year. They donated the church building to Fort Belmont where it was moved the 22 miles in 1999, facing eastward again as it had stood for the 97 years since it was built in Section 18. Hundreds now visit both buildings annually. Their first simple church building, from 1883 to 1902, still stands, by the cemetery, as the Delafield Town Hall in Section 15, Delafield Township, Jackson Co., Minnesota.

Maren (Mary) Mork Vane

Previously unpublished   *Form 291*   *Floie Vane*

The author is Mary Vane's grand-daughter

Maren Hansdatter Morka was born on December 16, 1867 in Lunner Parish in the Hadeland area of Oppland County, Norway. Her father was Peder Hansen Morka (1834-1886), a farmer on the farm "Morka". Peder's parents were Hans Hansen Morka (1805-1881) and Marte Pedersdatter Hÿtta (1807-1873). Maren was only two years old when her mother, Marie Hansdatter Raastad (1835-1870), died after the birth of her fourth child. Marie's parents were Hans Pedersen Raastad (1801-1859) and Marthe Larsdatter Framstad (1800-1870).

In 1871 Peder married Lisa Marie Haakenstad (1846-1918). That same year he sold his share of the Morka farm to his brother Hans and emigrated to the U.S. with his new wife and his four children. On April 15th, 1871 they sailed from Christiania (Oslo) on the ship *Concordia* and arrived in Quebec, Canada 37 days later. The family traveled via the McGregor route to Lincoln Township, Winnesheik County, Iowa. In 1876 they moved to Cerro Gordo Township in Lac qui Parle County, Minnesota, where Peder purchased the NW quarter of section 29. During his early years in America, Peder used "Hansen" or "Hanson" as his surname, but sometime during the 1880's he changed his last name to "Mork".

Maren's full siblings were Martha (1863-1952; m. James Edmond "Ed" Franklin), Hans P. (1864-1910; m. Olava J. Gulden),and Marie (1869-1952; m. Jacob A. Farmen). Maren's half-siblings (born to Lisa in the U.S.) were Edward P. (1872-1933; m. Carrie Ness), Karen/Carrie (1874-1915; m. John C. Skoien), Martin P. (1877-1974; m. Minnie S. Fossen), Louis/Lewis (1879-1945; m. Nettie Clausen), Anton P. (1882-1942; m. Gunhild M. Sorteberg), and Lena Petra (1885-1927; m. John A. Pederson). Most of these families lived in Lac qui Parle County. Also living in the county were some of Maren's father's siblings: Gjertrud Olson (1836-1905; widow of Ole Gulbrandsen Knarud), Martha Krugerud (1841-1902; Mrs. Halvor), Randi Pederson (1947-1908; Mrs. Anders), and Maren Kjerkeng (1852-1897; Mrs. Martin P.).

The Peder Mork family were members of Borgund Lutheran Church in Cerro Gordo Township. Maren was confirmed in this church in 1882. In 1884 she was working as a waitress in the hotel in Dawson, Minnesota, when she met her future husband James P. Vane.

On March 9, 1887, James and Maren were married by Rev. L.M.A. Hoff at his Cerro Gordo parsonage a few miles north of Dawson. Except for a short stay on a farm outside of town, James and Maren spent their married lives in the town of Dawson. They lived in several places in town, including rooms above the saloon. In 1912, James purchased the east half of block 37 in the NE section of Dawson, moved a house to the SE corner, and built a home for his family (NW corner of Walnut and Fourth Streets). One novel feature of the house was a dumbwaiter with which food could be lowered and stored in the cool temperatures many feet below ground level. This home was enlarged and remodeled several times. The house passed out of the family in 2009.

James and Mary Vane

James P. Vane was born Jens Peter Christensen on September 2, 1862 in Denmark to Christine Jensdatter and her third husband, Neil Christian Christensen. Jens was born on the Kobbermark farm in Lendum Parish in the Vendsyssel area of Denmark which at that time was part of Hjørring County. In 1879 Jens emigrated to the U.S. with his twin brother Christian Carl and his half-sister Anne Lucine and her husband Julius Jensen. They settled in Sundown Township, near Springfield, Minnesota, where they had relatives. After entering the United States Jens and Christian adopted the surname of "Vaen" after the birthplace of their father. Later they changed the spelling to "Vane" and Jens became known as James.

James and Maren became members of the Riverside Evangelical Lutheran Church on February 7, 1888. Their children were all baptized and confirmed in this church or in its successor, Trinity Lutheran Church. After the death of their first-born child during childbirth, James and Maren had seven daughters and five sons. Their children were: Jalmer Melvin (1889-1974; m. Tilla Alvina Lee), Oscar Carl Vane (1891-1972; m. Ida Victoria Johnson), Minnie Christine Vane (1892-1964; m. Ernest Noble Heath), Clara (1895-1999; m. Henry Augustin Anderson), Emma (1897-1987; m. Reinhold Lyman Kruger), Lillian (1899-1968; m. Edwin Bernhard Dravland), Mabel Vane (1901-1991; m. Howard Wesley Wilson), Alvin (1904-1966; m. Jessie Loretta Olson), Tilda (1905-1930), Martha (1908-2004; m. Alvin Jensen), Thorney (1910-1994), and Marvin (1913-1995; m. Marjorie Medcalf).

James established a general contracting and house-moving business. He dug the first wells in town and was the first to move a house in Dawson. For many years he had the largest house-moving equipment in Western Minnesota. The company prided itself in the carefulness of its moving which resulted in minimal cracking of plaster walls and windows. This was quite an accomplishment since in the early years the houses were moved by planks and rollers with horse power. At various times all five sons were employed in the business. In his spare time James would whittle wooden figures, many of which became toys for the children. He also made large concrete flower pots artistically decorated with stones. These pots can be seen today outside the home of relatives.

James and Mary Vane family - 1937

Maren was devoted to her husband, children and home. In addition to cooking and cleaning, she baked bread twice a week and sewed many of the clothes for her large family. She enjoyed making and stitching quilts, and for each of her daughters she made a lovely lone star quilt.

In March 1937, one hundred relatives and friends gathered at the Vane home to help James and Maren celebrate their golden wedding anniversary. In 1947 they celebrated their 60th anniversary. On their 62nd anniversary (March 9, 1949) James died at the age of 86. Maren died at age 92 on March 13, 1960 at the home of her daughter Minnie Heath in nearby Montevideo. James and Maren are buried in the southeast section of the Dawson Cemetery.

Hadelanders who served during the Civil War and Dakota Uprising 1861-1865

The following list of soldiers with roots in Hadeland who served during the Civil War or the Dakota Uprising was compiled by Ole P. Gamme. Drawn primarily from its database of Hadeland immigrants, research was also done in a variety of other sources. Along with their names, basic biographical information and the associated Emigrant Identification Database forms (available to members on the Hadeland Lag website) are listed. A handful of soldiers were identified as Hadelanders in other sources but it has not yet been possible to gather sufficient information to create a family form.

In 2012/2013, members were asked to submit stories about their Hadeland soldiers for the "Our Hadeland Ancestors" column. Those submissions follow this list.

- Abrahamsen, Gudmund (Gudmund A. Borch), born 22 Dec 1830 at Skaarud in Jevnaker, emigr. 12 Apr 1853, died 1864 in the Civil War. Form 264.
- Amundsen, Ingebret, born 24 Mar 1844 at Helgakerseiet in Gran, emigr. 10 Apr 1852, died 6 May 1862 in the Civil War. Form 500.
- Andersen, Anders (A. A. Egge), born 31 Mar 1839 at Egge in Brandbu, emigr. 21 Apr 1852, died 19 Dec 1919 in Freeborn Co., MN. Form 401.
- Andersen, Christopher, born 27 Apr 1839 at Raaseiet in Brandbu, emigr. 8 Apr 1861, died before 1907, maybe in Houston Co., MN. Form 167.
- Andersen, Erik (Erick Blegen), born 12 Apr 1846 at Blegen in Brandbu, emigr. 22 Apr 1852, died 7 Aug 1884 Otter Tail Co., MN. Form 756.
- Andersen, Gudbrand (Gilbert Anderson/Kristofferson), born 9 Sep 1841 at Olimbseiet i Jevnaker, emigr 9 Apr 1851, died 1915 in Hollandale, WI. Form 311.
- Andersen, Gulbrand (Gilbert Blegen), born 29 Dec 1842 at Blegen in Brandbu, emigr. 22 Apr 1852, died 11 Nov 1920 in Otter Tail Co., MN. Form 756.
- Andersen, Hans (Hans Blegen), born 27 Aug. 1849 at Blegen in Brandbu, emigr. 22 Apr 1852, died ? Form 756.
- Andersen, Paul (Paul A. Paulson Blisten), born 13 Jul 1843 at Løkeneiet in Lunner, emigr. 1 May 1849, died 29 Apr 1913 in Northwood, IA. Form 979.

- Andersen, Torsten (Thomas A. Thompson), born 1 Nov 1846 at Toverudeiet in V. Tingelstad, emigr. 11 Apr. 1861, died 1909 in Green Co., WI. Form 1363.
- Anderson, A. T. lived in Winneshiek Co., IA or Norge, James Co., VA after the war.
- Anderson, Ever, died 6 Feb 1905 in Kentucky?
- Christiansen, Svend (Sven Anderson), born 30 May 1839 at Skjerva in Lunner, emigr. 24 Apr 1849, died 1922 in Dakota Co., MN. Form 390.
- Christophersen, Anders (Andrew Christopherson Skute), born 1 Dec 1824 at Blegeneiet in Brandbu, emigr. 22 May 1852, died 28 Aug 1910 in Chippewa Co., WI. Form 1377.
- Christophersen, Nils (Nels Christopher Myrah), born 5 May 1844 at Dæhleneiet in Brandbu, emigr. 7 Apr 1854, died 19 Sep 1932 Benson Co., ND. Form 564.
- Christophersen, Ole (Ole C. Sorum), born 26 Feb 1831 at Holterbakken in Tingelstad, emigr. 15 Apr 1854, died 10 May 1896 Lafayette Co., WI. Form 184.
- Dahl, G. A., lived in Hollandale, Iowa Co., WI after the war.
- Engebretsen, Lars (Louis Rolfsen), born 9 Feb 1841 at Maurtvedten in Lunner, emigr. 8 Jun 1850, died 7 Jan 1936 in Racine Co., WI. Form 647.
- Eriksen, Christian (Christian Tandberg), born 14 Jan 1830 at Kløvstadeiet in Tingelstad, emigr. 31 Mar 1853, died 6 Oct 1911 in Rock Co., WI. Form 199.
- Eriksen, Erik (Erik Svendsrud), born 2 Dec 1839 at Svendsrud in Tingelstad, emigr.15 Mar 1861, died in the Civil War. Form 75.
- Eriksen, Hans (Daehlin), born 21 Mar 1834 at Dæhlin in Lunner, emigr. 20 Apr 1853, died 29 Jul 1899 in Worth Co. IA., Form 694.
- Eriksen, Ole Petter (Ole Peter Tandberg), born 4 Aug 1832 at Kløvstadeiet in Tingelstad, emigr. 31 Mar 1853, died 1920-1930 in Pierce Co., WI. Form 199.
- Eriksen, Paul, born 7 Feb 1808 at Drøvdal in Tingelstad, emigr. 8 May 1849, died 15 Jul 1863 in the Civil War. Form 851.
- Evensrud, Erick, died in the war.
- Falla, Gabriel Paulson, lived in Pine Knob, Crawford Co., WI after the war.
- Fosland, Ole, lived in Rock Co., WI after the war.
- Gudbrandsen, Anders (Andrew Gilbertson), born 21 Dec 1830 at Dvergstenseiet in Tingelstad, emigr. 22 Apr 1852, died 21 Apr 1907 in Monona Co., IA. Form 341.
- Gudbrandsen, Christian (Christ Ruden), born 30 Oct 1818 at Ruden in Gran, emigr. 5 Apr 1853, died 8 Apr 1890 in Hamlin Co., SD. Form 1233.
- Gudbrandsen, Gudbrand (G. Rostad), born 5 Apr 1827 at Raastad in Lunner, emigr. 13 Apr 1861, died 21 May 1896 in Rothsay, Otter Tail Co., MN. Form 419.

- Gudbrandsen, Gudbrand (Gilbert Vinger), born 4 Jan 1830 at Røisumseiet in Tingelstad, emigr. 11 Jun 1850, died 15 May 1925 Lafayette Co., WI. Form 422.
- Gudbrandsen, Gudbrand (Gilbert Gilson), born 6 Jun 1839 at Surka in Lunner, emigr. 1 Apr 1852, died 1916 in Waupaca Co., WI. Form 1312.
- Gudbrandsen, Peder (Peter G. Brynsaas), born 7 Feb 1841 at Dvergstenseiet in Tingelstad, emigr. 11 Apr 1854, died 29 Aug 1921 Nicollet Co., MN. Form 160.
- Gulbrandsen, Gulbrand (Gilbertson), born 5 Apr 1827 at Raastad in Gran, emigr. 13 Apr 1861, died 21 May 1896 in Otter Tail Co., MN. Form 419.
- Gulbrandsen, Tarald (Charles Gilbert), born 11 Oct 1837 at Næseiet in Brandbu, emigr. 18 Aug 1853, died 23 Jan 1886 in Huron Co., MI. Form 195.
- Guttormsen, Anders, (Andres Bakken), born 17 Jun 1839 at Kløvstadeiet in Tingelstad, emigr. 5 Apr 1853, died 12 Mar 1870 in Green Co., WI. Form 636.
- Guttormsen, Hans (Hans Bakken), born 8 Mar 1842 at Kløvstadeiet in Tingelstad, emigr. 5 Apr 1853, died ? Form 636.
- Guttormsen Iver (Iver Bakken), born 24 Jul 1836 at Kløvstadeiet in Tingelstad, emigr. 5 Apr 1853, died 8 Jan 1906 in Green Co., WI. Form 636.
- Guttormsen, Ole (Ole Bakken), born 3 Apr 1834 at Kløvstadeiet in Tingelstad, emigr. 5 Apr 1853, died ? Form 636.
- Halvorsen, Christoffer (Chris Albertson), born 24 May 1841 at Bjørge in Gran, emigr. 17 Mar 1849, died after 1910 in Jefferson Co., WI? Form 1270.
- Halvorsen, Halvor (Albert Albertson), born 1 May 1844 at Bjørge in Gran, emigr. 17 Mar 1849, died 29 Sep 1921 in Canyon Co., ID. Form 1270.
- Halvorsen, Lars, born 14 Sep 1837 in Toten, emigr. 1861, died 30 Aug 1862 in the Civil War. Form 830.
- Halvorsen, Ole (Ole H. Milesten), born 6 Feb 1840 at Milesten in Lunner, emigr. 18 May 1848, died 9 Sep 1863 in the Civil War. Form 986.
- Hansen, Anders, born 7 Dec 1834 at Dvergstenseiet in Tingelstad, emigr. 1861, died 10 Apr 1902 in Decorah, IA. Form 308.
- Hansen, Anders, born 4 Mar 1845 at Framstad in Gran, emigr. 15 Jun 1850, died 9 Feb 1930 Green Co., WI. Form 44.
- Hansen, Anders, born 7 Sep 1845 at Eggebraaten in Brandbu, emigr. 5 May 1850, died 30 Aug 1935 in Twin Valley, MN. Form 235.
- Hansen Even (Evan Skarrie), born 5 Mar 1840 at Skari in Brandbu, emigr. 18 Mar 1849, died 25 Dec 1875 in Fillmore Co., MN. Form 707.
- Hansen, Gudbrand (Gilbert H. Nass), born 26 Oct 1840 at Næseiet in Brandbu, emigr. 9 Apr 1861, died 19 Apr 1926 in Winneshiek Co., IA. Form 1091.

- Hansen, Halvor (Halvor H. Hofland), born 21 Sep 1833 at Rundeleneiet in Lunner, emigr. 18 Apr 1853, died 4 Jun 1864 in Georgia. Form 225.
- Hansen, Hans (Hans Loken), born 5 Apr 1839 at Raastad in Lunner, emigr. 19 Apr 1853, died 21 Jul 1915 Lafayette Co., WI. Form 1457.
- Hansen, Ingvold, born 23 Jul 1828 at Skjennumseiet in Jevnaker, emigr. 8 May 1852, died ? (after 1900) in Traill Co., ND? Form 1475.
- Hansen, John (John H. Bollerud), born 12 Jan 1830 at Baalerud in Brandbu, emigr. 20 Apr 1853, died 1912 in Moscow, Iowa Co., WI. Form 352.
- Hansen, Mons (Mons H. Grinager), born 7 Oct 1832 at Grinager in Tingelstad, emigr. 5 Apr 1853, died 30 Jan 1889 in Minneapolis, MN. Form 401.
- Hansen Ole (Ole H. Ness), born 15 Sep 1840 at Tomteiet in Brandbu, emigr. 22 Apr 1862, died 26 Dec 1919 Glenwood, IA. Form 138.
- Hansen, Paul (Paul H. Rosendahl), born 18 Oct 1838 at Dvergstenseiet in Tingelstad, emigr. 20 Apr 1852, died 30 Aug 1880 Houston Co., MN. Form 475.
- Hansen, Peder, born 10 Jan 1832 at Strande in V. Brandbu, emigr. 20 Jan 1854, died 18 Mar 1905 in Webster Co., IA. Form 506.
- Hansen, Tobias (Tobias Loken), born 21 Sep 1841 at Løken in Lunner, emigr. 19 Apr 1853, died 23 Aug 1888 Lafayette Co., WI. Form 1457.
- Henriksen, Anders (Andrew Hendrickson), f. 28 Jan 1825 at Lunderengen i Lunner, emigr. 15 Apr 1853, died 22 Dec 1888 Lafayette Co., WI. Form 567.
- Ingebretsen, Christopher (C. Emerson), born 12 Feb 1829 at Stomne in Lunner, emigr. 14 Apr 1853, died 27 Feb 1913 in Polk Co., WI. Form 1255.
- Ingebretsen, Hans (Hans Emerson), born 24 Feb 1831 at Stomne in Lunner, emigr. 14 Apr 1853, died 25 Dec 1910 in Green Co., WI. Form 1255.
- Iversen, Gunder (Gunder Everson), born 8 Aug 1823 at Sandviken in Jevnaker, emigr. 11 Apr 1862, died before 1870 in Iowa Co., WI? Form 1383.
- Iversen, Ole, born 11 Jan 1837 at Amundrudseiet in Tingelstad, emigr. 11 Apr 1853, died 28 Feb 1865 Prairie du Chien, WI. Form 518.
- Iversen, Peder (Peter Everson), born 17 Sep 1845 in Brandhagen in Brandbu, emigr. 23 May 1853, died 18 Jul 1873 in Mauston, Juneau Co., WI.
- Jacobsen, Anders, born 26 Oct 1845 at Nyhus in Brandbu, emigr.22 Apr 1852 from Brandbu, died ca. 1880 in Racine Co., WI? Form 245.
- Jacobsen, Christian, born 7 Jul 1848 at Nyhus in Brandbu, emigr. 22 Apr 1852 from Brandbu, died 25 Dec 1925 in Marshall Co., MN. Form 245.
- Jacobsen, Iver (Iver J. Sorlie), born 24 Jul 1835 at Sørlie in Lunner, emigr. 18 Apr 1853, died 4 Sep 1916 in Freeborn Co., MN. Form 225.

- Jacobsen, Jacob, born 5 Jan 1822 at Johnsrudeiet in V. Brandbu, emigr. 1852 from Christiania, died? (after 1910) in Franklin Co., IA? Form 1476.
- Jacobsen, Nils, born 25 Aug 1843 at Nyhus in Brandbu, emigr. 22 Apr 1852, died 1863 in the Civil War. Form 245.
- Jacobsen, Martin, born ca. 1828, lived in Walnut Grove, MN after the war.
- Jensen, Anders (Andrew Jackson), born 8 Apr 1830 at Sandbakken in Tingelstad, emigr. 11 Jun 1850, died 27 Nov 1897 in Green Co., WI. Form 637.
- Jensen, Christian (Johnson), born 26 Mar 1833 at Smedsrud in Gran, emigr. 9 Apr 1861, died 30 Jan 1901 in Argyle, Lafayette Co., WI. Form 943.
- Johannesen, Brede (Brady Skofstad), born 25 Dec 1844 at Paulsseteren in Tingelstad, emigr. 6 Apr 1853, died 14 Sep 1915 in Griggs Co., ND. Form 598.
- Johannesen, Halvor, born 3 Mar 1838 at Teslobakken in Brandbu, emigr. 8 Jun 1849, died after 1863 in the Civil War. Form 851.
- Johannesen, Jens (Jens J. Skofstad), born 9 Aug 1842 at Paulsseteren in Tingelstad, emigr. 6 Apr 1853, died 23 Mar 1864 in the Civil War. Form 598.
- Johansen, Iver, born 25 Feb 1818 at Kjoseiet in Brandbu, emigr. 28 Apr 1848, died Dec 1863 in the Civil War. Form 634.
- Johansen, Peder (Peder J. Hilden), born 25 Jul 1837 at Hildeneiet in Tingelstad, emigr. 29 Jun 1857, died 28 Jan 1914 in Montevideo, MN. Form 471.
- Johnsen, Anders, born 13 Jan 1829 at Høibyeiet in Lunner, emigr. 2 May 1852, died 24 Dec 1905 in Portage Co., WI? Form 438.
- Johnsen, Anders, born 12 Jul 1839 at Raaseiet in Brandbu, emigr. before 1865, died 1925 in Green Co., WI. Form 462.
- Johnsen, Lars, born 12 Mar 1832 in Kjevlingstuen in Lunner, emigr. 3 Jul 1857, died 1863-1865 in the Civil War. Form 201.
- Johnson, Ole, died before 1907 in WA?
- Larsen, Christian (Larson), born 28 Feb 1834 at Lyseneiet, emigr. 3 Apr 1856, died ? Form 638.
- Larsen, Erik (Erik Myhren), born 1 May 1823 at Askimeiet in Tingelstad, emigr. 1 Apr 1848, died 8 May 1877 in Green Co., WI. Form 638.
- Larsen, Erik, born 11 Feb 1831 at Framstad in Gran, emigr. 8 Jun 1849, died Sep 1863 in the Civil War. Form 851.
- Larsen, Fredrik (Nerengen), born 8 Mar 1825 at Stadumseiet in Gran, emigr. 29 Mar 1852, died 14 Apr 1907 in Iowa Co., WI. Form 425.
- Larsen, Hans, born 17 Jun 1828 at Framstad in Gran, emigr. 6 Jun 1849, died 11 Jan 1917 in Dickinson Co., IA. Form 851.

- Larsen, Martin (Pentbakken), born 19 Apr 1844 in Aker, Akershus, emigr. 1853, died 12 Oct. 1908 in Lafayette Co., WI. Form 116.
- Larsen, Mikkel (Mikkel Myhren), born 22 Oct 1824 at Lyseneiet in Tingelstad, emigr. 5 Apr 1852, died 18 Sep 1905 in Lisbon, Ransom Co., ND. Form 638.
- Larsen, Ole (Ole Bjorgeseter), born 7 Mar 1824 at Skjerva in Lunner, emigr. 15 Apr 1853, died 25 Sep 1897 in Moscow, Iowa Co., WI. Form 1130.
- Larsen Ole Christian, born 19 Nov 1842 in Aker, Akershus, emigr. 1853, died 9 Nov 1863 in Natchez, Adams Co., MS. Form 116.
- Larsen, Ole (Larson), born 19 Sep 1828 at Lyseneiet in Tingelstad, emigr. 10 Apr 1852, died 1864-1870 in WI or in the Civil War. Form 638.
- Larsen, Peder, born 26 May 1832 at Bilden in Tingelstad, emigr. 2 May 1851, died Apr 1924 in Blanchardville, Lafayette Co., WI. Form 544.
- Monson, Gilbert, died before 1907, lived in Ashby, Grant Co., MN?
- Monson, Mathias, died 1904 in Lime Grove, NE?
- Nilsen, Anders (Andrew Kjos), born 27 Aug 1829 at Kjos in Brandbu, emigr. 7 Apr 1854, died 12 May 1915 in Spring Grove, Houston Co., MN. Form 248.
- Nilsen, Hans (Myhra), born 12 Sep 1824 at Dæhleneiet in Brandbu, emigr. 22 Apr 1848, died 12 Feb 1867 in Spring Grove, Houston Co., MN. Form 566.
- Nilsen, Jacob (Jacob N. Nyhus), born 11 Apr 1819 at Nyhus in Brandbu, emigr. 22 Apr 1852, died 23 Jun 1862 in the Civil War. Form 245.
- Nilsen, Knud (Knudt Nelson), born 29 Jul 1834 at Gjefseneiet in Gran, emigr. 4 Apr 1861, died 11 Aug 1917 in Minneapolis, MN. Form 139.
- Nilsen, Torsten (T. N. Sandbeck), born 20 Sep 1844 at Haugseiet in Tingelstad, emigr. 15 Apr 1862, died 20 Dec 1925 in Divide Co., ND. Form 505.
- Norton, Christopher, born 31 Oct 1828 in Hadeland? Emigr. 1852, died 1905-1910 in Moscow, Iowa Co., WI. Form 88.
- Olsen, Anders (Andrew O. Tokerud), born 25 Sep 1843 in S. Land, emigr. 1864? died 3 Nov 1867 in Decorah, Winneshiek Co., IA. Form 450.
- Olsen, Carl, born 12 Jun 1841 at Hvalebyeiet in Gran, emigr. 20 Apr 1861, died before 1866 in the Civil War. Form 155.
- Olsen, Christian, born 15 Nov 1834 at Gunstadeiet in Jevnaker, emigr. 29 Mar 1852, died 11 Nov 1863 in Chattanooga, TN. Form 463.
- Olsen, Erik (Erik O. Dahl), born 26 Aug 1823 at Bratvoldseiet in Jevnaker, emigr. 5 Apr 1852, died 18 Jan 1894 in Iowa Co., WI. Form 312.
- Olsen, Gudbrand (Gilbert O. Melaas), born 30 Mar 1838 at Hytta in Lunner, emigr. 14 Apr 1853, died14 Mar 1872 in Winneshiek Co., IA. Form 361.

- Olson Hans (Hans Simonson) born 9 Aug 1840 at Harestuskogen in Lunner, emigr. 28 Mar 1851, died 24 Jan 1908 in Allamakee Co., IA? Form 1477.
- Olsen, Iver (Oleson) born 24 Oct 1839 at Johnsrud in W. Brandbu, emigr. before 1862, died 27 Nov 1926 in Fayette Co., IA. Form 383.
- Olsen, Ole (Rollin Olson), born 1. Nov 1831 at Gunstadeiet in Jevnaker, emigr. 8 Jun 1849, died 31 Mar 1898 in Green Co., WI. Form 462.
- Olsen, Peder, lived in Minnewaukan, ND after the war
- Olsen Simen (Simon Simonsen), born 3 Aug 1837 at Harestuskogen in Lunner, emigr. 28 Mar 1851, died in Allamakee Co., IA? Form 1477.
- Paulsen, Erik (Erick E. Paul), born 7 Apr 1841 at Retrum in Brandbu, emigr. 8 Jun 1849, died 3 Dec 1920 in Nobles Co., MN. Form 851.
- Paulsen, Gulbrand (Gilbert Paulson), born 11 Oct 1835 at Karlsrud in Jevnaker, emigr. 13 May 1850, died 29 Jan 1910 in Iowa Co., WI. Form 1223.
- Paulsen, Lars (Lewis Paul), born 6 Oct 1839 at Retrum in Brandbu, emigr. 8 Jun 1849, died 11 Sep 1922 in Dickinson Co., IA. Form 851.
- Paulsen, Peder (Peder P. Shager), born 16 Jan 1819 at Skiaker in Gran, emigr. 8 May 1849, died 16 Jul 1905 in Freeborn Co., MN. Form 496.
- Pedersen, Anders (Andrew Peterson Smerud), born 11 Dec 1840 at Engneseiet in V. Gran, emigr. 10 Apr 1852, died 6 Nov 1864 in Bardstown, KY. Form 462.
- Pedersen Peder (Peder Golie), born 20 Jan 1844 at Godli in Lunner, emigr. 15 May 1852, died 9 Mar 1920 in Sacred Heart, Renville Co., MN. Form 831.
- Raasum, Christian, ?
- Thorersen, Carl, born 15 Mar 1842 at Almseiet in Tingelstad, emigr. 15 Apr 1854, died 26 Nov 1864 in Little Rock, Arkansas in the Civil War. Form 307.
- Thorersen, Hans, born 4 Sep 1838 at Almseiet in Tingelstad, emigr. 15 Apr 1854, died 1865 in Arkansas in the Civil War. Form 307.
- Thorersen, Ole, born 3 Oct 1827 at Almseiet in Tingelstad, emigr. 28 May 1850, died 13 Sep 1913 in Dakota Co., MN. Form 307.
- Thorersen, Stephen, born 16 Aug 1830 at Alm in Tingelstad, emigr. 15 Apr 1854, died 22 Sep 1882 in Dakota Co., MN. Form 307.
- Torgersen, Christian, born 10 Jul 1840 at Gubberud in Brandbu, emigr. 5 Apr 1861, died Jan 1865 in the Civil War. Form 338.
- Torstensen, Anders (Andrew Thompson), born 25 Sep 1821 at Grimsrud in Brandbu, emigr. 11 Apr 1861, died 10 Nov 1903 in Lafayette Co., WI. Form 1363.
- Torstensen, Nils (Nels Thompson), born 5 Dec 1828 at Hvalebyeiet in Gran, emigr. 15 Apr 1853, died 27 Feb 1890 Green Co., WI. Form 75.

Rollin Olson   *published November 2012*

The book *Rollin Olson Civil War Letters* was translated and written by Morgan A. Olson about his great-grandfather who served in the Civil War. Morgan was instrumental in reviving the Hadeland Lag in the 1970s and was president of the Hadeland Lag from 1976-1985. Morgan's son James of Battle Lake, Minnesota, is a member of the Hadeland Lag. Two other great-grandchildren of Rollin Olson are Carol Olson Vind of Stillwater, Minnesota and her brother, Norman Olson of Dayton, Ohio.

Rollin Olson: Biographical Sketch written by Morgan A. Olson in the introduction to the book *Rollin Olson: Civil War Letters,* published in 1981.

Rollin Olson was born Ola Olsen, Nov. 1, 1831, at the Kalnebberud cottager home on the Gunstad farm in Hadeland, Norway. Kalnebberud and the Gunstad farm are a couple miles north of Jevnaker on the east side of the long lake called the Randsfjord in the district of Hadeland.

Ola was number six of seven children in the family of Ole Hansen and Kari (Iversdatter). The Hansen family were *husmenn med jord* (cottagers with a piece of ground) and all labored on the Gunstad farm. In return for their labor they had the privilege of living in a cabin on a small piece of land big enough for a yard and garden of their own, a short distance from the Gunstad farmstead.

Ola was the first of the family at Kalnebberud to leave the Gunstad farm and sail to America. The Jevnaker church records report that he left the parish April 18, 1849 and became a statistic in the column labeled *til Amerika.* Ola was among the earliest of many thousand people who emigrated from Hadeland in the following decades.

Poverty and the prospect of a dim future as a cottager's son on the Gunstad farm were motivating forces toward leaving home. Ola was $17^1/_2$ years old in the spring of 1849 when he left his Kalnebberud home and went to the seaport city of Drammen. He sailed from Drammen in June aboard a small sailing ship, the Norwegian bark *Benedicte* and arrived 56 days later in New York City, August 22, 1849.

It is assumed Ola Olsen followed the usual route from New York City up the Hudson River to Albany, then via Erie Canal boat to Buffalo, NY, and by boat through the Great Lakes to Milwaukee, WI. A family legend is that he worked his way from Buffalo to Milwaukee on a sailing vessel.

Ola hung around the Milwaukee docks in hopes of getting a job but with no special skills and the language barrier it was impossible. Luckily he met a Mr. Luraas, a pioneer Norwegian farmer from the Norwegian settlement at Koshkonong, WI. Mr. Luraas took pity on Ola and invited him to stay with his family on their farm for the winter of 1949-50 and he worked on their farm the next summer.

In the next years Ola found work in the pine forests of central Wisconsin during the winter and farm work or in the lead mines of Lafayette and Grant Counties in the summer.

He became acquainted with Norwegians in the area around Mineral Point, Argyle, Blanchardville and Jordan. In 1854 Ola married Mary Peterson (Smerud) who had arrived in America in 1852 with her widowed mother and brothers and sisters.

During several winters after Ola and Mary were married, Ola had the job as a foreman and his wife as a cook for a wood-chopping crew on Gilead Island, approximately 100 miles north of St. Louis, MO, on the Mississippi River. It was a winter job for a crew of 8 or 10 men who chopped and piled wood on the shore of the island. During the next summer, wood-burning steamboats would pick up the wood and use it as they plied the Mississippi River. It is assumed Ola's summer job was work as a farmhand in the Argyle and Blanchardville area of southern Wisconsin.

Daughter Caroline was born in 1855. A son, Morgan Peter, was born in 1859 in Waldwick Township of southeastern Iowa County, Wisconsin. This was near Moscow, WI, now a ghost town which had a very exciting history until the railroad bypassed it when it was routed through Blanchardville, WI.

President Abraham Lincoln was inaugurated for his first term as U.S. President on March 4, 1861. On April 14 Fort Sumter had fallen and Southern States began to secede from the Union. The next day, Aptil 15, President Lincoln issued a Proclamation calling for 75,000 militia men from the Northern States. Then on August 20, 1861, Lincoln made a specific request of Wisconsin's Governor Randall for five regiments from that state.

A group of leading Scandinavians met in Madison, WI, on Sept. 25, 1861 and decided to raise a regiment — 1,000 men. The later famous 15th Regiment Wisconsin Volunteer Infantry came into existence in December 1861 commanded by 32-year-old Hans C. Heg who had emigrated from Lier, near Drammen, Norway. The 15th Wisconsin consisted of Scandinavians, mostly Norwegians from Wisconsin and other Norwegians from northeastern Iowa, southeastern Minnesota and the Chicago, Illinois, area.

Ola Olson at age 30 became Rollin Olson as he joined the 15th Wisconsin Regiment. There is a legend that there were more than 100 Ole Olsons who enlisted in the 15th Wisconsin. The regimental commander asked Ole Olson to find other names by which to be identified. The legend continues that in the years Ola was foreman in the wood-chopping camp along the Mississippi River he was nicknamed "Roll In" Olson because each night he had to get his crew away from playing cards or other evening activities and to "roll-in" so they would be ready for work the next day. Hence the name Rollin Olson.

The name Rollin Olson ("son") was used in the Army record beginning with the date he was sworn in at Moscow, Wisconsin, December 4, 1861 with the official "muster-in date, Dec. 8, 1861."

The Army record provides the following vital statistic: "Five feet 9 inches high, light complexion, blue eyes, sandy hair and by occupation, when enrolled, a farmer."

The years in which Rollin served in the 15th Wisconsin Regiment are covered by the letters which are the purpose of this publication. Olson was discharged from the Army Hospital in Baltimore, MD, in time for Christmas at home with his wife and two children in December 1864.

Rollin purchased a farm in Jordan Township, Green County, WI, near the Jordan Lutheran Church. It is reported the family moved to their farm April 15, 1865, the day after President Lincoln was assassinated. On this farm four children were born: Clara in 1866; Oscar 1869; William 1873; Henry 1879.

Rollin was very well liked and acted as an ombudsman for people in the community. He participated in many community and public affairs. He held most of the elective minor local public offices at some time or other — school board, assessor, township chairman and member of the Green County board. He was federal census enumerator in 1880 and 1890.

Rollin Olson received the rank of Army 1st Lieutenant, Co. E, 15th Regiment Wisconsin Volunteer Infantry, as of June 20, 1889, which was retroactive to Nov. 10, 1864. From the Army official records: "Rollin Olson, 1st Lieut., Co E, 15 Regt Wis Inf. War Department, Adjutant General's Office, Washington June 20, 1889. Under the provisions of the Act of Congress, approved June 3, 1884, and the acts amendatory thereof, this officer is considered by this department as commissioned to the grade of first lieutenant, Co. E, 15 Regt. Wis. Inf. to take effect from Nov. 10, 1864, advice of T.A. Rossing, promoted." Rossing had been Rollin's company commander while both were on active duty.

Rollin passed away March 31, 1898, at the age of 66 and is buried in the Jordan Lutheran Church cemetery. "He was a man possessed of high moral character. He was a brave soldier, honored citizen and a noble father and husband. He built a reputation that will live forever in the minds of all who knew him." . . . quoted from a newspaper of the time.

Carol Vind, Stillwater, Minnesota, wrote:

Our great-grandfather Rollin Olson joined the 15th Regiment in Wisconsin in December 1861. He was taken prisoner on September 19, 1863 and was later sent to a hospital in Annapolis, Maryland. Rollin was discharged in time for Christmas 1864. He was granted the rank of 1st Lieutenant, Co. E, 15th Regiment Wisconsin Voluntary Infantry.

He told his wife Mary to save all the letters he wrote to her. She did this and in the 1920s they were found in the attic of my birthplace which was the Morgan Peter and Nellie Olson homestead in Willow Lake, South Dakota.

The letters were later given to my great-uncle Henry who was the youngest child of Rollin and Mary. His son Kenneth, a librarian, wanted them preserved and gave them to the archives of the Wisconsin Historical Association in Madison. They can be viewed and are in good condition.

When Morgan Albert Olson retired, he decided to translate the letters. He was allowed to copy them and in 1981 he completed the translation. He had them published and they were purchased mainly by relatives and friends. I understand James, Morgan Olson's son, has no more copies available so every book is precious.

Robert Brodin, Windom, Minnesota, sent the following article about Rollin Olson, the great-grandfather of his wife Rosalie.

Rosalie and I had been married for 30 years as of August 17, 1993 when after finding my paternal Wangen birth family of Freeborn County, Minnesota, we learned of certain "connections" between our two families four generations ago which we find very interesting.

On August 20, 1861, four months after the outbreak of the Civil War, President Lincoln requested five regiments of volunteers from the state of Wisconsin. Ola Olson was sworn in at Moscow, Wisconsin, on December 4 and "mustered in" on December 8. My birth father's mother's father, Lars Sebjornson (1832-1899) and Rosalie's father's mother's father, Ola (Rollin) Olson (1831-1898) were apparently "among the group of leading Scandinavians who met in Madison, Wis. and decided to raise a regiment — 1,000 men." And so the 15th Regiment Wisconsin Volunteer Infantry came into existence in December 1861 and consisted of Scandinavians, mostly Norwegians from Wisconsin and other Norwegians from northeast Iowa, southeast Minnesota and the Chicago area. Lars Sebjornson enlisted on January 18, 1862, shortly after his wife, Sigrid (Kittelson) Sebjornson (1834-1861), died on December 4, 1861 in childbirth with their third child, Ole Sebjornson (Madson). Lars and "Siri" were married November 3, 1857 and Seber Sebjornson (Madson) was born in 1858 and Gunhild Sebjornson (Anderson) in 1860. All three were raised by others. At his enlistment Lars, a Freeborn County, Minnesota farmer, was 5'7", light complexion, blue eyes and dark hair.

Lars was in Company K and Rollin in Company E of the Wisconsin 15th and Rev. Claus Lauritz Clausen was their first chaplain. Clausen was the second ordained pastor to the Norwegian Lutherans in America, being ordained October 18, 1843, just 15 days after the first, Rev. Elling Eielsen Sundve. Rollin Olson's letters home to his wife, Mary (Peterson Smerud) Olson (18371913) and two children: Caroline, 1855, and Morgan Peter, 1859, and which are compiled into a book entitled *Rollin Olson Civil War Letters* often refer to Rev. Clausen's helpfulness to the soldiers. While Company E called themselves "Olin's Rifles, Company K dubbed themselves "Clausen's Guards" in honor of the regiment's first chaplain.

As Rev. Clausen had officiated at Lars and Sigrid Sebjornson's marriage in 1857 at St. Ansgar, Iowa, so also did he officiate there at the September 20, 1863 wedding of Lars Sebjornson and Mrs. Clausen's niece, Bergethe Catherine "Betsy" Merkle (1845-1918), whose mother Turi

(Pedersdatter Brekke) Merkle (later, Mrs. Christian Jacobson), 1822-1865, was the sister of the second Mrs. Clausen, Bergethe (Pedersdatter Brekke) Hjorth Clausen, 1819-1887. Mrs. Lars "Betsy" Sebjornson was named for her Aunt Bergethe Clausen. It can be said of the Clausen's marriage that a widower married a widow because Rev. Clausen's first wife, Martha Rasmussen Clausen (1815-1846) died at age 31 after bearing their two sons, both named Martin Nicolai Clausen, the second of whom survived to become a civil engineer at Austin, Minnesota. Martha Clausen authored the *Lutheran Hymnary* hymn #51, "And now we must bid one another Farewell," which she wrote in Norwegian, *"Saa vil vi nu sige hverandre Farvel!"* and which first appeared in *Landstad's Hymn Book* which was used by the early immigrant church.

The second Mrs. Clausen was the young, childless widow of Hans Erasmus Hjorth, an Indiana extensive land owner. Besides raising Martin (1845), Rev. Claus and Bergethe Clausen had four sons: Charles (1852), a Washington State Auditor; Edward (1854), a druggist in Illinois and Washington; Lauritz (1856), an Austin, Minnesota lawyer; and Berger (after 1860), a Poulsbo, Washington druggist. These were my great-grandmother "Betsy" Sebjornson's first cousins. The Clausens also raised a daughter, Gunhild Jacobson, who became Mrs. Rev. Svein Strand of Estherville, Iowa, in later years. She was Bergethe Clausen's niece and "Betsy" Sebjornson's half-sister, the daughter of Turi (Pedersdatter Brekke) Merkle Jacobson and Christian Jacobson. Turi died when Gunhild was only four years old.

On September 19, 1863, one day before the Sebjornsons' wedding, Rollin Olson was taken prisoner by the Confederates at the Battle of Chickamauga, Georgia and he was imprisoned for a year at Libby Prison in Richmond and at Prison No. 3 at Danville, Virginia. After serving his three-year commitment, 1st Sgt. Rollin Olson was discharged December 8, 1864. Rollin purchased a farm in Jordan Township, Green County, Wisconsin, near the Jordan Lutheran Church. On this farm four children were born: Clara (Tollefson) in 1866, Rosalie's grandmother; Oscar in 1869; William in 1873; and Henry in 1879. Rollin died there March 31, 1898 at age 66 and is buried in the Jordan Lutheran Cemetery.

Private Lars Sebjornson was granted an honorable disability discharge on March 11, 1863 for an "injury of the spine and right hip" sustained at Island No. 10 on June 20, 1862, and returned to farm in Manchester Township, Freeborn County, Minnesota. Lars died there March 23, 1899 at age 66 and is buried at the rural Hartland Cemetery, Hartland, Minnesota. The Sebjornsons had 11 children, of whom Julia Catherine (Seberson — note the spelling change) Wangen (1868-1923) was third born and the mother of 10, including her sixth-born Joseph Raymond Wangen (1903-1945), my birth father, Donald LeRoy, a.k.a. Robert Merlyn Brodin (1933-).

After serving the Muskego (1843-1845), Koshkonong (1845-1846) and Rock Prairie (Lutheran Valley) (1846-1853) Churches in Wisconsin, Rev. C.L. Clausen led a caravan of 75 settlers, including his sister-in-law Turi Merkle and her daughters, Bergethe "Betsy" and Frances, and 40 covered wagons to northern Iowa in May of 1853. The covered wagons were pulled by oxen and about 300 head of cattle were driven along with the caravan. A woman who was a member of the party later wrote, "The journey lasted three weeks and most of us walked the whole way, driving the cattle. I remember that I carried children across creeks and rivers when we had to ford them." They chose for their settlement a site at the junction of Cedar River and a stream which Pastor Clausen called Deer Creek. He named the site St. Ansgar in honor of the "Apostle of the North, who brought Christianity to Denmark." Rev. Clausen was born in Denmark. There they built a church of stone which was for many years the sanctuary of the First Lutheran Church, St. Ansgar, Iowa. He also started about 26 other congregations in southeast Minnesota and northeast Iowa and one history account reads in Norwegian that it was he for whom the settlers in Belmont Township, Jackson County, Minnesota were assembled, in a home along the Des Moines River, and waiting to lead their worship service, when the Belmont Massacre occurred Sunday, August 24, 1862 in which 13 men, women and children were killed.

Clausen's first congregation after his October 18, 1843 ordination was at Muskego, Wisconsin where he served until 1846 and was their pastor when the Muskego Church was built in 1844 and dedicated March 13, 1845. That church now stands on the Luther Seminary Campus in St. Paul, Minnesota, where it was moved for preservation in 1904. According to Rosalie's mother's mother, Clara (Quammen) Anderson, her mother Annie (Halvorson) Quammen (1844-1920, Rosalie's great-grandmother, who was born March 29, 1844, was baptized in the "new" Muskego Church and presumably by the church's Pastor Claus Lauritz Clausen, Bob's great-grandmother's uncle! Pastor Clausen (1820-1892) died at his son's home in Washington and is buried with his second wife, Bergethe, at Oakwood Cemetery, Austin, Minn.

Additional Information

Robert Brodin added this information from the book *Dakota Dawn* by Gregory F. Michno. Jackson County's chapter 18 is the last in the book:

Here are the names of the 13 people who were killed in the August 24, 1862 Belmont massacre: Johannes Eske, Ole Olson Forde (Fyre, Fohre), Lars Larson Furnes (Furness, Furrenaes), Anna Knutsdatter Langeland Furnes, Lars G. Hjornevik, Anna Knutsdatter Bjorgo Langeland, Anna K.1 Langeland (a child), Agaata Langeland, Nikolai Langeland, Knut Langeland, Knut Haldorson Mestad (Midstad), Brita Andersdatter Rote Mestad, Mikkel Olson Slaabakken.

————— 〰〰 —————

Martin Larson (Pentbakken) *published November 2012*

Helen Loing wrote:

Martin Larson (Pentbakken) was born in a hospital (unusual for that time) in Oslo, on April 19, 1844. When he was 9 years old, he came to America with his parents and some of his siblings. The family came to Blanchardville, Wisconsin, and his parents homesteaded in nearby rural

Hollandale. After Martin grew up, he enlisted in the army on February 14, 1865, and he joined the Wisconsin Regiment. He was "mustered out" on June 21, 1866. He served on the frontier during the Indian attacks, and I was told by one of my mother's cousins that he guarded Indians during the Civil War. She said, "He was in a state where malaria was common, and when he returned, he often had attacks of ague and shivered with it in the summertime."

After returning to Wisconsin, he found that all of the land near Argyle had been claimed, so he homesteaded on land a bit further north, between Blanchardville and Hollandale. There were only wagon tracks and cow paths in those days, and Martin walked the 50 miles to Madison to file his claim and register the deed.

Martin was one of four Yellowstone Church members who served in the Civil War. In the book *Nordmaendene i Amerika* by Martin Ulvestad, 1907, there is an entry that reads as follows: "Martin Larson fra Hadeland, Route 1— Hollandale, Wisc. Member of Menige 4042." In a letter to one of her cousins, Clara Ingwell wrote, "This Martin Larson Pentbakken was a war veteran. I can still see him and Martin Larson Bilden sitting inside the altar rail at Yellowstone Church on Decoration Day as it was called then — Memorial Day now. They would march and command to each grave the wild flowers that we had picked the night before." Martin Larson died in 1908.

Martin Larson's older brother, Christian Larson, was also in the Civil War. He died of scurvy in the infamous Confederate prison camp at Andersonville, Georgia.

Christopher Larson *published February 2013*

Helen Loing and George and Nila Krenos submitted information:

Nila (Anderson) Krenos' ancestor, Ole Christian Kristoffersen was born Nov 19, 1842 Aker, Norway His parents were Lars Christophersen, born on Dec. 15, 1815 on the Hauer farm in Jevnaker, and Bertha Olsdatter, born on March 3, 1818 on the Broshaug farm in Hurdal, Norway. In America his name was changed to Christopher Larson when his father changed his surname to Larson. He is the older brother of Martin Larson.

When he entered the military service he was 19 years old and unmarried, 5'6" tall, light build with blue eyes, black hair, swarthy complexion. He enlisted for three years on 14 Aug 1862 at Argyle, Wisconsin, and was mustered in on 18 Oct 1862 at Camp Utley, Racine, Wisconsin. He was paid a bounty of $25 (of $100 total) at the time that he entered the service. He received the rank of private. He died on 9 Nov 1863, due to diarrhea, in the regimental hospital at Natchez, Mississippi. His effects, consisting of a hat, a blouse, a pair of trousers, a pair of shoes, three pair of socks, one haversack (editor's note: a haversack is a strong bag for personal belongings, which a soldier carried on his back or over his shoulder), one knapsack, one canteen and one rubber blanket and $27.15 money "that had been sent to his friends at Lafayette County, Wis. by the Adams Express Co."

The regiment left the state (Wis.) on Nov. 12, 1862 for Memphis. On Nov. 12, 1862 it left Memphis and joined the army under General Grant in his campaign in Northern Mississippi, preliminary to the campaign at Vicksburg. The regiment went into Mississippi and returned to Moscow, Tenn. on January 12, 1863 where it went into camp. On April 18, 1863 it went on an expedition in Mississippi. On May 17 the regiment embarked at Vicksburg. The Thirty-third arrived, by way of the Yazoo, at Snyder's Bluff on the 20th of May. On the 25th the regiment moved around to the left and took position beyond the 13th Corps. near the Hall's Ferry road. From that time until the surrender the men of the regiment took an active part in the siege. Their camp was so near the enemy's lines that they were all the time under fire. One of their number was killed by a Confederate sharpshooter while asleep in his tent. There was considerable fighting along the lines occupied by the Thirty-third, and on every occasion the men behaved themselves courageously.

After the surrender they marched with General Sherman's army against General Jackson. On the 18th day of August they took passage down river to Natchez where they did guard duty until Dec. 1, 1863.

Source: *Wisconsin at Vicksburg*, Madison, Wis. 1914.

Eric Olson Dalen   *published February 2013*

George and Nila Krenos wrote:

Erik Olsen Dalen enlisted in the Wisconsin Volunteers at Argyle, WI under the name and spelling Erick Olesen. He was age 42, signed his name with an "X", stated he was born in Norway, was a farmer, had blue eyes, light hair, complexion was florid, and his height was 5'7". He mustered in at Camp Randall, Madison, WI on March 9, 1865 as a Private in Company "C" 50th Wisconsin Volunteer Infantry Regiment. He was paid a bounty of $33.33 and $66.66 was due him. When he mustered out on June 12 1866 at Madison his clothing amount showed he had drawn $88.45 since enrollment and the amount due him was $35.42. Years ago we asked one of his granddaughters why a man 42 years old would enlist for one year for the sum of only $100 and she told us, "They needed the money."

Company "C", 50th Regiment, was recruited in the southern part of Lafayette County, Wisconsin by Oscar M. Dering, at that time Provost Marshal. He was subsequently elected Captain of the Company, organized and mustered into the Fiftieth Regiment under Colonel John G. Clark at Madison. They left by companies in April 1865 for St. Louis, MO., where they were assigned to quarters in Benton Barrack, Company C, under command of Capt. O.M. Dering, reported at Arrow Rock, whence they were delegated to Fort Rice, in Dakota Territory, arriving there on October 10, 1865. Company "C" whose term of service had not expired, having enlisted and mustered in 1864, reached Yankton, D.T. on the 8th of September 1865. They were on their way to Fort Rice, a distance of 700 miles, and had to walk the entire journey due to the lateness of the season and low water in the Missouri River.

Brigadier Alfred Sully had begun his preparations in early 1864 for the campaign against the hostile Sioux, who were west of the Missouri and south of the Cannonball River in present-day North Dakota. The expedition left Sioux City, IA early in May. They were late in starting having been delayed by the non-arrival of steamboats containing supplies and ammunition.

The various companies of many different outfits met at old Fort Sully near Farm Island, a few miles below present day Pierre, SD. The various troops were the 6th Iowa Cavalry, three Companies of the 6th Iowa Cavalry, Minnesota Cavalry, Colonel Pope's Battery and Brackett's Battalion and Companies A and B of the Dakota Cavalry."

The expedition left Fort Sully in late June 1864 taking three days to reach the mouth of the Little Cheyenne River (SD) where an engineer was killed by a small band of Indians. The command resumed its march and reached a point a few miles above the Cannonball River. Up to this point they had stayed on the east bank of the Missouri River. They now crossed the river and proceeded to erect many buildings of what is now known as Fort Rice. When the steamboats arrived and unloaded their supplies a storehouse was erected from logs to store all of these supplies. As with most early Missouri River military posts the logs necessary to construct the various buildings were from cottonwood trees. The roofs were covered with dirt.

Fort Rice was established in 1864 and is located on the right bank of the Missouri River. The nearest telegraph and railroad station was at Bismarck, 28 miles to the north. Ft. Sully was 258 miles distance by river and Sioux City, Iowa was 503 miles by land and 750 miles by river. The nearest Indians were on the reservations at Standing Rock (Sioux) Agency down the river and Berthold (Rees) Agency up the river. The buildings on Fort Rice were: quarters for four companies; officers' quarters, eleven sets; hospital; guard house; library; seven store houses, three quartermaster buildings, three commissaries, three ordinances, two cavalry stables and four quartermaster stables. All of the foregoing buildings were built of cottonwood and pine. Quartermaster stores were furnished from a depot at Jefferson, Indiana by rail to Sioux City,

thence by boat. Hay was furnished by contract. Beef was supplied on the hoof. Water was obtained from the Missouri River by water wagons and wood supplied by contract. Twelve months' subsistence was usually kept on hand.

Fort Rice was designed for four companies of infantry, It was later modified to accommodate cavalry. During 1864 and 1865 six companies of the 1st United States Volunteers (Galvanized Yanks) comprised largely of Confederate prisoners of war, were stationed at Fort Rice. These prisoners had volunteered to fight only against the Indians

Since Fort Rice had been established to serve as a base of operations against the Sioux Indians it was necessary for the garrison to be on the alert against Indian attacks. Although no assault was ever made on the Fort itself, a number of raids were made by the Indians on the horse and cattle herds belonging to the post or traders. Attacks were also made on haying and logging parties.

On May 31, 1866 Companies A, B, C, and D set out for Madison where they were paid and discharged from the service on June 14, 1866. The official returns of this regiment are very

incomplete and furnish very sparse data from which to compile a history. Company C only sustained the loss of 2 members who died from disease at St. Louis, Missouri.

Source: George W. Kingsbury, *History of Dakota Territory*, 1915, Vol.1 p. 354.

Read the full story of Erik's life in the article "Eric Olson and Christiane Andersdatter" in Volume One.

Gilbert Anderson *published February 2013*

George and Nila Krenos wrote:

Gilbert Anderson (Gudbrand Kristoffersen in Norway) was born Sept. 9, 1841 at Olumeie, Jevnaker, died Oct. 1915 in Hollandale, Iowa County, WI. He married Pernille Johansdatter Hagen, who was born Jan. 1, 1849 at Gjervikseiet in Brandbu, Norway. She died in 1911. Both are buried in Hollandale, WI.

Gilbert Anderson entered the army at the age of eighteen at Camp Randall, Madison, Wisconsin. He was a hired replacement for Mr. Gilbert Gribble, Waldwick Township, Iowa County who was subject to the draft. This young lad drove a team of mules on a subsistence wagon throughout the South for four years with the Union army. He volunteered on Sept. 18,

1861 and was in Company "E", 11th Infantry Regiment Wisconsin Volunteers. He mustered out on Sept. 5, 1865 and reached Madison, Wisconsin on September 18, 1865. This unit was organized to serve three years but ended up serving four years.

The greatest percentage of soldiers from Wisconsin in the Civil War were volunteers. There were very few drafted. Iowa County refused to encourage enlistment by the lack of appropriation of money for the support of the deserted families. The paltry sum of six dollars monthly was paid. No other appropriations were made. The care and support of volunteers' families were turned over to the townships in which they resided. Individual groups of citizens raised subscription money to subsidize their local recruits. A bounty of $200 was paid to volunteers. Any surplus on hand after the required number of men were paid was given to the families of men already in the army.

In the fall of 1861, after the threshing and plowing were done, the volunteers assembled at Camp Randall. The 11th Wisconsin Volunteer Infantry Regiment was organized at Camp Randall, Madison, Wisconsin and mustered into service on October 18, 1861. The regiment was ordered to St. Louis, Missouri, on November 19 and then to Sulphur Springs. It served on duty there and by detachment along the Iron Mountain Railroad until March 1862. The regiment also served in Mississippi, Western Louisiana and Texas. It participated in the siege of Vicksburg, the Battle of Port Gibson, the Battle of Champion Hill and the Siege of Jackson. The regiment lost 373 men during service. Six officers and 890 enlisted men were killed or mortally wounded. Four officers and 253 enlisted men died from disease.

Sources: Lyla (Anderson) Vinje 1990
  Roster of Wisconsin Volunteers, Madison, 1866 Vol. 1, p. 692.
  Military History of Wisconsin, Clarke & Co. Chicago 1866, pp. 569-573.
  Records & Sketches of Military Organizations, Democratic Publishing, Madison, 1904.

Nils Thompson *published May 2013*

Byron Schmid wrote:

Nils Thompson enlisted in Company A, 45th Wisconsin Infantry and served from February 8, 1865 to Sept. 27, 1865. Nils was born Dec. 5, 1828 in Hvalebyeit, Hadeland and married Anne Eriksdatter on Nov. 30, 1852. Their emigration registration is dated 15 April 1853 and their oldest son emigrated with them. Their children were Erik, Ragnhild, Ingeborg, Torsten, Caroline, Edward, Andrena and Ned. Nils died Feb. 27, 1890 in York Township, Green County, Wisconsin   Nils Thompson is one of eight Hadeland emigrant soldiers buried in Adams Lutheran Church Cemetery in Green County.

Nils Volunteer Enlistment Form

The Certificate of Service states that the 45th Infantry, of which Nils was a part, returned to Madison, Wisconsin on July 23, 1865.

Peder Shager   *published May 2013*

Frank Evenson wrote:

Peder P. Shager served in Minnesota's 10th Infantry Company E. He was born Jan. 16, 1819 in Hadeland, Norway. He came from Iowa in 1857 and settled in Hartland Township, Freeborn County, Minnesota. He enlisted in the Civil War on Aug. 13, 1862 at age 43 as a private and served 21 months in the Indian and Civil Wars. In 1882 he received a pension of $6.00 a month for injury to his abdomen. He died Jan. 16, 1905 and was buried in the Hartland Township Cemetery. The cemetery shows his death as July 16, 1908. Sources: Ulvestad, p. 327; FCHS); *Pensioners on the Roll as of Jan. 1, 1883, living in Minnesota*, published 1994, Park Genealogical Books, Brooklyn Park, Minnesota.

A Freeborn County history gives the following information: "Peter P. Shager, one of the early settlers of this county, is a native of Norway, born Jan. 16, 1819. He came to America in 1849 and resided in Dane County, Wisconsin one year, afterward in Columbia County until 1854, then went to Winneshiek County, Iowa. In the spring of 1857, he came to this county and settled in Manchester until enlisting on Aug. 15, 1862 in the Tenth Minnesota Volunteer Infantry, Company E, and served 21 months. After his discharge he located on a farm in section 34, Hartland, and has since devoted his time to its cultivation."

Information about the 10th Regiment Infantry shows that Company E detached at Island No. 10 from April 27-June 15, 1864, then moved to Memphis, Tenn. on June 19-20. They were part of Smith's Expedition to Tupelo, Miss. July 5-21, in Pontotoc July 11. They were near Camargo's Cross Roads July 13, near Tupelo July 14-15, at Old Town or Tishamingo Creel July 15, on Smith's Expedition to Oxford, Miss. Aug. 1-30, to Tallahatchie River Aug. 7-9, Abbeville Aug. 23, Mower's Expedition to Duvall's Bluff, Ark. Sept. 2-9. They were part of the March through Arkansas and Missouri in pursuit of Gen. Price on Sept. 17-Nov. 15. They moved to Nashville, Tenn. Nov. 24-30, were in the Battle of Nashville Dec. 15-16, in pursuit of Gen. Hood to the Tennessee River Dec. 17-28. They moved to Clifton, Tenn., thence to Eastport, Miss. Dec. 29-Jan. 4, 1865. They saw duty at Eastport, Miss. Until Feb. 6. They were in the Campaign against Mobile, Ala. and its Defenses March 17-April 12. They were part of the siege of Spanish Fort and Fort Blakely March 26-April 8, in the assault and capture of Fort Blakely April 9, the occupation of Mobile April 12. They were on the march to Montgomery April 13-25 and duty there until May. They moved to Meridian, Miss. and duty there until July, then moved to St. Paul, Minn. and mustered out Aug. 18, 1865.

During the service the Regiment lost 2 officers and 35 enlisted men who were killed and mortally wounded, and 4 officers and 111 enlisted men died of disease, a total of 152.

Peter John Hilden   *published May 2013*

Edward Usset wrote:

Edward's Great-Uncle Peter Hilden was born July 25, 1837 on the Hildeneiet farm at Tingelstad. His parents were Johan Pedersen and Kari Larsdatter, who were married July 20, 1837 in Gran. Peter emigrated to America in June 1857, served with the First Minnesota Heavy Artillery in the Civil War and died Dec. 25, 1913. Edward found the two following references to a Peter Hilden in the Civil War records and thinks that both might refer to his great-uncle.

> HILDEN, Peder F.: From Hadeland, Norway. Civil War: Private. Post war: Lived in Montevideo, Minnesota. *Sources:* Ulvestad, p. 291.

HILDEN, J. Peter: MN Hv Arty 1st Reg Co I. Residence not shown. Born in Norway. Civil War: Age 27. Enrolled 2 Feb 1865. Mustered 9 Feb 1865. Private. Discharged from the service with his company, 27 Sep 1865. *Sources:* MINN, p. 607; MCIW, p. 632.

Edward sent the following obituary for Peter Hilden from the *Montevideo (MN) Leader,* 30 January 1914 :

Peter J. Hilden, aged 76 years, 6 months, 3 days, died at his home in Montevideo Wednesday afternoon, January 28, 1914 of pneumonia.

Mr. Hilden was born July 25, 1837 at Gran, Norway and came to this country when 19 years old and settled in Goodhue County, Minn. He was married at Belvidere, Minn. to Miss Eveline Evenson Oct. 2, 1861, and served in 1st Minnesota Co. "I," during the latter part of the war. He was for many years a trusted employee of the Charles Betcher Lumber Company at Red Wing and also here and at Appleton, and was manager of the Company's business here for several years. He was a faithful member of the Masonic Lodge and of the Grand Army Post and was a charter member of the Eastern Star Chapter and he and his wife have long been members of the Methodist Church.

They moved to Montevideo from Red Wing about 35 years ago and have always lived in the house he built when they first came here. He leaves an invalid wife and two daughters, Mrs. Minnie Kendall of Montevideo and Mrs. Helma Nordstrom of Sacred Heart, all of whom were with him at the time of his death. Two other daughters, Caroline and Hannah, died some years ago. He also leaves three brothers, Lewis Hilden of Grantsburg, Wis., Thos. Hilden of Battle Lake, Minn., and Andrew Hilden of Baudette, Minn., and one sister, Mrs. Anna Hoff, of Battle Lake. Another sister, Mrs. Martha Swenson, died at Battle Lake last summer. Mr. Hilden was a man of few words and of retiring disposition but of sterling worth and as true as steel to his high ideals of justice and duty. He was a true man, a kind neighbor, and a faithful friend.   His funeral was under charge of the Masonic Lodge that he so much loved. "An honest man, the
"An honest man, the noblest work of God."

Jacob Nielsen Nyhus   *published February 2013*

Carol Harris Weber wrote:

Jacob Nielsen Nyhus was born April 11, 1819 on the Nyhuus farm and baptized April 18 in the Gran parish. He was the son of Niels Larsen Nyhuus and Berthe Jacobsdatter. Jacob married Kari Michelsdatter Roken in Gran on October 19, 1847. Jacob previously married Kari Nielsdatter Kjos on November 17, 1842. She died February 8, 1847 after giving birth to two sons, Niels and Anders.

Jacob, Kari and their 4 sons, Niels, Anders, Christian and Mikkel were entered in the Gran parish records as leaving Gran for America on April 22, 1852. They were located in the 1860 U.S. Federal census, living in Norway Township, Racine County, Wis. Jacob and Kari had 4 more children after their arrival in Wisconsin: Julius, Charles and Gulbjor, their only daughter., and Jacob, born in 1862, probably after his father was killed.

Jacob could not be located after the 1860 census and there was a reason. Jacob Nielsen had joined the Wisconsin 15th Volunteer Regiment, Company C, called the Scandinavian Regiment, to fight in the Civil War. The regiment was organized by Colonel Hans Christian Heg at Madison, Wisconsin and mustered into Federal service on January 31, 1862. The majority of its members were Norwegian immigrants (some records state as many as 90%), with the rest mainly Danish, Swedish and Dutch. Also appearing as Jacob Nelson, he was recorded on his enlistment papers as age 43 and married. He enlisted for three years on November 5, 1861 at Waterford, Wisconsin and was mustered in as a private on December 2, 1861 at Madison. The regiment lost 241 men who died of disease, one of them being Jacob. He died at Mississippi River Island No. 10 in Tennessee on June 23, 1862 and was buried at Mississippi River National Cemetery near Memphis, Tennessee.

Jacob was a distant relative of Carol's great-grandmother. The information was taken from a genealogy book about her family.

Ole Milesteen (Milestone) *published February 2013*

Carol Emerson Schwartz wrote:

Ole Milesteen (Milestone) emigrated from Hadeland, Norway, born "Ole Halvorsen" on the Milesten farm at Grua in Lunner on 6 Feb. 1840, son of Halvor Olsen Milesten and Else Larsdatter Olimb. He came with his parents and two siblings, Dorthe and Lars, from Lunner, Oppland in 1848. They came to Springfield Township, Dane County, Wisconsin, and by 1850 moved to Perry Township, Dane County.

At age 22 and unmarried, he enlisted for three years on 23 Dec. 1861 in Dane Co. and was mustered in on 1 Jan. 1862 at Madison, Wisconsin. He had the military rank of private in the Wisconsin 15th Infantry, Company "E." He was seriously wounded and taken prisoner at the Battle of Stone's River near Murfreesboro, Tennessee on 31 Dec. 1862. He was later paroled in a prisoner exchange and then taken to a parole camp in Annapolis, Maryland before being transferred to Benton Barracks in St. Louis, Missouri. He later returned to his company and was killed in the Battle of Chickamauga on 20 Sept. 1863. He is entered on the Roll of Honor for the 2nd Brigade, 1st Division, 20th Army Corps.

Ole was Carol's great-grandfather's brother.

Sources:

Naeseth, Gerhard B., *Norwegian Immigrants to the United States: A Biographical Directory, 1825-1850,* Vol. 3, 1847-48, edited by Blaine Hedberg, published by the Norwegian American Genealogical Center, Madison, Wisconsin, 2000, p. 217.

Ulvestad, Martin, *Norwegians in America, Their History and Record:* A translated version of the 1907 and 1913 *Nordmændene i Amerika,* edited by Deb Nelson Gourley, published by Asti My Asti Publishers, 2011, p. 64.

Wisconsin Historical Society Series 1200.

George Gilbert (Gulbrand Gulbrandsen) Vinger

published May 2013

John Monson wrote:

George (or Gulbrand) was the younger brother of my great-great-grandfather, Ole Gulbrandsen Roisum (Ole Gilbertson). He came to the United States from Norway in 1850 as a 20-year-old.

George did not want to serve in the Army in the Civil War. He was one of many people who opposed the war. These people who opposed the war were called "Copperheads" because some people who supported the war claimed they were "poisonous snakes who hid in the grass."

Gulbrand was 31 when the Civil War started in 1861. Gulbrand was living on his farm in York Township, Green County, Wisconsin when he was drafted in September 1864. He was able to delay his enlistment for several months. Gulbrand served in the U.S. Army, 46th Wisconsin Volunteer Infantry, Company A, as George Gilbert, enlisting on 8 February 1865 at Monroe, Wisconsin. The Forty-sixth Wisconsin Infantry Regiment was organized at Camp Randall, Madison, WI, the last Company being mustered into the service of the United States on March 1, 1865. The regiment left the state on the 5th of March, moving to Athens, AL on the line of the Nashville & Decatur Railway, and was engaged in patrol and guard duty in that vicinity until the latter part of September, 1865, when it was transferred to Nashville, TN. The Forty-sixth was mustered out of the service of the United States on September 27, 1865. It reached Madison, WI, on October 2, 1865, and was shortly thereafter disbanded.

Gulbrand's war service record describes him as follows: WI 46th Inf. Co. A. Residence: York, Green County, Wisconsin. Enlistment credited to Clarno, Green County. Born in Norway. Civil War: Farmer. Age 35. Married. Blue eyes, sandy hair, light complexion, 5'7". Enlisted for one year on 8 Feb. 1865 at Monroe, Green County, Wisconsin. Mustered 16 Feb. 1865 at Madison, Wisconsin. Bounty $100, $33.33 paid. Private. Mustered out with this Company on 27 Sept. 1865 at Nashville, Tennessee.

Gulbrand's views on the war were well known in the Argyle Community. An A. Anderson wrote to Rollin Olson, who was in service at the time, in either September or October 1864, including this note in the letter. "I can tell you Gulbrand Vinger also is drafted. He has not escaped and they say he is a Copperhead and therefore I wish him luck on his journey."[1] Those people in the northern states opposed to the war, or sympathetic to the South, were called Copperheads.

The author of the biography of Gulbrand and his son Christian written in 1901 obviously learned that Gulbrand had been a soldier, but probably knew none of the background history. He wrote: "Gulbrand G. Vinger served as a soldier in the Union army during the Civil War, making a record as a gallant and loyal son of his adopted country. He is now retired, enjoying the fruits of a useful and well-spent life.[2]

Please note: The insult "Copperhead" was used by Republicans to refer to those who opposed the war, the Peace Democrats, who were a very large minority in the North in early 1864. At that time "Copperhead" did not specifically refer to anyone's position on slavery. Only later in the 1800s did it come to imply that the person being insulted was both opposed to the war and in favor of slavery. Remember that until Dec. 6, 1865, slavery was legal in the United States, except for those states which had specifically outlawed it, and in the Southern Territory occupied by the North as of Jan. 1, 1863. This included most of Tennessee and large portions of Louisiana and Arkansas.

---

1 Olson, Rollin, *Civil War Letters,* no date, no page numbers
2 *Commemorative Biographical Record of the Counties of Rock, Green, Grant, Iowa; and Lafayette, Wisconsin*; published 1901, pages 750-751.

Anders Olsen Tokerud   *published November 2013*

Dave Gunderson wrote:

My grandmother had given me a picture of a Civil War soldier, shortly before she died in 1965. The only thing she knew was that his name was Anders Olsen Tokerud and he was my grandfather's uncle. As you well know, in the "pre-computer age", genealogy research was tedious. When I resumed research in the late 1980's, I found relatives that knew a little more. I was told he served in the Union Army from Wisconsin. There were at least 5 copies of the picture in the various branches of the family. All copies were treasured! You can see the stand where they clamped the neck so that the soldier did not move while the picture was being taken.

Private Anders Olsen Tokerud

From his uniform, he was clearly in the cavalry. I was advised that "Anders Olsen" would have been routinely modified to be "Andrew Olson." From my research, I had learned that only two men named Andrew Olson served in the cavalry in Wisconsin. I also learned that Ole Olsen Tokerud, the oldest brother of Anders had come with his wife Anna Jacobsdatter, and his brother Nils, in 1861. They came from the Bjoneroa of Hadeland. The whole family is on skjema 450. They initially settled by Yorkville, Wisconsin, just west of Racine. One of the two Andrew Olsons had enlisted in Company K, 2nd Wisconsin Cavalry on August 20, 1864, at Delavan, Wisconsin. That had to be the correct one.

You can write to the National Archives and request the Civil War service records of any soldier providing you have the name and exact unit. The current form is NATF Form 86. I did order the records. From them I learned that he was 5'7" tall, had blue eyes and brown hair. There are a number of websites that list information on Civil War Army unites. The 2nd Wisconsin Cavalry spent most of its time in 1864 and 1865 in southern Missouri and the Vicksburg area of western Mississippi. In the Civil War, the 2nd Wisconsin Cavalry Regiment had 24 men killed in action. 284 died of disease. As the Civil War ended, the United States Army began to shift large units to the Texas border with Mexico. Because Anders only had

two months left in his enlistment, he was discharged June 14, 1865, at Memphis, Tennessee.

How much money did he receive for his Civil War Service? He received a bonus of $100.00 [$33.33 paid on enlistment, the balance was paid on discharge]. He received $32.00 in pay every two months. In February, 1865, he was charged $.48 for losing ordnance. In subsequent years, I learned that Anders had been born at Hollingdalen in Sondre Land. With the exception of his brother Nils, everyone else in the family was born in Hadeland. My great grandmother, Elena Olsdatter Tokerud was born at Brunstad. My great, great grandfather, Ole Olsen Tokerud was born at Putten in 1805. His wife, Kari Nielsdatter was born at Avtjern in 1805. In 1866, the parents of Anders, his two sisters and one nephew came to the Decorah area. I'm sure that his hard-earned bonus and wages played a significant role in paying for their transportation from Hadeland.

I also learned that Anders Olsen Tokerud died November 3, 1867, age 24. He is buried at Washington Prairie Lutheran Church, just southeast of Decorah. I thought it would have been surprising if he didn't get malaria during his military service. I subsequently got a Minnesota veteran's flag marker for his grave so that he can be honored on Memorial Day with an American Flag. In Iowa, each cemetery gets $25.00 from the State for the upkeep of each veteran's grave.

The story doesn't end here! A few years ago, Ancestry.com put Civil War pension index cards on-line. As I knew Anders died in 1867, I was quite surprised to learn that he applied for a veteran's pension in 1906 in Manistee, Michigan! Again, you can also request pension records using Form NATF 85, from the National Archives. I did request the 1906 pension file. The pension file stated that Andrew Olson, "alias" Nils Olson, was a disabled veteran who deserved a pension. It stated that Andrew Olson, aka Nils Olson was born February 28, 1843. Unfortunately, the "real" Andrew (Anders) was born September 25, 1843. The brother Nils Olsen was actually born February 28, 1840 in

Anders Olsen Tokerud's gravestone

Sondre Land. For the fraudulent pension application, he changed his year of birth to the same year as that of his brother. However, he kept his month and day of birth! Clearly Nils Olsen Tokerud was in pretty poor health to try something like this. Obviously, he must have kept his brother's army discharge after his death in 1867. Nils did not get a pension! Nils subsequently died April 6, 1914. There was one other thing in the pension file that was quite interesting. There were actually medical records from the Civil War for Anders Olsen Tokerud. It said he had "remittent fevers" from October 14 to October 23, 1864; January 18 to February 2, 1865; March 17 to April 3, 1865; and April 13 to April 22, 1865. Clearly Anders had malaria.

His service in the Civil War clearly provided most of the money that allowed the rest of his family to leave Norway. They were very willing to pay for a cemetery marker for "*Ungkarl* Anders Olsen Tokerud!"

The National Archives has a very nice web site for requesting military service or pension records. Their website is www.archives.gov/con-tact/inquire-form.html.

At the 2013 stevne, Mr. Gunderson sponsored the showing of the feature movie "Lincoln" in honor of Anders Olsen Tokerud.

572

Hadelanders Who Served During World War I 1917-1918

   The following list of soldiers with roots in Hadeland who served during World War I was compiled by Ole P. Gamme of Kontaktforum Hadeland-Amerika. In 1921, lag members submitted the names of their veterans for publication in the lag yearbook. The yearbook is available in its entirety in the resources section of the Hadeland Lag website. Additions were made from the database of Hadeland emigrants and from submissions from current members. The associated Emigrant Identification Database forms (available in the Limited Access Archive on the Hadeland Lag website) are listed for individuals for whom the connection could be determined. A handful of soldiers were identified as Hadelanders in other sources but it has not yet been possible to collect enough information to create a family form.

- Pvt Alfred L Amunrud, Decorah, IA (1888-1954) Form 415
- Pvt Peder A Anderson
- Pvt Andrew Anderson, Plymouth, IA, (1896-1976) Form 2
- Pvt Oscar Alfred Alm, Binford, ND (1893-1951) Form 7
- Pvt Ole Alm, Minneapolis, MN (1887-1972) Form 6
- Pvt Edwin Alm, Randall, MN (1896-1979) Form 6
- Sgt Alfred Parnell Anderson Kindred, ND (1894-1984) Form 1619
- Pvt Carl Peter Amundson, Northwood, ND (1894-1971) Form 489
- Pvt Oscar C Anderson, Lanesboro, MN
- Pvt Axel Paulson Borgie, St Hilaire, MN (1894-1918) Form 1120
- Pvt Fred Bilden, Clermont, IA (1895-1967) Form 544
- Pvt Einar A Bakke, Maddock, ND (1897-1981) Form 661
- Pvt Bennie Alfred Benson, Cresco, IA (1895-1970) Form 1137
- Pvt Melvin Helmer Benson, Cresco, IA (1893-1973) Form 1137
- Pvt Julius Albert Bolson, Decorah, IA (1897-1961) Form 239
- Sgt Stephen Benjamin Bolson, Decorah, IA (1894-1970) Form 239
- Pvt Guldbrand Bjellum, Glasgow, MT (1893-1983) Form 1118
- Pvt Oscar M Blegen, Spring Grove, MN (1895-1983) Form 538
- Pvt Ignus T Blegen, Spring Grove, MN (1893-1974) Form 538
- Pvt John Christian Bjerke, Decorah, IA (1892-1975) Form 754

- Pvt Willie Borgie, St Hilaire, MN (1896-1972) Form 1120
- Cpl Harold Berg, Blanchardville, WI (1896-1978) Form 104
- Pvt Kristian Adolph Bartleson, Forest City, IA (1895-1972) Form 11
- Pvt Peter Bartleson, jr, Forest City, IA (1889-1970) Form 11
- Pvt Bernhard Bakke, Kempton, ND (1893-1965) Form 27
- Pvt Julius Blegen, Elgin, IA (1874-1939) Form 756
- Pvt Rudolph C Brandon, Campbell, SD (1891-1935) Form 16
- Pvt Joseph Bilden, Northwood, ND (1895-1972) Form 544
- Pvt Elmer O Broden, Montfort, WI (1892-1967) Form 386
- Pvt Edwin O Bjerke, Hatton, ND (1891-1970) Form 13
- Pvt Louis Bratvold, Maddock, ND (1898-1989) Form 347
- Pvt Ellef Hagbart Bratvold, Gem, ID (1889-1958) Form 477
- Pvt Emil Bratvold, Maddock, ND (1891-1987) Form 347
- Cpl Grover Carlson, Dawson, MN (1994-1969) Form 119 & 793
- Pvt Amund Olsen Chose (Kjos), Winnebago, IA (1890-1918) Form 1002
- Cpl James Carlin Dvergsten, Spring Grove, MN (1898-1973) Form 216
- Pvt Peter Arthur Dvergsten, Spring Grove, MN (1894-1957) Form 216
- Pvt Oscar Arnold Dahlen, Kindred, ND (1894-1918) Form 32
- Cpl Peder J Dahlen, Kindred, ND (1881-1953) Form 32
- Pvt Erwin S Dahlen, Kindred, ND (1896-1978) Form 32
- Pvt Grover Daves, Montfort, WI (1892-) Form 386
- Pvt George Dewey Davis, Montfort, WI (1898-) Form 386
- Cpl Norman A Eid, Flaming, MN (1896-1955) Form 40
- Pvt Albert Evans, Williams, IA (1889-1977) Form 995
- Sgt Anton J Eid, Flaming, MN (1891-1976) Form 40
- Pvt Sophus Evanson, Northwood, ND (1895-1974) Form 558
- Pvt Henry Edward Emberson, Blanchardville, WI (1899-1948) Form 1255
- Pvt John M Everson, Argyle, WI (1892-1972) Form 1624
- Pvt Perry O Everson, Argyle, WI (1891-1985) Form 1624
- Pvt Hans Edward Evenson, Northwood, ND (1890-1985) Form 558
- Pvt Albert Erickson, Christine, ND (1889-1973) Form 1337
- Pvt Carl Erickson, Christine, ND (1896-) Form 1337
- Cpl Frederick Tildman Erickson "Korson," Leonard, ND (1894-1922) Form 746
- Pvt Melvin P Enge, Davenport, ND
- Pvt Arthur Erickson, Valley Springs, SD (1888-1918) Form 859

- Pvt Garfield Oluf Fjeld, Hatton, ND (1893-1960) Form 786
- Pvt Oscar Edwin Flaten, Spring Grove, MN (1894-1973) Form 565
- Pvt Elmer Foss, Hagen, ND (1893-1967) Form 125
- Cpl Fredrick Foss, Hagen, ND (1895-1931) Form 125
- Pvt Henry Flaten, Hawley, MN (1895-1968) Form 860
- Pvt Magnus Flaten, Gildford, MT (18911983) Form 860
- Pvt Olaf Theodore Goodno, Dorchester, IA (1898-1987) Form 665
- Pvt Odin Einar Gjerdingen, Starbuck, MN (1895-1976) Form 330
- Pvt Albert H Gunderson, Northwood, ND (1890-1932) Form 153
- Pvt Harold Olaus Gunderson, Forest City, IA (1900-1949) Form 450
- Pvt Walter M Goodno, Darchester, IA (1893-1980) Form 665
- Pvt Peter Grina, Northwood, ND (1890-1955) Form 314
- Pvt Clarence Grina, Northwood, ND (1894-1918) Form 314
- Pvt Clarence Sigvald Gisleson, Orchard, IA (1894-1959) Form 49
- Pvt William Gilbertson, Hazel, MN (1897-1970) Form 1120
- Albert Theodore Gilbertson, Northwood, ND (1894-1969) Form 461
- Sgt Edwin N Gullerud, Maddock, ND (1893-1972) Form 56
- Cpl Bernie Gilbertson, Montford, WI
- Pvt Gustave T Gilbertson, Fennimore, WI (1891-1949) Form 468
- Quartermaster Arnold T Gulbrandson, Pequot, MN (1896-1953) Form 1620
- Pvt Oluf Helmey, Madison, SD (1889-1965) Form 22
- Pvt Dorf Henry Holverson, Clermont, IA (1888-)
- Seaman Howard M Hendrickson, Blanchardville, WI (1896-1981) Form 88
- Pvt Amos Henry Haug, Willow Lake, SD (1891-1968) Form 81
- Quartermaster Carl Gustave Hanson, Winchester, WI (1899-1975) Form 537
- Sgt Oscar Holman, Sedalia, Alberta, Canada (1897-1968) Form 917
- Quartermaster Leonard Alvin Haakenstad, Montevideo, MN (1898-1985) Form 79
- Pvt Lloyd A Hendrickson, Blanchardville, WI (1888-1962) Form 88 and 639
- Cpl Guy E Hendrickson, Blanchardville, WI (1893-1962) Form 88 and 639
- Pvt Andrew Hoff, Blanchardville, WI (1890-1954) Form 963
- Pvt David Hendrickson, Blanchardville, WI (1894-1918) Form 464
- Pvt Alvin A Halvorsen, Northwood, ND (1887-1970) Form 516
- Hassel N Halvorson, Northwood, ND (1894-1988) Form 516
- Pvt Joseph O Holt, Northwood, ND (1891-1983) Form 320
- Melvin Holt, Northwood, ND (1896-1960) Form 320

- Elmer Holt, Northwood, ND (1893-1980) Form 320
- Pvt Joseph Clarence Holte, Northwood, ND (1897-1967) Form 559
- Pvt Arthur Holverson, Moorhead, IA (1894-1919) Form 617
- Lt Arthur Edward Helo, Velva, ND
- Pvt Albert I Hagen, Northwood, ND (1889-1958) Form 466
- Pvt Joseph Hanson, White Earth, ND (1896-1982)
- Pvt Ole Ben Helgeson, Enderline, ND (1896-1971) Form 1537
- Pvt Theodore Daniel Hanson, Elgin, IA (1894-1956) Form 58
- Wag Peter C Hendrickson, Waukon, IA (1893-1979) Form 912
- Pvt Everett Andrew Hanson, Galveston Co, TX (1894-1971) Form 1236
- Pvt Leslie Julian Hanson, Galveston Co, TX (1891-1942) Form 1236
- Pvt Roy Hanson, Albert Lea, MN (1890-1969) Form 110
- Pvt Marvin Haugen, Glasgow, MT
- Cpl Everett L Heggen, Garretson, SD (1894-1968) Form 909
- Pvt Helmar W Hoff, Garretson, SD (1893-1919) Form 996
- Pvt Edwin Engebretson, Fertile, MN (1893-1918) Form 1143
- Pvt Sivert Ingebretson, Fertile, MN (1893-1975) Form 1143
- Pvt Frank Wilmer Ingwell, Blanchardville, WI (1895-1960) Form 87
- Pvt Grant Leroy Ingwell, Blanchardville, WI (1897-1972) Form 87
- Cpl Herman Johnson, Clermont, IA (1893-1969) Form 293
- Pvt Julius Jackson, Wilson, WI (1888-1938) Form 872
- Pvt Bernt Jackson, Wilson, WI (1887-1962) Form 872
- Pvt Lewis Jackson, Wilson, WI (1892-1952) Form 872
- Pvt Carmie Jackson, Wilson, WI
- Sgt Alvin R Jackson, Argyle, WI (1889-1969) Form 95
- Pvt Millard Johnson, Clermont, IA (1898-1927) Form 17
- Pvt Herman Johnson, Clermont, IA (1893-1969) Form 17
- Pvt Alvin Theodore Jorgenson, Grafton, ND (1896-1986) Form 135
- Sgt Arthur Edwin Kammerud, Rhinelander, WI (1895-1938) Form 106
- Sgt Jens Olaf Kittelsrud, Ethridge, MT (1892-1928) Form 969
- Pvt Edwin O Kjos, Flaming, MN (1896-1958) Form 684
- Sgt Julien L Knudson, Osage, IA (1892-1966) Form 49
- Herman M Knudson, Osage, IA (1887-1977) Form 49
- Pvt Martin Lahren, Mandan, ND (1895-1980) Form 1034
- Pvt Kristian Larsen, Meroa, IA (1891-1936) Form 670

- Pvt Amos C Lee, Moorhead, IA (1898-1994) Form 39
- Pvt Carl Lee, Osage, IA (1890-1922) Form 126
- Pvt Arnold M Lee, Jamestown, ND (1896-1985) Form 768
- Sgt Carl J Lee, Jamestown, ND (1887-1973) Form 768
- Pvt Orrin Leo Lee, Moorhead, IA (1900-1974) Form 34
- Pvt Norman Lee, Hudson, WI (1893-1970) Form 152
- Miss Karen Marie Lynner, Maddock, ND (1901-1990) Form 721
- Pvt Halvor Locken, Plaza, ND (1896-1971) Form 735
- Sgt Eddie Merkle Lee, Hudson, WI (1895-1963) Form 152
- Pvt Lloyd Palmer Larson, Argyle, WI (1897-1957) Form 544
- Sgt Alvin Palmer Larsen, Argyle, WI (1890-1985) Form 544
- Cpl Ingval Lynner, Clarkfiel, MN (1893-1975) Form 124
- Pvt Eli A Loe, Northwood, ND (1892-1976) Form 288
- Pvt Jule Larson, Montfort, WI (1892-1962) Form 382
- Denziel J Loe, Northwood, ND (1897-1963) Form 288
- Sgt Olaf L Larson, Montevideo, MN
- Pvt Herbert A Moe, Calmar, IA (1894-1959) Form 134
- Pvt Jesse Mahlum, Wadena, Sask, Canada
- Pvt Leo John Molstad, Hartland, MN (1897-1967) Form 130
- Pvt Martin Martinson, Fargo, ND (1891-1922) Form 137
- Pvt George Martinson, Fargo ND (1898-1975) Form 137
- Pvt Joseph Martinson, Minneapolis, MN (1895-1940) Form 137
- Pvt Arnold Gustave Melbostad, Spring Grove, MN (1894-1984) Form 515
- Pvt Palmer Hanson Molden, Mayville, ND (1892-1984) Form 516
- Pvt Gilman Morstad, Grand Forks, ND (1888-1918) Form 682
- Pvt Oscar A Mohagen, Grafton, ND (1899-1918) Form 135
- Wag Henry Oscar Nelson, Clermont, IA (1887-1959) Form 1160
- Pvt Edwin Clarence Nelson, Fennimore, WI (1893-1984) Form 430
- Mechanic Carl Benjamin Nelson, Excelsior, WI (1896-1971) Form 228
- Pvt Charles O Nelson, Elgin, IA (1892-1968) Form 614
- Pvt Earnest C Nelson, Fennimore, WI (1897-1959) Form 430
- Pvt Andrew Olerud, Wentworth, SD (1891-1966) Form 152
- Pvt Lloyd Olson, Argyle, WI (1893-1972) Form 1340
- Pvt Clarence Myron Olson, Argyle, WI (1888-1954) Form 507
- Cpl Richard Nels Olson, Austin, MN (1898-1972)

-
- Pvt Namen Joseph Olson, Blanchardville, WI (1890-1963) Form 1340
- Pvt Lars Onsager, Valley City, ND (1889-1966) Form 150
- Pvt Gustav B Onsager, Waukon, IA (1892-1963) Form 150
- Louis Teman Onsager, Vernon Co, WI (1892-1918) Form 156
- Pvt Palvin Paulson, Mayville, ND (1892-1966) Form 159
- Wag Alfred L Paulson, Plaza, ND (1894-1986) Form 711
- Pvt Clark Pederson, Ashby, MN (1894-1918)
- Pvt Anton G Pederson, Fertile, MN (1897-1986) Form 685
- Wag Peter Paulson, Plaza, ND (1895-1966) Form 711
- Pvt Alfred Pederson, Ashby, MN (1896-1982)
- Pvt George Pederson, Fertile, MN (1893-1958) Form 685
- Pvt Albee Paulson, Argyle, WI (1895-1980) Form 157
- Pvt Peder Pederson, New Richmond, WI (1888-1961) Form 218
- Pvt Hassel (Hazel) Peterson, C p V E Hdq Co 1, A P O 717, A E F
- Cpl Jonnie Peterson, Barronette, WI (1895-1974) Form 630
- Pvt Alfred Peterson, Barronette, WI (1889-1972) Form 630
- Pvt Arnold C Quenrud, Decorah, IA (1895-1954) Form 308
- Pvt Anders J Rekstad, Willow Lake, SD (1890-1949) Form 169
- Mechanic Hans A Rekstad, Willow Lake, SD (1890-1957) Form 169
- Pvt Gilman W Ruud, Northwood, ND (1891-1977) Form 449
- Cpl Andrew O Rossum, Seven Persons, Alberta (1888-) Form 171
- Pvt Harold Melvin Sandbeck, Williams, MN (1893-1951) Form 1199
- Pvt Peter Hanson Stadum, Sioux Falls, SD (1887-1976) Form 1244
- Lt Peter Bernard Saug, Osage, IA (1885-) Form 1013
- Pvt Helge Hanson Stadum, Sioux Falls, SD (1897-1996) Form 1244
- Lt Conrad E Sandvold, Moorhead, IA (1896-1989) Form 185
- Pvt Christian August Stensvold, Braham, MN (1897-1996) Form 1198
- Carl Oscar Stensvold, Braham, MN (1894-1918) Form 1198
- Pvt Pateo Oscar Sorum, Blancardville, WI (1893-1938) Form 184
- Pvt Julius Schoien, Elgin, IA (1889-1941) Form 58
- Pvt Christ Sherva, Ollie, MT (1893-1970) Form 324
- Pvt Justin Smedshammer, Litchville, ND (1897-1988) Form 179
- Pvt Ludvig Skjerva, Hawley, MN (1896-1977) Form 1222
- Pvt Peder Skari, Kindred, ND (1887-1975) Form 177

- Pvt Edwin Skari, Kindred, ND (1895-1949) Form 177
- Francis Schulkey, Grand Forks, ND (1898-1955) Form 493
- Pvt Alfred Simonson, Viking, MN (1896-1982) Form 732
- Cpl Lars J Smedsrud, Bottineau, ND (1898-1990) Form 693
- Albert H Gunderson, Northwood, ND (1890-1932) Form 153
- Mechanic Oscar Thompson, Elgin, IA (1889-1978) Form 891
- Pvt Olaf Thorson, Brandon, SD (1897-1984) Form 242
- Pvt Alfred Torgerson, Moorhead, IA (1890-1918) Form 1178
- Pvt Olaf Ingeman Tilleraas, Spring Grove, MN (1890-1981) Form 665
- Pvt Ingvald Tingvold, Canton, SD (1896-1978) Form 1322
- Pvt Iver Arthur Thorson, Spring Grove, MN Form 242
- Pvt Clarence E Thompson, Blanchardville, WI (1894-1941) form 75
- Pvt Walter M Teslow, Hayward, MN (1892-1975) Form 200
- Raymond L Teslow, Hayward, MN (1900-1951) Form 200
- Edwin Tingelstad, Silverton, OR (1890-1975) Form 202
- Pvt Stanley Tangen, Northwood, ND Form 493
- Pvt Melvin A Tveten, Maddock, ND Form 781
- Joseph Tandberg, Northwood, ND (1900-1918) Form 327
- Pvt Henry M Ulvick, Aneta, ND (1898-1985) Form 203
- Sgt Elmer Kenneth Walby, Hudson WI (1891-1966) Form 207
- Sgt Orville Perry Walby, Hudson WI (1891-1966) Form 207
- Gena Josephine Wamstad, Calmar, IA (1885-1951) Form 210
- Mechanic Harry Wold, Plaza, ND (1892-1972) Form 571
- Mrs Helene Framstad Wagner, Lincoln, NE (1891-1941) Form 205
- Pvt Walter Leonard Welo, Velva, ND (1896-1958) Form 1294
- Pvt George Watkins, Argyle, WI (1888-1949) Form 1145
- Pvt Orville Watkins, Argyle, WI (1894-1948) Form 1145
- Pvt Casper Miller Walby, Clear Lake, WI (1896-1967) Form 208
- Pvt Harry Norman Walby, Clear Lake, WI, (1894-1918) Form 208
- Pvt Arthur Manuel Walby, Clear Lake, WI (1891-1863) Form 208
- Pvt Clarence J Walby, Derona, WI (1892-1968) Form 567
- Arthur Walby, Osette, MT (1894-1973) Form 567
- Pvt John A Winden, Northwood, ND (1896-1918) Form 1092

Index by First Name

This index spans both volume one and volume two of the "Our Hadeland Ancestors" collection. Page numbers for volume two begin with 289.

Where only a first name appears in the text, if discernible an appropriate patronymic and/or surname has been added to the index to assist with identification.

Norwegian immigrants were unfamiliar with the idea of last name as family name. In Norway the third name was the name of the farm on which the individual resided; if residence changed, so did the 'last' name. This, coupled with a desire to Americanize both first and last names, meant that most immigrants tried out a variety of names and spellings before settling on a permanent moniker. Variations in spelling and alternative names that appear in the text are all included in this index.

This index is available to the public in the 'Resources' section of the Hadeland Lag website, www.hadelandlag.org

Anders Nilsen 552
Anders Nyhus 567,568
Anders O Daehlen 64,66
Anders Olerud 33,34
Anders Olesen 104
Anders Olsen 540
Anders Olsen 103,175,420,552
Anders Olsen Dælen 236
Anders Olsen Plomasen 176
Anders Olsen Tokerud 420,570-572
Anders Olsen Wamstad 459
Anders Olumeje 37
Anders Pedersen 439,495,501,
    512,553
Anders Pederson 494
Anders Pederson,Mrs 544
Anders Pederson Falla 494
Anders Plomasen 180-184
Anders Sandbakken 416
Anders Stadum 307
Anders Thoreson Kittelsrud 518
Anders Wahl 116,122,124
Anders Western 203
Andew Collier 276
Andrea Brauner 127
Andreas Andersen 511
Andreas Arnesen 79
Andreas Falla 488,491
Andreas Ingwell 415
Andreas Jensen Vaterud 375
Andreas Myhre 488
Andreas Nilsen Berger 61,62
Andreas P Overland 239
Andreas Thingelstad 51
Andreas Torsteinsen Hvamstad
    459,464
Andrena Thompson 564
Andres Anderson 143
Andres Bakken 549
Andres Gulbrandson 144,147
Andres Johnson 201
Andrew A Egge 56
Andrew Andersen 494
Andrew Anderson 79,563
Andrew Ayen 451
Andrew Bakke 326
Andrew C Bakke 322
Andrew Christofferson 239
Andrew Collier 275,280
Andrew Dybdahl 206,207
Andrew Eggebraaten 56
Andrew Ekonger 191
Andrew Gilbertson 140,141,143,548

Andrew Gulbrandson 144
Andrew Gulden 106
Andrew H Larson 126
Andrew Haga 53
Andrew Hagen 290
Andrew Harris 399
Andrew Hendrickson 550
Andrew Hilden 567
Andrew Hoff 565
Andrew Ingebretsen 31,32
Andrew J Haga 51
Andrew Jackson 551
Andrew Jenson 373
Andrew Johnsen 212,213
Andrew Johnson 201,297
Andrew Kanten 156
Andrew Kjos 552
Andrew Kolberg 242
Andrew Larson 172,173,507
Andrew Larson Dynna 468
Andrew Lee 298
Andrew Lofsvold 85
Andrew Moger 526
Andrew Nelson 271
Andrew O Rossum 578
Andrew O Tokerud 552
Andrew Olaf Scott 423
Andrew Olerud 577
Andrew Olsen 105
Andrew Olson 39,561
Andrew Opperud 540
Andrew Østen 28,29,30
Andrew P Ostlie 142,147
Andrew Peder Wek 321
Andrew Pedersen Kroshus 253
Andrew Pederson 143
Andrew Peterson 167,540
Andrew Peterson Smerud 553
Andrew Rasmus Wahl 116
Andrew Rekstad 159,162,165
Andrew Rufus Wahl 116
Andrew S Ellingson 408
Andrew Shoger 460
Andrew Simensen Østen 26,27
Andrew Stadum 306,307,308,309
Andrew Thingelstad 51,52,53
Andrew Thomas Wamstad 459
Andrew Tingelstad 235
Andrew Torgerson 367
Andrew Wahl 127,136
Andrew Wamstad 463,465-471
Andrus Olerud 34
Andy Gilbertson 388

Angela Bianco 183
Angela Charles 481
Angele Marion 361
Angeline Bjorgan 163
Ann Gilbertson 511-514
Ann Grinaker Johnsen 218
Ann Hewitt 477
Anne Hilden 99
Ann Maria Oleson 234
Ann Swingen 448
Anna Andersdtr Askim 32
Anna Arnesdtr Blekeneier 12
Anna B Bakken 133,134
Anna Berg 514
Anna Bertha Scott 423
Anna Borghild Karine Wahl 136,137
Anna Brørby 309,315
Anna C Nelson 481
Anna Collier 275,280
Anna Ericksdtr 200
Anna Erickson 246
Anna Erikine Gregersdtr Hultin Koller
    283
Anna Fensand 514
Anna Gilbertson 83,447,448,454,456
Anna Gilbertson Hanson 453
Anna Grinaker Johnson 223
Anna Gulbrandsdtr Gilbertson
    441,442
Anna Gulbrandson 466
Anna Haga 406,407
Anna Hansdtr 14
Anna Hansdtr Kingestuen 308
Anna Hansdtr Wang 532
Anna Hanson 296,454
Anna Haugtvedt 424
Anna Hilden Hoff 567
Anna Husby 194
Anna Irene Erikson 246
Anna Jacobsdtr Bakke 420
Anna Johanna Paulson 444
Anna Johansdtr 369
Anna Johnson 117,496,535,543
Anna Jorgensdtr 32
Anna Jorve 502,503
Anna Josephine Kjos 477
Anna Julia Osldtr Tokerud 421
Anna K Langeland 559
Anna Karine Hendrickson 454
Anna Karlsdtr 492
Anna Kjos 477,478
Anna Kjos Milsten 472,475,476
Anna Knutsdtr Bjorgo Langeland 559

Carrie Wamstad 459
Carrie Watrud 373
Carriene Peterson 468
Carriene Wamstad 467
Carroll Johnson 222
Carroll Lewis Klovstad 134
Carry Pedersen 445
Cary Holverson 456
Cary Rear 507
Caspar Andersen 38
Casper Edward Olson 39
Casper Larson Rud 507
Casper Miller Walby 579
Casper William Rud 509
Catherine E Skinner Wahl 116
Catherine Peterson 486
Chad Anderson 183
Charle LouAnn Bakken 134
Charlene Nelson 481
Charles A Johnson 542,543
Charles Arlandson 364
Charles Butler,Mrs 369
Charles Clausen 558
Charles Collier 280
Charles Edwin Lee 444
Charles Ekanger 191
Charles Eugene Flandrau 265
Charles Falk 478
Charles Falk,Mrs 242
Charles Francis Bakken 134
Charles Garfield Plomasen 181
Charles Gerard 527
Charles Gilbert 549
Charles Gutzmer 375
Charles Hanson 279,280
Charles Harper 341
Charles John Arlandson 366
Charles Johnson 477
Charles Keeney 158
Charles L Bell Dean 455
Charles Lafflin 97
Charles Nyhus 568
Charles O Nelson 577
Charles P Pedersen 446
Charles Peder Johnson 335,337
Charles Peder Pedersen 446
Charles Plomasen 182,184
Charles Rood 386
Charles Victor Lee 445
Charles Wamstad 468
Charley Lafflin 97
Charley Pedersen 445
Charlotte Amelia Aas 122

Charlotte Cornelia Anderson 134
Charlotte Jones 162
Charlotte Marick 32
Charlotte Olivia Nielsdtr 136
Charlotte Wahl 137,138
Charlotte Watrud 376
Charoline Western 203
Cherit Dilley 275
Cheryie Golpin 276
Chester Bourdeaux 361,362
Chester Gardas 361
Chester Nelson 481
Chester William Johnson 121
Chick Lafflin 97
Chris Albertson 549
Chris Hanson 441,455
Chris Sorum 94-101,380
Chris Vinger 417
Chrisian Nyhus 568
Christ Bjone 424,428
Christ Peterson,Mrs 203
Christ Ruden 548
Christ Sherva 578
Christen Christensen 236
Christen Frederik 209
Christen Horgen 342
Christen Jørgensen 288
Christen Lagesen 81
Christen Tobiason 82,84
Christian Andersen 473
Christian August Stensvold 578
Christian Bjone 426
Christian Carlson Berg 475
Christian Carl Vane 545
Christian E Milsten 478,479
Christian Engebretsen Hendrickson 511
Christian Ericksen Smedshammer 473
Christian Eriksen 548
Christian Fredrikson Fosse 83
Christian Frengen 514
Christian Gudbrandsen 548
Christian H Milsten 478,479
Christian Helgaker 319
Christian Hendrickson 512
Christian Jacobsen 550
Christian Jacobson,Mrs 558
Christian Jensen 336
Christian Jensen Johnson 551
Christian Kittelsrud 521
Christian Kjos 472,474,476,478
Christian Larsen 377

Christian Larson 550,560-561
Christian Magelson,Pastor 521
Christian Merle Lowe Sorum 100
Christian Merle Sorum 95
Christian Milsten 479
Christian O Bye 20
Christian Olsen 496,507,508,552
Christian Pederson 120
Christian Sherva 408
Christian Shoger 460
Christian Tandberg 548
Christian Theodore Gilbertson 131
Christian Thoreson Kittelsrud 515-522
Christian Torgersen 553
Christian Vinger 570
Christiane Andersdtr 37-41
Christiane Engebretsdtr 72
Christiane Nielsdtr 233
Christiania Ingebretsdtr 167,168
Christiania Ingebretsdtr Larsen Erickson 169
Christie Melbostad 254
Christin Pedersen 252
Christina A Gilbertson 452
Christina Enarson 137
Christina Oleson 234
Christina Tingelstad 235
Christine Amelia Gilbertson 453
Christine Anderson 396
Christine Campbell 235
Christine Damm 454
Christine Ericksdtr 37,38,39
Christine Eriksdtr Olson Dalen 394
Christine Gilbertson 447
Christine Hanson 374
Christine Hanson Davis 376
Christine Helgren 359,361
Christine Jensdtr 545
Christine Mohagen Stark 258,262
Christine Nickoline Mohagen 257
Christine Olsdtr 233
Christine Olsdtr Allergodt 233
Christine Olson 471
Christine Tingelstad 235
Christoffer Halvorsen 549
Christon Hanson 454
Christopher Andersen 547
Christopher Dybdahl 207
Christopher Gunderson 15
Christopher Ingebretsen Emerson 550
Christopher Kollecas 179

I-8

Gjori Nelson 23
Gjori Torstenson 20
Gladys Florence Lee 444
Gladys Irene Gilbertson 131
Gladys Johnson 411
Gladys Marie Christianson 487
Gladys Marjory Wek 321
Gladys Opal Torgerson 369
Glen Ruel Anderson 183
Glenn Haga 406,408,409
Glenn Johnson 335,337
Glorianne Nelson 527
Glynn H Rasmussen 457
Gordan Hiram Munger 120
Gordon Alfred Stark 262
Gordon Gilbertson 83
Gordon Grimson 341
Gordon Haga 411
Gordon Stark 261
Gordon Willard Pedersen 446
Gorm the Old,King 283
Goro Andersdtr 77
Goro Andersdtr Gunderson Marion 357-366
Goro Eidsand 213
Goro Engebrettsdtr Stomne 540
Goro Gamme 3
Goro Olsdtr 540
Goro Schiager 87
Grace Evelyn Aschim 76
Grace Geneva Vickerman 527
Grace L Larson 126
Grace Lenon 126
Grace Louisa Ryder 446
Grace Plomasen 176,181,184
Grant Leroy Ingwell 576
Greg Larson 172
Greg Plath 226
Gregers Hultin 283
Gregory F Michno 559
Grete Taaje 342
Grethe Johnsrud 390
Gro Thorson 175,180
Gro Thorson Plomasen 176
Grover Carlson 564
Grover Daves 564
Gubjor Larsdtr 381-383
Gubjor Larsen 377
Gubjør Pettersdtr 202
Gubjør Western 202
Gudbjør Andersen 37
Gudbjør Gudbrandsdtr Rua 42
Gudbjor Guttormsdtr 257,259

Gudbjor Harstira Berg Koller 275-280
Gudbjor Nyhus 568
Gudbjørg Andersdtr 75-78
Gudbjørg Jacobsdtr Røykeneie 171
Gudbrand Gilbertson 448
Gudbrand Gudbrandsen 548
Gudbrand Hansen 172,549
Gudbrand Hovland 11,12,15,16,19
Gudbrand Hvattum 537
Gudbrand Iversen Kjos 473
Gudbrand Jenson 501
Gudbrand Kristoffersen 563
Gudbrand Molden 132
Gudbrand Olsen 42,552
Gudbrand Olson Egge 440
Gudbrand Ostlie 146
Gudbrand Pedersen Gudmundshagen 235
Gudbrand Peterson Brynsaas 185
Gudbrand Povelsen Skjervum 302
Gudbrand Toverud 67
Gudmond Svingen 330
Gudmund A Borch 547
Gudmund Abrahamsen 547
Gudmund Johnsen Haga 403-412
Gudmund Lunder 429
Gudmund Lunder,Mrs 429
Gudner Ericksen Morstad 484
Gudrun Alida Bredesen Schau 75
Gudrun Koller 284
Gudrun Olsen 2
Gudrun Petersdtr Tvet 103
Gudrun Sterud 351
Gulbran Abrahamsen 507,512
Gulbran Henriksen 514
Gulbran Jerve 501,513
Gulbran Jorve 503
Gulbran Lia 399
Gulbran Ulrikson 144
Gulbrand Aarness 484
Gulbrand Abrahamsen 502
Gulbrand Abrahamson 495
Gulbrand Andersen 40,507,547
Gulbrand Andersen Koln 139-149
Gulbrand Andersen Vaterud 523,526
Gulbrand Anderson 139
Gulbrand Christopherson 40
Gulbrand Dihle 291
Gulbrand Gulbrandsen 416,493
Gulbrand Gulbrandsen Gilbertson 549
Gulbrand Gulbrandsen Lundberg 465
Gulbrand Gulbrandsen Røssum 90

Gulbrand Gulbrandson 83,463,467
Gulbrand Gulbrandson Dæhlin 440-458
Gulbrand Gulbrandson Lundberg 459
Gulbrand Guttormsen 257
Gulbrand Haga 410
Gulbrand Halvorsen 72
Gulbrand Halvorsen Koller 281
Gulbrand Hansen 81
Gulbrand Hanson 144
Gulbrand Hilden 160
Gulbrand Hovland 15-17
Gulbrand Iverson 151
Gulbrand Jenson 494,496
Gulbrand Jenson Falla 493,494
Gulbrand Jerve 491
Gulbrand Jorve 504,505
Gulbrand Larsen Koller 282
Gulbrand Lee 298
Gulbrand Mohagen 260
Gulbrand Oleson Roisum 416
Gulbrand Olsen 175
Gulbrand Olsen Gjefsen 341-347
Gulbrand Olsen Grevtegrev 523
Gulbrand Olson 441
Gulbrand Ostlie 147
Gulbrand Paulsen 553
Gulbrand Pederson 143
Gulbrand Petersen 505
Gulbrand Rapeshu Gilbertson 509
Gulbrand Ryen 406
Gulbrand Velohagen 82
Gulbrand Vinger 416-418
Guldbrand Bjellum 563
Guldbrand Gunderson 422
Guldbrand Huser 304
Gunda Ødegård Grina 290
Gunder Amundrud 302
Gunder Everson 550
Gunder Gunderson 15
Gunder Iversen 550
Gunder Johannesen 236
Gunder Johansen 501
Gunder Jorve 504
Gunder Olsen 357,422
Gunder Schiager 3,4,87
Gunerius G Elken 65
Gunerius Gundersen 357
Gunhild Halvorsdtr Kostvedt 487
Gunhild Jacobson 558
Gunhild M Sorteberg 544
Gunhild Myhrstuen 114
Gunhild Rosendahl 109

Gunhild Sebjornson Anderson 557
Gunnar Lee 172
Gunnar Thon 112,113,114,199
Gur Torgersdtr Flatin 20
Guri Haavland 103
Guri Hovland 11
Guri Nilsdtr Kloppa 10
Guri Svendsdtr 337
Guro Hovland 11,15
Guro Kristoffersdtr Gunderson 16
Gus Johnson 6
Gus Vinger 417
Gust Gilbertson 388
Gust Holte,Mrs 490
Gusta Avilde Finnerud 413
Gusta Gilbertson Lee 444
Gusta Rood 386
Gustav B Onsager 578
Gustav Christofferson 239
Gustav Gilbertson 83
Gustav Gudmundsen Haga 408
Gustav Gulbrandsen 83
Gustav Haga 406
Gustav Julius Lynne 486
Gustav Laumb 492
Gustav Newberg Enarson 137
Gustav Olson 149
Gustav Pedersen Erickson 444
Gustav Peterson 486
Gustav Rud 507
Gustav Tobiason 82
Gustav Vinger 418
Gustava Ostlie 147
Gustava Pedersdtr 143
Gustave Johansen 153
Gustave T Gilbertson 565
Gustina Iverson 409,410
Guthorm and Oline Mohagen 257-
  263
Guttorm P Hoff 66
Guttorm Petersen 85
Guttorm Reiersen 257
Guttorm Rognstad 85,86
Guy E Hendrickson 565
Guy Halvorson 456,457
Gwen Hamilton 480
Gwendolin Utigard 480
H A Skattum 66
H C Bjone 427
H Carlson,Rev 190
H E Jensen,Pastor 520,521
H E Rasmussen,Rev 438
H Elaine Lindgren 308

H Heyerdahl,Rev 90
H Holverson 456
H Thorsen 43
Haaken Ouren 47
Hal Arlandson 365
Halvdan the Black,King 230
Halver Halverson 456
Halvor Andersen 40
Halvor Anderson Kroshus 253
Halvor Bjertness 81,82,83,84
Halvor Gudmundsen Haga 408,410
Halvor Gulbrandsen 72,493
Halvor H Holland 550
Halvor H Melom 245,247
Halvor Haga 406
Halvor Halvorsen 549
Halvor Halvorsen Reah 408
Halvor Hansen 550
Halvor Hansen Rÿa 405
Halvor Hanson 493
Halvor Hovland 15,16,408
Halvor Johannesen 551
Halvor Knutson 104
Halvor Koller 281
Halvor Kristoffersen Skjervum 302
Halvor Kroshus 254
Halvor Krugerud,Mrs 544
Halvor Lageson 218,222
Halvor Lageson Olim 221
Halvor Larsen 72,167
Halvor Lynner 577
Halvor Melom 246
Halvor Olsen 35,244,270
Halvor Olsen Milesten 479,568
Halvor Pedersen 252,253
Halvor Sandbakken 416
Halvor Slaatland 244
Halvor Slaatland Johannessen 244
Halvor Steffensen Hovland 409
Halvor Tya 103
Halvor Velta 322-327
Halvor Vesland 45
Halvor Western 202
Han Gulbrandson 345
Hana Western 203
Hanna Birgitte Ulriksdtr 144
Hanna Erickson 7
Hannah 109
Hannah Bjone 426
Hannah Blegen 227,229
Hannah Buraas 148
Hannah Erickson 247
Hannah Hilden 567

Hannah Maasestad 16
Hannah Rud 507
Hannah Sorensen 423
Hans Lagesen 286
Hans A Rekstad 578
Hans Alm 151,154,160,161
Hans Amundsen Skirstad 85
Hans Andersen 103,547
Hans Andersen Haug 66
Hans Andersen Morstad 269
Hans Andersen Toso 125
Hans Andreas Hansen Blegen 227-
  231
Hans Bakken 549
Hans Bentsen 32
Hans Bjone 424-426
Hans Blegen 227,547
Hans Brynsaas 5,7
Hans Buraas,Mrs 140
Hans C Heg 555
Hans Christian Hanson 455
Hans Christian Heg,Col 568
Hans Christiansen 374
Hans Christianson Buraas 143,147
Hans Edward Evenson 564
Hans Egge 233
Hans Eid 277
Hans Ellensen 493
Hans Erasmus Hjorth 558
Hans Ericksen Alm 152
Hans Ericksen Flatla 540
Hans Eriksen Daehlin 548
Hans Gilbertson 83,342
Hans Grinager 69
Hans Grinager,Mrs 69
Hans Gudmund 433
Hans Gudmundsen Haga 409,410
Hans Gulbrandsen 343
Hans Gulbrandsen Collier 275
Hans Gulbrandsen Koller 275-280
Hans Guttormsen 549
Hans Guttormsen Mohagen
  257,258,259,260,261,262
Hans Haakenstad 439
Hans Haga 406,408
Hans Hansen 273,285,550
Hans Hansen Mork 544
Hans Hanson Skaarta 293
Hans Henriksen 511,513
Hans Hovland 12,16,17,19,408
Hans Ingebretsen Emerson 550
Hans Iversen Molden 132
Hans Iverson 150

Marjery Burns 104
Marjorie Elaine Lee 450
Marjorie Medcalf 545
Mark Anderson 341
Mark Borg 439
Mark Gould 116
Mark Twain 312
Markus Sterud 351
Marlene Braaten 435
Marlo Kenneth Wahl 130
Marlyn Johnson 528
Marlyn Johnson Sayles 523
Marquerite E Cleveland 122
Marshall Storvik 247
Marta Bredesen 75
Marta Olerud Aalberg 33
Marte Andersdtr 285
Marte Augedal 32
Marte Bredesdtr 339
Marte Carlson Vinger 416-418
Marte Christensdtr 81-84
Marte Christensdtr Gulbrandsen 83
Marte Engebrettsdtr Mortviet 540
Marte Gulden` 106
Marte Hansdtr 285,338,339
Marte Iversdtr 171
Marte Jensdtr 529
Marte Jonsdtr Rustad 518
Marte Kristiansdtr 248,357
Marte Lanning 104
Marte Larsdtr 418
Marte Olesdtr 104
Marte Olsdtr 103,199,507
Marte Olsdtr Larshus Gulden 107
Marte Olsen 105
Marte Paalsdtr Oppen 103
Marte Pedersdtr 493
Marte Pedersdtr Hytta 544
Marte Røisum 89
Marte Røssum 90
Martell Erickson 226
Martha Andersdtr Wahl Johnson 121
Martha Asmundsdtr 236
Martha Bolette Harrison 339
Martha Christine Jameson 409
Martha Eriksdtr Wien 222
Martha Eriksdtr Wien Grinaker 223
Martha Gilbertson 344
Martha Gilbertson Pederson 453,454
Martha Grinaker 225
Martha Gulbrandsdtr 493
Martha Gulbrandsdtr Gilbertson 442,
   445

Martha Haakenstad 431,432
Martha Haugtvedt 45
Martha Helgesen 474
Martha Henriksdtr 512
Martha Hilden Swenson 567
Martha Jensdtr 533
Martha Jensen 511-514
Martha Johnson 530
Martha Josephine Bergine Wahl 127
Martha Kjos 474,475,479
Martha Lia 397
Martha Marie Gulbrandson 466
Martha Mork Franklin 544
Martha Morstad 239
Martha Ness 291
Martha Olsdtr 507
Martha Olsdtr Vien 341-347
Martha Paulsdtr Sørumseie 79-80
Martha Pedersdtr Hoff 533
Martha Pederson 454
Martha Peterson 288
Martha Rasmussen Clausen 558
Martha Rosta 417
Martha Solem 494
Martha Vasie 491
Martha Vasjve Jenson 509
Martha Vane 545
Martha Wahl 136
Martha Wirstad 431,432
Marthe Alm 153,154
Marthe Amundsdtr 269
Marthe Andersdtr 79,139
Marthe Ellertsdtr 264
Marthe Engebretsdtr Hilden 31
Marthe Eriksdtr 39
Marthe Gilbertson Pederson 458
Marthe Gulbrandsdtr 202,275
Marthe Gulbrandsdtr Gilbertson
   440,441
Marthe Gulbrandsdtr Koller 282
Marthe Hansdtr 57
Marthe Helgesen Kjos 475
Marthe Henriksdtr 511,513
Marthe Horgen Quanrud 342
Marthe Ingebretsdtr 31,32
Marthe Iversdtr Wilkins 285
Marthe Jensdtr 530,531
Marthe Jensen 513
Marthe Jenson 488,501
Marthe Johansdtr 152
Marthe Johnsdtr 252
Marthe Jørgensdtr 207,208
Marthe Larsdtr Framstad 544

Marthe Lyseneiet 233
Marthe Maria Tertine Decimine
   Kittelsrud 521
Marthe Milsten 479
Marthe Paulsdtr Sørumseie 79
Marthe Pedersdtr 70,139,140,210
Marthe Pedersdtr Hvattum 58
Marthe Pedersen Eggebratten 445
Marthe Rasmundsdtr 440
Marthe Steffensdtr 200
Marthe Sterud 351
Marthe Wahl 127
Marthea Larsdtr 290
Marthia Anderson 140
Marthia Hofstad 203
Marthia Pedersdtr Anderson 139-
   149
Marthia Pederson 144
Marthin Kolberg 241,242
Martia Alm 152,159-166
Martin Adolph Gulbrandson 465
Martin Anderson 143,148
Martin Andreas Østen 26-30
Martin Berge 93
Martin Bollerud 452
Martin Clausen 558
Martin G Gilbertson 452
Martin G Ostlie 148
Martin G Peterson 185-187
Martin Gilbert Gilbertson 453
Martin Gonvick 477
Martin Gulbrandson 140,144
Martin Gundersen Jørve 501,
   504,505
Martin Haakenson 147
Martin Halbakken 196,199
Martin J Bearson 121
Martin Jacobsen 551
Martin Julius Kittelsrud 520
Martin Kjerkeng,Mrs 544
Martin L Pearson 43
Martin Lahren 576
Martin Larsen 344
Martin Larson 345,373,375,377,
   379,384,386,560
Martin Larson Bilden 385,559
Martin Larson Peintbakken 378
Martin Larson Pentbakken 385,552,
   559-560
Martin Larson Rud 507
Martin Larson,Mrs 373
Martin Laverne Gilbertson Jr 453
Martin Lund 491

Ole Jonsen Western 202
Ole Jorgensen 31,207
Ole Jørgensen Melaas 103
Ole Jorstad 318,319,320
Ole Jorve 503
Ole Kjos 474
Ole Knutsen 40
Ole Larsen 207,209,270
Ole Larsen Bjorgeseter 552
Ole Larson 171-176,552
Ole Larson Soug 343
Ole Lee 445
Ole Lia 397
Ole Milesteen 568-569
Ole Milestone 568-569
Ole Milsten 472
Ole Moger 50
Ole Myhre 488,491,495
Ole Myhre,Mrs 491
Ole N Kjos 475
Ole Neal Kittelsrud 521
Ole Nielsen Framstad 338
Ole Nokleby 488,491,496,499
Ole O Hovland 18-25
Ole Oddan 104
Ole Oe 44
Ole Ohe 46,47,48
Ole Olesen 209
Ole Olesen Stomne 540
Ole Olesen Tokerud 419-423
Ole Oleson Fohre 559
Ole Oleson Hovland 20
Ole Olesson Hovland 17
Ole Olsen 105,507,540,553
Ole Olsen Allergodt 233
Ole Olsen Dæhlin 532
Ole Olsen Gulden 103-106
Ole Olsen Helgesen Lee 444
Ole Olsen Hovland 10-14,15,17
Ole Olsen Hvamstad 467
Ole Olsen Lee 444
Ole Olsen Milsten 479
Ole Olsen Putten 419
Ole Olsen Tokerud 571
Ole Olsen Tvet Gulden 107
Ole Olsgaard 35
Ole Olson 440,510
Ole Olson Forde 559
Ole Olson Fyre 559
Ole Olson Kammerud 291
Ole Olson Lee 440
Ole Olson Tingelstad 232-236
Ole Ouren 47

Ole P Berger 64,65
Ole Pedersen 327,493
Ole Pedersen Brørby 412
Ole Pedersen Myhre 492
Ole Petersen 239
Ole Peterson Feum 297
Ole Petter Eriksen Tandberg 548
Ole Phillipson 416
Ole Plomasen 181,184
Ole Rekstad 159,162,163,
    164,165,166
Ole Rognstad 85-88
Ole Rossing 297
Ole Rossum 86,87,88
Ole S Jorve 502
Ole Sebjornson Madson 557
Ole Sigvart Andrew Østen 28
Ole Solsten 537
Ole Swingen 448
Ole T Olson 230
Ole Theodore Plomasen 176,180
Ole Thingelstad 51,52
Ole Thompson 286
Ole Thorersen 553
Ole Tollerud 197
Ole Torgerson 367
Ole Tosen Røsterud 10
Ole Toverud 67
Ole Wamstad 459,463,465-471
Ole Watrud 524
Ole Western 203
Ole Wien 67
Ole William Bredesen 75
Olea Lee 397-402
Olea Lia 397-402
Oleana Johnson 203
Oleanna Moen 418
Olena Gulbrandson 466
Olena Marie Borseth 465
Olga Bjone 424
Olga Estwick 246
Olga Josephine Østen 28
Olga Josephine Pederson 320
Olga Mathilde Wahl 130
Olga Mohagen 262
Olga Ostlie 139
Olga Ouren 47
Olga Skovly 342
Olga Tovson 168
Olga Vinger 418
Olin Nelson 448
Olina Abramsdtr 252
Olina Bengtsen 249

Olina Ohe 47
Oline Alm 154,160
Oline Alm Olson 155
Oline Andersdtr 103
Oline Eriksdtr 39
Oline Henriksdtr 511
Oline Jensdtr 531
Oline Johnsdtr 252,253
Oline Johnson 201
Oline Larsdtr 42,43
Oline Larsdtr Oe 45
Oline Lysgard Myrvold 542
Oline Mathea Olsdtr 138
Oline Mohagen 257-263
Oline Oe Grina 45
Oline Ohe Grina 290
Oline Pedersdtr 210
Oline Thingelstad 262
Oline Tingelstad 262
Oline Trulsdtr 410
Oline Wamstad 470
Olive Melom 246,247
Olive Tovson 168
Olive Wevik 191
Oliver E Gilbertson 452
Oliver Elmer Gilbertson 453
Oliver Enger Jr 391
Oliver F Enger 390,391
Oliver Gilbertson 453
Oliver Linsey,Mrs 466
Oliver Peder Pederson 321
Oliver Philip Bourdeaux 361-362
Oliver Rosendahl 109
Oliver Thompson 449
Oliver Tovson 168
Oliver Vinger 417
Olivia Melby 123
Olivia Melby Wahl 124
Olivia Olsen 357
Olle Amundsen Hilden 31
Olof Larsson Toneby 453
Olof Sigurd Gilbertson 131
Olous Gulden 104
Olous Olson 279
Oluf Bengtsen 249
Oluf Helmey 575
Omgebrot Olerud 33
Ora Melom 246
Orlene Mae Hendrickson 454
Orrin Alton Gilbertson 453
Orrin Leo Lee 577
Orris Christianson 131
Orvill Melvin Orstad 126

Thorsten Alm 57
Thorsten Gagnum 132
Thorsten Gilbertson 344,345
Thorsten Grinager 60
Thorsten Hvattum 299
Thorsten Nelson 23
Thorsten Paulson 344
Thorsten Steffensen 57,58
Thorval Gilbertson 83
Thorval Laumb 514
Thorvald Anvik 435
Thorvald Dihle 291
Thorvald Gulbrandson 83
Thorvald Haugtvedt 45
Thorvald Jorstad 316,318,319,321
Thorvald Kittelsrud 520
Thorvald Laumb 492
Thorvald Lind 283
Thorvald Pedersen 61
Thorvald Tobiasen 83
Thron Håkenstad 89-93
Thron Hokenstad 92
Thron Lunder 431,433,434,435
Thron Wirstad 429
Thrond Wirstad 431
Tila Gilbertson 388
Tilda Bently 409
Tilda Jensen 318
Tilda Johnson 201
Tilda Jorstad 318
Tilda Marie Jensen 320
Tilla Alvina Lee 545
Tillie Gulden 104
Tilman Conrad Paulson 443
Tim Burns 452
Timothy Francis Burns 453
Timothy Raphael Burns 453
Tina Kjos 478
Tina Swingen 334
Tina Tollefson 332
Tobias Gulbrandsen 81-84
Tobias Hansen Loken 550
Tobias Harris 15
Tollef Dahlen 466
Tollef Rosholdt,Pastor 44
Tolline Johansdtr 119
Tom Gunderson 15
Tom Halvorson 456
Tom Hvattum 299
Tom Paulson 442,443
Tony Birds Bill 353
Tony Trondsen 504
Torbjor Nielsdtr 236

Torena Samuelson 290
Torgeir Skjervum 302
Torger Hansen Sinnerud 473
Torger Larsen 42,43
Torger Larsen Oe 44,45
Torger Larsen Ohe 46-49
Torger Mikkelsen Gubberud 235
Torger Ohe 46,290
Torger Samuelson 290
Torgrim Larsen 418
Torina Gilbertson 342
Torina Myhre 491
Torjus Flom 257
Torrtin Paulson 442
Torstein Bredesen 75
Torstein Bredesen-Aschim 76
Torstein Olsen Hvamstad 459
Torstein Thorbjornsen 236
Torsten Anderen 548
Torsten Andersen Eidsand 213
Torsten Bredesen Gjefsen 336
Torsten Bronsaas 442
Torsten Nelson 23
Torsten Nilsen Sandbeck 552
Torsten Olsen Hilden 209
Torsten Paulsen 441,442
Torsten Paulsen Hvaleby 443
Torsten Paulson 440,453
Torsten Thompson 564
Torsten Torstenson 20
Torvald Laumb 491
Tosten Alm 207
Tosten Jensen 488,513
Tosten Jenson 495,501,513
Tosten Jørgensen 207
Tosten Myhre 488,491
Tosten Paulson 452
Tosten Vasie 491
Tosten Vasjve Jenson 489
Truman Melom 247
Trygve Sverre Hansen 138
Tune Anderson 15
Turi Merkle 558
Turi Pedersdtr Brekke Merkle 558
Turi Pedersdtr Brekke Merkle
   Jacobson 558
U S Grant,Gen 151
U V Koren,Rev 517,520
Ulrick Hanson Buraas 143,148
Ulrik Hansen Burås 144
Una Hunt 480
Uncle Anderson 296
Valborg Halvorsdtr 221

Valborg Halvorson 222
Valborg Jensdtr Lovlien 221
Valentine Nelson 445
Vent Blegen 174
Vera Augusta Sulsberger 457
Vera D Shurtliff 121
Vera Ion York 456
Vera Nevada Johnson 121
Vera Wahl 130
Verlyn Anderson 19,21,306,354
Vern Eslinger 411
Verna Evelyn Georgeson 320
Verna Melom 247
Vernon Eldred Vickerman 527
Vernon Gonvick 477
Vernon Irven Clay 457
Vernon L Larson 126
Vernon Larson,Mrs 468
Vicfor Gilbertson 288
Victor Allen Østen 28
Victor Arnold Lynne 486
Victor Johnson 466
Victor Østen 29,30
Vincent Buraas 140
Viola Almida Pedersen 446
Viola Kjos 475
Viola Marvita Lund 447
Viola Pedersen 445
Viola Vinger 418
Violet Esther Lee 444
Violet Lucille Munger 120
Violet Mae Vickerman 527
Violet Olina Kline 450
Virgil Allerson 126
Virginia Johnson 490
Virginia May Nelson 445
Virginia Nell Thompson 450
Vivian Caroline Peterson 240
Vivian Florence Plomasen 181
Vivian Plomasen 183
Vivian Utigard 480
Vivien Evangeline Thompson 451
Voyle Clark Johnson 335,336,337
Wallace Alm 157
Wallace Hodge 121
Wallace Melvin Swingen 448
Walter Eddie Norman Wahl 130
Walter Ferdinand Lynne 487
Walter Helstedt 411
Walter Lenoard Welo 579
Walter M Goodno 575
Walter M Teslow 579
Wanda Pauline Grover 255

www.ingramcontent.com/pod-product-compliance
Lightning Source LLC
Chambersburg PA
CBHW080227270326
41926CB00020B/4174